W9-BYQ-235

ILLINOIS CENTRAL COLLEGE
PN6120.C5K22 1975
STACKS
A treasury of Christmas plays :
A12900 302557

A TREASURY OF CHRISTMAS PLAYS

A Treasury of Christmas Plays

One-act, royalty-free plays for stage or microphone performance and round-the-table reading

Edited by

SYLVIA E. KAMERMAN

Publishers PLAYS, INC. *Boston*

CAUTION

The plays in this volume are fully protected by copyright law. All rights, including motion picture, recitation, television, public reading, radio broadcasting, and rights of translation into foreign languages are strictly reserved.

NOTICE FOR AMATEUR PRODUCTION

These plays may be produced by schools, clubs, and similar amateur groups without payment of a royalty fee.

NOTICE FOR PROFESSIONAL PRODUCTION

For any form of non-amateur presentation (professional stage, radio or television), permission must be obtained in writing from the publisher. Inquiries should be addressed to PLAYS, INC., 8 Arlington Street, Boston Massachusetts 02116

Library of Congress Catalog Card Number: 72–5242

ISBN: 0-8238-0203-5

MANUFACTURED IN THE UNITED STATES OF AMERICA

Preface

The forty one-act, royalty-free plays in this book were selected to convey to young people the important message and meaning of Christmas. This dramatic material can be effectively used in schools and in the community for classroom and assembly performance or club productions.

This volume includes traditional and modern one-act plays for young people—contemporary comedies, dramatizations of the Christmas story, serious dramas—all revealing the true spirit of Christmas. For variety and flexibility in planning programs, this book also offers reading plays which require no memorization and a minimum of rehearsal. These scripts may also be tape-recorded, broadcast over a public-address system, or used as part of the reading curriculum. With slight adaptations, they may also be successfully staged as "spotlight" productions, with or without scenery or special costumes.

It is hoped that the young actors and their audiences will find the real meaning of Christmas in these heartwarming dramas.

S. E. K.

TABLE OF

Junior and Senior High

Middle Grades

CONTENTS 

A TREASURY OF CHRISTMAS PLAYS

JUNIOR AND SENIOR HIGH

The Christmas Visitor

by Anne Howard Bailey

Characters

GERALD REMINGTON, *a well-to-do lawyer*
LAURA REMINGTON, *his wife*
BOY
SALLY BARTLETT, *a neighbor, in her late 20's*
CHARLES, *the Remington butler*
MRS. LESTER, *a social worker*
JAMIE, *a boy, about 6*
CAROLERS

SCENE 1

TIME: *Christmas Eve.*

SETTING: *The Remington living room, a fashionably furnished room in an expensive apartment building in a large city. A large, elaborately decorated Christmas tree dominates the room.*

AT RISE: *It is night, and the room is brilliantly lit.* CHARLES *stands on a ladder putting the finishing touches on the tree.* GERALD REMINGTON *stands by the window, looking moodily out at the falling snow.* CHARLES *turns, and holds out a large tinsel star.*

CHARLES: Where do you want this, Mr. Remington?

GERALD (*Looking at* CHARLES, *then out window again*): I don't care, Charles. Hang it anyplace.

CHARLES: I just thought—the star? (*He hesitates.*)

GERALD: Is there some special place for stars?

CHARLES: We always hang ours high, sir. To light you home by—and to wish on.

GERALD: Then let's not waste it, Charles. Even though I haven't any wish. Not a wish in the world. (*The door buzzer sounds.* CHARLES *starts down the ladder.*) And that will be Mrs. Remington—beautiful, bright, wearing Christmas cheer like a tinsel halo. (CHARLES *puts down star and opens the front door at right.* LAURA REMINGTON *bursts in. She is beautiful, artificially gay, and laden with Christmas packages of all sizes and shapes.*)

LAURA: Hello, Charles. A merry, *merry* Christmas Eve!

CHARLES: Good evening, Mrs. Remington. The same to you, Mrs. Remington. (*He tries to take some of the packages, but she walks to the couch and lets them all spill out of her arms.*)

GERALD (*Sardonically*): Yes—the same to you, Mrs. Remington!

LAURA (*Surprised*): Gerald. I didn't think you'd be home.

GERALD: Even the legal business shuts down for the happy holidays.

LAURA: But I didn't plan on you for this evening. You always stop by the club.

GERALD: Oddly enough, most people rediscover home on Christmas Eve. And—this is home. Daily maid service, garbage disposal, elevators and all!

LAURA: Well, I can't help it if I have plans. The Civic Council is judging the Outdoor Christmas Tree Contest tonight—

GERALD: And of course, you, the first woman president, must officiate.

LAURA: Naturally.

GERALD: Naturally.

CHARLES (*Clearing his throat*): Ah—if you'd like me to hang the star, Mr. Remington?

GERALD (*Picking up the star*): I think I'll reserve this last finishing touch for myself, Charles. Or better still, for Mrs. Remington. You're excused, Charles. (CHARLES *nods, takes ladder, and exits left.* GERALD *looks at the tree critically.*)

LAURA: Charles is rather artistic, isn't he? It's a lovely tree.

GERALD: By the tree's standards, or by ours? Maybe it doesn't like all this tinsel hanging in its hair. Maybe it's hungry for snow and thirsty for rain.

LAURA: Sentimentality doesn't become you, Gerald.

GERALD: No? I thought it went rather well with the season. (*He walks over to the stereo.*) Would you like to hear some Christmas music, Laura?

LAURA: Sorry. I haven't time.

GERALD: What a shame! May I comfort myself with the thought that you'll be pining for home and husband while you're out awarding blue ribbons for prize Christmas trees?

LAURA: Gerald, please. Don't let's quarrel.

GERALD: Is that what I'm doing? Quarreling? No, Laura, I'm asking for something. That I hoped you'd be able to give me. (LAURA *holds his gaze a moment, then turns abruptly away.*) No, I guess not. Not any more.

LAURA (*Apologetically*): You *do* understand about tonight, don't you, darling? And if you'd care to come with me . . . ?

GERALD: No, thanks. If I get desperate, I can always listen to the carolers. (*He walks to window and opens it. From offstage, noises of the street and* CAROLERS *singing "Joy to the World" are heard.*)

LAURA (*Sharply*): Shut that. I feel a draft. (*She starts putting on make-up at wall mirror. He shuts window.*)

GERALD: It's only fair to warn you. I haven't brought you a present because . . . well, I can't think of anything you don't have already.

LAURA: What a nice compliment, darling. To think your wife has everything! (GERALD *walks up behind her and puts his hands on her shoulders*)

GERALD: You're very beautiful, you know.

LAURA: Thank you, but that's only my reflection. (*She spins away from his grasp.*) It's late and I'm late, and if you really want to be a darling, you'll put those packages under the tree!

GERALD (*Surveying packages on couch*): What role are you playing? *Mother* Christmas?

LAURA: Heavens! Didn't I tell you? We're having company tomorrow. In fact, it's coming tonight.

GERALD: *It?* It—what?

LAURA: I don't know whether it's a boy or a girl.

GERALD (*Aghast*): Have you lost your mind?

LAURA: From the Orphans' Shelter, Gerald. The Welfare Committee passed a resolution last week that every member of the board should sign up for an orphan to spend Christmas Eve and Christmas Day in a home with a family. So what could I do? I'm first vice-president. The agency is delivering one sometime this evening.

GERALD (*Appalled*): Laura, haven't you any sensitivity, any depth of feeling at all?

LAURA: Surely you wouldn't begrudge an orphan a Christmas dinner and an armful of presents?

GERALD: I wouldn't have believed it. That you could be so thoughtless and selfish and callous.

LAURA: Selfish, Gerald? Callous? I believe it was your theory that no one has any business with children who isn't able to take proper care of them.

GERALD: That was when we were just starting out.

LAURA: I know. First we were too poor. Then we were too

busy and now . . . (*Her voice breaks*) You see, I'm only agreeing with you, Gerald. (*She exits quickly through front door.* GERALD *sighs, goes to stereo, and turns it on. A choir singing "Away in a Manger" is heard.* GERALD *hastily turns it off. He walks to the packages, rips the wrapping off one, revealing a child's carpenter set, with hammer, saw, etc. The buzzer rings.* GERALD *hurries to the door, and flings it open.*)

GERALD (*Eagerly*): Laura, I— (SALLY BARTLETT *leans against the door frame. She wears exotic slacks and blouse.*) Oh, Sally.

SALLY: Any room in your Christmas stocking for a next-door neighbor?

GERALD: Any time. Come in. (*She enters and they go to center.*)

SALLY: If you're not doing anything, I thought we might slide down a few chimneys together.

GERALD: Where are all your bright young men, Sal?

SALLY (*Shrugging*): Glamour's only an eleven-month asset. Come Christmas they head for a home-and-hearth type of girl. I was just putting a last-minute Christmas card down the mailbox when I saw Laura leave, so I thought as long as you were alone, and I'm alone . . .

GERALD: We could keep each other company. Great! Let's go out and find some really festive place.

SALLY: You're on! Give me time to get dressed, and bring your own mistletoe. (*She exits, leaving door open behind her.* GERALD *shakes his head. He starts toward door, then his eye falls on a smiling picture of* LAURA, *framed, on table beside couch. He picks up picture, sits on the couch, and stares glumly at it.*)

BOY (*At doorway*): Are you sad because you've lost the lady? (GERALD *jumps, as* BOY, *bareheaded and wearing a shapeless coat, walks in through open door and shuts it.*)

GERALD: How did you get in here?

BOY: I'm sure I have the right apartment. 10-D?

GERALD (*Nodding*): Yes. Then you're the boy from the Orphans' Shelter?

BOY (*Putting a card on the table by the entrance*): In case you should want me again sometime—you can look for me here.

GERALD: You shouldn't be wandering around the city by yourself, at night.

BOY: Are *you* afraid?

GERALD: Well, no. But then I'm a bit older than you are.

BOY (*Looking at* LAURA'*s picture*): Are you afraid for her?

GERALD: Why do you ask that?

BOY: She's a very beautiful lady. Is she always so sad?

GERALD: Sad? Laura? She's laughing in this picture. (*He holds the picture out.* BOY *looks at it and shakes his head.* GERALD *looks at the picture again. Thoughtfully*) You know—you may be right. (BOY *wanders over and looks at tree.*) Shall I turn the tree lights on?

BOY: If you want to.

GERALD: If I—? (*He laughs.*) I'm a little old for Christmas trees, son.

BOY: Why?

GERALD: When you grow up you'll find out that unless a house is filled with kids and laughter and excitement, Christmas doesn't mean much. (*He stops.*)

BOY: Then why did you decorate the tree?

GERALD: I don't know. Habit, I guess. We've always had a tree. I remember that first Christmas when Laura and I— (*He breaks off again.*)

BOY: Does your wife like Christmas trees?

GERALD: She did then. We bought the biggest tree we could find, but by the time we lugged it up four flights to our room, half the branches were broken off. It looked like a picked bird. (BOY *suddenly laughs and* GERALD *laughs with him.*) Would you like to unwrap some of your presents now?

BOY: That wouldn't be quite fair.

GERALD: Why not? They're yours. Look—here's one with the paper off. (GERALD *shows* BOY *the carpenter set.* BOY *looks at it gravely. He hefts the hammer.*)

BOY: It's too small for me. I can handle a real hammer.

GERALD: Can you? Are you a good carpenter?

BOY: Not yet. But I'm learning.

GERALD: You're quite a boy. How about some cake and milk? (BOY *nods and* GERALD *puts an arm around his shoulders.*) Then come with me. The kitchen's out this way. (*They exit left. There is the sound of a key in the lock. The front door opens and* LAURA *enters. She is clearly in a temper. She rips off her coat, throws it on couch.* GERALD *reappears, alone.*) I heard your key. I thought it was Charles coming back. Blue ribbons distributed so soon?

LAURA: Don't be clever, Gerald. I'm in a rush and a perfectly vile temper. The chartered bus broke down—and the Police Commissioner is getting a special car . . . (*She is prowling the room as she talks.*) It's snowing up a blizzard and the streets are jammed with those caterwauling carolers. . . . (*She starts toward door left.*)

GERALD: Wait a minute. Your guest is here.

LAURA: My what?

GERALD: Your charity case. Your orphan. It's a boy.

LAURA: Well, that's just dandy. Have Charles put him to bed, and tomorrow morning I'll—

GERALD: Charles isn't here. He's out.

LAURA (*Eyeing* GERALD *thoughtfully*): You're not going to be difficult, are you?

GERALD: He's a pretty interesting kid. Direct. Mind of his own. Funny what having a kid in the house will do for it—on Christmas Eve.

LAURA: For heaven's sake, Gerald! I'm in a *hurry!*

GERALD: You can be a little late, can't you?

LAURA: The Commissioner's going to phone me in thirty minutes. He's coming by to pick me up. And I want to change. (*She starts out, but* GERALD *suddenly yanks her back by her arm.*)

GERALD: Don't you care about anything but yourself?

LAURA: What's the *matter* with you?

GERALD: He's a nice kid, that's all. He's lonely. You're the reason he's here, so I think you ought to see him. Will you speak to him?

LAURA: That's ridiculous. He doesn't know me from Santa Claus, and I don't know him, so what difference does it make whether I see him or not?

GERALD: Aren't you even interested?

LAURA: If you're so interested, why don't you go talk to him?

GERALD: Because I'm not responsible for getting him here, and I've made other plans. (*He walks to closet by front door, and starts putting on hat and coat.*)

LAURA: Gerald . . . we can't leave a child alone in this apartment. (GERALD *deliberately buttons his coat. He doesn't answer.*) You told me you weren't going out. Surely you could wait till Charles gets back.

GERALD: I'm late now.

LAURA: But I'm chairman of the Tree Judging Committee. They're expecting me! The Commissioner is going to call me any minute!

GERALD: I'm sure it will make a charming anecdote for your next civic meeting. How the charitable Laura Remington rocked an orphan boy to sleep on Christmas Eve. Good night, my dear. Merry Christmas! (*He exits.* LAURA *gives a little cry of angry frustration. She chokes it back as the* BOY, *still in his shapeless coat, and holding a glass of milk, appears at door at left.*)

LAURA (*Seeing him*): Oh! I didn't hear you come in. I'm Mrs. Remington. I'll stay with you till our butler returns. Then I have to go out.

BOY: I don't mind staying by myself. I'm not afraid.

LAURA: That's out of the question.

BOY: Why? Do *you* mind being left alone?

LAURA: That's different. I'm a grown-up.

BOY: Yes. But, do you?

LAURA (*Suddenly*): I hate it.

BOY: Then I'll stay with *you*. Until Mr. Remington comes back.

LAURA: You might have a long wait.

BOY: I like Mr. Remington. We've been talking about Christmas trees, and he told me this was the prettiest he'd seen—except the first tree you had together.

LAURA: *That* one? (*She laughs.*) Why, all the branches were broken off, and— (*Suddenly she sobers. Her voice is low and sincere.*) He's right. It *was* a pretty tree.

BOY: Thank you for all the presents.

LAURA: Why, you haven't even looked at them.

BOY: My mother said you don't always have to see things to know they are there.

LAURA (*After a pause*): Suppose you knew something was there once; then it seemed to disappear and you can't find it anywhere. What would your mother say about that?

BOY: She'd say that no one sees past the wall he builds in front of his own heart.

LAURA (*Hesitantly, nervously*): I guess I'm a very silly, selfish woman.

BOY: No.

LAURA: What do *you* think of me?

BOY: I think you wish you had asked Mr. Remington to stay.

LAURA: You're a very observant boy. Talking to you, I feel . . . well, I feel as if we might be friends.

BOY: Yes.

LAURA: I'm glad you came to us for Christmas.

BOY: I wanted to come. (LAURA *smiles at him. He smiles back and crosses to her. She puts her hands on his shoulders.*)

LAURA: More milk?

BOY: Yes. (*She takes glass and starts out. She pauses and looks back.* BOY *has settled on the couch. His eyes are heavy. She smiles and exits.* BOY *droops, finally slumping into sleep.* LAURA *re-enters with a fresh glass of milk.*)

LAURA: If you'd like it warmed, I can— (*She breaks off as she sees the dozing* BOY. *She puts the milk down, crosses to him, and looks down at him tenderly. She bends and strokes a lock of hair back from his forehead.*) Pleasant dreams, little one. I'll try to make them come true for you. (*She glances at her watch, and pulls herself together briskly. She gently shakes the* BOY.) You can't sleep here, honey. Let's get you to bed. (BOY *half-wakens.* LAURA *helps him to his feet. He leans heavily against her. Half-supporting him, she steers him toward door at left. The phone rings.* LAURA *hesitates.* BOY *slumps more heavily against her. With a tender look, she hugs him closer. Slowly she moves on toward the door, helping the* BOY. *The phone continues to ring as they exit, then finally stops. Curtain.*)

* * *

SCENE 2

TIME: *Later that evening.*

SETTING: *The same as Scene 1. The lights are turned low, and the Christmas tree lights are on.*

AT RISE: LAURA, *wearing a long dressing gown, is curled up on the couch, dozing. A key turns in the front door. The door opens and* GERALD *enters. He looks tired and disgusted. He slams the door violently, waking* LAURA, *who smiles with pleasure when she sees him. Then her smile dies as she sees his frowning face.*

GERALD: I'm amazed. I thought you'd be out greeting Santa Claus.

LAURA: *I'm* amazed. I never expected you back this early.

GERALD: I don't like my tinsel with tarnish on it.

LAURA: Meaning?

GERALD: It's a little silly to celebrate love and good will to man.

LAURA: How true. For us, anyway.

GERALD: Why beat around the bush? Can't we face it—honestly and squarely?

LAURA: Are you implying that I've failed you? All right, Gerald. Maybe I have. But it takes two, you know— (*She gets up, turns her back and walks to the window. She dabs at her eyes surreptitiously.*)

GERALD: Laura . . . ?

LAURA (*Harshly*): Well? (GERALD *stops, rebuffed. Suddenly tree lights go out, leaving room dim.*)

GERALD: Nothing. The lights are gone.

LAURA: Yes. They are, aren't they? (*She turns toward him.*) What do you want to do about it? (GERALD *avoids her gaze. In some confusion, he picks up the toy hammer and fingers it.*)

GERALD: Clever set. The—er—boy liked it. Funny kid. Gives you the impression he's way ahead of you all the time.

LAURA: What do you want to do about *us,* Gerald?

GERALD: I'm not sure. What do you suggest?

LAURA: I've thought all this time we had *something.* Maybe just the weight of time and things shared. At least we've been together. Until tonight—

GERALD: Why drag tonight in? One Christmas Eve can't destroy everything.

LAURA: No? Somehow I think if tonight had been different, a lot that's been wonderful and good between us could have been saved.

GERALD: I don't think playing part-time mother is very admirable.

LAURA: What do you mean?

GERALD: It was a cheap trick—using a child's misfortune to feed your own vanity.

LAURA: Who walked out? *I* didn't!

GERALD: What?

LAURA: I couldn't leave. I've been here all evening. The Commissioner phoned about eight-thirty but I didn't answer the phone.

GERALD (*Quietly*): That wasn't the Commissioner. I phoned. (*Pauses, then, earnestly*) It wasn't much fun without you, Laura. It never has been. I got to thinking about you and the kid, and, well, it seemed stupid for me to be somewhere else, when I'd rather be here.

LAURA: It was really you who called?

GERALD (*Nodding*): Yes. When I didn't get an answer, I guess I saw red. I couldn't swallow the thought that you'd go off and leave a child alone.

LAURA: I intended to, you know. But . . . there's something odd about him. Detached—sort of apart from the world. Yet, I found myself drawn to him.

GERALD: Did you feel it? Honestly?

LAURA: I've never really thought I liked children. (*She turns away.*)

GERALD (*Walking toward her*): And yet—it's funny, but always in my mind, I picture you, holding a child.

LAURA: Gerald . . . (*She turns to him and puts out her*

hand. He is about to take it when a key turns in the lock. The front door opens and CHARLES *enters.*)

CHARLES (*Surprised*): Why, good evening, Mrs. Remington. Sir. I'm afraid I'm a little late. The crowds and—holiday spirit you know.

GERALD: We know, Charles. I'm beginning to feel a little spirit myself.

LAURA: We have an overnight Christmas visitor, Charles. A little boy. I wonder if you would look in on him. He's sleeping in my bedroom.

CHARLES: Yes, ma'am. (*He exits, peeling off his coat as he goes.* GERALD *and* LAURA *avoid looking at each other.* GERALD *walks to tree and touches one of branches.*)

GERALD: Maybe we ought to hang the star? (LAURA *looks at him questioningly*) Charles said a star is to light you home by—and to wish on.

LAURA: Do you have a wish, Gerald?

GERALD: Yes. Do you? (*Slowly, she nods*) Do you suppose they might even be the same? (CHARLES *reappears. He looks agitated*)

CHARLES: Excuse me, Mrs. Remington, you *did* say the visitor was in your bedroom?

LAURA: Why, yes. I put him to bed myself.

CHARLES: Well, he doesn't seem to be there now, madam.

LAURA: But that's impossible!

GERALD: Where could he be? (LAURA *rushes out, and* GERALD *follows.* CHARLES *remains, looking puzzled. A moment later,* LAURA *and* GERALD *re-enter. Both are baffled and disturbed*)

LAURA: Gerald, I tucked him in myself. Charles, search the apartment. He has to be somewhere! (CHARLES *nods and goes out.* GERALD *looks at* LAURA *with a frown.*)

GERALD: The bed didn't look as if anyone had slept in it, Laura.

LAURA: Gerald, I promise you. . . . I took him in, and I

put him down so carefully so he wouldn't wake and . . . (*She breaks off and covers her face with her hands.*)

GERALD: Don't. We'll find him. He's here someplace.

LAURA: No, no. I have the strangest feeling . . . (*She clings to* GERALD) Oh, Gerald, he was such a lonely little boy. And I feel we failed him.

CHARLES (*Reappearing in doorway*): I'm sorry, madam. There's no one in the apartment but the three of us. (*He exits.*)

LAURA (*Half hysterically*): But where could he have gone? And *why?* Oh, Gerald, what did I do . . . or not do?

GERALD (*Soothing her*): Perhaps it was both of us. Maybe he didn't feel he belonged here.

LAURA: But he did! He did! We have everything to offer a child—security, a good home, and love.

GERALD: Love?

LAURA: We *had* love, Gerald.

GERALD: But I haven't changed, Laura. It's still the same for me. (*The door buzzer sounds.* LAURA *turns with joyful relief to the door, and hurries to open it.*)

LAURA: Gerald . . . maybe it's him. The poor baby, he must have locked himself out. (*She flings the door open. On the threshold is* MRS. LESTER, *the social worker, holding* JAMIE, *a little boy of about 6, by the hand.*) Oh!

MRS. LESTER: Mrs. Remington? (LAURA *nods.*) I'm *so* sorry to be late, but the Christmas traffic, you know, and we've had a positive *rush* on holiday foster parents. (*She edges in, pushing* JAMIE *ahead of her*) This is Jamie, and he'll be with you over tomorrow. Jamie, say how-do-you-do to Mrs. Remington.

JAMIE: Hullo.

LAURA: But there's been some kind of mistake. You see, we already have a little boy from the Shelter. He came by himself, earlier.

MRS. LESTER: Oh, no. That's impossible. We *never* permit

our children out unattended. I mean, we're responsible for their welfare.

LAURA: I'm sure that's true, but all the same—

MRS. LESTER: Besides, Jamie was allotted to you the very day you phoned in. (*She flourishes a card*) You see, it's right here on the card. And when I realized who you *were* (*She simpers a little*), why, I wanted to bring him over personally.

LAURA: I don't understand. The other child came, and my husband and I just assumed . . .

MRS. LESTER: I assure you, Mrs. Remington, any other child who came here, claiming your hospitality, was unauthorized. (JAMIE, *not understanding anything but that he might not get to stay, puts his fist in his eye and starts to cry.*)

GERALD: Wait, perhaps we can settle this. (*He takes* JAMIE'S *hand.*) Don't cry, son. I think perhaps we have room enough for two Christmas visitors, don't you, Laura?

LAURA (*Smiling at him*): Yes, I think we do.

MRS. LESTER: Well, I must be getting along. But if I were you I'd check this other boy's credentials, and send him right back where he came from. Well, Merry Christmas! (*She smiles briskly, and exits.* LAURA *closes the door and looks at* GERALD.)

LAURA: But—where *is* he?

GERALD: I don't know.

LAURA: It's almost as if we dreamed he was here. (*With wonder*) But I held him . . . in my arms.

GERALD: Whoever he is, we have a lot to thank him for.

LAURA: Yes. (*She looks down at* JAMIE *and puts a hand on his head. He clutches her skirts and leans against her.*)

GERALD: You know, my dear, you've never looked more beautiful.

LAURA: Thank you, Gerald. (JAMIE *breaks away and goes to the tree. His eye is caught by the star, still unhung*)

JAMIE: Star . . . I want to hang the star! (LAURA *and* GERALD *do not immediately respond.*)

LAURA: I can't help feeling that somehow it was planned. Didn't he tell you his name, or where he came from?

GERALD: I never thought to ask. But (*Snaps his fingers*)—wait a minute. When he came in he said (*Groping*) . . . "In case you want me again, you can look for me here . . ." And he put something down. (*He moves to table, picks up card the* BOY *left.*) It says here . . . Bethlehem.

LAURA: Bethlehem, Pennsylvania?

GERALD: No. Just Bethlehem. (LAURA *and* GERALD *stare at each other, realization dawning*)

CAROLERS (*From offstage; singing the last stanza of "O Little Town of Bethlehem"*):

O Holy Child of Bethlehem,
Descend to us we pray;
Cast out our sin and enter in,
Be born in us today.

JAMIE (*From over by the tree*): I want to hang the star! (GERALD *puts out his hand to* LAURA. *She takes it, and they walk to the tree.*)

GERALD: All right, son. It *is* time we hang the star. (*He lifts* JAMIE, *and* LAURA *hands him the star. He stretches to hang it, as the curtain closes.*)

THE END

Merry Christmas, Crawfords!

by Mildred Hark and Noel McQueen

Characters

JOHN CRAWFORD
ALICE CRAWFORD, *his wife*
MYRA CRAWFORD, *15*
TED CRAWFORD, *13*
JANET CRAWFORD, *11*
BOBBY CRAWFORD, *8*
(Myra, Ted, Janet and Bobby: *their children*)
MAILMAN
BILL COLEMAN, *electric light repairman*
HELEN COLEMAN, *his wife*
JIMMY COLEMAN, *their 8-year-old son*
GRACE SAUNDERS, *a neighbor*
FRANCES SAUNDERS, *11*
LARRY SAUNDERS, *16*
MR. BASCOLM, *Mr. Crawford's boss*
MRS. BASCOLM
TEEN-AGERS

TIME: *Late afternoon, the day before Christmas.*

SETTING: *Crawfords' partly furnished living room. On rear wall center, there is a fireplace with mantel. Partially trimmed Christmas tree stands right, with lights strung on it, but unlighted. Ladder stands near tree, and two cartons sit next to it on floor. A small radio and a telephone are on table right and a television set left.*

AT RISE: MYRA *sits on floor, pinning up hem of curtains*

at window right. TED *sits on chair near phone, holding receiver to his ear.* JANET *and* BOBBY *are trimming tree.*

MYRA (*Getting up from floor after pinning up second curtain*): There, I've pinned up our old curtains. That will have to do till we can shorten them. At least the living room will look a little respectable for Christmas.

JANET (*Hanging ornament on tree*): And we have a Christmas tree, anyhow, if we don't have anything else. (*She steps back, looking at tree.*) Even if the trimmings are skimpy. . . .

BOBBY: Yeah, but Janet, where *are* all our decorations? We had lots more last year.

JANET: I don't know, Bobby. They must have gotten lost during the moving. If only I could find that box with the prettiest balls!

TED (*Into phone*): Hello. . . . Hello. . . . But I *have* been waiting, and this is important. (MR. CRAWFORD *enters left, holding out small Christmas angel.*)

MR. CRAWFORD: Myra, look what I found for our tree.

MYRA: Dad, the Christmas angel! Where in the world did you find it?

MR. CRAWFORD: With the kitchen pots and pans. I was unpacking them, and I found the angel in that old percolator we never use.

JANET: Oh, good! Let me have her, Dad. She goes right on the top of the tree. (*Takes angel, climbs ladder and puts angel on top*)

MR. CRAWFORD: There, that makes it look more like home, doesn't it? And what about the lights? Did you call the electric company, Ted?

TED: That's what I'm doing now. But I'm just waiting. They keep switching me from person to person.

MR. CRAWFORD: I can't understand it. I called them three times today and they were supposed to be here this morning. Well, tell them they've got to do something. It'll be getting dark and we can't be without lights for Christmas.

BOBBY (*Sadly*): The tree won't look right without lights.

MR. CRAWFORD: Tell them you're talking for me, Ted. I've got to find the big roaster or we won't be able to cook the turkey tomorrow. I've come across everything else—the old iron pot we use for camping, the waffle iron, the ice cream freezer (*As he goes off left*)—everything but the roaster!

MYRA: Poor Dad.

TED (*Into phone*): Hello . . .

BOBBY: We may not even have any turkey.

MYRA (*Motioning toward* TED): Shh-h-h.

TED (*Into phone*): Hello, I'm speaking for Mr. John Crawford. We've just moved into a new house and you were supposed to send someone to turn on our lights. It's 123 Acorn Street. . . . But you have all that information and you've got the order. The gas company and the phone company were here yesterday. . . . Oh. . . . You're what? . . . You're closing? . . . But what if the man doesn't come? . . . What'll we do? . . . Where can we call? . . . Oh, you think what? . . . Oh, I see. . . . What? . . . Well, yes, Merry Christmas to you, too. (*He hangs up.*) What nerve! She said Merry Christmas.

JANET: Merry Christmas without any lights?

TED: Oh, she says if he has the order, he'll get here. She thinks the snow may have delayed him.

BOBBY: But if he doesn't come, we won't have any lights on our tree.

MYRA: Tree lights? We won't have any lights at all! We'll be in total darkness.

JANET: Total darkness for Christmas! Can you imagine anything more depressing?

TED (*Sighing*): If you ask me, this whole holiday's depressing.

MYRA: Come on, Ted. We have to keep our spirits up for Mom and Dad's sake. They must feel just as bad as we do—in a strange town, without any of their old friends.

TED: Yes, I guess you're right. About the only person they've met is Dad's new boss.

JANET: That old Mr. Bascolm. All he could talk about was the Bascolm Manufacturing Company.

BOBBY: He's like Mr. Scrooge. Spoiling our Christmas.

MYRA: At least Dad has a good job there.

JANET: But why did it have to start now? I wish we could have waited until after the holidays to move.

MYRA: We couldn't, though. Dad's job starts the first of the year, and we were lucky to find this house and get moved in before then.

TED: It certainly is a mess, though. (*He is looking out window at right.*) Anyway, it looks like Christmas outside with all the fresh snow.

MYRA (*Looking out; wistfully*): Yes, don't the houses look pretty with snow on their roofs and the decorations out front? And look, the mailman is still delivering packages all up and down the street.

BOBBY: I guess he won't be delivering any packages to the Crawford house.

JANET: Packages? We won't even get any Christmas cards. There wasn't time to tell anyone about our change of address.

TED: The post office has our new address, so they'll forward our cards and packages eventually.

BOBBY (*Sadly*): Eventually—when is that? I wanted some presents for Christmas.

MYRA: There will be a few presents, Bobby. We didn't send all of them through the mail.

BOBBY: Oh, sure, the ones we brought for each other in

our suitcases—but what about Mom and Dad's presents for us? And Grandma and Grandpa's? The post office doesn't know where those boxes are.

TED: It's too bad they're lost, but maybe the post office will find them after the Christmas rush is over.

JANET: That's no fun.

BOBBY: Yeah. And after Christmas, they won't even be *Christmas* presents.

MYRA: I guess it won't seem the same, Bobby, but . . . (*She looks out window.*) Look, there's company arriving for Christmas across the street. They've got suitcases.

BOBBY (*Looking out*): I'll bet it's their grandpa and grandma.

JANET (*Sniffling*): Our Grandpa and Grandma are thousands of miles away—they won't get here on time.

TED: Come on now, Janet, cheer up, and put the rest of the stuff on the tree. Try to hang things that will cover that bare spot on the side.

JANET: Oh, all right, but I don't see why we couldn't at least have had a better tree. (*She hangs more ornaments.*)

BOBBY: You can't even buy a decent Christmas tree in this town.

MYRA: You can't buy a decent tree anywhere at the last minute, Bobby.

BOBBY: At home you could. Dad always took us to at least six places before we chose one.

MYRA: Yes, but that was at home—in the city. We don't know where to look for trees here in the suburbs.

BOBBY: Suburbs. I hate the suburbs! (MRS. CRAWFORD *enters left, carrying small box.*)

MRS. CRAWFORD: What's that, Bobby?

BOBBY: I said, I hate the suburbs.

MRS. CRAWFORD (*Cheerfully*): Why, Bobby, we've only been here one day. Give the new town a chance. (*Looking around*) Why, you kids have done wonders. The curtains look much better, Myra. And the tree looks great! You've done a fine job of decorating it. And I have a surprise for you. I found the box with the best Christmas tree balls.

JANET: Oh, Mom! (*Taking box*) Now we can really make the tree look nice.

MRS. CRAWFORD: Of course you can. And cheer up, Bobby, the Crawford family is going to have a Christmas dinner in spite of everything. Your father found the big roaster and now I'm going to make the stuffing for the turkey. (*She goes off left.*)

BOBBY: Oh, boy! Turkey with stuffing.

TED: Good old Mom. All she has to do is throw a few cheerful words around and things seem more like Christmas.

MYRA: Yes. (*Looking out right*) And—and look, the mailman is coming with a big package!

BOBBY: He is?

JANET: The presents!

BOBBY: I'll go! I'll go! (*He starts toward front door, right.*)

MYRA (*From window*): Never mind. I was wrong. He's taking the package to the house next door.

TED: Well, let's get the rest of the decorations on the tree. Open the box, Janet.

JANET (*Untying box*): O.K. (*She opens box; in dismay*) Oh, no! (MYRA, TED *and* BOBBY *rush over and look into box.*)

MYRA: Oh, dear, they're all broken!

BOBBY (*Shaking his head*): All busted! What's the use of trying to have Christmas when everything goes wrong?

JANET: Let's turn on the radio. Maybe if we listen to some Christmas carols we'll get into the right mood.

BOBBY (*Brightly, going to radio and turning it on*): That's a good idea!

TED: It would be a good idea if we had any electricity.

BOBBY (*Turning radio off*): Nuts. I forgot about that. We can't use the radio or the TV set. (MRS. CRAWFORD *enters left with hat and coat on.*)

MYRA (*Surprised*): Why, Mom—are you going out?

MRS. CRAWFORD (*Smiling*): Yes, I am.

MYRA: But I thought you were going to stuff the turkey.

MRS. CRAWFORD: No, I'm letting that go till this evening. In fact, we're letting everything go till this evening. Your father and I decided that straightening the house wasn't nearly as important as Christmas presents.

BOBBY: Presents?

MRS. CRAWFORD: Yes, we're driving over to the shopping center and shop like mad till the stores close.

TED: Hooray—Merry Christmas!

OTHERS: Merry Christmas! Merry Christmas! (MR. CRAWFORD *enters left, in hat and overcoat.*)

MR. CRAWFORD: Merry Christmas!

ALL (*Together*): Merry Christmas, Dad!

MR. CRAWFORD: I may look like Dad to you, but in fact, you are gazing at Mr. and Mrs. Santa Claus! We are about to climb into our sleigh and our trusty reindeer will whisk us away to the North Pole. And when we return—the Crawfords will have a Merry Christmas, indeed! (*He starts right with* MRS. CRAWFORD. *Phone rings. They stop and turn.*)

TED (*Laughing*): Better wait, Mr. Santa Claus, this may be for you. (TED *picks up phone.*) Hello? . . . Merry Christmas. . . . Oh, yes, sir. (*Holding out phone*) It *is* for you, Dad. It's Mr. Bascolm.

MRS. CRAWFORD (*Puzzled*): Mr. Bascolm? What in the world can he want with you on Christmas Eve?

BOBBY: It's old Mr. Scrooge!

MR. CRAWFORD: Shh-h, Bobby, he'll hear you. (*Taking phone from* TED) Hello, Mr. Bascolm. . . . Why . . . why. . . . Well, of course we're not very straightened around yet, but my wife and I were just going out to do a bit of last-minute Christmas shopping. . . . Yes. . . . Yes, we were just going out the door. . . . An—an office party? . . . Well—well . . . that's very nice of you to invite us, Mr. Bascolm, but I'm really afraid . . . Yes. . . . Yes, well, as I said we really have to do some shopping. Things have been a bit rushed, you know, and—but Mr. Bascolm, we just can't. . . . Well, of course, my wife will be glad to talk to Mrs. Bascolm. (*Putting hand over phone; to* MRS. CRAWFORD) He wants you to talk to Mrs. Bascolm. There's a party at the office, and—

MRS. CRAWFORD: But John, you know we can't go. I don't want to go. I—

MR. CRAWFORD: I know, I know, neither do I, so you tell her. He's putting her on now. (*Listening in phone*) Yes. . . . Hello, Mrs. Bascolm, here's Mrs. Crawford. (*Holding phone to* MRS. CRAWFORD)

MRS. CRAWFORD (*Taking phone*): Hello, Mrs. Bascolm. My, that is kind of you and your husband to want us to come to the party, but—but (*Weakly*)—but Mrs. Bascolm . . . Yes. . . . Yes. . . . Every year . . . all the office employees. . . . Well, of course, but—yes. . . . Yes, Mrs. Bascolm. Yes, I understand, and we'll be seeing you. . . . Goodbye. (*She hangs up phone.*)

MR. CRAWFORD: You—you didn't say we'd go?

MRS. CRAWFORD: What else could I say? They have it every year. All the office employees will be there. They are there right now waiting to meet us.

MR. CRAWFORD: Oh—oh—so they are waiting. (*He sighs.*) Well, then I suppose there's nothing else to do. We'll have to go right over.

BOBBY (*Almost in tears*): But—but what about our presents?

MRS. CRAWFORD: Bobby, we'll make it up to you. (*Turning to* MR. CRAWFORD) Oh, John, it isn't fair. All our Christmas plans are being spoiled because of your new job. I almost wish you still had your old one and we were back in the city.

MR. CRAWFORD: I know just how you feel. I'm disappointed, myself, but it's too late now—we have to go through with this party. (*To children*) Sorry, kids—I was wrong when I introduced you to Mr. and Mrs. Santa. (*With wry smile*) We're just Mr. and Mrs. Crawford, going to an office party.

BOBBY (*Angrily*): That rotten office! They ought to call it the Scrooge Manufacturing Company. They ruined our Christmas.

MRS. CRAWFORD: Oh, Bobby! I don't want to go to this party—but—but, I guess we have to go.

MR. CRAWFORD: Let's get it over with, dear. Come on. (MR. *and* MRS. CRAWFORD *cross to right exit.*) Goodbye!

MRS. CRAWFORD: Bye! (*They start to exit.*)

CHILDREN (*Calling, ad lib*): Bye! Have a good time! Hurry home! (*Etc.*)

MR. CRAWFORD (*Turning*): Oh, Ted—if the man ever gets here about the lights, you know where the fuse box and the main switch are.

TED: Yes, Dad. I'll show him.

MR. CRAWFORD: Thanks. We'll see you as soon as we can. Bye. (*They exit.*)

TED: Poor Mom and Dad. I guess they feel even worse than we do. And who knows if the man from the electric company will ever get here?

JANET: I don't know if I even care. (*Almost crying*) And —and no one could feel worse than I do.

BOBBY: Me too.

MYRA: But—it doesn't seem right to be miserable on Christmas, just because we've moved to a new place. Christmas ought to be everywhere.

BOBBY: But there ought to be presents.

TED: Oh, it isn't just the presents, Bobby. Christmas is more than just presents.

MYRA: Of course. It's—it's a kind of a feeling you get. And that feeling is made up of lots of things like—well, Christmas means surprises and secrets and sharing, and doing things for people and having them do things for you. Other years we've had all these things—friends and neighbors running in and out—

JANET: That's because we were back home. I agree with Mom. I wish we were back there right now. This afternoon I'd be going over to see Lizzie Slater's Christmas tree and tomorrow they'd all come over to see ours.

BOBBY: Sure, and I'd probably go sledding in the park with Tommy McGinnis. I miss Tommy.

TED (*Laughing*): I thought you were mad at Tommy. Last time you went out sledding you had a fight.

BOBBY: Well, here, there's not even anyone to fight with.

MYRA (*Laughing a little*): I know just what you mean. We've lost all our real friends. I was going to the holiday dance with Charlie, and now I don't know a single boy in town, so—well, even if they do have a dance, no one will ask me. (*Knock on door is heard.*)

TED: Well, I guess we'll get some lights, anyway. (*Crosses to door right and opens it, revealing* MAILMAN, *holding large package with torn wrapping paper*)

MAILMAN: You people expecting a package from out of town?

TED: A Christmas package! Is it really for us?

MAILMAN: The wrapping is so torn that all I can make out is the name of the street and (*Pointing*) over here it says from Mr. and Mrs. G . . . I can't make out the rest.

MYRA: Granger—that's Grandma and Grandpa's name.

MAILMAN: Granger, huh? I guess that must be it. Glad I found you in time. (*Putting down carton and holding slip and pencil out to* TED) Sign here.

TED (*As he signs*): I certainly will.

MAILMAN (*As he goes out right*): Merry Christmas! (BOBBY *pulls carton into middle of room.*)

BOBBY (*Excitedly*): Presents! We've got some presents!

JANET: Grandma and Grandpa's presents. They got here after all!

BOBBY (*Starting to rip open carton*): Let's take them out and put them under the tree.

TED: Now, wait, Bobby. Do you think we ought to, Myra, before Mom and Dad get home?

MYRA: No, I don't. We all wanted a surprise, and now we've got one. Let's save it to surprise Mom and Dad, too, when they get home.

TED: I agree.

MYRA: And this package has given me an idea. There must be other things we can do to surprise Mom and Dad. Let's try not worrying about ourselves so much and think of other things we can do to make it a Merry Christmas for Mom and Dad.

TED: I have an idea. (*He goes to carton near tree and takes out handful of Christmas cards.*) Here are some of last year's cards Mom saved. They'll look just as good as new ones if we stand them around the room. (*He stands cards on mantel.*)

MYRA: It makes it seem more like home already!

JANET: I want to put some around, too. (*Picks up handful of cards and looks left*) How about on top of the television set?

TED: That's fine. (*Puts more cards on mantel*) Bobby, why don't you put some on that table near the window?

BOBBY: O.K. (*Takes cards from carton and stands them on table at right*) I like this one with the big fat Santa.

MYRA: Why, the whole room looks more Christmasy. You know what? Mom was worrying because she hadn't had time for mince pies. But I'm going to make some Christmas cookies.

BOBBY: Cookies? You mean in the shape of stars and lambs and angels?

MYRA: Why not? Dad was unpacking the kitchen stuff and the cookie cutters must be there somewhere.

TED: I'd better get to work, too. I'll unpack all those cartons in Mom and Dad's room and put as much in place as I can. Will they be surprised!

JANET: May I help cut out the cookies?

MYRA: Maybe. But first you'd better finish the tree and get these boxes and the ladder out of the way.

JANET: All right, I'll hurry. (*She starts putting things on tree again.*)

BOBBY (*Looking out window right*): Hey, guess what? The electric company truck is outside! And here comes the man!

TED: Terrific! (*Goes right toward door*) Now our Christmas will really get started. We can have lights on the tree. . . . (*Opens door and admits* BILL COLEMAN, *who enters with toolbox*) Hello! We sure are glad you're here.

BILL (*Gruffly*): Is this the Crawford family? (*As* TED *nods*) Sign here. (*Holds out order book and pen*)

TED: But what's this for? We still don't have any lights, so why should I sign?

BILL: Just to show that I made the call.

TED: But what about the lights?

BILL: I've got an order just to hook 'em on, and there's no wire running from the pole out back.

MYRA: But that's terrible. Can't you run a wire?

BILL: Not today I can't. There's too much ice and snow on the pole to do it with my equipment. You'll have to wait until after Christmas.

JANET (*Sadly*): No lights after all.

BOBBY (*Almost crying*): Now our tree's no good.

JIMMY (*From offstage*): Hey, Dad! Dad! (JIMMY *rushes in; to* BILL) Hey, Dad, come out and look at my new sled!

BILL: Hold it, Jim. You can't come running into strange houses this way without being invited. What's the idea?

JIMMY: I saw your truck outside, so I knew you were here. Mom gave me my sled early because of the snow.

BILL: Oh, she did, did she? (*To others*) My son's just excited. Sorry that he bothered you this way. We'll be going now—I'll be back after Christmas to make the hookup. (*Turns to go with* JIMMY)

BOBBY: Just a second! (*They turn around.*) Could I—that is, would you let me try your sled?

JIMMY: Sure!

BOBBY (*Excited*): Neat-o! Oh, but we all have to plan a Christmas surprise for Mom and Dad.

MYRA: No, Bobby, I think going out for a while is a good idea. And sledding—why, that'll be just like home. There'll still be plenty for you to do when you get back.

BOBBY: O.K. Wait till I get my jacket! (*Rushes off left*)

TED (*To* BILL): I hope this is all right with you, Mr.—

BILL: My name's Coleman—Bill Coleman. We live just a few doors down the street. Sure, let the boys go sledding. (BOBBY *re-enters, wearing jacket.*)

BOBBY: Hey, Jimmy, does your sled steer?

JIMMY: Of course it does! I'll show you. (*Boys rush out right.*)

BILL: Well, see you after Christmas. (*Exits*)

MYRA: I guess it's not Mr. Coleman's fault about the lights, but he didn't try very hard, did he?

TED: Never mind. I'll go downstairs and see if there are any candles or flashlights in the basement. (*Exits left.*)

MYRA (*Looking out window right*): The boys are off in the snow with Bobby pushing the sled. Maybe he won't mind so much about the lights if he has fun sledding. (*Crossing left*) Guess I'll go to work on the cookies. Finish up the tree, will you, Janet?

JANET: O.K. (MYRA *exits left.* JANET *starts to trim tree.*

There is a knock on door. JANET *crosses to door and opens it, revealing* FRANCES.)

FRANCES: Hi. My name's Frances Saunders, and I live in the next block.

JANET: Oh, did you come over to get acquainted?

FRANCES (*Stepping inside, leaving door open*): No, I came over to get that Christmas package. (*Pointing to wrapped box*) It's our presents from Grandma and Grandpa.

JANET (*Startled*): Why—why, it is not! It's *our* presents from Grandma and Grandpa.

FRANCES: No. We asked the mailman, and he said he must have made a mistake and delivered it here. My big brother is coming over for it.

JANET (*Backing toward carton*): Well, you—you can't have it. (FRANCES *dodges around* JANET *and grabs string on carton.*)

FRANCES: We can too have it. It's ours! (JANET *also grabs string. They tug back and forth.*)

JANET (*Shouting*): It's ours, I tell you, it's ours! The mailman said so.

MYRA (*Rushing in left*): Janet, Janet—what's going on here?

JANET: She says this is their Christmas package, and it can't be.

MYRA: Let go of those strings. Both of you. (*As they let go, to* FRANCES) Now, who are you? What's your name?

FRANCES (*Excitedly*): I'm Frances Saunders and the mailman said our package was left here, and—and—(*Looking toward open door where* LARRY *has just appeared*) —and this is my brother, Larry. Larry, they won't let me have it.

LARRY (*Stepping in*): Frances, be quiet. You shouldn't have come here without me in the first place.

MYRA (*To* LARRY; *coldly*): Would you mind telling me

what's going on? I suppose you must be this girl's brother.

LARRY: Yes—I'm Larry Saunders. You see, we've been expecting the Christmas box that always comes from our grandparents, and when we asked the mailman about it, he said he probably left it here by mistake. (TED *enters left.*)

MYRA (*Pointing to package*): Ted, they say this is their package, not ours!

TED: Oh, they do? (*Going to box and pulling off string*) There's an easy way to find out. We'll look at the packages inside. (*He opens box, takes out package in Christmas wrappings, and reads tag.*) "To Mother, from Grandpa and Grandma."

JANET: See?

TED (*Taking out two more*): Oh-oh. (*Reads*) "To Frances from Grandpa and Grandma," and here's one to Larry.

FRANCES: There, what did I tell you?

JANET (*Stubbornly*): But it says from Grandpa and Grandma.

MYRA: But, Janet, lots of families have grandparents—

JANET (*Tearfully*): It's not fair. They were all the presents we had.

TED: It is too bad all right, but if they're not ours, they're not ours. Well, take 'em away, Larry.

JANET (*Crying*): Just everything has gone wrong. The Christmas tree balls were all broken, and then. . . .

FRANCES (*Interrupting*): Oh, who cares about a few Christmas tree balls? (*She rushes out, right.*)

LARRY (*Picking up box*): I don't know what's gotten into Frances. She doesn't usually act this way.

MYRA: I guess she's upset.

LARRY: Well, I suppose. But it's too bad you got the package first and—and had to be disappointed.

TED: It can't be helped. We just moved here, you see, and

none of our presents have come in the mail yet. The post office says they're lost. We wouldn't have minded about the package, except—well, we didn't have time to get ready for Christmas.

LARRY: Yeah, I understand. (*Going to door, with package*) Well, so long.

TED (*Closing door*): So long—Merry Christmas. (JANET *is sniffling a little.* TED *and* MYRA *stand looking at each other sadly.*)

MYRA (*Almost crying*): Oh, Ted. . . . (BOBBY *rushes in, right. His jacket is torn and dirty.*)

BOBBY (*Heatedly*): Say, where's that guy going with our presents from Grandma and Grandpa?

TED: They're not ours, Bobby. It was a mistake.

BOBBY: A mistake? But . . .

MYRA: Bobby Crawford, what have you been doing? Your clothes are a mess.

BOBBY: Oh, nothing very much. I—I had a fight with Jimmy.

TED: What?

BOBBY: Well, he said I wasn't as strong as he was because I came from the city. So we had a fight, and I washed his face with snow.

TED: But, Bobby, you shouldn't have done that. You—

MYRA: You picked a fine person to fight with, Bobby. Now Mr. Coleman will be furious with us, and we'll never get any lights.

JANET (*Looking out window*): And here comes that Frances, running up our walk. I don't want to see her again.

MYRA: Now, Janet, take it easy. We're getting in wrong with our neighbors as it is. (MYRA *opens door just as* FRANCES *appears in doorway, holding cardboard box.*)

FRANCES (*Holding out box*): See? I knew you didn't have to worry about a few Christmas tree balls. I ran home and told my mother, and she sent me right back with these. We've got lots of extras we never use. (*Holds out box to* MYRA)

MYRA (*Taking box*): Why—why, Frances, that's so nice! Janet, look!

JANET (*Peering into box*): Oh, they're beautiful! You—you mean we can use them on our tree?

FRANCES (*Excitedly*): Of course. And that isn't all. Everybody is coming to help.

MYRA: What do you mean by that?

FRANCES: When I told Mother how sad you all were when we took your—I mean, our presents away from you, she looked sort of cross the way she does sometimes when she's thinking. And then she said, "Why, it's terrible, just terrible!"

TED: But they *were* your presents.

FRANCES: That isn't what she meant. She said people who move into a new house always need help to get settled. And here we've all been thinking about our own Christmas and doing nothing about your family. Larry wants to help, too. He said we should all come over here and cheer up our new neighbors. (*To* MYRA) I think he mostly meant you!

MYRA (*Smiling*): He—he did?

FRANCES: Yes, and he's gone to get some of his friends, and Mother's on the way over, too. (*To* JANET) And . . . and may I help you finish decorating your tree?

JANET: Of course, Frances! (*They go to tree and hang balls on it.*)

TED: Well, if all the neighbors are coming to help, it sounds as though we may have surprises for Mom and Dad after all.

MYRA: You're right. But there's so much to do that I don't know where to begin.

FRANCES: You won't have to worry about that when my

mother gets here. She's the best organizer in town. Every year she organizes the voters' drive, and the PTA fair.

TED: That's quite a recommendation! (*Knock on door is heard.*) That must be your mother now. (*Opens door;* MRS. SAUNDERS *hurries in, carrying bulging shopping bag.*) Hello. You must be Mrs. Saunders.

MRS. SAUNDERS: Yes, I am. I just put a few things into this bag on my way out of the house.

BOBBY (*Looking into bag*): Mm-m-m! Oranges and cookies and candy!

MRS. SAUNDERS: Wait a minute! These are for Christmas—you can't eat them now.

MYRA (*Laughing*): That's right, Bobby. (*Going to* MRS. SAUNDERS) It's so good of you to come, Mrs. Saunders. I'm Myra Crawford, and this is Ted, and Janet, and Bobby—with the appetite.

MRS. SAUNDERS: We'll get acquainted as we work—there isn't much time. Where are your parents?

MYRA: Oh, they had to go to an office party where our dad has a new job.

MRS. SAUNDERS: Office party on Christmas Eve! Why, that's terrible. I'll bet you're hardly unpacked.

TED: We straightened up this room as well as we could, but the rest of the house is still kind of upset.

MRS. SAUNDERS: Naturally it is. I saw the moving van here yesterday, and I meant to come over, but there was so much to do that it slipped my mind. Well, when the others get here, you two will have to show them what things have to be moved, and how to arrange the rooms. Now, what about getting things ready for your dinner tomorrow?

MYRA: Oh, we've got a turkey, and Mom is going to stuff it when she gets home.

MRS. SAUNDERS: After the party? Nonsense. She'll be too

tired. We can take care of that right now. Is your phone in yet?

TED: Yes, it's right there. (*Points*)

MRS. SAUNDERS (*Going quickly to phone and dialing*): Helen is the best cook in town. She'll have that turkey ready for the oven in no time. (*Into phone*) Hello, Helen. . . . Yes . . . yes, I'm over at the home of that new family at 123, and they need a turkey stuffed for tomorrow. . . . Yes, that's what I said. . . . Then you'll be over? Yes. (*Laughs*) Then you're already acquainted with part of the family? . . . All right, hurry over. We haven't much time. (*Hanging up phone*)

MYRA: What did you mean, she's acquainted with our family?

MRS. SAUNDERS (*Smiling*): She says that Bobby, here, washed her son Jimmy's face with snow—and it hasn't been so clean in weeks!

BOBBY: You mean—she wasn't mad at me?

MRS. SAUNDERS: She didn't sound angry when she told me about it. (LARRY *and* TEEN-AGERS *are heard laughing and talking offstage.*) That must be Larry and his friends coming now. (TED *opens door.* LARRY *enters, followed by* TEEN-AGERS.)

LARRY: Now, one, two, three.

TEEN-AGERS (*Together*): Merry Christmas, Crawfords!

MYRA: Merry Christmas! Oh, this is wonderful.

LARRY: Merry Christmas, Myra.

MYRA: Merry Christmas, Larry.

MRS. SAUNDERS: Never mind the Merry Christmas until after we've done our work. Ted, you take some of this crew with you and put them to work.

TED: O.K. I guess the first thing is to lug a lot of stuff down to the basement, so that we can put the dining room furniture in place.

LARRY: Lead the way! (TED, LARRY, *and several* TEEN-

AGERS *exit left, laughing and talking.*)

MRS. SAUNDERS: Now, Myra, what needs to be done upstairs?

MYRA: Well, the bedrooms are still a mess, and there are linens to be put on the shelves, and the rugs can be unrolled, too, as soon as we get enough space cleared. (*She exits left, followed by other* TEEN-AGERS, *all talking happily.*)

MRS. SAUNDERS: Well, that's a start. Bobby, why don't you take that stepladder and put it away somewhere?

BOBBY: All right. (*He folds ladder and carries it off left.*)

MRS. SAUNDERS (*To* FRANCES *and* JANET): And when you girls finish with the tree, take both these cartons to the basement.

JANET: We will, Mrs. Saunders. Your Christmas balls do make the tree look better. If only we had lights.

MRS. SAUNDERS: You mean to say your lights aren't turned on?

JANET: No. Mr. Coleman was here and he says he can't fix them.

MRS. SAUNDERS: That's too bad. But, if Bill Coleman can't fix them, nobody can. We'll have to get you some candles for the mantel before it gets dark. (*Knock on door is heard.* MRS. SAUNDERS *opens it, letting in* HELEN COLEMAN, *carrying wrapped pie, and* JIMMY, *carrying candlesticks with candles.*) Oh, good, Helen, glad you came so fast.

HELEN: Hello, Grace. Glad to help.

MRS. SAUNDERS: And, Jimmy, we were just saying we needed candles for the mantel.

JIMMY: Dad said there were no lights here, so Mom said to bring these. (*Hands candlesticks to* MRS. SAUNDERS)

MRS. SAUNDERS: Thank you—they'll be just fine. (*She puts them on mantel.*)

BOBBY (*Rushing in left*): Wow, are they getting things straightened out in a hurry! (*Seeing* HELEN *and* JIMMY) Oh—hello.

HELEN: Hello, Bobby. Why did you run away so fast when I came out on the front porch at our house?

BOBBY: Well, I—I thought you'd be mad because I was fighting with Jimmy.

HELEN: Oh, I don't suppose it's the last fight you two will have. But I wanted to give you this mince pie to bring home.

BOBBY: Mince pie?

HELEN: Yes, I heard you telling Jimmy your mother wouldn't have time to make any and we had three.

BOBBY (*Taking pie and holding it up*): Hooray! Look, Janet! We've got mince pie for Christmas! (*He puts it on table.*)

JANET: I—I guess we're getting almost everything for Christmas. (*Tree lights come on.*) Oh, look—the lights are on!

BOBBY: The lights are on!

FRANCES (*Looking at tree*): It's beautiful!

MRS. SAUNDERS: Yes, there's nothing as beautiful as a Christmas tree, I always say.

JANET (*Picking up carton*): Let's take the cartons out and tell everyone to come and look at the tree.

FRANCES: All right. (*Picks up other carton and runs off left behind* JANET)

JANET (*From offstage*): Everybody come and see the tree! The lights are on!

MRS. SAUNDERS: And Bill said he couldn't fix them. Was he trying to fool somebody?

HELEN: No, he was serious when he talked to me—I guess he managed, anyhow. Well, I can't stand here looking at the tree if I'm going to get that bird stuffed before their parents get home. (*She turns toward kitchen, just as* JANET *and* FRANCES *re-enter left, with* MYRA, TED, LARRY, *and* TEEN-AGERS *following them. All exclaim as they see tree. Front door opens and* MR. *and* MRS. CRAWFORD *enter, followed by* MR. *and* MRS. BASCOLM. MR. BASCOLM *carries large package wrapped in Christmas paper.*)

MR. CRAWFORD: What's this? We have company!

BOBBY (*Rushing forward*): I'll say, Dad. They're straightening up the whole house, and Mrs. Coleman brought a mince pie, and Mrs. Saunders some cookies and candy, and Mrs. Coleman is going to stuff the turkey and—and wow, you've got a present!

MR. CRAWFORD: Just a minute, Bobby! One thing at a time. Will someone please tell me what's been going on here?

MRS. SAUNDERS: Well, I guess I'd better, as I've been sort of organizing things. I'm Grace Saunders and you must be Mr. and Mrs. Crawford, and I recognize Mr. and Mrs. Bascolm from pictures I've seen in the paper. The rest of us are just neighbors who have come in to help your family get comfortable in time for Christmas.

MRS. CRAWFORD (*Almost crying*): Why—why—if that isn't the nicest thing I've ever heard of in all my life. I don't know how to thank you.

MR. CRAWFORD: I've already made one speech today, to thank Mr. and Mrs. Bascolm and my new friends at the office. They insisted we go to what they called an office party, but it was really just an occasion for them all to give us a present for the family. So I'll just say what I said before. It's pretty wonderful to move to a new job and a new home, feeling that you'd lost all your old friends, and then to find—well, that you have many new friends all around you. Thank you all. (*Everybody applauds.*)

MR. BASCOLM: Well, I'd applaud, too, if I could put this package down.

MRS. CRAWFORD: Of course! Let's put it right under the tree.

MRS. BASCOLM: My, your tree is beautiful.

MRS. SAUNDERS: And the lights just came on—we don't know how, because Bill Coleman said he couldn't fix them. (BILL *enters left.*) Why, Bill! How did you do it?

BILL: I really didn't do much except tell Mr. and Mrs. Brady next door that there were no lights here, and I couldn't run a line from the pole. So they said to run one from their meter for a day or two. They're too old to get out much, but they told me to come in and say Merry Christmas to you from them.

MRS. CRAWFORD: Of all things! Just everybody is making Christmas nice for us. I can't believe it.

BOBBY: Boy, I like the suburbs. (*Everyone laughs.*)

MR. BASCOLM: It seems to me that I've heard that voice before. (*Laughing*) Yes, sir, it was when I called on the phone today. I distinctly heard him say, "It's old Mr. Scrooge."

BOBBY: Well—well—I—I—

MR. BASCOLM (*Pretending to be angry*): Yes, young man? What have you got to say for yourself?

BOBBY: Well, I—I—

JIMMY: Mr. Bascolm, what he meant was that you are a real good guy like Scrooge in the end of the story.

BOBBY: Yes—yes, that's right, Mr. Scrooge—I mean, Mr. Bascolm.

MR. BASCOLM: Oh. (*Indicating* JIMMY) I take it this boy is a friend of yours.

BOBBY: Him? (*Giving* JIMMY *playful shove*) Sure. He's Jimmy Coleman. He's my buddy. (*All laugh.*)

MR. BASCOLM: Well, that's fine. You stick with him and

you'll do all right. And as long as I'm the nice Mr. Scrooge, I'll say *(Waving arm to include everyone)*—God bless us every one!

ALL: Merry Christmas! (*Curtain*)

THE END

A Room for a King

by Graham DuBois

Characters

MICHAEL, *the innkeeper*
SARAH, *his wife*
ELIZA, *his mother*
RUTH, *a kitchen maid*
JACOB, *a guest at the inn*
ADAH, *his mother*
ENOS, *a shepherd*
WISE MAN
MARY } *in tableau*
JOSEPH } *in tableau*

TIME: *The night of Christ's birth.*
SETTING: *The yard of the inn at Bethlehem.*
AT RISE: SARAH *is sitting on the bench as* MICHAEL *enters from the inn.*

MICHAEL (*Rubbing his hands in satisfaction*): It has been a good day, Sarah. The inn is full. All the rooms are taken—all but one, and that I'm reserving for a very special guest.

SARAH: I am glad that you are pleased, Michael.

MICHAEL (*Sitting beside her*): Well, you don't seem very much impressed. We are making money. Travelers have been flocking here all week on their way to Bethlehem to pay their taxes. Some of them are people of importance—and you sit here staring at the sky.

SARAH (*Quietly*): What do you mean by people of importance? That old lady who has sat here watching and listening?

MICHAEL (*Impatiently*): Of course not! She's probably only the wife of some fairly well-to-do farmer.

SARAH: That tall man who seems afraid to lay his bundle down?

MICHAEL: I should say not. He's only a little merchant. At least that's what he says he is.

SARAH: You sound suspicious.

MICHAEL (*Glancing about him*): I am. I can't quite make out what he is doing here. Why won't he let that precious bundle out of his sight? Why does he spend so much time in his room? He has been out of it only once today, and then he walked around this yard looking over his shoulder as if he thought somebody was spying on him.

SARAH: It seems to to me that everybody is waiting for something to happen. There's an air of expectancy in the night. The world is holding its breath. (*A donkey brays.*)

MICHAEL: Stupid beast!

SARAH: What was that?

MICHAEL: That confounded donkey.

SARAH: Not the little animal that poor woman was riding? I watched her from my window. I thought she would faint before her husband could get her to the door of the inn. I do hope you gave them a comfortable room, Michael.

MICHAEL: I gave them no room at all—the paupers! What they could pay was insufficient for their bed in the straw of the stable.

SARAH (*Rising and pointing to the stable*): You don't mean you made them pay for that wretched place?

MICHAEL: I do indeed! Why shouldn't they? They are lucky to get it.

SARAH: May God forgive you! You don't know what you have done. (*Sits and bows her head*)

MICHAEL: Why are you so upset? I might have turned them away.

SARAH: You might have given them a room at the inn.

MICHAEL: There was no room.

SARAH: You had one room; you still have it. Let us move them in there before it is too late.

MICHAEL (*Looking at her in amazement*): Surely you don't mean my royal guest chamber?

SARAH: I do mean that.

MICHAEL: Sarah, you are mad! You know that room is always reserved for the great of the world. I have wonderful news for you. One of Herod's representatives was here this morning. Do you realize that Herod himself may pass this way tonight?

SARAH: A greater one than Herod may pass this way.

MICHAEL: What do you mean? (*Looks at her, puzzled*) I'll wager you've been with that soothsayer again. She always upsets you. I can see that far-away look in your eyes as if you saw and heard strange things.

SARAH (*Raising her eyes to the heavens slowly*): I do see and hear strange things. I see the lovely face of a newborn babe. I hear angelic voices making music in the night. (*Bows her head. A Christmas carol comes from the stable*) Don't you hear them, too?

MICHAEL (*Listening*): I hear nothing but the wind in the trees.

SARAH: There was a song in the stable.

MICHAEL (*Listening*): Just the stable boys singing as they feed the animals. I'll have to warn them: they might disturb the people at the inn. (*Listens*) And I hear that miserable donkey again. He must go. (*Rises*)

SARAH (*Laying a hand on his arm*): No, Michael; for my sake, let him stay. Perhaps he hasn't had enough food.

MICHAEL: He hasn't had any—unless his wretched master broke the locks on my bins.

SARAH: Michael! You can't mean that you let that poor little animal go hungry?

MICHAEL: Why not? He's his owner's responsibility, not mine. (*Turns toward stable*) I'll turn him loose to forage by the roadside. There's plenty of grass along the road.

SARAH: No, Michael; he's too lame and tired. (JACOB *enters from inn, carrying a bundle under his arm, his hat drawn far down over his face.*)

JACOB: I can't stand it any longer.

MICHAEL: Why, what is wrong, sir? Your room is comfortable I hope?

JACOB: It's not the room: it's that donkey. I can't bear to hear him braying.

MICHAEL: As I thought! I was afraid he would annoy my guests. I was just going to turn him out.

JACOB: No; you don't understand. I know what a donkey needs when he brays like that. I had one as a pet when I was a child. He wants food. You probably don't realize that he is hungry.

MICHAEL: I do realize it, sir, but his owner made no provision for his food, and the rule of the inn is that—

JACOB (*Feeling in his pocket*): Oh, is that all? (*Draws out a coin and hands it to* MICHAEL) Will that be sufficient?

MICHAEL: More than sufficient, sir. You are generous. I'll attend to it at once. (*Turns toward stable*)

JACOB: No—if you will permit me, I'd like to feed the donkey myself.

MICHAEL: Certainly. (*Draws key from pocket*) Here is the key to the feed bins. (*Hands key to* JACOB)

JACOB: Thank you. (*Walks toward stable*) I'll return it immediately. (*Enters stable*)

MICHAEL (*Sitting on bench and shaking his head suspiciously*): A strange fellow! Did you notice how tightly he held that bundle under his arm? Did you see how he wears his hat? So far down over his face it almost hides his eyes. He won't let you get a good look at him. He turned his face away when I handed him the key. I'd give a fortune to know what he has in that bundle. Why did he have to take it into the stable with him?

SARAH: Maybe he wanted to offer it to that poor woman as a pillow. (ADAH *enters from the inn.* MICHAEL *rises.*)

MICHAEL: Is there something I can do for you, madam?

ADAH (*Looking around her nervously*): I—I was just wondering whether any more guests have arrived at the inn.

MICHAEL (*Surprised*): Why, no, madam. It is getting late for travelers, you know; and, besides, the inn is full. Were you expecting somebody?

ADAH: No—no. Tomorrow I go to the tax offices to pay my taxes. I'd—I'd feel safer if I found someone to go with me. My cousin lives near Bethlehem, but I do not know his house. I—I thought perhaps he might drop in here for a cup of wine.

MICHAEL (*Looking at her suspiciously*): Hardly at this hour.

ADAH (*Turning away reluctantly*): Well—good night. (*She walks to inn door and turns.*) If you hear of anybody who will go with me, will you let me know?

MICHAEL: Certainly, madam. (*She enters inn. He sits on bench.*) Another queer character! I knew when she came that she wasn't the type I generally accept as guests, but it was getting late, and so I took her in.

SARAH: And gave her that wretched, dark little room in the corner.

MICHAEL: It was good enough for a woman of her position. (JACOB *enters from stable*) Hush! Here he comes.

JACOB: Well, I think that poor little donkey will be quiet for the rest of the night. (*Walks to bench and hands the key to* MICHAEL) Thank you. (*Walks to inn door*) He's eating as if he hadn't had any food for a week. (*Enters inn*)

MICHAEL (*Pockets key. Triumphantly*): Do you notice anything strange about him now? (*Nods toward inn*)

SARAH (*Quietly*): I can't see that he has changed in the past few minutes.

MICHAEL: I'm afraid you are not very observant. He no longer has the bundle. (RUTH *enters with the bundle in her hands.*) What have you there?

RUTH (*Looking cautiously about*): A bundle that man left in the stable.

MICHAEL: Give it to me. (RUTH *hands him the bundle.*)

SARAH: Perhaps he forgot it. We must return it to him.

MICHAEL (*Impatiently*): Don't be stupid! This may hold the secret of what that man is. (*Examines bundle*)

SARAH (*To* RUTH): Where did you find it? On one of the food bins?

RUTH: No; in the straw. I ducked behind a stall and watched him hide it there.

MICHAEL: That settles it. (*Begins to unwrap the bundle*) We'll soon know what this rogue is doing at a respectable inn.

SARAH (*Protestingly*): You have no right to tamper with another's property.

MICHAEL (*Holding up uniform*): As I thought! (*Meditatively*) Now I remember. Only yesterday it was. I heard a man in one of the shops say an officer had left his legion. The hunt was on. (*Examines uniform*) This is an officer's uniform. (*To* RUTH) Go into the inn and make sure that man doesn't leave his room without being seen. (RUTH *walks to door of inn and enters.*) Sarah, there is a magnificent reward offered for him—enough to build an addition to the inn.

SARAH (*Stunned*): Michael, you can't mean that you would—

MICHAEL (*Putting uniform on bench*): Well, Herod will know how to deal with him. (*Rubs his hands in satisfac-

tion) Wife, we are made. Herod will be delighted with our loyalty.

SARAH: You don't mean that you would turn this poor man over to the authorities?

MICHAEL: What else? He is a deserter, isn't he? The penalty is death.

SARAH: From what is he deserting? From things worse than death. From one of the most hated tyrants this world has ever known. From cruelty and greed and murder. From—

MICHAEL (*Clapping his hand upon her shoulder*): Peace, woman! You know not what you say. (*Looks fearfully about him*) Herod's spies are everywhere. Our very servants may be in his employ.

SARAH: That is what this poor man would desert. Maybe he has felt something strange and wonderful in the night, just as I feel it deep within my heart. (*Looking at sky*) Maybe that star has guided him to the inn.

MICHAEL: What star?

SARAH: That star in the East. (*Pointing*) Don't you see it?

MICHAEL (*Staring at sky*): The sky is full of stars. They all look alike to me.

SARAH: There is one that is different—so full and bright and lovely that it makes all the others seem dim.

MICHAEL (*Impatiently*): I tell you the sky is just as it has always been at this season.

SARAH (*Shaking her head sadly*): I'm afraid you are blind, Michael.

MICHAEL: Blind? The physician examined my eyes only yesterday. He says they are unusually strong for a man of my age. He told me—

SARAH (*Gently*): There are some things that one must see only with the eyes of the heart. (*Listens*) The song again! Don't you hear it now? (*Christmas carol is heard from the stable*)

MICHAEL (*Listening*): There is no sound—absolutely nothing. Even the wind is still.

SARAH (*Sadly*): How deaf you are, Michael!

MICHAEL: My ears are as good as yours, woman.

SARAH: There are some things which only the ears of the heart can hear.

MICHAEL: What things? (*Sneeringly*) Music and song from a stable, I suppose?

SARAH: Yes, music and song and the words of an old prophecy have been ringing in my ears all day. "O Bethlehem, tiniest of townships in all Judah, out of you a king shall come to govern Israel." (WISE MAN *enters left.*)

MICHAEL: Hush, wife! Say no more. Here comes a representative of the king. (*Rises, to* WISE MAN) I bid you welcome, sir. I have been expecting you.

WISE MAN: The King will come tonight. You should feel honored that He has chosen your inn.

MICHAEL: I do, indeed, sir. I have been preparing for him all week. The royal chamber is at his disposal.

WISE MAN: You have done well. There is no chamber in all the world worthy to receive Him. Your name will be cherished by future ages because He was born here.

MICHAEL (*Amazed*): Born here? I don't understand. I thought—

WISE MAN: He will arrive tonight. (*Looks at sky*) It is getting brighter. Soon it will be as bright as day. The sky will be flooded with light, and hosts of angels will fill the air with song.

MICHAEL: I—I don't know just what you— (*A Christmas carol from the stable.*)

WISE MAN (*Bowing his head and listening*): The loveliest music I ever heard! (*Puzzled*) But it doesn't seem to come from the inn; it seems to be coming from the stable. (*Turning toward stable*) I'll go see that the boys are attending to our camels. In the meanwhile, make sure that the royal chamber is ready. (*Walks to stable*)

MICHAEL: I will, sir. (WISE MAN *enters stable*) Is the man mad? (*To* SARAH) We have important work ahead of us. (SARAH *rises.*) Go see that the maids have overlooked nothing in the royal chamber. (SARAH *walks to inn door*) We have to watch those stupid girls every minute. (SARAH *enters inn as* ELIZA *enters from left.*)

ELIZA (*Walking to bench*): Such a chase as I have had! (*Sits*) I'm all out of breath.

MICHAEL (*Surprised*): Mother! You shouldn't be out on the highway at night. (*Eagerly*) Did you happen to see that fine gentleman who just arrived?

ELIZA: Yes, he and several others like him passed me.

MICHAEL: Tell me, didn't his dress strike you as strange? If he's a representative of Herod, wouldn't his attire be more like what we see in Bethlehem?

ELIZA: You must remember, son, that we don't see ambassadors of Herod very often.

MICHAEL: That's true. But he talked so incoherently. Angels and light and song!

ELIZA: Probably just his manner of speaking. These minions of Herod, you know, have to talk in exaggerated terms when they mention the king.

MICHAEL: You are right. (*Thoughtfully*) I didn't know that Herod was expecting a son.

ELIZA: Probably keeping it a secret. He has to be careful. There are many, I understand, who would destroy him and his offspring.

MICHAEL: That's it. Herod realizes that my inn would never be suspected. He and his wife are coming here so that the news will not leak out. Mother, after this event my inn will be known throughout the world. (*Rubbing his hands*) People will bid for the honor of sleeping in a room where a future king was born. I'll be rich beyond my wildest dreams. . . . But you haven't told me what you were doing on the highway at this hour.

ELIZA: It was Ruth who was responsible for my going out into the night.

MICHAEL (*Amazed*): Ruth? Not that silly maid who is always daydreaming in the kitchen?

ELIZA (*Nodding*): I saw her from my window. She was gazing up at the sky. A moment later she ran down the highway, and as soon as I could I followed her.

MICHAEL: Disobedient wretch! I ordered her not to take her eyes off the door of that man with the bundle. (*Turning toward the inn door*) I'll have to make sure that he's still there.

ELIZA: It's no use, Michael.

MICHAEL: Why not?

ELIZA: He has gone.

MICHAEL: Are you sure? (*Sinks down upon the bench*)

ELIZA: Yes; he went out the front door a moment after she left.

MICHAEL (*Pounding the palm of one hand with his fist*): The miserable fool! This may cost me a handsome sum. (*Rises*) But he can't have gone very far. Come, Mother. (ELIZA *rises.*) I have a dozen men posted along the highway to let me know the moment they spot Herod's retinue approaching. (*Walks toward portal left, followed by* ELIZA) They can tell us in what direction this deserter went. (*They go out as* ADAH *enters from the inn.*)

ADAH (*Walking toward the bench*): How very still the night is! (*Sits and looks at the sky*) That star is getting nearer and brighter. It's almost directly over the stable now. (JACOB *enters from the stable door. He stands irresolute for a moment, and then walks stealthily toward the inn door.*)

ADAH: Jacob! Come back. Don't be afraid.

JACOB: Who are you? I know you not.

ADAH: My son! You are running away from something, but you can't outrun a mother's love.

JACOB: *Mother!* (*Walks toward bench, his arm outstretched*) You must not stay here. (*Kneels and enfolds her in his arms*) There is danger now wherever I am. I am an outcast, a deserter. That hateful uniform beside you is the badge of Herod's cutthroat army.

ADAH (*Fingering uniform*): You mean—this is yours?

JACOB: It was mine. I tore it off when I got your message. I hid it in the straw, but they found it, and now there is no chance of escape. This miserly innkeeper has seen to that. (ENOS *enters from stable and stands unnoticed, watching them.*)

ADAH: You did get my message, then? I wanted you to know that your little sick Caleb was calling you.

JACOB (*Rising*): How is he? Is he better? What does the physician say?

ADAH (*Shaking her head sadly*): He is no better. He is still calling you. The physician says unless the child can see you, he may—

JACOB: No, Mother! Don't say it. I can't bear it. (*Sinks down upon bench*)

ADAH: I had to come to Bethlehem to pay my taxes. I planned to appeal to Herod's officials. I thought they might grant you a leave of absence.

JACOB (*Laughing bitterly*): How little you know those heartless brutes!

ADAH: I thought I would stay at our cousin Enoch's house, and he could go with me to the tax offices, but I couldn't find it. Do you know where Enoch lives?

JACOB: Yes. He hid me there the night I deserted. He gave me these clothes. He wanted me to leave this uniform with him, but I wouldn't consent because it would have endangered him and his family.

ADAH: But why did you come to this inn—under Herod's very nose?

JACOB: That was my reason for coming here, Mother. I knew his men would search for me outside Bethlehem. I hid that uniform so deep in the straw that it wouldn't have been uncovered for weeks. Somebody must have seen me.

ADAH: We must do something, Jacob. You can't just stay here and let them take you.

JACOB: There is only one thing left for me to do, Mother. I'll have to fight my way out of here if I can. There is no other way.

ENOS (*Advancing toward bench*): There is another way.

JACOB (*Springing up from bench*): Who are you?

ENOS: Just a humble shepherd, my friend. I and others were watching our flocks when the star and an angel host appeared to guide us to Bethlehem.

JACOB: How dare you eavesdrop upon me and my mother?

ENOS: I didn't mean to eavesdrop. I happened to overhear your mother and you talking about a sick child. I had a child once.

JACOB: But what can you do?

ENOS: I can put you on the road that leads to your child.

JACOB: It's impossible. How could you do that? The innkeeper's men have surrounded this place. They would fall upon me like hungry wolves if I attempted to leave now.

ENOS: They won't recognize you.

JACOB: There's not one of them who hasn't seen me. Why wouldn't they recognize me?

ENOS: We shall exchange clothing.

JACOB: No! Do you suppose I would let another suffer in my place? The person who aids a deserter receives the same punishment as the deserter himself.

ENOS: I have lived here all my life. I know every path and

cave in these hills. I have a much better chance of getting away than you have.

ADAH: Listen to this good shepherd, my boy.

JACOB: No; I can't accept such a sacrifice.

ENOS: Your child is calling, my friend.

JACOB (*Hesitating*): If I only thought you could get away!

ENOS: Your mother is in danger, too, you know. She has been here at the inn with you.

JACOB: But you owe me nothing. Why are you doing this thing?

ENOS: In the name of a child who died; in the name of a child who is to be born tonight.

JACOB (*Yielding*): What would you have me do?

ENOS: Take me to your room. You will put on this shepherd's garb. Then you can walk boldly out of the yard with your mother. Come! We haven't a moment to lose; the innkeeper may be back at any moment. (*He leads* JACOB *to inn door and turns to* ADAH.) You wait here, madam, until your son returns. (*He and* JACOB *enter inn.* MICHAEL *and* ELIZA *enter left.*)

MICHAEL: You heard what they said. He tried to sneak past them, but they made him turn back to the inn. (*They walk to inn door and stop.*)

ELIZA: None of them had seen Ruth.

MICHAEL: No matter. It's a good riddance. She wasn't worth her salt. And, besides, she might try to claim part of the reward. Let us see if he has gone back to his room. (*They enter the inn.*)

ADAH (*Bowing her head in prayer*): God, help them both to escape, and find a refuge for them and for all poor hunted creatures. (SARAH *enters from inn.* ADAH *raises her head.*)

SARAH (*Advancing toward bench*): Forgive me for disturbing you. (*Sits on bench*) I believe you were praying.

ADAH: Yes, I was. I was praying for two brave but discouraged men. Do you often pray?

SARAH: Yes. I pray for the little children in this tortured world, that they may be given a better opportunity than we have had. And all day I have known, somehow, that tonight a child would be born who would bring a new promise and a new hope.

ADAH: You have felt it, too? There is something in the night, an air of hushed expectancy that, in spite of sorrow and danger, fills my heart with awe and happiness. (MICHAEL *and* ELIZA *enter from the inn.*)

MICHAEL: Did you lock the outer door?

ELIZA: Yes. To leave the inn he must pass through the yard.

MICHAEL: Good. There is no avenue of escape for him now.

ELIZA: Is he in his room?

MICHAEL: Yes. I listened at his door. I heard his voice.

ELIZA: His voice? Was he talking to himself?

MICHAEL: No, there was another man in his room with him. That has me puzzled. His voice seemed familiar.

ELIZA: Just some guest probably, who dropped in for a chat.

MICHAEL (*Advancing to bench and addressing* ADAH): Couldn't you sleep, madam?

ADAH: I was restless, and the night was so beautiful that I came out for a breath of air. (JACOB, *in* ENOS's *clothes, enters from the inn.*)

MICHAEL (*Angrily*): What are you doing here, you rogue?

SARAH (*Rising and laying a restraining hand on his arm*): Now, Michael, don't lose your temper. The poor fellow means no harm.

MICHAEL: I have told these thieving shepherds to keep away from the inn. (*To* JACOB) Why are you sneaking about at this hour? Were you trying to rob me or my guests? (*Pauses*) Well, why don't you answer me? Don't just stand there gaping like an idiot.

ADAH (*Rising*): I think I can answer for him. This poor shepherd knows the way to my cousin's house. He has promised to take me there. (*Walks to* JACOB *and takes his arm*) I can promise that he will give you no trouble.

MICHAEL: Well, get him out of here as soon as you can. (ADAH *leads* JACOB *to gateway left*) I don't feel safe as long as one of these miserable creatures is near my inn. (ADAH *and* JACOB *go out.*)

ELIZA: I'll look around to see if he has taken anything.

MICHAEL: And make sure the deserter is still in his room. He's the most valuable thing we have. (ELIZA *enters inn.*)

SARAH: Michael, how can you be so utterly heartless—on this night of all nights?

MICHAEL: This night is the same as any other to me. A deserter comes to my inn. It is my duty to turn him over to Herod's representatives. (*Struck by a sudden thought*) Why, one of Herod's representatives is here! I never thought of that. (*Turns toward inn*) I can deliver this rogue to him.

SARAH (*Holding him back*): No, Michael! For my sake! For the sake of the child we never had, I beg of you that —(ELIZA *enters from inn, leading* ENOS *in* JACOB'S *clothes.*)

ELIZA: I was just in time, Michael. He was trying to pick the lock on the front door.

MICHAEL (*Brushing* SARAH'S *hand from his arm*): We'll put the rascal into safe hands. (*Advances to* ENOS) Herod's men will see to it that you have no locks to pick. (*Lays a hand on* ENOS'S *shoulder*) Come with me, my fine rogue. (*The* WISE MAN *enters from stable.*)

WISE MAN: What is all this commotion? This should be a night of peace and happiness.

MICHAEL: You are a representative of the king, are you not, sir?

WISE MAN: I hope I am.

MICHAEL (*Triumphantly*): Then I turn over to your custody this man who has betrayed the king, a traitor, a deserter. (*Tears hat from* ENOS's *head*) Look on this scoundrel's face and— (*Stands back in amazement*) Why —why—this is not the man. We—we have—been tricked. This fellow is one of those wretched shepherds. But he's guilty too. He helped a deserter to—

WISE MAN: Set this man free at once. He has served the King.

MICHAEL (*Bewildered*): Served the king? I tell you he—

WISE MAN: He helped a King's father and mother find their way to this inn. He ministered to their lame donkey. And tonight he left his flocks to follow that star. (*Points to heavens*)

MICHAEL (*Looking upward*): What star? I see a million stars.

WISE MAN: Your eyes are so blinded by selfishness that you can't see the loveliest star that ever illumined the darkness of this world. (*A Christmas carol from the stable.* ENOS *kneels and folds his hands in an attitude of adoration.*)

MICHAEL: Don't kneel to me for mercy, fellow. Save your pleas for the king.

WISE MAN: He's not kneeling to you. He's kneeling because of the song.

MICHAEL: I hear no song.

WISE MAN: Your ears are so dulled by the sound of money jingling in your coffers that you can't hear the sweetest music that ever gladdened the hearts of men.

MICHAEL: I'm afraid you don't understand, sir. When the king arrives, I'll—

WISE MAN: The King has arrived.

MICHAEL: He has arrived? It's impossible, sir. My men along the highway would have—

WISE MAN: The King whom you turned away from your royal chamber was born in a manger. The Prince of Peace lies in your stable.

MICHAEL (*Bewildered*): The Prince of Peace? (*Beginning to understand*) You mean the old prophecy has—

WISE MAN: Has been fulfilled. And you were blind and deaf to everything that was taking place within your own walls—except those things which filled your pockets.

MICHAEL (*Sitting on bench*): I didn't know. Can a man be blamed for what he doesn't know?

WISE MAN: Your lack of knowledge is no excuse. (*Indicating* ENOS *and* SARAH) These people didn't know, either, but they had something mightier and more beautiful than knowledge—they had faith. (ADAH *and* JACOB *enter left.*)

SARAH (*Looking at them in astonishment*): You dared return—even though you knew it might mean prison and death?

JACOB (*Pointing to* ENOS): That man had risked his life for me. I couldn't let him take the penalty alone.

ADAH: It was when we saw the star and heard the song that we knew we had to come back—even though we came with empty hands.

ENOS (*Showing his hands*): I, too, have nothing to bring.

WISE MAN: My companions and I brought rare gifts—gold and frankincense and myrrh—but I tell you what you offer the Child is more precious than any of these—love of your fellow man.

MICHAEL (*Sitting with bowed head and speaking disconsolately*): I saw no star; I heard no song.

WISE MAN (*Laying his hand on* MICHAEL'S *shoulder*): Poor, lonely man, groping in your blindness! (*A Christ-

mas carol is heard faintly from the stable.) Come kneel with us before the manger. Perhaps then you may find a star that will lighten your darkness, and hear a song that will banish your loneliness. (*The Christmas carol becomes louder. All kneel facing the stable. A part of the stable wall is drawn aside, revealing the tableau of the Christ Child in the manger, with Mary and Joseph kneeling in adoration*)

THE END

Monsieur Santa Claus

by Helen Louise Miller

Characters

ANDRE, *an exchange student from France*
MIM SUTTON, *a hostess*
BINKY SUTTON, *her younger sister*
JAY, *Mim's boy friend*
MR. SUTTON
MRS. SUTTON
BEV
STEVE
DOROTHY
DAVE
RUTH
KEN
FAYE
FRANK
} *guests*
2 DELIVERY BOYS

TIME: *A few days before Christmas.*
SETTING: *The Sutton living room. A Christmas tree stands in one corner, and the room is decorated for Christmas.*
AT RISE: ANDRE *is stretched flat on his stomach on the sofa, reading a book. The radio is playing Christmas carols.*

ANDRE (*Sitting up and staring in disbelief at the book*): No! No! This cannot be! Nevair! Nevair! Nevair! Eet ees too much! I would disgrace myself! (*Closes book with a bang, rises, and slams book on sofa. Thrusts hands in pockets, and strides about the room.*) A surprise party! That ees all I need! I could nevair go through wis eet. Nevair! (*As he strides up and down stage, he collides with* BINKY *who enters with a pile of packages.*)

BINKY (*As packages spill*): Oops! Watch what you're doing, Andre.

ANDRE: So sorry, Binky. Permit me. (*Stoops to pick up packages*)

BINKY (*Crossly as she also scrambles for packages*): You've done enough harm. I'll pick them up myself. What are you doing in here, anyhow, at this time? I didn't know you were home. (*Collects packages and puts them under tree*)

ANDRE: I was reading. Binky, you must tell me somesing. (*Grabs hold of her wrist.*)

BINKY: Don't be so mysterious. What do you want to know?

ANDRE (*Pulling her over to sofa and picking up book*): It's this . . . this . . . how you say? This annual. This yearbook from zee last term. Look. Here ees picture. Underneath it say: "Santa Claus stages surprise party at home of Foreign Exchange Student." Binky, there ees somesing going on here tonight. I feel eet. Eet ees in zee air. Everysing so hush-hush! So—how you say—*mysterieux*.

BINKY: Andre, you're just getting all steamed up over nothing. Where did you get hold of that yearbook anyway?

ANDRE: In zee bookcase. I was looking at it to take my mind off Christmas.

BINKY: To take your mind off Christmas! Why, Andre, I can hardly wait for Christmas. Think of all the plans we've made. The fun we'll have! And your first Christmas in America!

ANDRE: Ees also first Christmas away from home! (*Turning aside*) Everywhere I go ees Christmas. Zee streets all decorated! Zee store windows, since Halloween! Zee programs at school! Zee Christmas trees for sale! Zee carols on zee radio! I have all zee time zee lump in zee throat!

BINKY: I know how you feel, Andre, especially about the carols. (*Turning off radio*) I can get pretty lumpy over *Silent Night* even right here at home.

ANDRE: And now this, this I read in zee yearbook. Please, Binky, if there ees surprise party, tell me. How you say—tip me off.

BINKY: You know those snooty seniors wouldn't tell me anything if they could help it. Remember I'm only a Freshman. According to Mim I'm much too young to take part in any of their affairs. Take the Holly Hop for example. I'm not even supposed to be old enough to go to that.

ANDRE: Binky, you are what you call "stalling." Ees not Holly Hop we talk about. Ees surprise party. Now come on. You are my friend, n'est-ce pas? When I first come here, you say we stick together. Come on now, tell me what you know about this party.

BINKY: But, Andre, I can't do that. The kids will kill me. (*Claps hand over her mouth*)

ANDRE (*Triumphantly*): Then there ees surprise party, like in zee yearbook!

BINKY: Andre, I didn't say that. You're just guessing. (*Catching hold of him, as he starts to run out*) Andre, Andre, where are you going?

ANDRE: I must get out of here. Surprise party I cannot

take. I am too emotional. My heart, eet ees moving too fast.

BINKY: Now, you listen to me, Andre Beaucaire. If the cat's out of the bag, I can't very well put it back again. But you can't run away from that surprise party. The Student Advisory Board has worked on it day and night, and you're not going to spoil it for them by walking out.

ANDRE: But don't you see, Binky, they are so kind—so good. They give me so much, and I—what have I to give them? They come wis zee presents, et moi, I have nothing. You know I have so leetle spending money.

BINKY: But you don't need to give them anything, Andre. They don't expect it.

ANDRE: But what ees Christmas wis all getting and no giving? Giving ees zee heart of Christmas.

BINKY: Oh, dear! I know how you must feel, but how can I make you understand? You are giving us all something just by being here. Mother always says the most important thing is to give yourself.

ANDRE: Your Mamma—she say that?

BINKY: I've heard her say it a thousand times. And I know she's right. What are a few shirts and ties and gift certificates . . .

ANDRE: Gift certificates?

BINKY: Yes, gift certificates . . . little slips of paper that you can cash in at a store for whatever article is named. I have a gift certificate in one of those boxes for Dad. After Christmas he can take it down to the Men's Shop and get any hat he wants. Then I'm sure of the color and size.

ANDRE: Clevair! Very clevair!

BINKY: Andre, you're not listening to me. Now, please, please, be sensible about this. Mim and the rest of the crowd would never forgive me if they ever found out I told you. But I'm supposed to see that you are here about seven-thirty. I have orders not to let you out of my sight.

ANDRE: You are my leetle shadow?

BINKY: Right. And I'm going to keep tabs on you.

ANDRE: Then you will have to be quick on zee feetsies, leetle shadow, because in France I was champion cross-country runner. Look behind you! Someone ees coming. (*As* BINKY *turns,* ANDRE *runs off stage.*)

BINKY: Andre, Andre, come back here. You can't do this. Andre, Andre. (*She runs after him, calling desperately. Almost immediately,* MIM *and* JAY *enter, laden with packages.* MIM *is holding up a tie not yet in the box.*)

MIM: I do hope Andre likes this tie I got for him, Jay. The clerk said it is an import.

JAY: Probably imported from Coney Island.

MIM: What's the matter with you lately? You're so cynical.

JAY: Not cynical, just practical. After all, a tie is a tie. He'll wear it around his neck, same as anyone else.

MIM: You sound as if you hope he'll choke.

JAY: Maybe I do.

MIM: Jay Taylor, what a horrible thing to say about Andre! I don't think you even like him.

JAY: Sure, I like him. He's the sharpest tennis player I've ever seen, and he's a good egg. But what am I supposed to do? Stand here and grin like a Chessy Cat while my girl wraps up a Christmas present for another guy?

MIM: Now that's my idiot boy friend talking. You know perfectly well Andre is not just another guy. He's . . . well . . . he's an all-school project!

JAY: I'll buy that all right. At least, he's an all-girl project. Since that Andre Beaucaire moved in, the rest of us fellows might as well pull up stakes and head for the Klondike.

MIM: You ought to be ashamed of yourself. (*Finishing wrapping tie*) After all, you voted for this Foreign Exchange Student the same as the rest of us. And think how lucky we are to get a wonderful boy like Andre. Suppose he had turned out to be on the goony side.

JAY: Maybe I could take the guy better if he had buck teeth and a wart on his nose. I never voted for a combination of Beau Brummell and the Three Musketeers.

MIM (*Smiling fondly*): He *is* cute, isn't he? All the girls are crazy about . . . (*Catching herself in time*) About his accent and his manners.

JAY: Yeah, he makes the rest of us feel like the original Hick from Punkin Crick!

MIM: Jay, you're impossible. Where's your present?

JAY: Right here. I'll put it under the tree with the rest. (*Does so*)

MIM: What did you get?

JAY: A book.

MIM: That was sweet of you, Jay. He loves to read.

JAY: He'll love to read this all right. It's called, *Going Steady, U.S.A.*

MIM (*Whirling around in anger*): Jay, you are absolutely hateful. One more crack like that and you can just pack up and go home, Christmas or no Christmas.

JAY: O.K., O.K., Mim, I was only kidding, but look at it my way. Here you are, knocking yourself out over this guy. It's "Andre" this, and "Andre" that! You can't go to the movies because you're helping Andre with his English, or you're teaching Andre American rock, or you're going to the library with Andre.

MIM: Well, for goodness' sake, I'm only trying to make the poor boy feel at home. After all, he's a guest in our house, a guest in our school, and a guest in our country.

JAY: Sure, but is it part of international goodwill to give him dancing lessons?

MIM: Oh, don't be so huffy! I just want him to catch on to our dances before he goes to the Holly Hop.

JAY: Does he have a date?

MIM (*Stalling*): Now, Jay, it's a little bit early.

JAY (*Belligerently*): I'm asking you, Mim Sutton, does Andre have a date for the Holly Hop?

MIM: Well, not exactly . . . but if the worst comes to the worst . . .

JAY: What are you hinting at?

MIM: Well, now, I couldn't let him go stag, could I?

JAY: You mean to tell me with all those girls at school falling over themselves to get a date with Andre, you are actually considering . . .

MIM: Down, boy, down! I didn't say I was going to the dance with him, did I?

JAY: No, and you'd better not.

MIM: In spite of Andre's continental air, he's really shy about asking a girl for a date. He has to know a girl pretty well.

JAY: He knows Binky well enough, doesn't he?

MIM (*In great disgust*): Binky! Why, Binky's just a child! He couldn't take a Freshman to the Holly Hop.

JAY: Why not? Is there a law against it?

MIM: There's no point in arguing with you. Andre is a stranger here, and he's homesick. How would you like to be in a strange country at Christmas time?

JAY: Oh, what's the use? I just can't win. (*Doorbell rings, there are a couple of off-stage "Yoo-hoos," and* BEV *and* STEVE *enter dragging a lightweight cardboard carton big enough for a boy to crouch inside. It is wrapped in white paper and decorated with a big red satin bow. The lid swings open at the top.*)

BEV: I hope this is big enough.

STEVE: It's the only one we could find.

MIM: Did you bring the suit?

STEVE: It's inside the box, whiskers and all.

MIM: Good. Then Jay can try it on for size.

JAY: Who? Me? What's the big idea? (BEV *gets Santa Claus suit from box.*)

STEVE: You'll probably need a couple of pillows to stuff him out, good and fat.

MIM (*Hustling* JAY *into the suit*): You know you're always good at things like this. The idea is when Andre opens the box, you will pop out and distribute the gifts. "Emcee" the whole party, in fact.

JAY: Suppose he doesn't open it right away? Do I just stay in there and quietly suffocate?

STEVE: That's the idea, chum.

BEV: Don't be silly. Mim will see to it that he opens this package first. (*All help bundle* JAY *into the Santa Claus suit.* MR. *and* MRS. SUTTON *enter.*)

MR. SUTTON: Well, I see you have Santa Claus under control.

MRS. SUTTON: Is everything ready?

MIM: The gang should be here any minute, Mother. Doesn't Jay look wonderful?

MR. SUTTON: I think he could do with another pillow. What do you think, Steve?

STEVE (*Getting pillow from sofa and stuffing it in where it will do the most good*): That should put a few more pounds on him.

MRS. SUTTON: I'm so nervous about the cake. Andre told me about a recipe of his mother's and I'm afraid he left something out.

MR. SUTTON: When are you expecting Andre to show up?

MIM: Binky has her orders to have him here promptly at seven-thirty.

MRS. SUTTON: He's been spending every evening in the library until nine. Poor boy! I'm afraid he's working too hard. (*Doorbell rings.*)

BEV: Here they come. Shall I open the door?

MIM: Go ahead. (*Exit* BEV.) Jay, you'd better get into the box.

JAY: Not till the last minute. I might get claustrophobia. Besides, there's plenty of time. I'll take charge of the loot. (DOROTHY, DAVE, RUTH, KEN, FAYE, *and* FRANK *enter, all bearing gifts. Greetings are exchanged.*) Right this way, boys and girls, give your presents to old Santa Claus.

DOROTHY (*Handing package to* JAY): Here's the sweater I made. It's a little lumpy in spots, but the blue just matches his eyes.

DAVE (*Handing package*): Socks are my contribution.

RUTH (*Handing package*): I got him a whole dozen of ball point pens. He's always borrowing mine in study hall.

KEN: I'm on the practical side, too. I got him a slide rule.

FAYE: He's always admired those billfolds in the school colors. (*Hands present to* JAY)

FRANK (*Handing envelope*): Ten free haircuts should see him through most of the school year.

MRS. SUTTON: Andre will be thrilled to pieces. I can hardly wait to see his face.

MR. SUTTON: He's a good kid, Andre. We want to make this the best Christmas he's ever had.

STEVE (*To* JAY): Better hop into the box, Santa dear, or you'll be caught with your beard showing.

JAY: O.K., O.K. But remember, he has to open this box first.

STEVE: Mim and I will take care of that. Now get in there, squat down and shut the lid.

JAY (*In a muffled voice*): It's hot in here. What if I have to sneeze?

DAVE: We'll all make so much noise, he won't hear you.

RUTH (*Giggling*): I feel so nervous.

FAYE: So do I.

BEV: Surprise parties are always a strain.

DOROTHY: Suppose he doesn't show up?

KEN: He's bound to show.

FRANK: Where do you suppose he is? It's after seven-thirty now.

MRS. SUTTON: He's been spending hours at the library.

FAYE: But we don't have any school assignments now.

MIM: Don't worry. Wherever he is, Binky will track him down. She's the original bird dog.

KEN: You know, I feel sorry for the poor guy, in a way.

GIRLS: Sorry? Why?

KEN: Well, gee whiz, how would you like to walk in here all unprepared and have a whole surprise party blow up in your face like a sky rocket? (*Sound of door*)

MIM: Sh! Here they are. Douse the lights! (*Black-out*)

JAY (*From box*): Hurry up! I'm dying.

ALL: Sh-h-h!

BINKY: Never mind. It's only Binky. (*Lights on*)

ALL: Binky! Where's Andre? (*Etc.*)

BINKY: He's not coming.

ALL: Not coming!

MRS. SUTTON: I knew it would be hard to pry him away from that library.

BINKY: He's not in the library.

MIM: Then where is he?

BINKY: I have no idea.

JAY (*Popping out of box and mopping his forehead*): What goes on? What is this? How long am I supposed to stay in that box while we wait for him?

BINKY: You might as well come out. I told you he isn't coming.

JAY: What do you mean he isn't coming? What are you talking about?

MIM: It was your business to get him here.

BINKY (*Sitting down and mopping her face*): I'm bushed.

I've chased that boy clear down to the shopping center and lost him in the traffic. He didn't win that cross-country medal for nothing.

BEV: But what happened? How did he find out?

MIM: Binky, I bet you let it slip. You never could keep a secret.

BINKY: I didn't tell him, honest I didn't. He got hold of last year's classbook and saw the pictures of the surprise party you staged for Ilse Haabe. Somehow or other he smelled a rat, and he skeedaddled.

MRS. SUTTON: But it's so unlike him. You can always count on Andre to do what is expected of him.

MIM: Well, this time, he surely did the unexpected.

MR. SUTTON: Most ungrateful of him, I must say, after you kids went to all this trouble.

BINKY: I don't think he meant to be ungrateful, Dad. He . . . he . . . just couldn't face it.

RUTH: What's so hard about facing your friends at Christmas time?

BINKY: That's just it. We *are* his friends, of course, but we're *new* friends. He's two thousand miles from his own friends, and his family.

MRS. SUTTON: I was beginning to think he was getting homesick.

MIM: But that's why we're giving this party . . . to help him forget.

DOROTHY: I guess you can't forget your own people at Christmas.

RUTH: But we wanted him to have a real American Christmas.

JAY: Maybe what he really wants is a French Christmas.

BINKY: He's not bothered about the nationality of Christmas, Jay . . . it's something else.

ALL: What?

BINKY: It's the presents.

ALL: The presents?

JAY (*Thoughtfully*): I think I understand, Binky. We've been so busy trying to give him things for Christmas that we've forgotten what a guy wants most is to *give,* not *get.*

BINKY: That's almost exactly what he said, Jay.

MR. SUTTON: You're right, son. Giving is the best part of Christmas. In our enthusiasm we've forgotten how much he would want to give us something in return.

KEN: And he's allowed to bring so little money out of the country, he couldn't afford it.

MIM: He hardly has enough money to send gifts to his family. (*Doorbell rings. To* JAY) Quick! Quick! It might be Andre after all. (*Helps* JAY *scramble back into the box.* MR. SUTTON *goes to door.*)

DELIVERY BOY: Package for R. K. Sutton. Sign here, please. (*As* MR. SUTTON *signs,* DELIVERY BOYS *drag in large packing box with placard addressed to* MR. SUTTON.) Thank you, sir. (DELIVERY BOYS *exit*)

MR. SUTTON: I wonder what my family's been up to. Here, some of you boys give me a hand with this thing. (BOYS *help open the box.*)

MIM (*To* MRS. SUTTON): Oh, Mother! You finally got him the Hi-Fi set after all!

BINKY: Why didn't you tell us about it?

MRS. SUTTON: Honestly, I don't know anything about it. Are you sure you two aren't up to something again?

MIM: I didn't get him anything that big. Maybe Binky's fine hand is in this.

BINKY: Cross my heart, it's a surprise to me, too.

MR. SUTTON (*Untying last of string*): Thanks, boys. I can take over from here. (BOYS *move aside.*) The lid is nearly off. (*He opens the lid, and out pops* ANDRE *in complete Santa Claus regalia.*)

ANDRE: Joyeux noel, mes amis!

JAY (*Popping out of his box*): Merry Christmas, everybody!

ANDRE *and* JAY (*Pointing at each other in astonishment*): You! What are you doing here?

ALL: Andre! (*Many ad lib remarks and laughter*)

JAY: This is a switch, if I ever saw one.

ANDRE (*Over hubbub*): Please, please! I have zee short speech!

JAY: Quiet! Quiet! Monsieur Le Santa Claus has the floor.

ANDRE: When my nose first smell a Christmas surprise, I theenk, and I theenk, and I theenk. What can I give my so good friends in this land where everybody have everysing? I must give somesing . . . or I burst! Noël eet ees not Noël wisout zee giving. Since Thanksgiving Day, I get zee funny feeling in zee stomach . . . no . . . no . . . not in zee stomach . . . in zee heart. Eet ees zee homesick pain. When I see zee lights and zee store windows, zee pain eet ees worse. When zee music play, when zee carolers sing, I am very sad. How will I play Monsieur Le Santa Claus to all my friends here in America? What will I give Mamma Sutton who feed me so much I gain fifteen pounds? (*All laugh.*) What will I give Papa Sutton who take me into his house like son? What for Mimi? What for Binky? What for Jay? What for all my classmates? Then Binky . . . she tell me what to do.

BINKY: Why, Andre Beaucaire, I never said one word!

ANDRE: Mais oui. You tell me what to do. You tell me about gift certificates.

BINKY: But, Andre, you don't get gift certificates for nothing. You have to pay at the store.

ANDRE: I do not get my gift certificates at store. Binky, she tell me somesing else . . . somesing Mamma Sutton say.

MRS. SUTTON: Dear me, what did I say?

ANDRE: Binky say you teach her zee most important gift is

to give yourself. So I get busy. I make zee gift certificates. (*Gets out of box. Going to* MRS. SUTTON *and handing her an envelope*) To Mamma Sutton, wis love from Andre, gift certificate, good for one dozen dishwashings and two dozen floor scrubbings.

MRS. SUTTON (*As guests applaud*): Why, Andre, that's a wonderful present.

ANDRE (*To* MR. SUTTON): For Papa Sutton, gift certificate, good for one dozen car washes and six lawn mowings.

MR. SUTTON: Hey, this is all right. I wish the rest of my family would catch on to this system.

ANDRE (*Bowing to* MIM): To Mimi, and all zee girls (*Gives envelope to each girl*) One French lesson every day, boy friends permitting. (*All cheer and applaud. To* JAY) To my good friend, Jay, and to all zee boys (*Hands envelope to each boy*) Free tennis instruction wis special tips on zee Beaucaire smash serve.

BOYS: Thanks, Andre. Do you really mean it? (*Etc.*)

STEVE: Our school will have the best tennis team in the country, if Andre takes us on.

MR. SUTTON: I must say, Andre, you're a fast worker. How did you manage all this? The packing box, the suit and everything?

ANDRE: I have zee leetle secret. I get job.

ALL: A job?

ANDRE: I get zee Christmas job. I need money for presents to go to France. So I go to shopping center. All last week when you theenk I am in library, I work in store.

MIM: But Andre, you don't know enough English to be a clerk.

ANDRE: I was not clerk. I was Monsieur Le Santa Claus in zee toy department.

ALL (*Laughing*): Oh, no! You weren't! (*Etc.*)

ANDRE: Eet ees not hard to learn to say, "And what do you want for Christmas, my leetle man?"

MR. SUTTON: So that's where you got the Santa Claus suit and the delivery service.

ANDRE: My boss, he ees very nice man. He understand.

JAY: I'm afraid we haven't understood a lot of things, Andre, but something tells me we'll do better from now on. And now it's *my* turn to play Santa Claus. All those presents under the tree are from your friends here at Whittier High.

ANDRE: For me? All of them?

JAY: All of them. But first (*Digging in his pocket for envelope*) here is a little present from me.

ANDRE (*Opening envelope*): Two tickets to the Holly Hop! Thank you, Jay. Thank you very much. Eees just what I needed.

JAY: I was afraid of that . . . er . . . I mean . . . I felt sure it was. And, well, it's a little awkward to say this, Andre, but, well, if you have any trouble lining up a date, (*Looks at* MIM *significantly*) I think I know a girl who would enjoy going with you.

ANDRE (*With a grin*): Thanks, mon ami. There are many customs here in America, I do not understand . . . customs . . . well, like going steady, par example . . . but I theenk I catch on. As for zee date, I do not anticipate zee trouble. You see, I still have one gift certificate I have not yet delivered. (*Walks over to* BINKY) To Binky, zee one who ees young enough to understand zee most, one gift certificate for zee Holly Hop.

BINKY (*In a transport of delight*): Oh, Andre! Andre! Do you mean you'll really take a Freshman?

ANDRE (*With a bow to* MRS. SUTTON): If zee Freshman's Mamma will permit.

BINKY: Oh, Mother, Mother, may I go? Please!

MRS. SUTTON: You're a bit young for the Holly Hop, dear, but if it's all right with your father.

MR. SUTTON: It's all right with me, chicken. Anything for international peace and goodwill! And now, what do you say we have a little music? (*Turns on radio to Christmas music*)

BINKY: Not any Christmas music, Dad. It gives Andre a lump in his throat.

ANDRE: Not any more, Binky. Zee lump eet ees quite disappeared. Listen . . . I can even sing zee words. (*Entire group joins in Christmas carol as curtains close.*)

THE END

Christmas Spirit

by Earl S. Dias

Characters

SALLY GILLUM, *seventeen*
MRS. GILLUM
MR. GILLUM
TOM GILLUM, *eighteen*
BOB ABBOTT, *Tom's friend*
MR. GRIGGS, *a Laneville selectman*
MISS PENNYPACKER, *librarian*
MRS. GRAY

TIME: *About 8:30 on Christmas Eve.*
SETTING: *The living room of the Gillum home, located in a New England village.*
AT RISE: SALLY *is inspecting the Christmas tree.* MRS. GILLUM *sits on the sofa, her hand on her forehead.*

MRS. GILLUM: Goodness, I have a headache that seems to go right down to the tips of my toes.

SALLY (*Standing back to admire tree*): It's all this Christmas rush, Mother. You've been on the go for over a week now. And, golly, we have so many cousins and uncles and aunts to buy presents for. It's a wonder that you're still up and around.

MRS. GILLUM: Oh, I don't mind Christmas shopping, Sally. It's rather fun to buy gifts for people, anyway. I really enjoy trying to decide what particular present will please each person.

SALLY: Well, I don't.

MRS. GILLUM: You mean you don't like shopping?

SALLY: It's bedlam! And the stores are so crowded—even in a one-horse town like ours.

MRS. GILLUM: One-horse town? You'd better not let your father hear you talk that way about Laneville.

SALLY (*Picking up one of presents and moving it to another place under the tree*): Oh, it's fine for him. He can get his writing done here easily enough. Heaven knows there's plenty of peace and quiet. In fact, the place is a morgue.

MRS. GILLUM: But that's what is so pleasant about it, Sally. After the hustle and bustle of New York, Laneville is positively heavenly. And your father has really made progress here on his new novel.

SALLY: That's something, I suppose. Personally, though, I think the place is full of hicks. You can almost see the hay in their hair.

MRS. GILLUM: That isn't a very nice thing to say. I think the people here are very pleasant and friendly.

SALLY (*Crossing and sitting in chair at left of table*): Friendly? They're a lot of cold fish, if you ask me. I've heard of New Englanders and how they're supposed to be reserved and rather distant. Well, I've found out.

MRS. GILLUM (*Sighing*): You don't seem to have much Christmas spirit, Sally.

SALLY: Christmas spirit? That's a joke, Mother. Christmas is nothing but a commercialized affair, anyway. The only ones it benefits are the merchants. They're making money hand over fist, just as they do on Mother's Day and Father's Day and all those other so-called sentimental occasions whose whole purpose is to make everyone spend as much money as possible.

MRS. GILLUM: Goodness, you're getting cynical!

SALLY: I just see things as they are. And honestly, Mother, if I have to spend much more time in this ghost town, I'll lose my mind. I dread going back to Laneville High after Christmas vacation.

MRS. GILLUM (*Dryly*): Your father and I have noticed that you don't seem to be very happy there.

SALLY: Happy! The place gives me the creeps. A lot of kid stuff about Saturday night dances and silly basketball games. At Miss Fenwick's School in New York, we concerned ourselves with important things.

MRS. GILLUM: Such as?

SALLY: The latest books and plays and concerts—you know, things that really matter.

MRS. GILLUM: Your father and I have thought of sending you back to Miss Fenwick's for the last half of the school year.

SALLY (*Rises and goes over to hug her mother*): Oh, Mother, have you really? That would be just wonderful! (*She stretches happily*) Back to civilization once more. (MR. GILLUM *enters from right.*)

MRS. GILLUM: Well, John. You've worked late tonight.

MR. GILLUM (*Sighing wearily and sitting in chair at right of table*): Yes, the writing was going well, and I didn't want to leave it. One of my characters has me on the run, though. She's a woman—one of those slinky, attractive creatures—and she seems to keep popping into the book when I least expect her.

SALLY (*Laughing*): Why, Dad! I didn't know you were interested in such types.

MR. GILLUM: I'm interested in them only as characters in a novel.

MRS. GILLUM: I should hope so!

SALLY: Do you remember last Christmas Eve? We all went to Mr. Hammond's wonderful party, and then on

Christmas Day we went to the theatre. Oh, New York is the place to be on holidays—or any other day.

MRS. GILLUM: That's all I've had from her for the last hour, John.

MR. GILLUM: I take it Laneville doesn't agree with you, Sally.

SALLY: Or I don't agree with it.

MR. GILLUM: Strange, because your brother likes it here very much.

SALLY: Of course he does. Tom's a hero at school—football and basketball and all that sort of adolescent drivel. Besides, he's very fond of Sue Benson, too—and she's enough all by herself to make him think Laneville's wonderful.

MR. GILLUM: At least he's entered into the spirit of things. You, on the other hand, have been rather aloof. Why haven't you taken part in more school activities and learned to know some of the local young people better?

MRS. GILLUM: Don't you know, John? Your daughter thinks the entire population of Laneville is composed of hicks.

MR. GILLUM: Indeed?

SALLY: They don't have any sophistication whatsoever.

MR. GILLUM: I've found them to be intelligent and well-informed.

SALLY (*Laughing*): I gathered that from your short story.

MR. GILLUM: You mean "A Village Incident"?

SALLY: Yes, the one that came out in the *Saturday Evening Post*. You made that small town sound like paradise. (*Shakes her head*) Laneville is a far cry from paradise, as far as I'm concerned.

MR. GILLUM: It's a very pleasant place. And you'd be surprised how many townspeople have spoken to me about the story. They're delighted that I used Laneville as a setting.

SALLY: It's probably the first publicity the town has received since the Revolutionary War.

MRS. GILLUM: I've told Sally she can probably go back to Miss Fenwick's for the last half of the school year.

MR. GILLUM: Yes, she can—if she wants to.

SALLY: I do want to, Dad, very much.

MR. GILLUM (*Sighing*): I'll miss you, Sally, but if it's what you really want, I'll get a letter off to Miss Fenwick's tonight before I go to bed.

SALLY (*Jumping up and going over to kiss her father on the forehead*): Thank you, Dad. You're a darling.

MR. GILLUM (*Looking at watch*): Hmm—nine o'clock. Where's Tom tonight?

SALLY: My glorious-voiced brother is out singing Christmas carols with some of his pals.

MRS. GILLUM: Why didn't you go with them, Sally?

SALLY (*Contemptuously*): Kid stuff.

MRS. GILLUM: I think it's a very charming custom. You don't seem to have any Christmas spirit at all.

SALLY: Christmas is commercialized just like—

MRS. GILLUM: Please, Sally, spare us the sermon. We've been all over that once before. (*Voices are heard outside singing "Silent Night."* MRS. GILLUM *picks up her knitting,* SALLY *re-arranges decorations on Christmas tree, and* MR. GILLUM *picks up some typewritten pages from table and reads them over, correcting them occasionally with a pencil. When the song is over,* MR. GILLUM *smiles.*)

MR. GILLUM: Very well done. I couldn't even hear Tom's monotone.

MRS. GILLUM (*Pretending to be angry*): Tom is *not* a monotone! Besides, anyone sounds wonderful when he's singing Christmas carols. (*The carolers now sing "Adeste Fidelis." When the singing is completed, there are cries of "Good night," "See you tomorrow," and*

"Merry Christmas." Then TOM GILLUM *enters at upstage center, followed by* BOB ABBOTT.)

TOM: Hi, folks—and Merry Christmas!

BOB: Merry Christmas, everybody!

TOM: I've brought Bob back for a soda. After all that singing, we need to wet our whistles.

MRS. GILLUM: There's plenty in the refrigerator.

MR. GILLUM: Your caroling was excellent.

TOM: You bet. We're full of the good old Christmas spirit. Come on to the kitchen, Bob.

BOB: Want to join us, Sally?

MRS. GILLUM: Yes, Sally, why don't you have a cold drink with the boys?

SALLY: No, thank you. I'm too comfortable right here.

BOB (*Disappointed*): O.K.

TOM: My sister is Little Miss Comfort herself, Bob.

SALLY: Ha! Ha! Very funny. (TOM *and* BOB *exit right, with* BOB *casting a last look at* SALLY, *who ignores him.*)

MRS. GILLUM: I think you might have been a little more hospitable, Sally.

SALLY: Tom is hospitality personified. He doesn't need any help.

MR. GILLUM: That Bob Abbott seems to be a very fine boy.

SALLY: He's all right, I guess.

MR. GILLUM: You don't sound too enthusiastic.

SALLY: He's so much like Tom—crazy about sports and dances and that sort of thing.

MR. GILLUM: Aren't those natural interests for young people?

SALLY: There are other things in life. Besides, Bob is like all New Englanders. Why, I don't think he ever spoke ten words to me before tonight.

MRS. GILLUM: And how many words have you spoken to him?

SALLY: It's certainly not *my* place to make advances to the male population of Laneville. (*Doorbell rings.*)

MR. GILLUM (*Rising*): I'll get it. (*He goes to door and opens it, ushering in three visitors.*) Well, this is a surprise. Merry Christmas to you all! Let me take your coats. (*The three enter, give him their wraps, and then go to greet* MRS. GILLUM. MISS PENNYPACKER *is a tall, lean woman of indeterminate age. She is carrying a long, narrow, attractively-wrapped package.* MRS. GRAY *is stout and jolly-looking.* MR. GRIGGS *is about* MR. GILLUM'S *age. He carries a scroll.* MR. GILLUM *takes the wraps and exits with them at right, returning a moment later.*)

MRS. GILLUM (*Rising and coming forward to greet the guests*): How are you, Miss Pennypacker? How nice to see you, Mrs. Gray. And you too, Mr. Griggs. Merry Christmas. (*The three smile and respond "Merry Christmas."*)

MR. GRIGGS: I suppose you're wondering just what the three of us are doing here. Well, we're not trying to imitate the Three Wise Men of old, but we do come, like them, bearing gifts.

MISS PENNYPACKER (*Holding up her parcel*): Indeed we do.

MRS. GRAY: And happy to do it!

MRS. GILLUM: Gifts? Why, how lovely! But what have we done to deserve such kindness?

MR. GRIGGS: Well, as Laneville's selectman, I suppose I had better act as spokesman.

MISS PENNYPACKER: Please do, Mr. Griggs.

MR. GRIGGS: Thank you, Miss Pennypacker.

MRS. GRAY: I can't think of anyone who could do the job more nicely.

MR. GRIGGS: And thank you, Mrs. Gray.

MISS PENNYPACKER: I always love to hear Mr. Griggs speak

at our town meetings. He always says just the right thing in just the right words.

MRS. GRAY: Indeed he does.

MR. GRIGGS: Please, ladies, spare my blushes. Anyway, Mr. and Mrs. Gillum, although my companions, I assure you, are overestimating my poor talents, I do have something to say—if you'll bear with me.

MR. GILLUM: Of course. (*Smiling*) I'm on tenterhooks.

MR. GRIGGS: Not to keep you in suspense any longer, I'll get down to business. You see, Mr. Gillum, we citizens of Laneville are extremely grateful to you.

MISS PENNYPACKER (*Nodding vigorously*): Yes, indeed.

MRS. GRAY: We're more than grateful.

MR. GRIGGS: And a group of us, at a meeting the other night, decided we ought to show some concrete evidence of our gratitude.

MR. GILLUM: All this is very flattering—but grateful for what, may I ask?

MR. GRIGGS: For several things. First of all, we like the way in which you have, in a short time, adjusted yourself to our Laneville way of life. Second, your presence in our community has brought us honor and some degree of fame.

MRS. GRAY: It was your story that did it, Mr. Gillum.

MISS PENNYPACKER: Such a lovely piece of writing—and how admirably you captured the spirit and the essence of Laneville in it.

MRS. GRAY: We mean, of course, "A Village Incident."

MR. GRIGGS: You see, Mr. Gillum, all of us thought it remarkable that an outsider such as yourself could get to the very heart of what we stand for here and what our mode of living means to us.

MISS PENNYPACKER: And we want you to know how much we appreciate and admire what you've done.

MR. GRIGGS: I haven't much more to say. But, as selectman, I have been authorized to have this scroll prepared. (*He gives it to* MR. GILLUM) It's not much, perhaps, but please believe that what it says is sincerely meant and that it reflects accurately the sentiments of Laneville's citizens.

MR. GILLUM: Why, thank you. I—I just don't know what to say.

MRS. GRAY: Please read it aloud, Mr. Gillum.

MR. GILLUM (*Opening the scroll*): "To our friend and neighbor, John Gillum, the affection and respect of his Laneville neighbors is evidenced in this scroll. For his ability as a writer who understands the human heart and for his understanding of our community, we offer him our friendship and admiration. And to a new but already well-loved citizen of our town, we extend the hand of neighborliness."

MRS. GILLUM: Why, John—that is wonderful!

MISS PENNYPACKER (*Coughing slightly*): Ahem!

MR. GRIGGS: Oh, yes, Miss Pennypacker also has something for you that we hope you'll like.

MR. GILLUM: Well, this really *is* Christmas for me!

MISS PENNYPACKER (*Handing package to* MR. GILLUM): Because I am the librarian in Laneville, our committee thought I was the logical person to present this to you. We have had your story bound in leather for you. We all thought it would be most appropriate.

MR. GILLUM: I can't think of anything that would have pleased me more.

MRS. GRAY (*Smiling*): It's my turn now, I think.

MR. GILLUM: You mean there is more?

MRS. GRAY: Really, it isn't much, but we hope you'll like it. As president of the Laneville Historical Society, I've been instructed by our members to present you and your entire family with a life membership in the Society. (*She hands him a certificate*) This includes you, Mrs. Gillum, and your son and daughter.

MRS. GILLUM: Thank you very much.

SALLY: It's very thoughtful of you.

MR. GILLUM: I hardly know what to say, although, (*Grinning*) I'm supposed to be a man of words. But I want all of you to know how much I appreciate your kindness. You merely illustrate what I've known all along—that Laneville is a neighborly place.

MR. GRIGGS (*Begins to applaud and is joined by* MISS PENNYPACKER *and* MRS. GRAY): Bravo!

MRS. GILLUM: Won't all of you please have some refreshment with us? John, let's go into the dining room for a snack.

MR. GILLUM: Wonderful idea.

MRS. GRAY: Thank you. I'm supposed to be on a diet—but certainly one ought to be able to cheat a little on Christmas Eve.

MRS. GILLUM (*Laughing*): Indeed one should. (*She leads way to door right and all but* SALLY *exit.* MRS. GILLUM *stops at door*) Coming, Sally?

SALLY: I'm not hungry, Mother—thanks. (SALLY *rises and goes to table at center. She takes up scroll, which* MR. GILLUM *has left on table, and reads it aloud. Then she sets scroll down on table once more, goes to sofa, sits down, and seems to be very thoughtful. After a moment or two,* BOB *enters from right.*)

BOB: Hi.

SALLY: Hello, Bob. Where's Tom?

BOB: He's helping your mother with the refreshments. Say, isn't it wonderful about your father? The old town has really gone all-out for him.

SALLY: It's very nice.

BOB: That story of his was good.

SALLY: I didn't know you'd read it.

BOB: Sure. I've been wanting to tell your father how much I liked it—but, well, you know—it's kind of hard to tell the author exactly how you feel about his story.

SALLY: And you New Englanders have never been famous for talking a lot.

BOB (*Smiling*): I guess that's right. (*Seriously*) You know, parts of your father's story reminded me of Thoreau. It has the same viewpoint that *Walden* does.

SALLY: Dad would be flattered to hear you compare him to Thoreau. I had no idea *you* were a Thoreau fan.

BOB: Gosh, yes. His writing is always meaty—something you can sink your teeth into. Emerson is the same way, too. You really have to think when you read him. Last summer I read Emerson's essay on "Self-Reliance" a dozen times or more—and I found something new in it each time.

SALLY (*Enthusiastically*): I've read it several times, too. When I was to Miss Fenwick's in New York, I thought it was wonderful. (*Slowly*) But I didn't expect you to feel that way.

BOB: What do you mean, Sally?

SALLY: I've always thought that about all you were interested in was football and baseball.

BOB: There's nothing wrong with football and baseball—but for Pete's sake, I know there are other things in life.

SALLY: It just seems strange to hear you talking about Thoreau and Emerson. I never realized—

BOB (*Grinning*): In other words, you thought I had a pointed head or something.

SALLY (*Upset*): Oh, no—it was just that I never thought of you as liking books.

BOB: Well, after all, how would you know I liked to read? You hardly speak to me at school. In fact, you just brush by me in the corridor with your head way up in the air.

SALLY (*Heatedly*): That's not true. It's just that everyone at Laneville High seems so reserved. They hide in their shells like turtles all the time.

BOB: You just don't understand. Some of the kids are shy, and they don't want to impose themselves on anyone. But you should have heard what the boys said when you first came.

SALLY: What do you mean?

BOB: They were all talking about how pretty you were—and what an addition you made to the school.

SALLY: Not one of them has even hinted he was glad to see me around.

BOB: They were all afraid to talk to you. Some of the fellows began to think you were conceited, and that you looked down on them because you came from New York. I remember back in October, some of the kids wanted to ask you to be a cheerleader—but they didn't dare. They thought you'd laugh right in their faces.

SALLY: But I would have loved being a cheerleader!

BOB: I'm sure you could be one next year. I'll be glad to tell them if you want me to.

SALLY (*Thoughtfully*): No—I think it might be nice if I told them myself.

BOB: Great! Wish I were going to be around to see you in action.

SALLY: But where are you going?

BOB: To Harvard—I hope.

SALLY (*Impressed*): Harvard!

BOB: Sure. My father went there and my grandfather and my great-grandfather.

SALLY: Golly!

BOB: Sally, there's been something I've wanted to ask you—but I've been afraid you'd give me the cold shoulder.

SALLY: Go ahead, Bob.

BOB (*Squaring his shoulders*): Well, here goes. You probably know that during Christmas week there's always a big dance in Laneville. We have it to celebrate the anniversary of the Battle of Laneville—that was back in the Revolution when a band of Laneville volunteers foiled a British raid on the town.

SALLY: I've heard of it.

BOB: The dance is a costume affair; everyone goes dressed in clothes of the Revolutionary period. You probably think that's silly, though.

SALLY: I think it sounds like a lot of fun!

BOB: You really mean that?

SALLY: Of course I do.

BOB (*Grinning*): Well, then, I guess it's safe to ask you. (*Gulping*) Will you go with me?

SALLY: I'd love to.

BOB: Great! That makes this a really merry Christmas for me.

SALLY (*Thoughtfully*): For me, too. (MR. *and* MRS. GILLUM, TOM, MISS PENNYPACKER, MRS. GRAY *and* MR. GRIGGS *enter from right. The guests have their wraps on. They move toward upstage door.*)

MRS. GILLUM: And thank you again for coming. You've been very kind.

MR. GILLUM: I never shall forget this night.

MR. GRIGGS: Nor shall we.

MISS PENNYPACKER: It's so wonderful to have a really distinguished writer in our midst.

MRS. GRAY: And I do hope, Mr. Gillum, that you'll be with us a long time.

MR. GILLUM: I assure you I haven't any intention of leaving Laneville.

MRS. GILLUM: It's too nice a place to leave.

TOM: I second the statement!

MR. GRIGGS: Good for you, Tom. And now, ladies, we had best be going. Merry Christmas, everyone. (*All those on stage now shout "Merry Christmas!"* MISS PENNYPACKER, MRS. GRAY, *and* MR. GRIGGS *exit.*)

MR. GILLUM: Now, wasn't that a wonderful gesture on their part? I don't know when I've encountered such friendly people.

TOM: You ought to run for selectman yourself, Dad. You'd be a cinch to win.

MR. GILLUM (*Laughing*): No, thanks. I'll keep out of politics and stick to my typewriter.

BOB: I have to be going; it's getting late. Thanks for the soda—and thank you, Sally.

SALLY: Thank *you.*

TOM: Say, what's going on here?

BOB (*Banteringly*): Nothing that concerns you, old boy.

TOM: Hmmm.

BOB: Good-night, everybody—and Merry Christmas.

ALL: Merry Christmas. (*After a final smile in* SALLY'S *direction,* BOB *exits upstage center.*)

TOM: My, my! Looks serious.

SALLY: What are you talking about?

TOM: That smile Bob just gave you.

SALLY: There was nothing wrong with the smile.

TOM (*Whistling*): I'll say there wasn't! Say, Mom, are we going to open our presents at midnight as usual?

MRS. GILLUM: Indeed we are.

TOM: I think I'll take a little nap until then. You'll call me when it's time, won't you?

MRS. GILLUM: Of course.

TOM: Good. See you later. (*He goes to door right and pauses there*) Boy, what a smile that was! (TOM *exits right.* MRS. GILLUM *goes over to Christmas tree and begins to rearrange some of the gifts.*)

MR. GILLUM: I suppose this is as good a time as any for me to write that letter to Miss Fenwick's. If you're going to go there next month, we'd better make arrangements as soon as possible.

MRS. GILLUM: That's a good idea, John.

SALLY (*Joining mother at tree*): Dad, I—I don't think you need to write that letter.

MR. GILLUM: Not write it?

SALLY: No, I've changed my mind.

MR. GILLUM (*Smiling*): That's a woman's privilege.

MRS. GILLUM: That's wonderful, Sally. I'd so much rather have you here with us.

SALLY: And I'd rather be here.

MR. GILLUM (*Comes to tree and puts arm about* SALLY'S *shoulders*): Changed your mind about Laneville?

SALLY: Yes, Dad, I have. It's hard to explain and I don't suppose I can put it into words the way you could, but I think I've been a bit hard on Laneville.

MR. GILLUM (*Going to table and picking up the scroll*): Did this have anything to do with your change of heart?

SALLY: Yes, that—and a lot of other things I didn't understand before tonight. I guess I never understood that you have to give in order to get—that in order to have friends you have to be friendly. Maybe it's something like Christmas. It's really more fun when you give presents as well as get them.

MRS. GILLUM: I'm glad to hear you say that, dear.

SALLY: I just wish I'd realized a lot sooner how stand-offish I was being.

MR. GILLUM: Maybe such things take time, Sally.

SALLY: Anyhow, I don't need to make a New Year's resolution to like Laneville. I *know* I'm going to like it.

MR. GILLUM (*Teasingly*): Any particular person in Laneville you know you're going to like especially?

SALLY: Oh, Dad! Bob's a nice boy, and I do like him very much—but I'm thinking of other things besides Bob. I could have joined some of the school clubs, I could have tried out for a part in the school play, I could have done so many things. I'm just lucky I have a second chance to prove myself. Did you know they wanted me to be a cheerleader, and they were afraid to ask me?

MR. GILLUM: You'd make a mighty pretty cheerleader.

SALLY: I'm going to ask if I can be one next year.

MR. GILLUM: Good girl!

SALLY: I think Tom's idea about a nap until midnight is a good one. I'll go to sleep now—but remember to wake me for the festivities! (*She waves at her parents, calls "Merry Christmas" as she reaches the door, and then exits as her parents say "Merry Christmas."*)

MR. GILLUM: Now that's the best Christmas gift of all. Good will toward men. I think Sally's found the meaning of those words.

MRS. GILLUM: Yes, she's grown up a bit tonight, John.

MR. GILLUM: And now, how would you like me to read you what I've written today?

MRS. GILLUM: You mean about that slinky, attractive woman that keeps popping into the book?

MR. GILLUM: Well, she does make an appearance.

MRS. GILLUM: Just to show that I'm full of the Christmas spirit, too, I'll come along with you, John. As you've said, good will toward men—and women, too, slinky or otherwise. (*They exit arm in arm, chuckling, as the curtains close.*)

THE END

The Trouble with Christmas

by Paul T. Nolan

Characters

TAMMY
DEBRA
HARRIETT
THOMAS
RICHARD
MISS EMILY, *a little old lady*
SANTA CLAUS

SETTING: *A conference room. Downstage center there is a long conference table with five chairs around it. Up right is a captain's chair with a small table next to it. Upstage center, against wall, is a larger table. There is a concealed exit behind it. Up left is a pile of Christmas materials, including a small fir tree in a stand, a folding cardboard fireplace, several boxes of Christmas tree decorations including ornament for top, white table-cloth, candlesticks with red candles, centerpiece and five boxes wrapped with Christmas paper. A rocking chair is a little downstage from these articles. There are doors downstage right and left.*

AT RISE: DEBRA, HARRIETT, THOMAS, *and* RICHARD *are seated around conference table.* TAMMY, *standing at end of table, is orating.*

TAMMY: And so, fellow committee members, I say the trouble with Christmas is—

DEBRA: You should say the troubles with Christmas *are.*

HARRIETT: That's right. What's wrong with Christmas is plural.

THOMAS: Christmas is commercial and phony.

RICHARD: Hypocritical baloney.

TAMMY: Even the music is bad.

DEBRA: And the decorations are sad.

HARRIETT (*Strongly*): And Santa Claus is a cad.

THOMAS (*Turning to look at* HARRIETT): Santa Claus a cad! I wouldn't go that far. (TAMMY *sits.*)

RICHARD: Neither would I. (*Nostalgically*) When I was a little boy, Santa gave me a very fine electric train, with two tunnels.

HARRIETT: Don't be childish, Richard. Your father gave you that train. And he probably paid too much for it because it was Christmas. There is no Santa Claus, Richard.

RICHARD: Then how come he's a cad?

HARRIETT: That's *why* he's a cad!

RICHARD (*Dreamily*): My father broke my train. It was an accident.

TAMMY: You see, Richard? Harriett's right. Shoddy merchandise.

RICHARD: It was not! My father didn't need to break shoddy things—he could break good things. He was a very strong man.

HARRIETT: I'll bet your mother was stronger. Women are stronger than men. That's a proven fact now.

RICHARD: Oh, yeah? Then how come Santa Claus is a man?

HARRIETT (*Heatedly*): There is no Santa Claus.

TAMMY: But if there were, he'd be a woman.

THOMAS: My father is stronger than my mother, but she's smarter.

HARRIETT (*Rising*): Everybody, listen to me. We're getting away from our purpose. We are here tonight for just (*Pounds table with fist*) one reason: to get rid of everything that's wrong with Christmas.

TAMMY: Christmas is just another male chauvinist institution.

DEBRA: Right on, sister!

HARRIETT: Look, Tammy, do you think Christmas would be any better if Santa Claus were a woman?

RICHARD: I don't think so. Not with his white beard.

THOMAS: The witches in *Macbeth* have beards, and they're women.

HARRIETT: Tammy, you see what happens when we don't stick to the subject? We're all in favor of women's lib, peace, progress, and protection of the environment. But, tonight—on the twenty-fourth of December—we have only one cause. We're going to get rid of Santa Claus.

RICHARD: If he doesn't exist, why do we have to get rid of him?

HARRIETT: It's the idea we're going to get rid of. If Santa Claus really existed, we could just expose him.

DEBRA: Yes, we could be kind and retire him.

TAMMY: Or send him to Siberia. But since he's an idea, we've got to wipe him out.

DEBRA: Without mercy.

RICHARD: I thought we were in favor of mercy.

THOMAS: Not for bad ideas.

HARRIETT: Then are we all in agreement that Santa Claus must go?

DEBRA: I agree. (*Points at fir tree*) He's mean to trees.

THOMAS: I agree. (*Points at packages*) He's all show—like those packages there. Gift-wrapped boxes with nothing in them.

TAMMY: I agree. Santa's a phony.

RICHARD (*Slowly*): Well, I suppose I agree. But I'm not giving back that very fine train he gave me. I've kept it all these years, and when I have a son, I'm going to give it to him.

HARRIETT: You do that, Richard. But not on Christmas, and don't tell him it's a present from Santa Claus.

TAMMY: Just look at the evidence we've collected—all the empty trinkets of Christmas. (*Stands and crosses to tree*) When we put on our exhibit, people will really see what meaningless stuff this is. (*Holds up tree*) Look at this miserable little tree. (*Sets tree down; dramatically*) For that tree alone, Santa Claus stands condemned. (HARRIETT *joins her.*)

HARRIETT (*Holding up package*): And when we open these fake packages and the public sees there's nothing inside, everyone will agree with us.

DEBRA: Santa Claus must go!

RICHARD: Are you sure all the packages are empty? I was hoping that maybe I'd get. . . .

HARRIETT: They're empty, Richard. We wrapped them ourselves.

RICHARD: I know that. But strange things happen on this night. Remember last year? We all agreed that Santa had to go, and then before the meeting was over, we were all singing Christmas carols.

HARRIETT (*Firmly*): It will be different this year.

DEBRA (*Standing*): This is the year we get Santa Claus.

TAMMY (*Chanting*): Let's get Santa! Let's get Santa! (*Begins to march around stage, holding tree, chanting.* HARRIETT, DEBRA, *and* THOMAS *quickly get in line and follow her, chanting loudly.* RICHARD *shrugs, gets up and starts to follow them, walking slowly and chanting without enthusiasm. Suddenly* MISS EMILY *enters. She is a little old lady, in Victorian clothes, carrying a gift-*

wrapped package which she puts with other packages. She begins to chant happily. Others stop their chanting and look at her in surprise.)

MISS EMILY (*Chanting alone*): We're going to get Santy. We're going to get Santy.

HARRIETT (*Angrily*): Who are you?

THOMAS: What are you doing here?

TAMMY: This is a private meeting of young people to wipe out all the evils of the world.

DEBRA: Most of which were started by people of your generation.

MISS EMILY: I know and I agree. And you're going about it in the right way. (*Chants*) Let's get Santy. Let's get Santy.

HARRIETT: Now, wait a minute. Who are you?

MISS EMILY: Why, I'm Miss Emily, just a little old lady passing by. But when I heard you chanting that you wanted to get Santa Claus, I knew I'd found what I was looking for. Santa Claus always comes to young people who want him, and I must see him tonight.

DEBRA: Miss Emily, I'm afraid you don't understand.

MISS EMILY (*Happily*): Yes, I do. I was young once, and every Christmas Eve I waited for Santa to come. I always had a glass of milk and a few cookies for him. I want Santa Claus, too.

TAMMY (*Putting down tree*): We don't want him. We want to get rid of him.

MISS EMILY: Oh, I see. Well, before you send him to his next visit, may I talk to him? It's about my little niece, Sally. I thought she wanted a pink scarf, but today she told me she wanted a blue one. But when we wrote to Santa, we asked for a pink one. Now I must tell him it should be blue.

HARRIETT: Miss Emily, you still don't understand.

TAMMY: There is no Santa Claus.

MISS EMILY (*Smiling*): You're just fooling. I remember once a little girl wrote to the Baltimore *Sun* and asked if there was a Santa Claus. And the editor said—in the paper, too—"Yes, Virginia, there is a Santa Claus." Why, that same editorial is still being printed today.

THOMAS: He just wrote that to get people to buy his paper.

RICHARD: I don't know about that. Editors usually tell the truth. There are laws, you know.

HARRIETT (*Angrily*): Oh, Richard, stop being an idiot.

THOMAS: Miss Emily, we don't want to hurt your feelings. But we have investigated Santa Claus thoroughly . . .

TAMMY: And scientifically.

DEBRA: And objectively.

HARRIETT: And we agree, democratically, there is no Santa Claus.

MISS EMILY: There is so.

HARRIETT: Miss Emily, have you ever seen Santa Claus?

MISS EMILY (*Crossing to chair and sitting*): When I was a little girl, I wanted a china tea set. And my daddy didn't have any money, so he told me to ask Santa Claus. And Christmas morning, there it was. That proves there's a Santa Claus.

RICHARD (*Nodding*): Just like the time Santa gave me a train—with two tunnels.

TAMMY: Both of you know where you got those presents. Your parents gave them to you and said they were from Santa Claus.

MISS EMILY: I don't believe my parents would have done that. I've heard people blame others for things that are bad, but I've never heard anyone blame someone else for something that's good.

RICHARD: That's right. My father always took credit for my good looks, and he blamed my mother's side of the family for my brains. If my father had given me that train, he'd have told me.

HARRIETT: Well . . . I'll admit it's a little strange, and not normal psychology at all. That's another thing that's wrong with Santa Claus! He makes people behave strangely.

TAMMY: And just for one day, too. Everyone is disappointed later.

DEBRA: Miss Emily, you don't think those department-store Santas are real, do you?

MISS EMILY: Of course, I don't.

RICHARD: They're just Santa's helpers.

TAMMY: They're just a bunch of actors helping themselves. I know. My Uncle Charlie works every year as a Santa Claus, and he just tries to get kids to ask their parents for the rotten toys the store is trying to sell.

MISS EMILY: That is disgraceful. Poor Santa Claus.

HARRIETT: There is no Santa Claus!

TAMMY: There never has been a Santa Claus!

DEBRA: There never could be a Santa Claus! (SANTA CLAUS *enters. He looks worn out, his beard is thin, and his suit is patched. All stop and look at him in disbelief.*)

SANTA CLAUS: Excuse me. I thought I heard my name mentioned.

MISS EMILY: It is Santa Claus! It really is!

TAMMY: It is not. It's probably my Uncle Charlie.

RICHARD: It could be Santa Claus.

HARRIETT: It could not. There is no Santa Claus.

THOMAS (*Going to* SANTA CLAUS): What's the matter? You look sick. (*Takes his arm*) Let me help you to this chair, so you can sit down. (*Leads him to captain's chair.* SANTA *sits.*) Maybe we'd better call a doctor.

MISS EMILY: No, that won't be necessary. I know what Santa needs. (*Exits quickly*)

HARRIETT (*Concerned*): He does look sick. (*To* SANTA) Look, old man, we don't have anything against you personally. We know that you must need a job badly to dress up like this.

DEBRA: It really is terrible that people will make a tired old man dress up like Santa—for the (*Cynically*) spirit of Christmas.

TAMMY: You Santa Clauses ought to unionize. This costume they gave you is terrible. It's full of patches.

SANTA CLAUS: Thank you, children, for your concern. I *am* tired. This job gets harder every year. I don't mind the long trip, but everyone seems angry at Santa these days. Why, tonight some children threw snowballs at me.

TAMMY: That wasn't very nice of them.

THOMAS: Look, don't you think we'd better call your family or friends to take you home?

SANTA CLAUS: Oh, no. I still have work to do. (MISS EMILY *returns with a glass of milk and plate of cookies. She puts them on the table next to* SANTA. *He takes a bite from one cookie and a sip of milk, then brightens and suddenly recovers. He stands up straight and begins to laugh loudly.*) Ho, ho, ho! (*All step back in amazement.*) All right, children, I'm your old Santa again. Come and tell me what you want for Christmas.

RICHARD: Well, Santa, there's this book about trains that I've been wanting for a long time, but I don't know the author or title. I remember seeing it when I was a child . . . it has a red cover.

MISS EMILY: Santa, I don't want anything for myself, but—

HARRIETT (*Interrupting*): Richard—Miss Emily—have you two lost your minds? This isn't Santa Claus. It's just a tired old man—a victim of the commercialization of Christmas.

RICHARD: Just because you don't want anything for Christmas, Harriett, don't try to keep me from getting what I want.

HARRIETT: I want lots of things. I need an umbrella, for example. But Santa Claus isn't going to give me one, because there isn't any Santa Claus.

MISS EMILY (*Pointing at* SANTA): There he is.

HARRIETT: He's an old man with a fake beard and a patched costume. (*Starts toward* SANTA) I'll pull off his beard and you can see for yourself.

SANTA CLAUS (*Covering his beard with his hands*): Please, young lady, not you, too! This is a real beard, but all evening people have been pulling it to prove it isn't. Soon, I won't have anything left.

HARRIETT: All right. The beard may be real, but you're not.

SANTA CLAUS: Would you believe me if I said I were Santa Claus?

MISS EMILY: I would. I do!

RICHARD: I might. I'd like to.

HARRIETT: I wouldn't, and nobody else would.

TAMMY: It would be unscientific to believe in Santa Claus.

DEBRA: And much too subjective for someone as objective as I.

THOMAS: And it would be commercial, too.

HARRIETT: And undemocratic. Four of us say you are not Santa Claus, and we're the majority.

RICHARD: I didn't say he was Santa Claus. I just said he might be.

MISS EMILY: Why, of course, he's Santa Claus. You can see him.

HARRIETT: I just see a man dressed like Santa Claus. It's just like this stuff here (*Indicates tree, packages*)—all pretense.

MISS EMILY: I rather like that little tree. Besides, it's real.

SANTA CLAUS: Why don't we all sit down and talk about this?

HARRIETT: There's nothing to talk about. Christmas is a big fake, and it's all because of Santa Claus.

THOMAS: That's right. If it weren't for Santa Claus, there wouldn't be all the commercialism.

DEBRA: And the phoniness.

TAMMY: And the corny music.

RICHARD: I like the music—I really do. I like everything about Christmas.

HARRIETT (*Pointing to packages*): Including this commercial stuff here?

SANTA CLAUS (*Kindly, but with authority*): Now, everyone listen to me for a moment.

HARRIETT: I'm not going to listen to you any more—

SANTA CLAUS: I've listened to you and to millions like you. Don't you think it's fair to give me a chance?

THOMAS (*Going to chair at table and sitting*): That's fair. Let him speak.

DEBRA (*Sitting at table*): I guess it's only democratic.

TAMMY (*Sitting*): And maybe even objective.

RICHARD (*Sitting*): I want to hear him.

MISS EMILY (*Sitting in rocker*): He may tell us a story.

HARRIETT (*Bored*): I know it's going to be a story. (*To* SANTA) Well, go ahead. Talk.

SANTA CLAUS: Won't you please sit, too, Harriett?

HARRIETT: I don't want to sit. (*Pauses*) How do you know my name?

SANTA CLAUS (*Standing*): All right, then you can be Santa's helper. (*Waves his hand at Christmas objects*) These, I assume, are your evidence that Christmas and Santa Claus should be abolished. Is that correct?

HARRIETT: This stuff is just like you. Fake. (*Picks up tree*) Look at this tree.

SANTA CLAUS: Well, well. It does look a little puny. But

let's give it a chance. Set it up on that table next to my chair, will you, please, Harriett?

HARRIETT (*Backing away, still holding tree*): I will not. I'm not going to be part of any stupid game! (RICHARD *gets up and goes over to* HARRIETT, *reaching for tree.*)

RICHARD: Here, let me take it, Harriett. (*He grabs one end of tree.* HARRIETT *does not let go.*)

HARRIETT: Stop it, Richard! (*They both tug at tree.*) You're being taken in by this old fraud.

THOMAS: Let Santa have a chance, Harriett.

DEBRA: You said you would.

HARRIETT (*Slowly letting go of tree*): I did, didn't I? Well, you win, Richard, but I'm not going to believe a word of it. (*Folds her arms and stands belligerently while* RICHARD *puts tree on table.*)

RICHARD (*Stepping back to look critically at it*): It still looks terrible.

TAMMY (*Rising*): It needs some decorations. (*Gets box of decorations and joins* RICHARD) I'll trim the tree, and you can help me, Richard. (*They begin to trim tree.*)

SANTA CLAUS: I think that little tree might just surprise us.

HARRIETT (*Picking up cardboard fireplace*): I suppose this will give us a nice warm fire, too. (*Shakes her head*) I'd like to see you go up and down this fireplace.

SANTA CLAUS: Well, maybe I could, if it were set up.

DEBRA (*Rising*): I'd like to see that! I'll set it up. (*Takes fireplace, goes upstage and sets it up around table*)

SANTA CLAUS: Thank you, Debbie.

HARRIETT: Her name is not Debbie. It's Debra.

DEBRA: My grandfather used to call me Debbie. (*Pauses*) I liked it when he called me Debbie. You can call me Debbie, Santa.

MISS EMILY (*Picking up tablecloth*): I guess I'd better set the table.

THOMAS: Wait a minute! Wait a minute! What's happening here? This isn't supposed to be a Christmas party. We brought this stuff to show what's wrong with Christmas.

MISS EMILY: Well, you can't show it unless folks can see it. Come on, Tommy, help me spread the cloth.

HARRIETT (*Indignantly*): Tommy! Do you think he's a child?

THOMAS: Oh, I don't mind. (*Helping* MISS EMILY *shake out and arrange cloth*) All right, we'll set the table.

HARRIETT: Thomas, not you, too!

THOMAS: Setting the table doesn't mean I believe in Santa Claus. It's just that we ought to be pleasant to each other. (THOMAS *and* MISS EMILY *place candlesticks, candles, and centerpiece on table.* DEBRA *finishes setting up fireplace and stands back to admire it.* RICHARD *and* TAMMY *put ornament on top of tree and move back. Lights dim and soften. Spotlight shines on top of tree.* HARRIETT *furiously turns her back;* SANTA *beams.*)

RICHARD: The tree looks good now, doesn't it?

TAMMY: Not bad. Not bad.

DEBRA: This fireplace looks almost real.

THOMAS: I wish we had some real food. We could have a feast.

HARRIETT (*Bitterly*): Are you all satisfied?

RICHARD: We ought to sing some Christmas songs. Come on, everybody, let's sing "Jingle Bells." (*Starts singing alone*) "Jingle bells, jingle bells—"

HARRIETT (*Striding to center*): Richard, be quiet. I'm ashamed of all of you. You're acting like children. And why? Because an old man tricks you into turning the conference room into a fake Christmas scene. I'll bet you all believe he's Santa Claus now, don't you?

RICHARD: I do.

HARRIETT: You would, Richard. But the rest of you—you

have some sense. What has changed? Nothing. (*Picks up pile of packages*) These boxes are still empty, and you'll notice that our Santa Claus didn't come with a pack.

MISS EMILY (*Going to* HARRIETT *and taking boxes*): That's right. We forgot the presents. Richard, help me pass them around.

RICHARD (*Going to* MISS EMILY *and taking some packages*): I hope there's one for me. I didn't write to Santa this year.

HARRIETT: Everyone's gone mad!

TAMMY: Oh, Harriett, we don't believe in Santa Claus. I just wanted to see if I could—well, I mean—I don't believe in Santa Claus. I'm not stupid.

HARRIETT: I should hope not.

MISS EMILY (*Reading tag on package*): The first one's for Tammy.

TAMMY: For me?

MISS EMILY: I'll put it at your place, dear. (*Puts package on table.* DEBRA, TAMMY, THOMAS, *and* RICHARD *sit at table.*)

HARRIETT: Who put name tags on those boxes?

THOMAS: I didn't . . . . Well, only one, for a joke.

RICHARD (*Reading tag*): And here's one for Thomas. (*Sets package on table*)

THOMAS: I didn't make out that tag.

MISS EMILY (*Reading tag*): And here's one for Debra. (*Sets package on table*)

RICHARD: And one for Sally. (*Pauses*) Hey, there's no Sally here. Who's Sally?

MISS EMILY (*Taking box and putting it on table*): That's my niece. (*To* SANTA) I meant to tell you, Santa, Sally wants blue.

SANTA CLAUS: Oh, it's blue, Miss Emily.

MISS EMILY: Thank you, Santa.

RICHARD: And one for Harriett. (*Puts package on table*)

HARRIETT: Just what I've always wanted—an empty box. This is going to make me angry!

MISS EMILY: And the last one's for Richard! (*Hands him package*)

RICHARD (*Taking package*): I'll bet it's that book on trains I've been wanting.

HARRIETT: I'll bet it's not. I wrapped that package myself, and it's just like you, Richard—full of hot air. (*To* SANTA) You're a very clever man, whoever you are. You ought to be selling patent medicine with a carnival. You really are a confidence man.

SANTA CLAUS: Thank you, my dear. I hope I am a confidence man. (*Moving to upstage center*) I hope that I can give people confidence—confidence in their goodness. Sometimes I seem old-fashioned and sometimes new-fashioned, and sometimes I may not seem to be telling the truth. There is a great deal of generosity in this world, but you have to have some confidence to see it. And you have to know how to look. Those are the real gifts I try to bring—faith in goodness, generosity, and vision. I'm sorry people use my name for things they shouldn't, but you don't throw away good money just because there are some counterfeit bills around, do you?

HARRIETT: Aha! I knew it would get to money.

RICHARD (*Unwrapping package and holding up book with red cover*): It is! It's the book on trains I've been wanting. Thank you, Santa Claus.

SANTA CLAUS: Well, Harriett, what do you say about Santa now?

HARRIETT: Not a thing. You're the big talker. You talk.

SANTA CLAUS: Do you want to tell Richard that Santa Claus did *not* give him that book?

HARRIETT (*Nervously*): I don't want to tell him anything. Besides, it's just a book.

RICHARD: How did you know I wanted this book, Santa? I didn't write you.

SANTA CLAUS: Harriett told me. (HARRIETT *looks up, startled.*)

RICHARD: Harriett! She doesn't believe in you. How could she talk to you?

SANTA CLAUS: I guess she didn't know it was me.

RICHARD: I still don't know how Harriet knew I wanted that book.

DEBRA: There's no secret about that. You talk about that book all the time.

TAMMY: Harriett, did you give Richard that book?

HARRIETT: Why should I do a stupid thing like that? (*Points at* SANTA CLAUS) He gave it to him. He said he did.

TAMMY (*Tearing off wrapping paper and holding up framed picture*): It's the picture I've been wanting! (*Others begin to unwrap their presents.* HARRIETT, *intrigued, moves closer to table, watching.*)

MISS EMILY (*Holding up opened package to show blue scarf*): I knew it would be blue! Sally will be so happy in the morning.

THOMAS (*Opening box and holding it up to show ring*): Look at this ring, everybody! This is the one I've been telling you about. (SANTA *quietly goes to fireplace.*)

DEBRA (*Holding earrings up to ears*): These are the very earrings I wanted. (SANTA *exits through small door behind fireplace, unnoticed.*)

HARRIETT (*Bitterly*): Well, hooray for everyone. (*They turn to look at her.*)

TAMMY: What about your present, Harriett? (*Hands her package*)

HARRIETT (*Opening it slowly*): I know it's going to be an umbrella. But I'm not going to believe. I'm not going to believe. (*Opens package and holds up umbrella*) I don't believe it! (*Lamely*) Thanks, somebody. I can sure use this.

RICHARD: Thank Santa Claus. He's the one who gave it to you.

HARRIETT (*Dropping umbrella furiously*): I'm tired of this Santa Claus business. Somebody here was nice enough to give me a gift. I thank him. But it wasn't that character over there. (*Turns to point at* SANTA CLAUS) He's gone! Where did he go? (*They turn to look.*)

MISS EMILY: I'll bet he went up the fireplace. And I forgot to look.

TAMMY: He is gone. That's for sure.

DEBRA: He was here, wasn't he?

RICHARD: I saw him. At least, I think I saw him.

THOMAS: Well, Harriett, was he here? Is there a Santa Claus?

HARRIETT: There is no Santa Claus, and he wasn't here.

RICHARD: My book is here.

HARRIETT: Then somebody here gave it to you. There is no Santa Claus.

DEBRA: There couldn't be a Santa Claus.

TAMMY: And next year, we're really going to prove it.

DEBRA: Yes, just wait until next year.

THOMAS: That's what we said last year.

HARRIETT: Well, next year, we'll do it right. But since we are all here, and the place is decorated, and it is Christmas Eve, what do you say that we sing one Christmas song. There is one—just one—I almost like. (*Offstage music for a Christmas song is heard. All start singing;* MISS EMILY *goes slowly down left; music stops.*)

MISS EMILY: Merry Christmas to all, and to all a good night! (*Exits.*)

ALL (*Calling after her*): Good night!

THOMAS: Next year, Harriett?

HARRIETT (*Shrugging*): Or the year after. You know, Christmas isn't so bad (*Firmly*)—as long as it only comes once a year. (*Lights fade to single spot on tree; music is heard from offstage; actors hum; and curtain falls.*)

THE END

The Humblest Place

by Graham DuBois

Characters

ETHAN, *an innkeeper*
MARTHA, *his wife*
SHEPHERDS
SARAH, *a maid at the inn*
WOMAN, *a servant to the Three Wise Men*
THREE WISE MEN
JOSEPH
ONE OF HEROD'S MEN

TIME: *The early morning of Christ's birth.*
SETTING: *The yard of the inn at Bethlehem.*
AT RISE: MARTHA *is seated on the bench.* ETHAN *enters from the inn.*

ETHAN (*Approaching the bench, rubbing his hands gleefully*): Well, all the rooms are taken—except the one at the end of the passage. (*Sits*) It's not often that I can rent that room. But I shall do so tonight.

MARTHA (*Surprised*): Not that dreadfully dark little hole in the corner? There is hardly enough space to turn around.

ETHAN: Who wants to turn around at this hour? All a weary traveler is interested in is dropping upon a bed for a long, refreshing sleep.

MARTHA (*Sighing*): I'm afraid there's nothing refreshing about that room—if one can call it a room. Not a breath of air! And no light ever enters.

ETHAN: What need of light for those who will be up at the crack of dawn? These travelers have come to Bethlehem to be taxed, and the tax offices open early. There is such demand for rooms tonight that I even plan to rent space in my stable.

MARTHA: What kind of person would be fool enough to take it?

ETHAN: Not the sort I usually accept here, I admit. But it is getting late, and travelers have plenty of money. (*Jingles coins in his pockets*) I can ask more than I generally get for my finest quarters. Perhaps some mother, obliged to take her child with her to Bethlehem, may come along. I'll make an exception to my rule not to accept children. Straw can be a comfortable bed for a woman, and the child could sleep in the manger.

MARTHA (*Indignantly*): And you would put a child in that wretched place?

ETHAN: Why not? I'll wager it would be better quarters than many children have tonight.

MARTHA: May God forgive you! What if the child you put in that manger should be—(*Shudders*)

ETHAN (*Putting his hand on hers*): Why do you shudder? You are trembling.

MARTHA: I just thought of an old prophecy, which says that out of Bethlehem will come forth one who is to be ruler of Israel. What if that child is to born here?

ETHAN (*Laughing mirthlessly*): You are much too gullible, dear. The only thing that ever comes forth out of Bethlehem is the demand for taxes. Don't let your mind dwell on these old prophecies. Think of the future. We'll soon have enough to build an addition, and when that happens our inn will be the finest in the empire.

These rooms will be filled by the rich and mighty. They will ring with the merriment of noble guests.

MARTHA: They will be empty without the laughter of little children.

ETHAN (*Still absorbed in his dream of the new inn*): I'll build a special room for you. It will have all that— (*A Christmas song offstage*) What is that caterwauling? Why do these good-for-nothing shepherds have to disturb the peace of my guests? (*Rises*) I'll get a soldier. I'll—

MARTHA (*Laying a hand upon his arm*): Sit down, Ethan, and listen to the song. It is very beautiful, and it is not loud enough to disturb anybody. (ETHAN *sits. They listen until the song fades and the* SHEPHERD *enters from the highway.*)

ETHAN (*Rising*): What do you want?

SHEPHERD: We followed the star.

ETHAN: What star, idiot?

SHEPHERD (*Pointing to the heavens*): That star above your stable. We followed it all the way down from the hills. It moved before us.

ETHAN: Well, follow it off my premises.

SHEPHERD: We can't. (*Points*) Don't you see? It has stopped right above your stable. Just as the angel told us it would.

ETHAN: Angel? What angel?

SHEPHERD: While we were in the fields, keeping watch over our sheep, an angel appeared to us. We were sore afraid, but the angel said, "Fear not, for I bring you good tidings of great joy."

ETHAN: What foolishness! The only angel you heard was in your befuddled brain.

SHEPHERD: The angel said we would find Him here.

ETHAN (*Puzzled*): Find *him?* Who?

SHEPHERD: The King.

ETHAN (*Angrily*): Get out of here, numskull! The only king you will ever find is king of the dunces, and you'll find him right among yourselves.

SHEPHERD (*Walking toward portal*): I'll go—but we'll be back. (*Exits*)

ETHAN (*Sitting*): Stupid beast! Wastes my time talking about angels and kings, and stars that move and then stand still.

MARTHA (*Quietly*): I have a strange feeling that he may be right.

ETHAN (*Astounded*): What? Do you mean to tell me that you actually believe what that ignorant boor said?

MARTHA (*Meditatively*): I hardly know what I believe. (*Looks toward the heavens*) There is something strange about that star—strange and beautiful as if it were the only star that had ever been in the heavens. See how it shines through that black cloud—like a jewel against the bosom of the night.

ETHAN (*Looking upward*): It looks just like a million other stars that I have seen. (SARAH *enters from stable, walks to portal, and stands there, staring down the highway*) Why are you standing there, girl, gaping down the highway?

SARAH: I'm watching the donkey, master.

ETHAN: Watching a donkey? What is so unusual about a donkey? Dozens of them pass this way every day.

SARAH: But this little beast seems so weak and tired. He is just limping along. An old man is leading him. There's a woman on the donkey's back.

ETHAN: Some peddlers probably. What are they doing out at this time of night when most decent citizens are in bed?

SARAH: They are stopping near the stable. He is helping the woman off the donkey's back.

ETHAN: Well, I don't want them hanging around my property. They'd better not come here hawking their wares. I'll send for the soldiers if they do.

SARAH: The woman is sitting at the side of the road. Her face is buried in her hands. She seems ill.

ETHAN (*Angrily*): That is none of our business. Have you nothing better to do than waste your time gawking at some miserable creatures on the highway? Get back to your place in the stable.

SARAH (*Turning from portal*): Yes, master. (*Walks to door of stable*) I shall be there if you need me. (*Exits as* JOSEPH *enters through portal*)

ETHAN (*Rising. To* MARTHA): I guess this is one of the vagabonds she was talking about. (*To* JOSEPH) What do you want, old man?

JOSEPH: Shelter for the night, I beg of you.

ETHAN (*Firmly*): There is no room at the inn.

JOSEPH: I do not expect a room at the inn. I only ask some corner of your stable for a few hours.

ETHAN: Are you prepared to pay well for it?

JOSEPH: I have no money—except what I brought for my taxes.

ETHAN (*Coldly*): We don't harbor beggars here.

JOSEPH (*Proudly*): I am no beggar. I am just a poor man in desperate need. And my wife is too ill to travel further. We have come all the way from Nazareth.

ETHAN (*Laughing cynically*): That is not much of a recommendation in Bethlehem. We are in the habit of saying that no good can come out of Nazareth.

JOSEPH (*Imploringly*): Please, sir, show me some mercy. My wife is tired and sick, and I am so feeble that I could hardly help her down from the donkey's back.

ETHAN (*Sternly*): You have heard me. Leave this inn at once or I'll call the soldiers. (*Calling*) Sarah!

SARAH (*Appearing in doorway of stable*): Here I am, master.

ETHAN: Help this man's wife to mount the donkey and send them on their way.

JOSEPH (*Stretching out his arms to* ETHAN *imploringly*): My wife is too ill to go on. We have no place to lay our heads.

ETHAN (*Coldly*): That is no concern of mine. (*To* SARAH) What are you waiting for? Do as I bade you.

SARAH: Yes, master. (*Takes* JOSEPH *gently by the arm*) Come with me, sir. (*Leads him to portal*) Maybe I can— (*They go out.*)

ETHAN (*Indignantly*): Impudent rogue! Standing there arguing with me after I had told him there was no place. (WOMAN, *carrying three small metal caskets, enters through the portal*) What do you want, woman?

WOMAN: I am seeking lodging for the night.

ETHAN: Accommodations are very scarce. I suppose you are prepared to pay a satisfactory price?

WOMAN (*Shrugging her shoulders*): The price is no consideration. I serve one of the wealthiest men in the East. He and his two companions are the most powerful citizens in our country. They are known everywhere as wise men.

ETHAN (*Puzzled*): But if they are from some foreign country, they don't have to pay taxes here. What are they doing in Bethlehem tonight?

WOMAN: They have come to find the King.

ETHAN (*Even more bewildered*): The king? What king? Where is he?

WOMAN: He has not yet been born.

ETHAN (*Looking at her skeptically*): Why did they bring you with them?

WOMAN: They thought I might be able to tend the mother.

ETHAN: And do they know where this king is to be born?

WOMAN: They said he would be born in Bethlehem. I

overheard them telling Herod that it was so written by a prophet.

ETHAN (*Impatiently*): There are hundreds of houses in Bethlehem. Whereabouts in Bethlehem?

WOMAN: Here—at your inn.

ETHAN (*Amazed*): Here? You mean in my royal chambers?

WOMAN (*Shaking her head*): No; my master said it would be in the humblest place.

ETHAN: The humblest place? What did he mean by that?

WOMAN: In a manger—in your stable.

ETHAN (*Angrily*): Don't jest with me, woman. That is the most absurd thing I ever heard. The idea of a king being born in a stable!

WOMAN (*Turning toward portal*): I can only tell you what my master said. (*Walks toward portal*) If you have no room, I shall have to look elsewhere.

ETHAN (*Raising a hand*): Wait! I couldn't show such discourtesy to your master as to turn away one of his retinue. I still have one most comfortable little room. (*Calls*) Sarah! (*To* WOMAN) The maid will see that you are taken care of. The price will be ten pieces of silver.

WOMAN (*Feeling in her pocket*): Very well. (*Draws out some coins and hands them to* ETHAN) There you are.

ETHAN (*Pocketing coins*): Thank you. You are fortunate to find such comfortable quarters at this hour. (SARAH *enters from stable*) Sarah, show this lady to that little room at the end of the passage. (SARAH, *followed by* WOMAN, *exits into inn.* ETHAN, *jingling coins in his pocket, walks to bench.*) I told you I could do it. (*Sits*) I should have asked more. Why are you sitting there with your head in your hands?

MARTHA (*Sadly*): It's that poor couple you turned away. I can't get them out of my mind.

ETHAN (*Impatiently*): It's that queer woman who just

came. She has upset you with her wild babbling about a king to be born in our stable. How can you believe such nonsense? I tell you the woman is mad.

MARTHA: Her words gave me a strange feeling.

ETHAN (*Sarcastically*): Like the star, I suppose.

MARTHA: Yes—like—like that. As if something new and beautiful and wonderful was about to be born into the world.

ETHAN: I almost wish I hadn't rented the room to that fool woman. I can see that she has had a bad effect upon you.

MARTHA: But she hasn't, Ethan. Somehow I feel strangely happy—I know not why. But with the happiness is mingled sadness at the thought of that poor couple wandering helpless in the night, and regret that we may have lost a glorious opportunity.

ETHAN (*Angrily*): A glorious opportunity! An opportunity to harbor two worthless vagrants who might have robbed our guests and made off with our cattle.

MARTHA (*Emphatically*): They were not vagrants. Of that I am sure. Who knows but that they may be destined to become—(HEROD'S MAN *enters through portal and stands looking about.*)

ETHAN (*Touching* MARTHA'S *arm warningly*): Be careful now. It is one of Herod's men. I'll attend to this. Let me do the talking. (*Rises*) Is there something I can do for you, sir?

HEROD'S MAN: I was sent by King Herod to visit your inn.

ETHAN (*Bowing*): I am honored, sir. I am at your service.

HEROD'S MAN: Herod's representatives are searching about Bethlehem for a new-born child. Three persons, calling themselves wise men, informed the king that he was to be born in our village. They said the child was to be a king. Herod is alarmed lest the people be aroused. Is there such a child here?

ETHAN: I can assure you, sir, that there is no child whatsoever here. We seldom accept children at the inn for fear they may disturb our guests.

HEROD'S MAN: Nevertheless, I must search the premises. It is my duty to carry out Herod's orders.

ETHAN: Suit yourself, sir. Come with me. (*Walks toward inn*) I shall be glad to show you through the inn. (*Enters inn, followed by* HEROD'S MAN)

SARAH (*Entering from inn, her hands to her face*): Oh, I have done something awful. The master will never forgive me.

MARTHA: Why, Sarah, what has happened? (SARAH *walks toward bench*) Sit here and tell me what is the matter. (*Indicates bench*)

SARAH (*Sitting*): That old man and his wife and the poor little donkey. They were so pitiful. I couldn't bear the thought of their traveling the highway tonight.

MARTHA (*Patting* SARAH'S *hand consolingly*): Never mind, child. It isn't your fault. The master told you to send them off.

SARAH (*Weeping*): That's just it. It's the first time I have ever disobeyed.

MARTHA (*Eagerly*): You mean that—

SARAH: I—I didn't. I didn't send them off.

MARTHA (*Clasping her hands and raising her face heavenward*): Oh, thank God!

SARAH (*Looking at* MARTHA *in amazement*): You mean that—that I didn't do wrong—that I won't be punished?

MARTHA: The master may punish you, Sarah, but I am quite sure that God never will.

SARAH (*Wiping her eyes with a corner of her apron*): I guess the master will send me away. But I couldn't help it. That sick woman is so weak and yet so beautiful and —and holy-looking that I gave them my place in the stable.

MARTHA: You have done a very lovely and righteous thing, Sarah. (*A Christmas song is sung offstage. She and* SARAH *sit listening to the song.* WOMAN *enters from inn and stands near door, listening until the song ceases.* MARTHA *turns to* WOMAN) Couldn't you sleep in that little room? Have you come out for a breath of air?

SARAH (*Rising and pointing to bench*): Sit here, madam.

WOMAN (*Walking to bench*): Thank you. (*Sits. To* MARTHA) No, I had fallen asleep, but your husband and some other man are rousing all the guests, and so I thought I would wait out here until they had finished.

ETHAN (*Followed by* HEROD'S MAN, *entering from inn*): I have shown you everything. We have nothing to hide here.

HEROD'S MAN: I am quite satisfied. I am sorry I had to disturb you. But I have my orders, you know. (*Looking at stable and pointing*) What's that over there?

ETHAN: Only my stable. (*Jocularly*) You'll find nothing to interest you there—unless you think a couple of cows and a few sheep might be royal parents.

HEROD'S MAN: I'd better take a look. (*Walks to stable*) I have to report to my superiors that I've made a thorough inspection. (*Enters stable*)

ETHAN (*Turning toward bench and rubbing his hands in satisfaction*): You see, Martha, how wise I have been in not encouraging my patrons to bring children here? If I—

SARAH (*Tearfully*): Oh, master, that man will—

ETHAN (*Turning to look at* SARAH *in surprise*): Why, what's the matter with you, girl? What are you crying about? You are trembling like an aspen tree.

HEROD'S MAN (*Entering from stable*): Nobody in there—except an old man and his wife.

ETHAN (*Amazed*): An old man? His wife?

HEROD'S MAN: Employees of the inn probably.

ETHAN (*Regaining his composure*): Yes; of course, of course. Employees of the inn.

HEROD'S MAN (*Walking to portal*): Certainly nothing about them to suggest royalty. (*Exits*)

ETHAN (*Turning in fury to* SARAH): So that's it! That's why you are weeping and trembling. You have disobeyed my orders. Do you realize that in hiding those miserable people in the stable you have deprived me of considerable income? Tonight a place in the straw is worth as much as one of my finest rooms. (*Points to stable*) Get in there at once and see that those tramps and their donkey leave immediately.

SARAH (*Sobbing*): I—I can't, master. They are not able to travel tonight. I only gave them my place in the straw. I was going to sleep on the ground.

ETHAN (*Angrily*): Unless you do as I say, I'll—

WOMAN (*Rising. To* ETHAN); If this poor couple could pay, how much would you ask?

ETHAN: Let me see, now. On a night like this, with hundreds of travelers moving toward Bethlehem to pay their taxes, and the town over-crowded, any sleeping space is valuable.

WOMAN: Very well. Name your price.

ETHAN: Ten pieces of silver.

WOMAN: Agreed. (*Feels in her pocket, draws out some coins, counts them, and hands them to* ETHAN) See if that is correct.

ETHAN (*Counting coins*): Correct. You have made a shrewd bargain. (*Pockets coins*) I might have asked much more.

WOMAN (*Walking toward* SARAH): And now I will go into the stable. (*Follows* SARAH *to stable*) Maybe I can help that poor woman. (*Enters stable with* SARAH)

ETHAN (*Jerking his thumb toward the stable and then tapping his forehead suggestively with his finger*): That woman must have lost her mind. (*Sits on bench*) I thought she had a queer look in her eyes when she came here.

MARTHA: May God forgive you!

ETHAN (*Turning to* MARTHA *in amazement*): Forgive me? Forgive me for what?

MARTHA: For making a profit from human suffering.

ETHAN: I only did what any other enterprising innkeeper would do under the circumstances. That woman is crazy, I tell you. If I didn't take her money, somebody else would.

MARTHA (*Quietly*): Perhaps she is not as crazy as you think.

ETHAN: If she's not a crazy woman, I never saw one. First, she comes here and rents the poorest room we have, and then she pays good money so that two tramps whom she had never seen may sleep in my stable. (*Points to stable*) And she's in there now, probably handing out more money.

WOMAN (*Entering from stable*): The woman is desperately ill. (*Walks toward bench*)

ETHAN (*Rising*): Sit here, madam.

WOMAN (*Sitting*): Thank you, Mr. Innkeeper. The maid tells me that there's a physician here. May I ask that you call him to tend that poor woman, who is in dire need?

ETHAN: You ask the impossible, madam. The physician accepts only noble persons as patients. What would he think of me if I asked him to go into my stable to look after a penniless tramp?

WOMAN (*Sighing*): I suppose there's no use in my saying more. You wouldn't understand me if I told you that he will never have a patient as noble as she. (*Rising and turning her eyes to the heavens*) I have a feeling that the moment is not far off—the greatest moment in the history of the world. I'll get the gifts for the king. (*Walks *to inn)* If my master arrives, tell him that I am here. (*Exits into inn*)

ETHAN (*Looking at* MARTHA *in amazement*): What is that mad woman talking about—the greatest moment in the history of the world?

MARTHA: Oh, Ethan, that is something each of us must understand for himself. (*Lays her hand on his arm*) Don't you feel it in the night? Don't you hear it in the song the shepherds sing? Don't you see it in the star shining above the stable?

ETHAN (*Drawing away from her irritably*): I hear nothing, woman, in the noise those howling shepherds make. I see nothing in a star that is like any other star that shines over Bethlehem almost every night. What you feel is in your own imagination.

MARTHA (*Nodding toward inn*): That woman feels it.

ETHAN: That crazy woman is likely to feel anything.

MARTHA: Sarah, a poor servant girl, feels it.

ETHAN: I am not surprised at anything that stupid creature feels. She belongs to a class that thrives on superstition, Martha, but I am surprised that you, an intelligent woman, should be taken in by these two fools.

MARTHA: That simple shepherd feels it. He left his flocks on the hillside to follow the star. There is something lovely and mysterious about this night.

ETHAN: Those lazy shepherds will leave their flock upon any pretext. I am amazed that you swallowed this incredible yarn.

MARTHA (*Quietly*): Sometimes the truth is the most incredible thing in the world.

ETHAN (*Nodding toward inn*): What did that crazy creature mean by speaking of gifts for a king?

MARTHA: You remember those little metal caskets that she brought with her? I believe they must contain something very precious for the King.

ETHAN: What are you talking about? What king?

MARTHA (*Touching his arm gently*): I'm afraid I'll never be able to make you see. Try to understand what the rest of us feel tonight—the soft but brilliant light of yonder star, the tender hush of expectancy, as if the whole world were waiting for the birth of a new hope and a new leader.

ETHAN: You are talking nonsense!

MARTHA (*Imploringly*): Oh, Ethan, I beg of you, act before it is too late.

ETHAN: Act? What do you mean? What would you have me do?

MARTHA (*Pointing toward stable*): Move that poor woman and her husband into your royal chambers.

ETHAN (*Staring at* MARTHA *incredulously*): Have you completely lost your mind? Would you ruin my reputation for running the most exclusive inn in this vicinity? Would you make me the laughingstock of all Bethlehem? (*Laughs cynically*) I suppose you would have me move the donkey into the royal chambers, too. What do you suppose would become of my inn if I followed such stupid advice.

MARTHA: I think it would become a shrine for all the world. I think your name would go down the ages as the man who had given shelter to the King. But you must act at once: that woman said the moment was at hand.

ETHAN: Ah, that's it—that woman! I should never have taken her in.

WOMAN (*Entering from inn, carrying the three metal caskets*): I shall have these gifts ready for my master and his companions. (*Walks toward bench.* ETHAN *rises and motions to her to take his place.*) One of these belongs to each of them. (*Sits*) Perhaps you would like to see what they have brought the King.

MARTHA (*Eagerly*): I would, indeed!

WOMAN (*Opens one of the caskets.* ETHAN *stands to one side, watching curiously*): This is Casper's gift.

MARTHA (*Amazed*): Pure gold!

ETHAN (*Much impressed*): Enough for a king's ransom.

WOMAN (*Opening second casket*): Balthazar will present this.

MARTHA (*Bending over casket*): Myrrh. As fragrant as the woodland on a May morning.

WOMAN: The most precious that Arabia can produce. (*Opens third casket*) Melchior sought many days to find this.

MARTHA: Is that frankincense?

WOMAN: It is, indeed—the finest in the world.

SARAH (*Entering from stable*): The dearest little boy!

ETHAN: What do you mean? Has one of those shepherds dared to bring his child here?

SARAH: No, master; he is the son of that poor woman who came on the donkey. Born only a few minutes ago.

WOMAN (*Joyfully*): It is the king!

ETHAN: In my stable! (*Pounds his fist against his palm in despair*) I am ruined! The news will spread that I permit beggar children to be born here, and no guests will come to my inn. (*Enter* THREE WISE MEN *through the portal.*)

FIRST WISE MAN: We seek a child who has just been born.

ETHAN: There is no child here, gentlemen, except the child of two vagrants who was born in my stable.

FIRST WISE MAN: He is the one we seek. (*To* WOMAN) Have the gifts ready. (*Walks to stable door*) I shall see if the mother is ready to receive us. (*Enters stable*)

ETHAN (*Amazed*): The gifts are for *him?* Can it be that I—(*A Christmas song offstage*) What is that? Those confounded shepherds again! I'll put a stop to this. (*Takes a few steps toward stable*)

MARTHA (*Imploringly*): No, Ethan! For my sake. (*Clasps her hands and raises her face toward the heavens in an attitude of devotion*) It is the song the angels sing when there is rejoicing in heaven. (*Everybody, except* ETHAN, *listens in rapt attention until the conclusion of the song, and then the* FIRST WISE MAN *enters from the stable, followed by* SARAH.)

FIRST WISE MAN (*To* ETHAN): You didn't realize, last night, that you were to have the privilege of entertaining an infant king and his mother.

ETHAN (*Astonished*): You are mistaken, sir. No royal mother is here, no infant king.

FIRST WISE MAN (*Pointing to stable*): Even now he lies within your stable walls.

ETHAN (*Forcing a laugh*): Surely, sir, you do but jest. There is nobody in that stable except two miserable beggars from Nazareth and—

FIRST WISE MAN: And their son—the King of Kings.

ETHAN (*Dazed*): The King of Kings? And I never knew!

FIRST WISE MAN: You should have known. A shepherd in the hills told me he had informed you of the coming of the King, and you drove the poor fellow off.

ETHAN: How could I know he was telling the truth?

FIRST WISE MAN: If it had not been for your humble kitchen girl, you would have also driven off the Saviour of mankind.

ETHAN: I had no way of recognizing his parents. They were dressed like vagrants.

FIRST WISE MAN: But my maid here (*Points to* WOMAN) must have told you of the prophecy.

ETHAN: I didn't know who she was. I didn't believe what she said.

FIRST WISE MAN: Oh, you of little faith! Think of the glory that might have been yours if you had had more faith in your fellow men. You could have been the first to serve the King.

ETHAN: Is it too late to serve him now? Isn't there something I can give him to make up for—

FIRST WISE MAN: Yes, there is one thing—the greatest gift that any man can offer.

ETHAN (*Eagerly*): And what is that?

FIRST WISE MAN: Yourself.

ETHAN: How can I do that?

FIRST WISE MAN: By taking less thought of yourself and more of others; by seeing to it that there is always room at your inn for some weary traveler without money and without friends. And, above all, by finding room in your heart for the King. (*Several* SHEPHERDS *enter through the portal, bearing gifts—fruit, eggs, flowers of the field, etc. A Christmas song is heard from offstage. A part of the stable wall is drawn aside and the tableau of the manger is revealed. All kneel in an attitude of devotion.*)

THE END

Little Women

by Louisa May Alcott
adapted by Olive J. Morley

Characters

Meg, Jo, Beth, Amy — *sisters*
Mrs. March, *their mother*
Aunt March, *their aunt*
Hannah, *the family servant*
The Hummels, *two German children*

Time: *A few days before Christmas, 1862.*
Setting: *The living room of the March home in New England.*
At Rise: *The March sisters are grouped around the fire.* Meg, *a sweet-faced, very womanly "little woman" of sixteen, sits upstage, busy sewing. Gentle* Beth, *aged thirteen, is at her feet on a low stool, knitting. Fifteen-year-old* Jo, *tall, colt-like and boyish in manner, lies on the hearth-rug, with some knitting beside her. Fair-haired, self-important little* Amy, *aged twelve, sits in the center, sketching.*

Jo: Christmas won't be Christmas without any presents.
Meg (*Sighing*): It's so dreadful to be poor! (*She looks at her frock distastefully.*)

AMY (*With an injured sniff*): I don't think it's fair for some girls to have lots of pretty things, and other girls nothing at all.

BETH: We've got Father and Mother and each other, anyhow.

JO: We haven't got Father here, and we shan't have him for a long time. (*There is a little sniff from* AMY, *and* BETH *wipes away a tear.*)

MEG: Now, girls, you know the reason Mother proposed not having any presents this Christmas was because it's going to be a hard winter for everyone; and she thinks we ought not to spend money for pleasure when our men are suffering so in the Army. We can't do much, but we can make our little sacrifices, and ought to do it gladly. But it's awfully hard. (*She sighs.*)

JO: Still, I don't see how the little we can spend would do any good. Anyway, we've each got a dollar, and the Army wouldn't be much helped by our giving that. I agree not to expect anything from Mother or you, but I do want to buy *Undine and Sintram* for myself; I've wanted it *so* long.

BETH: I planned to spend my dollar for new music. (*She sighs.*)

AMY: I shall get a new box of Faber's Drawing Pencils. I really need them.

JO: Mother didn't say anything about *our* money, and she won't wish us to give up everything. Let's each buy what we want, and have a little fun. I'm sure we work hard enough to earn it.

MEG: I know *I* do—teaching those dreadful King children nearly all day, when I'm longing to enjoy myself at home.

JO: You don't have half as hard a time as I do. How would you like to be shut up for hours with a nervous, fussy old lady, who keeps you trotting, is never satisfied, and worries you till you're ready to cry?

BETH: It's naughty to fret—but I do think washing dishes and keeping things tidy is the worst work in the world. It makes me cross, and my hands get so stiff, I can't practice well at all! (*She looks at her hands, gives an audible sigh.*)

AMY: I don't believe any of you suffer as I do, for you don't have to go to school with impertinent girls, who plague you if you don't know your lessons, and laugh at your dresses, and label your father if he isn't rich, and insult you when your nose isn't nice.

JO (*Laughing*): If you mean *libel,* say so, and don't talk about *labels* as if Papa were a pickle bottle.

AMY (*With offended dignity*): I know what I mean, and you needn't be *statirical* about it. It's proper to use good words, and improve your *vocabilary.*

MEG: Don't peck at one another, children. Don't you wish we had the money Papa lost when we were little, Jo! Dear me, how happy and good we'd be, if we had no worries.

BETH: You said, the other day, you thought we were a great deal happier than the King children, for they were fighting and fretting all the time, in spite of their money.

MEG: So I did, Beth. Well, I think we are; for, though we do have to work, we have lots of fun, and are a "pretty jolly set," as Jo would say.

AMY: Jo does use such slang words. (JO *immediately sits up, puts her hands in her pockets, and begins to whistle.*) Don't, Jo, it's so boyish.

JO: That's why I do it.

AMY: I detest rude, unladylike girls.

JO: I hate affected, niminy-piminy chits.

BETH (*Sweetly*): Birds in their little nests agree. (*Everyone laughs.*)

MEG: Really, girls, you are both to be blamed. You're old enough to leave off boyish tricks, and behave better, Josephine. It didn't matter so much when you were a little girl; but now that you are so tall, and turn up your hair, you should remember that you're a young lady.

JO: I'm not! And if turning up my hair makes me one, I'll wear it in two tails till I'm twenty! (*She pulls off her hair net, and shakes down her long hair.*) I hate to think I've got to grow up and be Miss March, and wear long gowns, and look like a China aster. It's bad enough to be a girl, anyway, when I like boys' games, and work, and manners. I just can't get over my disappointment in not being a boy, and it's worse than ever now, for I'm dying to go and fight with Papa, and instead I have to stay at home and knit like a poky old woman. (*She shakes her knitting till the needles rattle and the ball bounds across the room.*)

BETH: Poor Jo! It's too bad! But it can't be helped; so you must try to be contented with making your name boyish, and playing brother to us girls. (*She strokes* JO's *hair.*)

MEG: As for you, Amy, you are altogether too particular and prim. Your airs are funny now, but you'll grow up an affected little goose if you don't take care.

BETH: If Jo is a tomboy, and Amy a goose, what am I, please?

MEG: You're a dear, and nothing else. (*Hugs* BETH) But look, girls, it's six o'clock. Marmee will be here any minute now. (*She rises and lights the lamp on the bookcase.* AMY *shakes up the cushions in the easy chair* MEG *has vacated.* BETH *sweeps the hearth and* JO *holds up an old pair of slippers to the fire.*)

Jo: These are quite worn out. Marmee must have a new pair.

Beth: I thought I'd get her some with my dollar.

Amy: No, I shall!

Meg: I'm the oldest!

Jo: But I'm the man of the family now that Papa is away, and *I* shall provide the slippers, for he told me to take special care of Mother while he was gone.

Beth: I'll tell you what we'll do. Let's each get her something for Christmas, and not get anything for ourselves.

Jo: That's like you, dear! What will we get?

Meg: I shall get her a nice pair of gloves.

Jo: Comfortable slippers, best to be had.

Beth: Some handkerchiefs, all hemmed.

Amy: I'll get a little bottle of cologne; she likes it, and it won't cost much, so I'll have some left to buy my pencils.

Meg: How shall we give the things?

Jo: Put them on the table, and bring her in and see her open the bundles. Don't you remember how we used to do on our birthdays?

Beth: I used to be *so* frightened when it was my turn to sit in the big chair, with the crown on, and see you all come marching round to give the presents, with a kiss.

Jo: We'll let Marmee think we are getting things for ourselves and then surprise her. We must go shopping soon, Meg. There's hardly any time left, with all we have to do about getting the play ready for Christmas night.

Meg: Oh, we'll have time to go tomorrow afternoon. And, anyway, I don't mean to act any more after this time. I'm getting too old for such things.

Jo: You won't stop, I know, as long as you can trail around in a white gown with your hair down, and wear gold-paper jewelry. You are the best actress we've got, and there'll be an end of everything if you quit the boards.

We ought to rehearse tonight. Maybe we could go over a few scenes before Marmee gets home. (*The girls move the table back, leaving a space in the center of the stage where the acting will take place. All exits and entrances refer to this area, so that none of the girls actually leaves the stage during the rehearsal.*) Come here, Amy, and do the fainting scene. You're as stiff as a poker in that.

AMY: I don't care. I never saw anyone faint, and I don't choose to make myself all black and blue, tumbling flat like you do. If I can go down easily, I'll drop; if I can't, I shall fall into a chair and be graceful. (*Arranges chair at back*)

JO: Do it this way; clasp your hands like this. (*She demonstrates.*) Then, stagger across the room, crying frantically, "Roderigo! Save me! Save me!" (JO *screams melodramatically and does a beautiful stage fall.*)

AMY (*Feebly imitating, with her hands stretched out stiffly like a doll*): Roderigo! Save me! Save me! (*She moves across the stage jerkily, falls into the chair awkwardly, slides off it and falls on to the floor with a squeaky "Ow!"*)

JO: It's no use! Do the best you can when the time comes, and if the audience laughs don't blame me. Come on, Meg. We'll do the caldron scene. (BETH *hurriedly places a coal scuttle in the center.* MEG *seizes a witch's hat from the corner, and a cloak which has been hung up on the door.* JO *pulls off the tablecloth and drapes it around herself in the form of a cloak, puts on a broad-brimmed hat with a feather, and proceeds to hitch up her skirts. She then puts on a pair of riding boots which have been hidden between the bookcase and the door.*) Ready, Meg? (*In a theatrical voice*) What ho, witch! I need thee! (*Claps her hands*) Fetch me the potions whereby I may win the fair Zara's love and kill my enemy Roderigo.

MEG (*Comes forward and stirs the "caldron" while she chants*):

Hither, hither, from thy home,
Airy sprite, I bid thee come!
Born of roses, fed on dew,
Charms and potions canst thou brew?
Bring me here, with elfin speed,
The fragrant philter that I need;
Make it sweet, and swift and strong;
Spirit, answer now my song! (AMY *dances daintily forward from the back. She has twined leaves in her hair, and carries a poker with wandlike effect in one hand, and a pepper shaker in the other.*)

AMY (*In a sing-song voice*):

Hither I come,
From my airy home,
Afar in the silvery moon;
Take the magic spell,
Oh, use it well!
Or its power will vanish soon! (*She hops gracefully out, then, suddenly remembering the philter, she runs back and places the pepper shaker before the coal scuttle.*) Oh, I forgot! (*She exits hastily.*)

JO: *Amy!*

MEG: Now come hither, naughty sprite! Bring the draught that shall quench light! (BETH *enters, rather shyly, and places a salt shaker before the caldron.* MEG *and* BETH *both exit.*)

JO: Well, not *bad,* I suppose. Now, we'll do the death of Hugo. Beth, you must be the servant. (*Enter* MEG, *smiling craftily. She waves her wand, an umbrella; then, hearing* JO *make stamping noises at the back, she hides behind chair.*)

JO (*Entering*): Ah ha, my handsome Roderigo, soon you will be dying at Zara's feet, and she will be mine! (*She gets three cups and a tray from the mantelpiece and places them on the table. She then takes the two philters, the pepper shaker and the salt shaker, from her boots. She pretends to empty the contents of the salt shaker into one cup and places the cup on the tray, muttering*) Death to Roderigo. (*She then takes the pepper shaker.*) And now for the love potion. Half for Zara and half for myself. (*She pretends to empty the pepper shaker into the other two cups. She places one of these cups on the tray and the other on the table within easy reach. She claps her hands.*) Minion! Minion! (BETH *enters, holding the toasting fork absentmindedly.*) Put that down, you dear little goose. (*Evilly*) I have evening refreshment prepared for the prisoners. Bear these two cups to them—the one on the left to Roderigo, the one on the right to Zara, and take care not to make any mistakes.

BETH: But—but, sire.

JO: Now you beckon me downstage. (BETH *does so.*) That's right. (*As* JO *and* BETH *stand whispering, downstage.* MEG *comes out of hiding, and quietly switches the cups —putting both love potions on the tray which* BETH *will carry to the prisoners and leaving the death potion for* JO *to drink. She then hastily hides.*)

BETH: The one on the left to Roderigo, the one on the right to Zara. (*She goes to the table and picks up the tray.*)

JO: Begone, I say, begone! (BETH *exits, taking tray.* JO *sits down at table and picks up poisoned cup.*) Ah ha— Ah ha! Love potion do your work! (*She drinks and then gasps.*) I have been tricked! (*She dies in horrid agony, rolling on the floor. All shriek with laughter.* JO *sits up and rubs her elbows.*)

MEG (*Removing her hat and smoothing her hair*): It's the best we've had yet.

BETH: I don't see how you can write and act such splendid

things, Jo. You're a regular Shakespeare. (*She abstractedly picks up the toasting fork with a slipper at the end of it.*)

JO: Well, I do think *The Witch's Curse* is rather a nice thing. But I'd like to do *Macbeth.*
"Is that a dagger that I see before me?" (*She makes passes at the toasting fork.*)

MEG: No, it's the toasting fork with Marmee's slipper at the end of it instead of the bread. Beth's stage struck! (*All go into peals of laughter. Enter* MRS. MARCH, *carrying a shopping bag. She is a motherly looking woman with a can-I-help-you look about her.*)

MRS. MARCH: Glad to find you so merry, my girls.

GIRLS: Marmee!

MRS. MARCH (*During the following speeches the girls are helping* MRS. MARCH *off with her cloak and bonnet, and ensconcing her by the fire, where* BETH *and* AMY *divest her of her shoes and put on the warm slippers.*): Well, dearies, how have you got on today? There was so much to do for the soldiers, getting the boxes ready to go tomorrow, that I didn't come home to dinner. Has anyone called, Beth?

BETH: No one, Marmee.

MRS. MARCH: How is your headache, Meg?

MEG: Oh, it's worn off, thank you, Mother.

MRS. MARCH: Jo, you look tired to death. (*To* AMY) Come and kiss me, baby. (AMY *runs to her and sits on her knee. After a brief hug, she joins the other girls, who are now getting tea.* MEG *is arranging the table, and* AMY *removes some of the paper bags from* MRS. MARCH'*s shopping bag, which she has put on a chair or on a corner of the table.* BETH *quietly goes back and forth from living room to kitchen, left, bringing in bread, milk, etc.* JO *goes out for wood, and overturns everything she touches with a great clatter.*)

AMY (*Peeping into one of the bags*): Ooh! Muffins!

MEG: Now, Amy, don't be greedy.

AMY: Can't I have just a taste?

MEG: They have to be toasted. You shall help Beth do them. (AMY *and* BETH *get busy at the fire, toasting and buttering muffins.*)

JO: And don't lick the butter, you disgusting child! (*As she sees* AMY *licking already greasy fingers.* AMY *quietly sticks out her tongue.*)

MRS. MARCH (*Reprovingly*): Amy! (AMY *looks shamefacedly down.*) Now, come, girls, be happy together. Remember, it's Christmas time. Besides, I have another treat for those who are good. (*She looks at* AMY, *and then draws a letter out of her bag.*)

JO: A letter!

OTHERS: A letter!

ALL: Three cheers for Father! (*All run to their mother.* JO *leans over the back of her chair,* MEG *sits on the arm,* AMY *on her knee, and* BETH *at her feet.*)

MRS. MARCH: Yes, a nice long letter. He is well, and thinks he will get through the cold season better than we feared. He sends all sorts of loving wishes for Christmas, and an especial message to you girls. (*Reading*) "Give them all my dear love and a kiss. A year seems very long to wait before I see them again, but remind them that while we wait we may all work, so that these hard days may not be wasted. I know they will remember all I said to them, and conquer themselves so beautifully, that when I come back I may be fonder and prouder than ever of my little women." (*There is a moment's serious pause.*)

AMY (*Hiding her face in her mother's shoulder*): I *am* a selfish girl, but I'll truly try to be better, so he mayn't be disappointed in me by and by.

MEG: We all will. I think too much of my looks, and hate to work, but won't any more, if I can help it.

JO: I'll try to be what he loves to call me, "a little woman." (BETH *wipes her tears.*)

MRS. MARCH: And now, dears, what about tea? Is the kettle ready, Beth?

BETH: It's just on the boil. (*Sound of carriage wheels offstage*)

ALL: Whoever can it be? Perhaps it's Sallie Moffat. Or Mr. Lawrence. (*Etc.*)

AMY (*Running to the window*): It's Aunt March!

JO: Christopher Columbus! Whatever have we done to deserve this? (*General consternation. The girls hurry round tidying the room.* BETH *hurriedly makes the tea.*)

MRS. MARCH: What can she want at this hour of the day? Put that chair tidy, Meg. Jo, do push your stage properties out of sight. You know how they irritate her. Make the hearth tidy, Beth, and get another cup. Come here, Amy, and let me re-tie that sash. (HANNAH'*s* face *appears at the door. She is a red-faced, middle-aged servant with a practical, cheerful disposition.*)

HANNAH (*In a stage whisper*): It's your aunt! (*Then she steps back*) Please step this way, ma'am. (*She opens the door and stands behind it, announcing*) Miss March. (*Enter* AUNT MARCH. *She is an autocratic old lady.* HANNAH *retires, with a suspicion of a wink.* AUNT MARCH *stands, leaning on her cane, surveying the family.* MRS. MARCH *comes forward to greet her.*)

MRS. MARCH: I'm so glad you've dropped in. You're just in time for a cup of tea.

AUNT MARCH: Oh, I've not come for tea. Had mine long ago. And so would you if you hadn't spent all your day down at those stupid packing rooms. It's no place for a woman with a family. But there, it's no good talking to the mule-headed. (*Sharply*) How's March?

MRS. MARCH: We've heard from him today. I've just been reading the girls his letter. He's standing the hardships a great deal better than we expected.

AUNT MARCH: No business to be there at all. I told him so at the first. But March is a fool! He never would listen to common sense, any more than you. (MRS. MARCH *purses up her lips.*) He'll get pneumonia, that'll be the next thing. You mark my words. (*Points her cane at* MRS. MARCH) A man of his physique won't stand up to an Army winter. And black's expensive, and won't suit *you,* my lady. (*Points her cane at* MEG) Well, don't come to me. Remember, I told you so.

BETH (*Almost crying*): Oh, Marmee, does she mean Father's going to die?

MRS. MARCH (*Comforting her*): No, no, dear. Of course not. It's only Aunt's way. (*She looks across at* AUNT MARCH *imploringly, but the old lady ignores the look, and gazes round the room with disapproval.*)

MEG: Won't—won't you sit down, Aunt? (*There is an atmosphere of discomfort among the girls, who of course are still politely standing.* MEG *pulls forward the chair by the fire.*)

AUNT MARCH: Not by the fire. Brings out my rheumatism. Thank you, child. (*As* AMY *places a chair for her a little left of the table and arranges a cushion*) I see you've brought up one of them with some social promise. (*Seats herself, and the others do likewise, except* AMY, *who stands by her chair.* AUNT MARCH *pulls her curls playfully.*) She won't look so bad when she's a few years older. You must marry well. (*Looking at* AMY *critically*) You shall have the turquoise ring when you come out.

AMY (*Ecstatically*): Oh, Aunt! Not the *turquoise!*

AUNT MARCH (*Patting her hand*): There, there, child. Wait till you've grown a bit, and we'll see. (*In moving *the chair,* AMY *has unwittingly disclosed one of* JO's *riding boots which had been hastily pushed underneath it.*) What's *this?* (*She raises it on the end of her cane.*) Some tomfoolery of yours, I'll be bound, Josephine.

JO: Oh, we're only getting up a pl—(*Stops and puts her hand over her mouth as* MRS. MARCH *signals to her*)

AUNT MARCH: Getting up a pl—, indeed! Some theatricals, I suppose. (*To* MRS. MARCH) I told you not to encourage her in that nonsense. It leads to no good!

MRS. MARCH (*With an effort not to show her irritation*): These are only harmless little home entertainments. I can't take the girls much to the theatre, as you know, and they must have some amusement.

AUNT MARCH: Oh, they get enough of that, by the way I see Josephine gallivanting with young Lawrence.

MRS. MARCH (*To* AMY): Pass Aunt a cup of tea, dear. (AMY *does so.*)

AUNT MARCH: Thank you, child. (*Bent on getting a rise out of* MRS. MARCH) A young tomboy, that's what she's becoming. She'll do some harum-scarum thing, and disgrace the family.

MRS. MARCH (*Quietly*): Well, we're only young once, and I thoroughly approve of Laurie as a companion to the girls. He's a bit wild at times, I own, but he's steady enough underneath.

AUNT MARCH: Oh, I dare say. The Lawrences have money. You've shown more sense there than I gave you credit for. It isn't the *boy* I object to, it's the tutor. And that brings me to the reason for my visit. (*Looks hard at* MEG) I've seen that young man come this way a great many more times than is good for him, *and* you!

MEG (*On the defensive*): Mr. Brooke is kindly helping me with my German.

AUNT MARCH: And teaching you a great many other things besides.

Mrs. March *and* Meg: Aunt!

Mrs. March: I must really beg you not to put such ideas into the girls' heads.

Aunt March: Oh, *I* haven't put them there. It's young Brooke, by the way she's blushing.

Meg (*In an agony of confusion and anger*): I'm *not* blushing, and I don't know what you mean. Mr. Brooke is only a friend.

Aunt March: Oh, I've heard of those friendships. They weren't allowed when *I* was a girl. (*To* Mrs. March) But you'll go your own way, and bring up your girls as you please, to marry penniless tutors and be nothing but a burden on the family. After your own troubles with March I should have thought you would have more sense.

Meg (*Tossing her head*): I shall marry whom I choose!

Aunt March: No doubt you will, and your mother will let you—the more fool she. But when Cooke's out of work and the cupboard's bare, don't come to me.

Meg: I certainly shall never do that, Aunt March.

Aunt March: Well, I'll remember that you've said it. This Looke hasn't any rich relations, has he?

Meg: No, but he has many warm friends.

Aunt March: You can't live on friends. Try it, and see how cool they'll grow. He hasn't any business?

Meg: No. Mr. Lawrence is going to help him.

Aunt March: That won't last long. James Lawrence is a crotchety old fellow, and not to be relied on. Young Looke probably thinks *you've* got rich relatives. Well, warn him not to look this way. I've a better use for my money than helping poverty-stricken teachers.

Meg (*With heat*): Mr. Brooke wouldn't dream of such a thing! He's honest and good and means to stand on his own feet. He wouldn't marry for money any more than

I would. He's above such meanness. And, anyway, I'd far rather be the wife of a poor man, who loves me, than have carriages and a mansion and no one to care for me in it!

AUNT MARCH: Highty-tighty! Is that the way you take my advice, miss? You'll be sorry for it, by and by, when you've tried love in a cottage and found it a failure.

MEG (*Sharply*): It can't be worse than some people find in big houses! (AUNT MARCH *puts on her glasses and gives* MEG *a long look.*)

AUNT MARCH (*In a conciliatory tone*): Now, Meg, my dear, be reasonable. I mean it kindly, and don't want you to spoil your whole life by making a mistake at the beginning. You ought to marry well, and help your family; it's your duty to make a good match, and it ought to be impressed upon you.

MEG: Father and Mother don't think so.

MRS. MARCH: Money is a needful and precious thing, and when well used, a noble thing—but I never want my girls to think it is the only prize to strive for. I'd rather see them poor men's wives, or even happy old maids, than *un*happy wives or unmaidenly girls, running about to find husbands.

AUNT MARCH (*Turning to* MEG): It's easy to see that your pa and ma, my dear, have no more worldly wisdom than two babies.

MRS. MARCH *and* MEG: I'm glad of it!

AUNT MARCH: Well, I wash my hands of the whole affair! You're a willful child, Meg, and you've lost more than you know. (*Rising, and waving away the plate of muffins which* AMY *is offering*) No, I won't stop. I'm disappointed in you. If you mean to marry this Cooke, not one penny of my money goes to you. Don't expect anything from *me*. Your Mr. *Rooke's* friends must take care of you. I'm done with you forever! (*She exits in high dudgeon.* MRS. MARCH *follows her out, looking vexed.*)

MEG: Of all the interfering old ladies—!

JO (*In horror, to* MEG) : *Don't* say you've gone and fallen in love!

MEG: Well, and why ever shouldn't I?

JO (*Ruffling her hair*): Oh, it'll be dreadful!

AMY: I think it is a most interesting event, don't you, Beth?

BETH: Yes, very.

AMY: We can all be bridesmaids in pale blue with pink nosegays, and you can have a lovely wedding cake with doves in white icing on it.

JO: It'll be the end of everything. They'll go lovering round the house and we shall have to dodge. Meg will be absorbed, and no use to me any more. (MRS. MARCH *re-enters.*) And just when I'd planned for her to marry Laurie!

MRS. MARCH: Don't worry about the future, Jo. I think it can safely take care of itself.

JO: Well, I hate to see things going all criss-cross and snarled up, when a pull here, and a snip there, would straighten them up. I wish wearing flat irons on our heads would prevent us from growing up. (*All laugh, except* MEG, *who still looks embarrassed and annoyed. There is a knock, and* HANNAH *enters.*)

HANNAH: Oh ma'am, there're some little German beggar children at the door. Shall I send them packing?

MRS. MARCH: Send them packing! Hannah, it's Christmas time! I could never send anyone from my door at such a season. Bring them into the warmth.

HANNAH: Well, I never! In with the young ladies! There never was such a critter for giving away more than you've got.

BETH: Oh, please bring the little children in, Hannah. (*Exit* HANNAH)

BETH: I'll cut some more bread.

MRS. MARCH: That's right, Beth.

HANNAH (*Off*): Now wipe your feet on the mat and mind you behave in front of the young ladies. (*Enter* HANNAH *with the two Hummel girls. They are pathetically ragged and dirty, and look half starved*)

MRS. MARCH: Come along in, dears.

BETH (*Coming forward*) : Come to the fire, children. (*She leads them to it. They stretch out their hands to the blaze.*)

CHILDREN: *Das ist gute!*

MRS. MARCH: Poor things! They look as if they'd never seen a fire.

JO: Haven't you one at home? (CHILDREN *shake their heads.*)

BETH: They look so hungry. (CHILDREN *look hungrily at the full table.*) Come to the table and have some tea. (*The girls begin to feed them.*)

AMY: Have some muffins. (CHILDREN *devour these ravenously.*)

MRS. MARCH: Have you no food at home? (CHILDREN *shake their heads.*)

MRS. MARCH: No fire and no food! How many are there of you? (CHILDREN *look puzzled, then show seven fingers*)

JO: Seven of them!

MRS. MARCH: Have you a father and mother?

OLDER GIRL: *Mutter.* (*She cradles and rocks her arms*)

BETH: I know, she means they've a mother with a tiny baby. Oh, Marmee!

MRS. MARCH: And no fire or food! (*She looks at the well-spread table and the faces of the girls.*) Girls, I can't help thinking of another little baby who had no warm home on the first Christmas of all—only a draughty stable.

Don't you think, for His sake, we ought to do something for this one?

JO: I think we're greedy, selfish pigs! Here we've been grumbling about our small troubles and thinking ourselves poor, and these people have nothing at all! Let's bundle everything together and take it to them.

BETH: Oh, do let's! (*They get busy;* MEG *superintends the packing of food in* MRS. MARCH*'s shopping bag*)

MRS. MARCH: Hannah, get some wood. We must make them a fire.

HANNAH (*Exits, grumbling slightly, though good naturedly*): Well, if I ever come across the like!

MRS. MARCH (*As business proceeds*): That's right, Meg.

BETH: Here's some tea. (*She produces the teapot.*)

AMY: I'll carry the muffins.

JO: Mind you don't eat any of them! (HANNAH *re-appears with wood.*)

BETH (*To* CHILDREN): Now you'll show us the way, won't you, dears?

CHILDREN: *Der Angel-Kinder!* (*They begin to sniff.*)

BETH (*To* CHILDREN): Oh, please don't cry. Everything is going to be all right.

JO: Come on, everyone! Let's sing "Deck the Halls." It's such a cheerful carol. (*The girls begin to sing as they snatch bonnets and cloaks from pegs on the door or hall outside.* BETH *shares hers with* CHILDREN *and putting an arm around each, she leads off, the others following, carrying baskets or bags of food.* AMY *clutches the bag of muffins.* JO *brings up the rear with a basket of wood.*)

HANNAH (*Standing with her hands on her hips, and watching them go out*): I've never seen the like! Giving away their food and leaving nothing for themselves! Christmas angels they are, and may the good Lord bless them!

THE END

Room for Mary

by Muriel B. Thurston

Characters

MOTHER, *Sarah Warren*
JANE, *in her early twenties*
MARTHA, *college girl*
ANNE, *in her late teens*
PEGGY, *typical teen-ager*
MARY, *a young woman*

SETTING: *Living room.*

AT RISE: MOTHER *is busily dusting in the living room, while humming a Christmas carol. The phone rings and she crosses the room to left to answer it.*

MOTHER: Hello, Sarah Warren speaking. Oh, hello Reverend Young, how are you? . . . Fine, thanks. . . . Oh, a Merry Christmas to you, too! I dare say you're busy the day before Christmas. . . . Yes, I guess we all are. . . . Oh, we're expecting John home from Albany tonight. Yes, he's been there on business these past two weeks. Well, as a matter of fact, we're having a regular home-coming here—Jane is taking a few days off from her job in New York and Martha arrives from college any minute. . . . Yes, she stopped off in New York with a friend for a few days on her way home. . . . Well, we are pretty excited of course—Peggy and Anne and I are all in a dither getting ready. But we're all planning to attend Christmas Eve service tonight. . . . (*Laughs*) . . . That's right. . . . (*Listens, interjecting occasionally*) . . . Oh! . . . Oh, my . . . isn't that a shame! . . . Well, the poor soul. . . . A little boy, how nice. . . . Yes, I can imagine it would. . . . Why, Reverend Young, you know I'd be happy to take her in under ordinary circumstances, but with the girls coming home and so much excitement about Christmas, I don't know. . . . But it *is* Christmas Eve and we'll make out somehow. . . . You tell her she's most welcome. Yes . . . that's all right. I'll see you then. Goodbye. (*Hangs up receiver, puts hand to head and sighs and resumes work at greater speed. Door slams and* PEGGY *enters left, wearing a heavy winter coat over blue jeans.*)

PEGGY: Hi, Mom! What's new? (*Takes off coat, gloves, etc., and scatters them as she flops in chair and reaches for apple*) Believe me, no cherubs for *me* when *I* get married! These two kids I've been taking care of today have me worn to a *frizzle!*

MOTHER (*Chuckling*): You mean "frazzle" dear.

PEGGY: Either way, I'll never be the same! The baby's cute, 'though he does holler a lot these days.

MOTHER: Teething, probably.

PEGGY: That's what his mother says. Little Carol was into everything—I didn't have a minute's peace.

MOTHER: Sounds like somebody aged two I used to know! (*Smiles at her*)

PEGGY (*Rises and crosses to* MOTHER *and hugs her as she goes off to kitchen at right*): You *know* I was a beautiful, well-behaved little angel—just look at me now!

MOTHER (*Wearily*): Yes, just look! (*Indicates scattered clothing*) Come back here and pick up this mess. (PEGGY *returns from kitchen with handful of Christmas cookies and assumes grotesque position across chair with maga-*

zine in her hand.) Really, Peggy! The rest of the girls might appreciate some of those cookies too, you know. (ANNE *enters right.*)

PEGGY: Aw, Mom, I'm a growing girl!

ANNE: You certainly *are!* And if you don't stop feeding your face so much you'll soon burst at the seams! Hello, Mother. (*Crosses and kisses her*) Heard from Dad or the girls?

MOTHER: Not yet, dear, but I expect them any minute. I guess Dad must be driving slowly. It's snowing in Albany. Oh—Peggy, put all these things away for me while I fix my hair.

PEGGY (*Absently*): Mmmmmm.

ANNE: Guess I'll clean up a bit too. Mother, don't you think Peggy should change? That outfit looks terrible for Christmas Eve—especially for a family reunion.

MOTHER: Yes, Peggy, you'd better change.

PEGGY: For goodness' sake, Mom, what for? Everyone knows me here and I hate all this frilly business.

ANNE: You don't have to be frilly to be clean and neat, and *personally,* I'm sick and tired of seeing you looking a mess. (*Flounces out right.* PEGGY *springs up and snatches her clothing and with exaggerated motions flounces after* ANNE, *mimicking her.*)

PEGGY: Deah me! Two years ago we were just a gal in jeans ourself, but l-ooook at us n-ow! (MOTHER *laughs, and picking up cleaning equipment goes to the kitchen. The front door opens and* JANE *and* MARTHA *quietly enter left.*)

JANE (*Laughs*): Well, well, a royal reception!

MARTHA: Hi ho you all—two tired travelers are looking for a "room at the inn!" How about it? (MOTHER *and* ANNE *rush in right—there are warm welcomes and a general removing and hanging of wraps, etc.*)

MOTHER: I was just fixing a cup of tea. How wonderful,

now we can talk a bit. Anne, dear, bring in the tea and cookies, and you two just sit down and let me look at you! It's *so* good to have you home again!

JANE: It's good to be home too, Mother. Oh, those city crowds!

MOTHER: I can imagine. Well, we'll have a real home Christmas and a grand time all together.

MARTHA: Sounds wonderful—oh, I have so much to tell you I don't know where to begin. Where's Dad?

MOTHER: He'll be arriving home soon—he's been in Albany on business. (PEGGY *enters in skirt and sweater, still mimicking* ANNE, *who follows with tea.*)

PEGGY: How do I look now, Mother deah? (*Sees sisters and resumes normal enthusiasm*) Jane and Martha! Hi, you two! Gosh, it's good to see you! Did you bring me something super from Santa?

JANE: Hasn't changed a bit—how's the world been treating you, kitten?

PEGGY: Oh, I guess I'll stand up under the strain. Ummmm, FOOD!

ANNE: Honestly, Mother, she must have a bottomless pit for a stomach.

PEGGY: You're just jealous because you have to starve yourself to keep that wan, mysterious look to fascinate Bill. Little does he know you're just *hungry!*

ANNE: Mother, make her stop!

JANE: Aha, a new love interest!

MARTHA: Listen to who's talking!

MOTHER (*Laughs and holds up her hands*): Wait a minute, things are progressing too fast. I have a problem to present to you before you get too involved here.

PEGGY: Fire away, old dear.

ANNE: Peggy!

MOTHER: Reverend Young called just a few minutes before you all came home, and he told me a rather sad story.

MARTHA: Oh, oh, here we go again—he knows where to find a soft heart.

JANE: What is it this time, Mother?

MOTHER: Well, I'll admit it touched me because it concerned a young girl—a displaced person just about your age. She and her husband arrived in this country a few days ago and were going on to Kansas where he has been promised work. However, she had a baby boy the day they reached our town and he had to go on without her. She's to follow him as soon as she is able to travel, but in the meantime she has just been discharged from the hospital and she's weak and frightened and has no one to care for her and no place to go.

PEGGY (*Disinterested tone*): How sad, how sad.

MARTHA: Wait, Mom, let *me* finish the story. So, our beloved Pastor thought and thought, "Now who would take these people in and work her fingers to the bone to take care of them? Aha! Just the ones—Sarah and John Warren."

MOTHER: I believe his *main* thought was that you girls could make her feel at home and include her in your Christmas fun.

JANE: Oh, but Mother, over Christmas—a perfect stranger in the house.

MARTHA: And we'd looked forward to just a family holiday together!

PEGGY: A baby howling around here all Christmas day—horrible thought!

MOTHER: Well, I wondered how you'd feel—I'm sure Dad and I wouldn't mind.

ANNE: No, you wouldn't mind—you'd just fuss over her and wear yourselves out seeing that she had a nice Christmas and you wouldn't have any fun at all! I vote NO—let's have a family time—no outsiders.

JANE: I suppose it sounds dreadful, but I *am* tired of confusion and I *would* like a relaxing time—perhaps a few friends in tomorrow night for a while. Jim Harwood is driving over for the evening, and I know Martha would like to have Ed over for a while . . .

PEGGY: Aha, Jim Harwood, so that's the new heart-throb!

ANNE: Oh, Peggy, don't be so infantile! Bill is coming, too.

MARTHA: That sounds like fun to me.

PEGGY: Well, if we're making it a party, I'm going to invite Squinty Miller for me.

JANE: *Squinty*—that sounds like quite a character!

ANNE: You hit the nail right on the head that time!

PEGGY: Well, *I* like him—he's an authority on bugs.

MARTHA: Oh, divine!

MOTHER: I don't see why this person would disturb your plans. There will probably be a half a dozen others here too before you get through and she'd have a wonderful time.

ANNE: Oh, Mom, let's face it, we'd all feel uncomfortable and have to spend half our time making sure she was enjoying herself, instead of having fun ourselves.

JANE: Besides, have you forgotten how much care a new baby is, Mother?

MOTHER: This all sounds a wee bit selfish to me—where's your real Christmas spirit, girls? I always thought my family had plenty of it!

ANNE: We do, Mother, but we're thinking of you, too, you know.

MOTHER: Well, I'm going upstairs to do some last minute wrapping—you think it over and decide while I'm gone. (MOTHER *exits and front doorbell rings.* PEGGY *answers it and comes back with large package. Meanwhile* ANNE *starts fixing tree.*)

PEGGY: Jane, it's for you—quick, open it and let's see what's in it—it looks yummy!

JANE: Relax, chum, it contains my presents for everyone

—all wrapped and ready for the tree. I'm sure glad it arrived on time. I might as well arrange them now and have it over with. The tree looks lovely, Anne.

ANNE: It needs a little more work here and there.

MARTHA: Get away from that suitcase, Peggy—that one has presents in it—unwrapped, so no peeking! You might take the other one upstairs for me, though, like a good girl.

PEGGY: Who was your maid at college? Good old Peg! (*Takes suitcase off. Others work on tree, arrange packages, etc.* MARTHA *opens large package.*)

JANE: I suppose we'd better make up our minds about this refugee of Mother's. It *is* too bad she'll be alone over Christmas.

ANNE: Well, I don't have to think it over. As Peg says, imagine a howling baby in the house.

MARTHA: Well, I think someone will find a place for her—one of *us* would have to move out of a bedroom to make way for her.

JANE: Then we're agreed—no room in *this* inn, eh girls?

MARTHA: Sounds a little cold-blooded, but that's the way it is. (PEGGY *returns bedecked in* MARTHA's *formal gown, heavily made up with an absurd hairdo adorned with a large flower. She has on saddle shoes and makes an elaborate entrance.*)

MARTHA (*Horrified*): Peggy! Take that off this minute!

ANNE: See what I have to put up with, girls? (PEGGY *circles the room making all sorts of wild gestures and posing, while* MARTHA *follows her.*)

MARTHA: Peggy! Be careful with that gown! (MOTHER *enters.*)

MOTHER: Peggy, what on earth are you doing? Go and take that oufit off immediately and scrub that stuff off your face. If your father ever walked in now you'd frighten him to death! Well, girls, what did you decide?

JANE: Mom, we decided against her coming. We think some other church family should do it for a change.

MARTHA: Yes, can't she go somewhere else?

MOTHER (*Sarcastically*): I dare say there's an empty stable somewhere.

ANNE: Oh, Mother, that's not *fair*.

MOTHER: I'm sorry—I'm quite disappointed in all of you, and I don't know what Dad will say. . . . (*Phone rings.*) I'll get it. (*Girls talk softly among themselves, obviously worried about* MOTHER's *reaction.*) Hello. . . . Yes, this is Sarah Warren speaking. (*Aside to girls*) It's a long distance—who on earth— Oh yes. Oh John! What are you doing so far away? We've been expecting you any minute. . . . (*Alarmed*) . . . Has anything happened? . . . Oh *no!* . . . Oh, John, are you badly hurt? . . . But, John, that means you won't be with us for Christmas! I'm coming right up there—where are you? . . . Oh, but John, we've never been separated at Christmas-time. . . . Yes, I guess so, but it won't be the same. . . . You're sure you'll be able to come home the 26th? . . . We'll wait and have our Christmas then . . . well, all right, we'll call tomorrow to see how you are, and tell you about our day. What number shall I call? . . . All right. Please take care of yourself, dear. We'll miss you. . . . Yes, goodbye. (*Hangs up with bewildered look on her face, crosses to chair. Girls cluster around.*)

JANE: Has something happened to Dad, Mother? Tell us, quickly.

MOTHER: He was in an auto accident. No one was hurt too badly, but your Dad injured his shoulder a little and the doctor insists he stay until the day after Christmas to make sure there's no other injury and to prevent shock.

PEGGY: That means Daddy won't be home for Christmas?

MOTHER: I wanted to wait until the 26th to celebrate, but he won't let us. He wants to think of us all celebrating just as we always do. He says they have a little celebration for the hospital patients, so he'll make out all right. I guess we'll just have to carry on as best we can . . . but it will seem strange.

ANNE: Poor Dad, all alone for Christmas. (*The girls all look at each other.*)

JANE: It seems awful when it's someone you love who is to be alone.

MARTHA: Dad always gets such a big kick out of all the Christmas doings.

ANNE: I guess we've been pretty selfish thinking about our fun, girls. That little refugee's husband is probably worrying about her holiday just as we are worrying about Dad's.

JANE: That's true. Tell you what—let's change our minds and concentrate on giving her a marvelous time, and that will help us to get through Christmas until Dad gets here.

ALL: All right, let's!

MARTHA: We'll have our Christmas presents tomorrow and then rewrap them and have another celebration when Dad comes so he won't miss the fun.

PEGGY: Two for the price of one!

MOTHER: Thank you, girls. I knew I could count on you! But we'd better get busy—I'm expecting her any minute!

JANE: Mother! We might have known!

ANNE: Oh, but girls, there'll be nothing under the tree for the mother and her baby.

JANE: We all have plenty of nice things we can share with her. Mom and I will be in charge of that!

MOTHER: I've saved a box of toys for my prospective grandchildren—things you girls hardly touched—they will do for the baby. They're at the top of the stairs, Martha. Oh—Peggy and Anne, bring the old bassinet and the box of baby things. I've set them out too. You two will have to bunk on the studio couch in the den. (PEGGY, ANNE *and* MARTHA *exit right while* JANE *takes a small package from her purse.*)

JANE: Here, Mother, I just bought this perfume for myself —perfume does a lot for a woman's morale! And I have a new slip too in my suitcase.

MOTHER: That's very generous, dear—you always buy such wonderful perfume. Do you think Dad and I should give her a check? She could probably use it.

JANE: I think you could do it graciously without hurting her feelings.

MOTHER: All right, I'll do that then. (*Girls enter in a burst of noise and enthusiasm and set up bassinet.* ANNE *finds rattle and ties it to tree with a pretty bow, then leaves.* PEGGY *opens box of baby clothes and sets bonnet on her head.*)

PEGGY: Look, Mom, I told you I was a beautiful baby.

JANE: Peggy, for goodness' sake—go and change! If that poor girl walks in here now she'll think she's been sent to the insane asylum!

PEGGY (*Still rummaging*): She'll have to get used to me sooner or later!

MARTHA (*Opening suitcase*) : Here, Mother, I just finished knitting this sweater—will it do?

MOTHER: Oh, that's lovely, Martha—you do knit so beautifully.

MARTHA: Take it easy on that dress, Peg!

PEGGY: Relax, dearie. What on earth can I give her? Most of my things are wrecked before I have them an hour.

MOTHER: You have that lovely necklace and bracelet Aunt Dot sent for your birthday—you've never worn them.

PEGGY (*Pretending heartbreak*): My one touch of glamour!

Ah, me, such sacrifice. (*Goes off right.* ANNE *returns.*)

ANNE: My contribution—my new scarf and gloves.

MOTHER: Oh, nice, Anne—I'm glad these things are all so pretty—it'll be a lovely Christmas for a lonely girl. (PEGGY *enters, carrying jewelry box.*)

MOTHER: Thanks, Peggy.

JANE: All this time we've never asked her name and I want to write this card. What is her name, Mother, do you know?

MOTHER: I was just thinking of it, and it gave me the queerest feeling. Her name is *Mary.* (*All stop short.*)

PEGGY (*Softly*): Well, can you *beat that!* (*Doorbell rings and* MOTHER *straightens her dress and pats her hair and goes to door. She returns with* MARY *and the "baby," wrapped in a blanket.*)

MOTHER: Mary, this is my family, and we all want you to know how happy we are that you've come to spend Christmas with us.

MARY (*In broken English*): Oh, thank you so much—you are so kind. (PEGGY *takes the baby and puts it in bassinet and fusses over it, while* ANNE *stands by softly exclaiming and admiring.* MOTHER, MARTHA *and* JANE *help* MARY *to unwrap baby and settle her in chair, making soft conversation as the curtain slowly closes.*)

THE END

Violets for Christmas

by Marguerite Kreger Phillips

Characters

MAGGIE } *scrub women*
HEN }
MRS. DALTON, *the office manager*
A SPECIAL SANTA CLAUS
MRS. PENNINGTON

TIME: *A few days before Christmas.*
SETTING: *The office of the Give-Christmas-Cheer Society.*
AT RISE: MAGGIE *is busily mopping the floor of the office. She hums "Jingle Bells" as she moves about. She stops for a moment to look at the red boxes on the desk, shakes one, listens to the bells attached to the box, laughs, looks over her shoulder to see if anyone heard them, puts the box down and goes back to her mopping.* HEN *enters from downstage right carrying a pail that has water up to the top, which spills over as she walks. She laughs as she mops the water up, then starts to work downstage of the desk.*

MAGGIE: You're sure putting your heart into your mopping this morning!
HEN (*Almost singing*): When I heard the bells ringing, I felt happy all over. Christmas bells do that to me.
MAGGIE: You always were a softie. Did you have coffee?

HEN (*Licking her lips*): I sure did—with lots of rich cream floating around the cup. I jes' felt like I was afire —nice and warm inside.

MAGGIE: A body needs something warm. I wouldn't be needin' much urgin' if another cup came my way.

HEN (*As she wrings out her mop*): One to a customer. Only the Santas get all they want. We're not s'posed to be charity cases. We work for a livin' . . . I do—(*With a sly wink and a cute toss of her old head*) do you?

MAGGIE: Humph! What do you think? My old man would turn over in his grave if he could see his Maggie piloting a dirty mop over the floor of an office for old transients.

HEN (*With a gay laugh*): It's the truth. I pray for the poor fellas every night. I sure do, but I kinda get cold all over when I see them start out. My feet jes' ache.

MAGGIE (*As she rests her chin on top of the mop handle and speaks with cynicism*): Faith and why is that? It's not your feet that are after trampin' up and down and it's not you that has to bow and smirk over every penny. (*Now pantomimes like a begging Santa on a corner.*)

HEN (*Pointing at her with interest and nodding applause*): That's jes' it. I was thinkin' 'bout that cold wind blowin' down their backs. My old back wouldn't take it.

MAGGIE (*Suddenly changes to a listening attitude towards door upstage center*): Footsteps in the hall. I wonder now is it Mrs. Dalton heading this way? (HEN *takes a peek at door, then back she rushes to her pail with a wave at* MAGGIE *who turns to her pail. Both women are now mopping away as* MRS. DALTON *enters in street clothes. She greets the women with a nod as she removes hat and coat and hangs them up. Then she removes gloves, puts them in the desk drawer and rubs her hands vigorously as she speaks.*)

MRS. DALTON: Good morning, girls. Hard at it, I see.

(MAGGIE *puts mop in pail. She winks at* HEN *unseen by* MRS. DALTON.)

HEN (*By way of making conversation*): But not too hard.

MRS. DALTON (*Now frowns as she sees* MAGGIE *just sloshing her mop up and down in the pail*): Maggie, will you stop limbering up that mop?

MAGGIE (*Not at all chastened by her cross tone.* HEN *giggles and gets very busy*): My mother always said a good mopper warms up herself as well as the mop.

MRS. DALTON: That will do, Maggie. We have to finish up around here. It has to be clean when the Santas come back. Even if you girls are full of the joy of Christmas and want to relax . . . I still have to remind you that the work must be done.

HEN: So they can get it all muddy again?

MAGGIE: That's what I say, too!

HEN: I don't know why that has to be . . . we mop and mop and in they come with their big feet and then it's all mud again. (*Stops mopping and suddenly grabs her back*) I got a little crick in my back this mornin'.

MRS. DALTON (*Amused; she sees through them both*): And you, Maggie? What ails you?

MAGGIE: Not a word did I say of complaint, but I could use some more coffee. (*Getting a black look from* MRS. DALTON *she starts mopping with energy.*)

HEN: You said it. (HEN *now sings in rather a sweet old voice as she mops*) "Jingle bells, jingle bells,
Jingle all the way. Oh, what fun—" (*Stops suddenly and speaks across to* MAGGIE) And it sure gives you the poke that lifts. (*Even* MRS. DALTON *joins in the laugh at this and then* MAGGIE *and* HEN *move downstage.* MRS. DALTON *inspects the red boxes on her desk and rearranges them, lifts up some record books from desk drawer and opens one before speaking.*)

MRS. DALTON: Maggie, will you finish this side near the desk first?

HEN (*As* MAGGIE *moves upstage above desk at left and* HEN *takes the right*): I never saw so much mud for the Christmas season. It gives me plenty to do, all those old shoes bringin' in so much mud.

MAGGIE: It's thankful they should be to have the shoes and feet left in them after bein' on them from morn to night.

MRS. DALTON (*Looks up from her work*): By the way, girls, your handsome, mysterious friend only turned in fifty cents last night.

MAGGIE (*They both stop mopping*): The tall one with the young man's walk?

HEN: And such a sad look.

MRS. DALTON: The one with the air of mystery, the young one. The one the supervisor thinks is up to some tricks.

MAGGIE: Not him. He's not got a tricky bone in his body.

MRS. DALTON: He certainly didn't get much out of the Christmas crowds yesterday.

MAGGIE (*Her Irish ancestry creeps into her speech occasionally*): The dirty spalpeens! The back a'me hand to them!

HEN: I know where I'd use my hand on some of those women in their mink coats. They walk past the old Santas and drop a thin dime in the box.

MAGGIE: Wouldn't you think they'd take pity on the lad?

MRS. DALTON: Everyone doesn't have Christmas in his heart as you and Hen do. And will you tell me how they would know he was a lad under that beard?

HEN (*Laughs*): That's right, Maggie, how would they know?

MAGGIE (*Grumbling and sloshing her mop about*): All those snooty society dames go prancin' by with their heads in the air—may the banshees take over their dreams and leave them bedraggled lookin' in the mornin'.

MRS. DALTON (*Nodding her head*): My sentiments too, Maggie. (*Then suddenly leaning forward and speaking as if her words had great import.*) I noticed that our nice friend had warm gloves on last night when he checked in.

HEN *and* MAGGIE (*Almost simultaneously*): He did?

MRS. DALTON: Either he used some of the money or a good Samaritan gave them to him. They were too expensive to be his own . . . that is, none of the other men could own such gloves. (*Both scrub women are thrilled to be included in this talk.*) But I can't understand him taking that much money for gloves—he just doesn't seem that kind. (*She sighs.*)

HEN: I can tell from that sigh you consider him honest. I say some woman done him wrong. (*Stamps her mop and spills some water*) Making a mess of his life like I'm making a mess of this floor.

MAGGIE (*Now leans on the desk as she looks at* MRS. DALTON, *her mop dragging behind her*): Fifty cents. Glory be an' is that all the poor boy could squeeze out of the tightwads? Believing that is hard, but—

MRS. DALTON (*Cutting in*): All pennies too. From children most likely.

MAGGIE (HEN *continues to mop slowly finishing the place from door upper right to desk and outer door but she listens and turns to nod her head keeping in the conversation that way*): Surely ya' don't think he would be having sticky fingers?

MRS. DALTON: A thief?

MAGGIE: Call it that.

MRS. DALTON (*Looks across her desk. Her eyes seem focused on some distant spot*): They are transients off the highways and byways of life, the men we take in here.

Who knows what they hide under that Santa Claus costume? The supervisor takes them in if they look like they need help—mentally or physically, but mostly they come to our door begging for work because of empty stomachs.

MAGGIE (*With a sniffle*): And the sad hearts they be hiding.

MRS. DALTON (*Suddenly very business-like*): But come, come, we can't worry about their hearts. It's hard enough to watch these boxes and keep track of what they turn in at night.

MAGGIE: I wouldn't put it past some of those old trailers to be slippin' a quarter in their pants now and agin, but not *him!*

HEN (*Waving at the boxes*): I thought the boxes were locked.

MRS. DALTON: Sometimes people just hand the men the money.

MAGGIE: (*Thinking hard*): Sure he's bowed down with a trouble a' some kind.

HEN: Give him another chance.

MAGGIE (*Now smiles broadly and coaxingly to* MRS. DALTON): Today might be the day.

HEN: Let some of your Christmas spirit slip over on him.

MAGGIE (*Suddenly very serious*): Maybe 'twill be he'll land a gold piece this day. (*Then she glares from one to the other daring them with her eyes to contradict her.*) Who's here to say it can't happen?

MRS. DALTON: Of course I shall give him another chance. I think he's honest, but on the other hand, I have a boss, too, and just because this Santa is so handsome and polite—

MAGGIE (*Cutting in with shriek*): Oh, then you did look under his beard! How else would you know he was handsome?

MRS. DALTON (*Laughs*): His eyes!

MAGGIE (*Turning to* HEN *with a pleased smile of recollection*): And wasn't he the gentleman? Sure and didn't he take time out to speak a pleasant word yesterday to a couple of old shawls like us?

HEN (*Thrilling at the remembrance as she leans on her mop and gazes heavenward*): Lordy! What a man that is under all that red calico. I still say some woman done him wrong. (*Just at this moment the* SANTA CLAUS *under discussion appears at door upper right. He is tall and thin in spite of the costume and as he hesitates in doorway holding his Santa cap with beard attached in his hand,* HEN, MAGGIE *and* MRS. DALTON *stare entranced at his sad handsome face.*)

SANTA CLAUS (*As he now comes down towards the desk*): Could I trouble you a moment? (*As* SANTA *moves down to desk at left center* HEN *and* MAGGIE *move their pails downstage right as in a dream and then stand, a picture of mops, pails, opened mouths and stretched necks.*)

MRS. DALTON (*Recovering her poise*): You . . . you startled me without your beard—you are so much younger.

SANTA CLAUS (*Now his turn to be confused as he realizes he is no longer disguised*): I shouldn't have come in here without it. Will you pardon me? (*He includes* HEN *and* MAGGIE *in his bow, then hurriedly dons cap and beard.*) I hope you didn't see my face clearly. (HEN *pokes* MAGGIE *at this.*)

MRS. DALTON (*Forcing herself to be so business-like*): I'll forget your face at once. We're not interested in the faces of the men that come here to beg, it is the money that they turn in. Now what is your difficulty?

SANTA CLAUS: You make it difficult but I do want you to know that I will do better today. I am going to try other corners. (*Now holds up his gloves*) These gloves —I saw you looking at them last night when I checked in. They were . . . were given to me as a present before I came begging at your door.

MRS. DALTON (*Tries to cover his embarrassment by speaking brusquely*): We all hope you have luck today. (HEN *and* MAGGIE *nod vigorously and beam from ear to ear.*)

SANTA CLAUS: Thank you. I seem to attract only the children. I—I am afraid it is my fault. I try to avoid the adults because—well—(*He looks helplessly about and* MAGGIE *and* HEN *lean forward.*)

HEN (MRS. DALTON *raises both hands in a wave to shush her*): You're afraid of runnin' into somebody that knowed ya before.

SANTA CLAUS (*Gives* HEN *a little nod of his head and speaks sadly*): Yes, and I need to be here. These other Santas are helping me.

MRS. DALTON: The supervisor is thinking of dismissing you.

SANTA CLAUS: Because of that paltry fifty cents I turned in? Would he really make me leave? Put me out?

MRS. DALTON (*Quickly*): Oh, no, we never put anyone out in the cold at Christmas time. (*Then she stops to gesture sharply to* MAGGIE *and* HEN.) Girls! Get to your mopping! It is almost time for the Santas to file out. (HEN *and* MAGGIE *become very active but stay in the background and we know they are not missing a single word.*) You may stay here, sleep here until you find other work, but unless you make a better report tonight you can't play Santa any more. The superintendent thinks maybe you haven't enough Christmas spirit to *play* Santa.

SANTA CLAUS (*Despair in his voice*): But that is why I came here. I wish I might explain more fully, but you are entitled to know this much. . . . I am trying to humble myself—to learn what it really feels like to be poor.

MRS. DALTON (*Cuts in sharply and she is puzzled*): Forcing

yourself to be a beggar? You mean you really want to learn how to beg? You're trying to help yourself that way?

HEN (*Impulsively leaning forward*): Mrs. Dalton, that poor man's lost in this wicked city. He's trying to find Christmas.

SANTA CLAUS (*Relief in his voice as he turns to* HEN): How could you know? That's it—(*Turns quickly back to* MRS. DALTON) Don't report me yet, give me another day here. I'll approach everyone that passes and bring back a full box. Now I must join the others. (HEN *has remained immobile, her mouth open as* SANTA *moves quickly off up right.*)

MAGGIE (MRS. DALTON *too is speechless and is looking towards up right*): It's the old Saint himself. He's masquerading. Come to earth to sort out the divils from the angels.

HEN (*Now speaks with awe in her voice*):
Could be he's a shepherd seekin' His stable—
While the shepherds watched their flocks by night—
All seated on the groun'
The angel of the Lord come down, and
Glory shown 'round.
(*Tense with excitement*) That's what it is. I jest bet he's one of them shepherds. My mother always said if you looked hard enough you could see the shepherds on the city streets at Christmas time.

MAGGIE (*Giving her a slap*): And blessings on you for being an old softie.

MRS. DALTON (*Blows her nose—she's the softie—then covers up by speaking crossly*): Get to work! What do you think you get paid for? Standing around reciting poetry?

HEN (*Turns back to her work but manages to get in*): I was only cogitating on the glory of the Lord.

MRS. DALTON: We've done enough cogitating—shall we work for a change?

HEN (*Pushing the mop and almost grumbling*): We all do funny things when our hearts are broken.

MRS. DALTON (*Her voice is kind again*): Why, Hen, do you think he has a broken heart?

HEN (*Giving the mop a bang on the floor*): I do! Didn't you hear what he said? I'm trying hard to be humble—that's what he said, and no man is going to do that unless he's crushed.

MRS. DALTON (*Skeptically*): And that means he has a broken heart?

HEN (MAGGIE *is opened-mouthed at* HEN'S *wisdom*): Some woman has told him he's too proud to take her money —maybe the one that give him them gloves.

MRS. DALTON: What a silly idea—(*Then pulls up short to think*) or is it such a silly idea? You may have hit on something. A poor young man in love with a rich girl—maybe he even is married to her and she keeps waving her money in front of his face—

HEN (*Has leaned forward on her mop, intent on every word*): A straight guy wouldn't take that. He'd have pride. I know I'm right.

MRS. DALTON: Then you would be clairvoyant.

HEN: Sounds good. Maybe I am. Clairvoyant's a nicer name than *Hen*rietta . . . nobody ever remembers to put in the "rietta" part. Just plain old Hen. (MAGGIE *and* MRS. DALTON *laugh.*) You'll find out old clairvoyant's right. I heard his vocal cords moanin'.

MRS. DALTON: Well, between you two he's bound to turn out to be something. Hen, you said a moment ago he was a Christmas shepherd, and Maggie said he was old Saint Nicholas himself. Now, that's enough fooling. Get to work and not another word about this. It's none of our business anyway. (*Now there is a busy half-minute and both* MAGGIE *and* HEN *are bending down wringing out their mops when the front door from the street up-stage center bursts open.* MRS. PENNINGTON *enters. She is young, pretty, and wears a fur coat with a huge bunch of violets pinned on the shoulder.* MAGGIE *and* HEN *raise up slowly as if seeing an apparition, their mops sliding toward the floor as they stare.*)

MRS. PENNINGTON (*Crosses down to desk*): I am Mrs. Pennington.

MRS. DALTON (*Extremely cool. The name means nothing to her*): Yes?

MRS. PENNINGTON (*Slightly taken aback—hesitates a moment*): I . . . I want to do something for you.

MRS. DALTON (*Thinking she has a philanthropist on her hands*): That is very kind of you. We need all the money we can get to pay for the Christmas dinners. We have empty stomachs to fill.

MRS. PENNINGTON (*Her chin raised*): Oh! you misunderstand—

MRS. DALTON (*Giving her a close look as she cuts in*): You said you wanted to help us.

MRS. PENNINGTON (*Nervously*): I do. I mean I want to work. I want to work for you.

MRS. DALTON (*Freezing up*): I'm sorry. We do not employ people like you. (*Gives her a very thorough look from head to toes.*) Old down-and-outers get our jobs. Men, the forgotten men. The ones that have no hope, no friends, no one to love them—nothing left for them but to beg.

MRS. PENNINGTON (*Looks away and repeats the last words to herself as if disturbed by them*): Nothing left for them but to beg—oh, no!

MRS. DALTON (*Thinks the "oh, no" is contradicting her speech*): Oh, yes, that's the kind that come here and ask for these begging jobs.

MRS. PENNINGTON (*Shakes her head*): That would be dreadful. (*Then looks directly at* MRS. DALTON) Will you listen to me patiently . . . will you try to understand? I need something you can give me.

MRS. DALTON (*Who is trying but is fast losing her patience and beginning to doubt the woman's sanity*): What did you say your name was?

MRS. PENNINGTON: I am Mrs. Pennington.

MRS. DALTON: Well, Mrs. Pennington, I am a working woman. You are not. Please will you go out the way you came in and not waste our time . . . unless you wish to fill one of these? (*Shakes one of the boxes under her nose and the bells tinkle*) We have a poor man that hasn't been able to fill his box. He has a hard time begging. He seems new at it. Give him a start. (*The old girls now pick up their mops. Again* MRS. DALTON *pushes a box at her but* MRS. PENNINGTON *backs away.*)

MRS. PENNINGTON (*Tears in her voice*) : You still misunderstand. I'll make it worth your while . . . I'll pay you for letting me work. (*She looks intently at* MAGGIE *and* HEN *and is suddenly inspired.*) Work like that! I want to work with my hands—menial work—(MAGGIE *and* HEN *look at their hands then back at her.*)

MRS. DALTON (*Firmly*): We employ only people who *need* help.

MRS. PENNINGTON (*A catch in her voice*): I need it . . . please . . . it is the only kind of medicine that will help me.

MRS. DALTON (*Now really thinks* MRS. PENNINGTON *is unbalanced but tries the box again*): A donation perhaps?

MRS. PENNINGTON (*A pleading note creeps into her voice*): This is the Christmas season. Put it down to the star in the East, candles burning in the window—people do odd things at this time of the year. Put it down to anything you like, only let me work here.

MRS. DALTON (*Frowning now*): But why here?

MRS. PENNINGTON: You said this is where men come for help—broken, sick, forsaken—(*Her voice breaks.*)

MRS. DALTON: What's that got to do with you?

MRS. PENNINGTON: I am seeking something . . . this is where I must try. Believe me, I am sane, but heartbroken. (MRS. DALTON *shakes her head, completely baffled, while* HEN *gives* MAGGIE *a sharp dig with her elbow.*) Please let me work here. (MRS. PENNINGTON *now moves quickly across to* MAGGIE *and* HEN.) These women—(*Points to mops*) There, that is what I want to do. Get my hands dirty, make my back ache—let me take their place? (MRS. PENNINGTON *now looks directly at* MAGGIE *as she reaches into her purse.*) I will make it right for you. (MAGGIE *moves a step to her and bites her lip as she casts a look at* MRS. DALTON. MRS. PENNINGTON *now looks from one scrub woman to the other.*) Surely one of you would help me out. Will one hundred dollars cover the charges? Don't ask me why I want to do this seemingly crazy thing . . . just help me to do it. (HEN *gasps and her eyes pop as she stares at the handful of bills and* MAGGIE *quickly looks from* MRS. DALTON *who shakes her head "no," then back to* MRS. PENNINGTON.) I'll need your apron.

MRS. DALTON (*As* MAGGIE'S *hand yanks at her apron string and it hangs ready*): Maggie! No!

MAGGIE: But, Mrs. Dalton—

MRS. DALTON: I said no!

MRS. PENNINGTON (*Now takes a bill from the handful she holds and presses it into* MAGGIE'S *hand*): You must take this. (MRS. DALTON *stares and seems unable to speak.*)

MAGGIE: O.K., here's your apron. (MAGGIE *takes the bill, hands* MRS. PENNINGTON *the apron and with a wave at*

HEN *and* MRS. DALTON *is out the door downstage right in a flash.*)

MRS. DALTON (*Suddenly jumps and runs around her desk crying out*): Maggie, Maggie, come back here—you can't do that. (MRS. PENNINGTON *puts out a hand to stop* MRS. DALTON *and a door slams off.*)

HEN (*With a delighted chuckle*): Too late, Mrs. Dalton, too late!

MRS. PENNINGTON (*Shows* MRS. DALTON *the bills in her hand*): I gave her only a twenty-dollar bill. Please add the rest to your fund? (*Now* MRS. PENNINGTON *forces the handful of bills upon* MRS. DALTON, *who moves dazedly back to her desk.* MRS. PENNINGTON *removes her fur coat and tosses it over a chair down right. Then she ties* MAGGIE'S *old apron around her waist while* HEN *stares open-mouthed.*)

HEN (*Sees* MRS. PENNINGTON *bend down with her white kid gloves still on to pick up mop*) : If you expect to get them hands dirty—(*Points at gloves*)

MRS. PENNINGTON (*Embarrassed*): Oh! My gloves. (*She moves over to desk which has an open space on it near the red boxes and places her gloves there.* MRS. DALTON *just sits and stares unable to cope with the situation. Then as* MRS. PENNINGTON *turns to mop and pail* MRS. DALTON *realizes she still holds the rest of the money and hastily shoves it into the desk drawer.*)

HEN (*Smiles at* MRS. PENNINGTON): Bare hands will get you closer to the manger.

MRS. PENNINGTON (*Stares for a moment, puzzled*): The manger?

HEN: The Christ child's manger—don't you remember about little Jesus in the manger?

MRS. PENNINGTON (*Astounded as she looks into* HEN'S *earnest face*): How can you know that I have been away from that manger?

HEN: You're wantin' to be humble—to get yourself dirty. (MRS. PENNINGTON *bows her head and* HEN *moves up to door at upstage right and looks out. Then* MRS. PENNINGTON *moves downstage. Her back is to desk and she struggles with mop and pail. As she wrings the mop out, the dirty water covers her hands. She shivers, but keeps bravely struggling.*)

MRS. DALTON (*To* HEN): Hen, are they starting?

HEN (*Over her shoulder*): There they go, the poor old guys—out to beg. Out into the cold, cold world. Nobody to love them any more. (*The tinkling of bells can be heard offstage.* HEN *turns and comes back to pick up her mop and works some distance away but watches* MRS. PENNINGTON *out of the corner of her eye as* MRS. PENNINGTON *faces downstage trying to mop.*) Hope folks are good to the old Santas. I hope they don't freeze their toes. (*Now the tall young* SANTA *comes rushing in from upstage right and as he talks* MRS. PENNINGTON *stops mopping as if hearing a familiar voice and turns to look directly up and over at his back.*)

SANTA CLAUS: I'm sorry to bother you, but we're one box short. I gave out the last one and I need one for myself. This is to be a big day for me and I can't get along without a box.

MRS. DALTON (*Beaming*): I'll knock on this one and give it good luck. (*As she reaches for the box she knocks the white gloves off the desk to the floor.* SANTA *bends at once to pick them up.* MRS. PENNINGTON *drops her mop, rushes to his side and reaches for the gloves as he lifts his head.*)

MRS. PENNINGTON: Thank you—they're my gloves. (*They now stand both holding onto the gloves, staring into each other's eyes. There must be a pause giving him time for realization.*)

SANTA CLAUS (*Choking with emotion*): Helen! It *is* you?

MRS. PENNINGTON: Yes, Jim, and I was sure it was your voice.

SANTA CLAUS (*Removes his beard and cap quickly and now clutches them in one hand together with the gloves*): But Helen, what are you doing here?

MRS. PENNINGTON (*Looks up at him adoringly*): I've found you. (*They are completely oblivious of* MRS. DALTON *who sits tensely still clutching the red box she had meant to hand* SANTA, *and* HEN *who leans on her mop gaping.*)

SANTA CLAUS: But that apron?

MRS. PENNINGTON (*Now holds tightly to his arm*): Jim, when we quarreled again, and oh, how much quarreling we've been doing . . . you left. *I* was the one that needed to go. It was my pride, my money, my love of clothes and jewels and society . . . you knew we were losing all the fine things of life, but I wouldn't listen. I was trying to change you . . . then you left—

SANTA CLAUS (*With deep feeling*): Helen, I had to get away. I felt that I must learn how to be humble again.

MRS. PENNINGTON: I searched the hotels, then suddenly I thought—why Jim is somewhere trying to find peace and where else would that be but among the poor . . . and I decided to humble myself, to make myself worthy of you when I found you . . . and I came here. Oh Jim, is it too late for us to learn to be humble together? (*He embraces her.*)

HEN (*As if unable to control her voice she speaks out suddenly with deep religious feeling*):
"And the angel of the Lord came down
And glory shone 'round them."

SANTA CLAUS (*They both look up startled at her voice and realize where they are*): Oh, Helen, these good people—these *are* good people! (SANTA *looks from* HEN *to* MRS. DALTON.) You will pardon us . . . this is my wife.

(MRS. DALTON *is weeping.*) Helen has found me . . . we have both learned much . . . thank you for all your kindness, your understanding. (*They turn to move off upstage center when* SANTA *stops suddenly and looks down at his hand in which he still clutches his beard and hat and the gloves.*) Here I am moving off with your property. (*He hands* MRS. DALTON *the hat and beard. She takes them and wipes her eyes but can say nothing. Then as he turns to hand his wife her gloves,* MRS. PENNINGTON *suddenly remembers her coat.*)

MRS. PENNINGTON: Oh, Jim, my coat . . . I had forgotten. There, on the arm of that chair. (SANTA *now gets the coat and hands it to* MRS. PENNINGTON, *assisting her into it.*)

SANTA CLAUS (*As* MRS. PENNINGTON *adjusts her coat he again turns to* MRS. DALTON): May I keep this costume? (MRS. DALTON *nods yes. She is too choked up with tears to speak and she hands him back the hat and beard.*)

MRS. PENNINGTON: You're going down the street in that?

SANTA CLAUS (*As if testing her*): Would you be ashamed of me?

MRS. PENNINGTON (*With deep feeling*): No, Jim, no, it brought us together. (*Now turns impulsively to* MRS. DALTON.) May I keep this old apron? (MRS. DALTON *again nods yes then turns to stare in utter amazement when* MRS. PENNINGTON *suddenly crosses down to* HEN, *unfastening her violets as she does so, and then holds them out to* HEN.) And to you who brought me closer to the manger, please have these. (HEN *slowly reaches out, the mop slides unheeded from her hand to the floor and she takes the violets, then stands holding them cupped in both hands staring down at their loveliness as though she had never seen violets before.* MRS. PENNINGTON *moves quickly back to* SANTA, *takes his arm and without another word or look at the occupants of the room they move off at upstage center and out of their lives.* MRS. DALTON *turns to follow them with her eyes, but* HEN *never moves, just stands staring down at the violets. Then* MRS. DALTON *sighs, opens her desk drawer and pulls out the handful of bills.*)

MRS. DALTON (*Waving them at* HEN) : Eighty dollars—good old sentimental greenbacks! This will buy a lot of dinners for our poor people.

HEN (*Looks up startled but only for an instant. Her eyes go back to the violets. She holds them to her nose, takes a deep breath, then holds them against her shoulder*): Gollee! I always wanted violets for Christmas. (*Quick curtain*)

THE END

Season's Greetings

by Helen Louise Miller

Characters

KIM RICHARDS, *an inexperienced secretary*
JEFF TYLER, *an ambitious art student*
MR. TYLER, *Jeff's uncle, a Christmas card artist*
MRS. DELANEY } *neighbors*
MRS. MARTINKA }
MR. CANFIELD, *a greeting card agent*
JIM, *the elevator boy*
FRED }
JOE } *the brass trio*
BILL }
DELIVERY BOY

TIME: *The day before Christmas.*

SETTING: *The living room studio of Joshua Tyler, furnished in modernistic style. An easel, center back, displays a large, gaudy, extreme cubist design, and a weird modernistic sculpture stands on desk downstage left, next to which stands a typing table.*

AT RISE: KIM RICHARDS *is typing, scrutinizing her notes from time to time. The telephone on the desk rings.*

KIM (*At phone*): Mr. Tyler's studio. No, Mr. Tyler is not in. I'm expecting him shortly. You're what? Oh, you're calling about the ad in the morning paper. That's splendid! Mr. Tyler will be . . . (*In a tone of disbelief*) What? What did you say? There must be some mistake. (*Coldly*) I'm afraid I haven't the slightest idea what you're talking about. (*Pause*) You may call again if you like, but I know Mr. Tyler will not be interested. I'm sorry. Thank you. Goodbye. (*Hangs up*) Of all the crazy people in the world. (*Enter* JEFF TYLER *bearing a large poinsettia.*)

JEFF (*Bright and breezy*): Hiya, Beautiful! Where shall I put this?

KIM: Right here on the desk. What a beauty! Is it for Mr. Tyler?

JEFF: It is. The elevator boy asked me to bring it in with me. Hope the old boy appreciates it. Looks expensive.

KIM: I hope so, too. But he seems to hate all kinds of Christmas decorations. Won't have them around! Not even a sprig of holly!

JEFF: He doesn't need any decorations, not with such a beautiful secretary. Which reminds me . . . how come you're here chained to that typewriter the day before Christmas?

KIM: 'Cause I'm a working girl, and the minute my boss gets back, we're going to tackle a pile of correspondence this high. (*Gestures*) Your uncle's a busy man, Mr. Jeff.

JEFF: What's the idea of that *Mister* Jeff routine? Did we, or did we not, grow up in the same block?

KIM: We did, but now that I am your uncle's secretary, I should show you more respect.

JEFF: Respect? I can't remember much respect between us when I dipped your pigtails in the inkwell, back in fifth grade.

KIM (*Laughing*): That was a long time ago.

JEFF: It sure was. And you've passed from pigtail to pony-tail with flying colors. That hairdo's very becoming, I might add. Though it would look better with a spray of mistletoe over one ear.

KIM: Don't bother. And now, if you'll excuse me . . . (*Starts to type*)

JEFF: Come off it, Kim. Even if Uncle Josh is your boss, I'm still not above pulling your hair or chasing you around the block with a dead mouse!

KIM: You'd catch it from your uncle if you tried any tricks like that today.

JEFF: I caught it then. But it didn't seem to do any good. I went right on pursuing you. Only now, instead of a mouse, I could chase you with orchids, and boxes of candy, and bottles of perfume, and theatre tickets, and—

KIM: Jeff Tyler, you behave yourself! And get out of here before your uncle comes back. I don't want him to think I'm wasting my time, when I should be on the job. I have pages and pages of shorthand notes to type.

JEFF: Shorthand? What does a pretty girl like you need to know about all those little pothooks and curlicues?

KIM: She needs to know plenty, if she wants to be a good secretary. And that's what I want to be, Jeff. I know your uncle hired me just because he knew my parents and felt sorry for me because I needed a job. But I'm determined to make good.

JEFF: Well, don't be so grim about it. You'll do all right. After all, Uncle Josh doesn't expect perfection.

KIM: Oh, but Jeff, he does. Or, at least, it seems to me that he does. You see, I'm not really very good. I'm slow, and I make mistakes; and sometimes, this old shorthand nearly drives me crazy. And, then, he goes so fast in dictation and uses so many words we never had in school, I can't keep up with him.

JEFF: Why don't you tell him to slow down, and ask him to spell the words you don't know?

KIM: It's easy to see you've never tried being a secretary! And you just don't know your uncle!

JEFF: What do you mean I don't know my uncle? I've been in and out of his house for seventeen years, haven't I? He's almost like my second father.

KIM: But you've never worked for him! Honestly, he can be so sarcastic when you make a mistake! It just sends goose bumps all down my spine. Then I get so tied up in knots, I make more mistakes than ever.

JEFF: You sound as if you need a holiday. And this is the season. Why don't you take the day off?

KIM: I did leave early yesterday afternoon, and when I said something about today, he just gave me one of his iceberg looks and said . . .

JEFF: Now don't tell me he said, "Bah! Humbug!" and pulled the old Scrooge act on you!

KIM: Not quite that bad. But he gave me to understand it was to be business as usual.

JEFF: Uncle Josh wasn't always like this, Kim. He used to be a lot of fun. It's this Christmas card business that's getting him down.

KIM: But why should it? It must be wonderful to design Christmas cards. Think of the pleasure they give people.

JEFF: That's not the way Uncle Josh looks at it. He says Christmas cards are just a racket. You see, he wanted to be a serious artist, a portrait painter. Well, he never seemed to make the grade, and finally, he settled for this. I know he hates it.

KIM: But he shouldn't. Nothing is appreciated more than a beautiful Christmas card.

JEFF: I know. But he says they're just a commercial scheme to bring in money instead of good will. Besides that, he's running out of ideas.

KIM: Maybe that's why he's turning out stuff like that.

(*Indicating easel*) He seems to go in for all these abstract designs. They don't seem to be a bit Christmasy to me.

JEFF: Me either. Personally, I just don't get it.

KIM: Neither does Mr. Canfield, his agent. At least that's what he said when he was here last week to look over the new sketches. He said that one (*Pointing to easel*) should say "Jolly Nightmare" instead of "Merry Christmas." He's coming back today to see if your uncle has turned out anything new.

JEFF: Yes, I know. That's one reason I popped in. I wanted to show him this. (*Places his own drawing on easel*)

KIM: Oh, Jeff, that's terrific! It makes you feel good just to look at it.

JEFF: I hope it makes Mr. Canfield feel the same way. It sure didn't have that effect on Uncle Josh.

KIM: Didn't he like it?

JEFF: Like it? He called it a warning to termites! He said it was all he needed to convince him he'd be wasting his time to send me to art school.

KIM: Oh, Jeff! What a shame!

JEFF: Never mind! I'll get there—uncle or no uncle! That's why I want to see Mr. Canfield. He's chairman of one of the scholarship committees. When Uncle Josh said he might drop in this morning, I made up my mind to be Jeffrey on the spot! Where *is* Uncle Josh anyway?

KIM: Out scouring the town for a lost picture.

JEFF: How could he possibly lose a picture?

KIM: When Mr. Canfield was here last week, he tried to get your uncle interested in doing some old English Christmas scenes. He brought along part of his collection for inspiration, and poor Mr. Tyler has managed to lose one.

JEFF (*With a whistle*): Canfield will be burned up! Those prints are valuable!

KIM: Mr. Tyler is plenty upset. He had it in an envelope he was taking to the Art League. He's advertised, but so far, no results.

JEFF: Boy, oh boy! I can see this isn't going to be a merry Christmas for Uncle Josh. No wonder he's lost his Christmas spirit.

KIM (*Laughing*): You know that's funny!

JEFF: What's funny?

KIM: What you just said about your uncle losing his Christmas spirit. That's what the phone call was about.

JEFF: What phone call?

KIM: The one right before you came in. Some man kept insisting your uncle should drop in at the Fifty-Six Supper Club tonight, and they'd guarantee he'd find his lost Christmas spirit.

JEFF: How crazy can these advertisers get!

KIM (*With a puzzled frown*): Yes, it sure was crazy . . . and yet . . . oh, my goodness! Jeff! Quick! My steno pad! (*Leafs madly through her notebook*) Oh, no! No! It can't be! It isn't possible!

JEFF: What's the matter, Kim? You're white as a ghost! You're not going to faint, are you?

KIM: Faint? Oh, if I only could! Jeff, I have to get out of here before your uncle comes back.

JEFF: It's too late. Pull yourself together. Here he comes. (*Covers his own painting with original cubist painting on easel*)

KIM: Oh, dear! What will I do? (MR. TYLER *backs into the room arguing with a* DELIVERY BOY *who is carrying a Christmas tree.* MR. TYLER *wears overcoat and carries a large envelope.*)

MR. TYLER: I tell you you can't bring that thing in here. It's not for me.

DELIVERY BOY: Your name's Tyler, isn't it? And this is Number 9, Mayfair Apartments, isn't it?

MR. TYLER: Yes, but . . .

DELIVERY BOY: Then it's for you, all right. Where do you want me to put it?

MR. TYLER: I want you to put it back where you got it. Is that clear?

DELIVERY BOY: But I can't do that, sir. Tony wouldn't like it.

MR. TYLER: Tony? Who's Tony?

DELIVERY BOY: Tony Tonelli, down on the corner. You buy your oranges from Tony. He thinks you're a swell guy. The tree's from him.

MR. TYLER: That's very good of him. But just the same I did not order a Christmas tree from Tony or anybody else.

DELIVERY BOY: Who said anything about *order?* The tree is a *present* from Tony. You don't have to pay. He sent it on account of your ad!

KIM: Oh, no! (*To* JEFF) I must get out of here. (JEFF *stops her.*)

MR. TYLER: My ad? What ad? I certainly didn't advertise for a Christmas tree.

DELIVERY BOY: No, no. I mean your ad in the Lost and Found section. Tony says to tell you he knows just how you feel, and maybe the tree will help.

MR. TYLER: I don't understand. How could a tree possibly help?

DELIVERY BOY: Oh, I don't know exactly. But, well, it's a funny thing about Christmas trees. They kind of get you! Maybe when you start putting it up and trimming it and everything, well, maybe you'll find what you lost.

MR. TYLER: But I did find what I lost. I have it right here! It wasn't lost after all. I had merely left it in the Library.

DELIVERY BOY: Good! I'll tell Tony. And in the meantime, have a merry Christmas. (*Exits*)

MR. TYLER: Of all the confounded lunatics! Jeff, get this thing out of here in a hurry. (*Briskly takes off coat, puts it on chair.*)

JEFF: But Uncle Josh . . .

MR. TYLER: You heard what I said. Now get busy. Wait a minute. You can take that monstrosity with you. (*Points to poinsettia*) Where did it come from?

JEFF: The elevator boy asked me to bring it in when I came up.

KIM: There's a card, sir. Shall I open it?

MR. TYLER: By all means.

KIM (*Opens card and reads it*): "Maybe this will help restore your lost Christmas spirit. A Friend."

MR. TYLER (*Roaring*): My what? What's that about my lost Christmas spirit? Read that again.

KIM (*In a faint voice*): "Maybe this will help restore your lost Christmas spirit. A Friend."

MR. TYLER: What is this? Some sort of joke? What's going on here? Jeff Tyler, do you know anything about this?

JEFF: Who? Me? Look here, Uncle Josh. I just came in a few minutes ago. Ask Kim. I didn't even know you'd lost anything till Kim told me. (*Phone rings and* MR. TYLER *seizes it.*)

MR. TYLER: Yes. Yes, this is Joshua Tyler speaking. What? No, I've certainly no intention of spending my Christmas Eve at the Fifty-Six Supper Club! What's that? It will what? Bring back my lost Christmas spirit? What in blazes are you talking about? My ad? What ad? In the morning paper! No, I certainly have not seen it, but you may rest assured I'll have a look at it as soon as I hang up this phone. Goodbye. (*Hangs up*) Kim, get me the morning paper.

KIM: Yes, sir. (*As she gets paper, a knock at the door is heard.* JEFF *opens it.* MRS. DELANEY *enters.*)

MRS. DELANEY: Oh, Mr. Tyler. I'm so glad you're in. (*Apologetically*) Oh, I'm sorry. I didn't know you had a visitor.

MR. TYLER: That's quite all right, Mrs. Delaney. This is my nephew, Jeff. And, of course, you know my secretary, Kim. Jeff, this is Mrs. Delaney. She's my neighbor across the hall.

MRS. DELANEY: That's just why I've come, Mr. Tyler. Because I *am* your neighbor. You know, I just said to Ed the other evening, we're all so busy and rush around doing so many things that we just don't take the time to be neighborly any more. And do you know what Ed said to me, Mr. Tyler? (MR. TYLER *shakes his head.*) Ed said, "Kitty, you're right, absolutely right." And then I said, "Now take Mr. Tyler—lives right across the hall, and he's never once been inside our apartment." And then this morning when I saw your ad . . . (*Gets handkerchief from pocket*) Well, I was just so touched that I said to Ed, "Well, you just never know what heartbreak and loneliness go on right under your nose, do you?" And do you know what Ed said, Mr. Tyler? (MR. TYLER *is speechless.*) Ed said, "Kitty, you go right over there to Mr. Tyler's apartment after you've washed the dishes and invite him over here for Christmas Eve. And don't take no for an answer!" That's just exactly what Ed said, Mr. Tyler, and I want you to know that we'd both be terribly happy if you'd come. Nothing fancy, just the family . . . but, well . . . we have all our decorations up and if I do say so myself, the apartment looks beautiful. How about it, Mr. Tyler?

MR. TYLER: I . . . er, I certainly appreciate your invitation, Mrs. Delaney, but . . . well . . . I really have another engagement.

MRS. DELANEY: Oh, dear! Can't you possibly come? Ed will be so disappointed.

MR. TYLER: I'm afraid I can't make it tonight, Mrs. Delaney . . .

MRS. DELANEY: Then how about tomorrow? Couldn't you have your Christmas dinner with us, Mr. Tyler?

JEFF: My uncle has a standing invitation for Christmas dinner at our house, Mrs. Delaney.

MRS. DELANEY: Oh! (*Brightly*) Well, perhaps you'll find time to drop in during the holidays. You know Ed and I are great admirers of yours, Mr. Tyler. Every time we get one of your cards, Ed frames it and hangs it in his den. There's one thing that made us laugh at your ad, Mr. Tyler.

MR. TYLER: What was that?

MRS. DELANEY: All that modesty! Referring to yourself as an "unknown artist"! I just said to Ed, "Imagine that, Ed! Mr. Tyler—an unknown artist!" And Ed said to me . . . Know what he said, Mr. Tyler? Ed said, "Any time Mr. Tyler's an unknown artist, so is Leonardo da Vinci!"

MR. TYLER (*With a forced smile*): That's a real compliment.

MRS. DELANEY: Well, so long, Mr. Tyler, and a merry Christmas to you. (*Glancing at* KIM *and* JEFF) With these young people around, I bet you'll have your Christmas spirit back in no time. (*Exit* MRS. DELANEY.)

MR. TYLER: And now I think we've had just about enough of this! Kim, the paper, if you please!

KIM (*Who has been looking through paper during* MRS. DELANEY'*s visit*): Oh, Mr. Tyler! It's worse than I thought! It's . . . it's really terrible!

JEFF (*Looking over her shoulder*): Nothing could be that bad, Kim. Where is it? Let me see.

MR. TYLER (*Taking paper*): I'll do the looking. After all, this is *my* advertisement. Now, where is it?

KIM (*Weakly*): The third from the bottom.

MR. TYLER: Great Caesar's ghost! (*Reading*) "Lost: Old-fashioned Christmas spirit by unknown artist. Finder please return to Joshua Tyler, 9 Mayfair Apartments. Liberal reward." By Jove! I'll sue them! No newspaper can make a laughing stock of me! Kim, get me the *Daily Herald*. Ask for the Managing Editor.

KIM: But, Mr. Tyler! Please! It's not the newspaper's fault!

MR. TYLER: Not the newspaper's fault? Of course, it's their fault.

KIM: No, sir. It's not their mistake. It's mine.

JEFF: Are you sure, Kim?

KIM: Yes, I'm sure. It's my wretched shorthand. (*Getting steno pad*) Look! Here are my notes. See. I meant to write: Lost: Old-fashioned Christmas *print* by unknown artist. Instead . . . see . . . right here's the mistake.

JEFF: Gee whiz! Those pothooks all look alike to me.

KIM: But they're all different. Oh, Mr. Tyler, if only I had typed up my own notes, I would have caught it. But I left early yesterday and gave them to Jeannie at the main desk. She typed exactly what I have here. I can't explain it, except . . . well, I guess my mind was on Christmas instead of on my work.

MR. TYLER: It's incredible! Simply incredible! No one but an imbecile could make such a mistake! Kim—*you're fired!*

JEFF: Uncle Josh!

KIM (*Almost in tears*): He's right, Jeff! I *am* an imbecile! He has every right to fire me! Now I'll never be a secretary! Never! No one will ever hire me again.

JEFF: Don't take it so hard, Kim. After all, there are other jobs and certainly Uncle Josh will give you references.

MR. TYLER: What sort of references could I give a little scatterbrain who could get her employer into such a mess as this! She's made me a laughing stock, a public joke! Lost my Christmas spirit, indeed!

JEFF: But it's true, Uncle Josh! You *have* lost it!

MR. TYLER: What?

JEFF: You lost it long ago! Ever since you've been designing Christmas cards you've been soured on the whole idea.

KIM: Jeff, there's no use talking.

JEFF: But it's true. Look at this place! Not a sprig of holly, not a candle or a bit of evergreen until good old Tony sent the Christmas tree! For years you haven't done any Christmas entertaining. You don't even do Christmas shopping . . . you just send checks. You turn off the radio so you won't hear the carols. You won't even accept our invitation to Christmas dinner.

MR. TYLER: You know I must watch my diet.

JEFF: That's not the real reason. You're just afraid of Christmas.

MR. TYLER: Afraid of Christmas?

JEFF: Well, what other reason could you have for acting like this? You don't even wish your neighbors a merry Christmas when you meet them in the hall.

MR. TYLER: Why should I? By the time I've thought up forty-eleven different ways of saying "Merry Christmas" and painted forty-eleven designs to go with them, I don't feel like saying "Merry Christmas" to my own grandmother! As for my neighbors, they don't care any more about it than I do.

JEFF: Is that so? What about Tony Tonelli and Mrs. Delaney, and—and that friend who sent you the poinsettia? You're just sore, Uncle Josh! Sore because you're painting Christmas cards instead of landscapes, or por traits or murals or something the world would call grea art with capital letters. Well, that's where you're wrong Uncle Josh. Your Christmas cards will mean just a much to the people of this world as any other form o art you might have chosen. You'd realize that, if you'c only give yourself half a chance.

MR. TYLER: Is that so?

JEFF: Yes, that's so. You used to paint beautiful Christma cards, the kind that people love.

MR. TYLER: A lot of sentimental foolishness!

JEFF (*Indicating easel*): And I suppose *this* isn't foolish ness? Uncle Jeff, I think you ought to thank Kim fo making her mistake. You really *have* lost your Christma spirit, and that's a terrible thing to happen to anybody whether he's an artist or a cobbler. (*A knock at the doo is heard.*)

KIM: I'll get it. (*Opens door. Enter* MRS. MARTINKA, *a frai old lady carrying a small parcel.*) Oh, hello, Mrs. Mar tinka. Can I do something for you?

MRS. MARTINKA: Mr. Tyler? Is he at home? Can I pleas to see him?

KIM (*Doubtfully*): Well, yes, he's here, Mrs. Martinka but . . .

MRS. MARTINKA (*Catching sight of* MR. TYLER): Oh, ther he is. I must see him. I will take only a little of his time (*To* MR. TYLER) Excuse, please, Mr. Tyler. I read you ad by the morning paper. So sad it was! I just had t come.

MR. TYLER: Please, Mrs. Martinka . . . it was a mistake

MRS. MARTINKA: Yes, yes, a big mistake to lose Christma spirit. I know. Since last year I know. In hospital I was Thought I had no friend in the world. And then the begin to come. Friends, neighbors, the good people i this apartment house. They give me Christmas car shower. It rain. It pour. Christmas cards all over my bed. Nurses pin them on wall. And yours, Mr. Tyler, all those little angels. So beautiful! So sweet! They make me feel better just to look at them. I keep every one in big scrapbook!

MR. TYLER: That was nice of you, very nice, Mrs. Martinka, but . . .

MRS. MARTINKA: So when I read your advertisement I understand. You too lose Christmas spirit. So maybe I bring it back to you. (*Extending parcel*) In Poland, where I come from, it is custom to exchange *Oplatki* with our friends.

OTHERS: *Oplatki?*

MRS. MARTINKA: *Oplatki* is small wafer. See, just big enough for envelope. Same size as greeting card. Only we do not write on them. We *eat* them. We break them and share them with our friends on Christmas Eve. I bring you *Oplatki,* Mr. Tyler. Share it with your loved ones. It will bring back your Christmas spirit . . . just like greeting cards bring back mine. You try?

MR. TYLER: Very well, Mrs. Martinka. I'll try. And thank you. Thank you very much. (*As* MRS. MARTINKA *is about to exit, there is a fanfare of horns and a brass trio strikes up "It Came Upon a Midnight Clear." When they reach the third phrase,* MR. TYLER *speaks.*) Jeff! Jeff! Make them stop that racket. Tell them to move on.

JEFF: I'll try, sir. (*As* JEFF *goes to door,* FRED, JOE *and* BILL, *the brass trio, enter.* MRS. MARTINKA *exits.*)

MR. TYLER: Kim, don't just stand there. Get rid of those banshees at once.

FRED: Merry Christmas, Mr. Tyler.

JOE: Excuse us, Mr. Tyler. We didn't know you had company. We just came about your ad.

BILL (*Who has an extra trumpet tucked under his arm*): I guess you don't know me, Mr. Tyler. I'm Bill Adams from the third floor. Mom and Dad got to talking about your ad this morning. You know, the one about losing your Christmas spirit, and, well, Fred and Joe and I got to thinking maybe we could do something about it.

KIM: Oh, really, boys, that was nice of you, but, there's really nothing to do. You see . . .

BILL: Sure, there's something we can do, and we're here to do it. You see, Mr. Tyler, we always play in the courtyard here at the apartment on Christmas Eve, and then we go out into the neighborhood. Always before we've had a quartet but this year, Dan Green moved away, and so we're short a trumpet player. Dad thought that maybe . . . well . . . there's nothing to boost a guy's Christmas spirit like Christmas carols.

MR. TYLER: Who did you say you are, young man?

BILL: Bill Adams. My Dad's name is Punky Adams. Used to go to high school with you. That's how he knows you can play a trumpet. He says you used to be a real hot jive man.

MR. TYLER: Punky Adams? You mean Punky Adams lives right here in this apartment house?

BILL: Sure. He and Mom often wanted to come down and call, but, well, I guess they're sort of on the timid side when it comes to celebrities.

MR. TYLER: Celebrity? Who's a celebrity?

BILL: Why, gee whiz, you are, Mr. Tyler. You're a real artist. Mom and Dad have a whole collection of your Christmas cards. They're real fans of yours.

JOE: How about it, Mr. Tyler? We're going down to the furnace room for a rehearsal. Want to come along?

JEFF: Go ahead. I dare you, Uncle Josh.

MR. TYLER (*Reaching for trumpet*): I haven't played a trumpet for years.

FRED: Once a trumpeter, always a trumpeter, Mr. Tyler.

JOE: Let's have a chord, Bill. (*The three boys play the opening chord of a carol;* MR. TYLER *joins in, a little sour, but loud.*)

BILL: Not bad, Mr. Tyler. Now let's hit it again. (*On the second chord,* MR. CANFIELD *enters, wearing hat and coat, carrying a brief case.*)

MR. CANFIELD: Well, well, well! Bless my soul, Tyler! What's going on here?

KIM: Oh, Mr. Canfield, let me take your coat and hat. (*He removes and gives* KIM *overcoat and hat.*)

MR. TYLER: Oh, hello, Canfield. You know Kim, and my nephew, Jeff. These are some of the boys who live here in the house.

BILL: We just dropped in to ask Mr. Tyler to play trumpet in our Christmas quartet.

MR. CANFIELD: Well, I didn't know you were a musician, Tyler, as well as an artist.

BILL: We'll be shovin' off, Mr. Tyler. But that trumpet will be waiting for you.

MR. TYLER: Thank you, boys. I'll—I'll think it over. (*Exit* FRED *and* JOE.)

BILL: We'll just leave the trumpet here in case you want to warm up a bit. (*Leaves trumpet and exits*)

KIM: And now, if you'll excuse me, Mr. Tyler, I'll get my things. (KIM *turns to exit;* JEFF *tries to stop her.*)

JEFF: No, Kim—wait! (KIM *shakes her head, gestures* JEFF *toward* MR. CANFIELD, *and hurries offstage.* JEFF *hesitates a moment, as if about to follow her, then turns to listen to* MR. CANFIELD.)

MR. CANFIELD (*Surveying room*): Well, Tyler, this place looks a bit more like Christmas than it did the other day, when I was here. I'm glad to see you at least broke down and got a tree. Maybe there's hope for you yet.

MR. TYLER: What do you mean by that?

MR. CANFIELD: Just what I said. I don't mind telling you, my friend, unless you get rid of some of these freakish ideas and get closer to Christmas, you're through. Do you have anything else to show me beside this unlikely daub? (*Gestures toward easel*)

MR. TYLER: I told you the other day, Canfield. This is my new line. I'm sorry if you don't like it.

MR. CANFIELD: What about that old English idea? Didn't you get any inspiration from those prints I gave you?

MR. TYLER: Inspiration. Humph! I got nothing but trouble from those prints, Canfield, nothing but trouble. In fact, one of them cost me my secretary.

MR. CANFIELD: What do you mean? (*He idly picks up painting on easel, thereby revealing* JEFF'*s Christmas picture.*)

MR. TYLER: It's a long story, most of which is too incredible to believe, but—

MR. CANFIELD (*With a whistle of surprise*): Say, what's this? Now here's something like it! Old man, you've been holding out on me. Now this is more like your old style.

JEFF: Do you really like it, sir?

MR. CANFIELD: Like it? Why, this is the real thing. It carries an honest-to-goodness message of Christmas that people will recognize the minute they see it. (*Clapping* TYLER *on back*) Congratulations, Josh. You're getting back in the groove.

MR. TYLER: Sorry, Dick. But it's the wrong groove. That's not my design. The artist is a younger man.

JEFF: Golly, Uncle Josh! Please don't be sore. I know you don't like this sort of thing any more, but I wanted Mr. Canfield to see it.

MR. CANFIELD: This boy has talent, Josh. He should be in art school.

MR. TYLER: I know it, and that's where I want to send him, but . . .

JEFF: Gee, Uncle Josh, listen to what you're saying! You just said you really want to send me to art school.

MR. TYLER: Of course I do. But when I see you doing stuff like this, I get scared. I'm afraid you'll turn out like me.

MR. CANFIELD: What's so bad about that? Josh Tyler is only one of the most outstanding Christmas card designers in the country. (KIM *enters with coat, hat, suit-box and brief case.*)

MR. TYLER: So what? Can't you understand, Canfield? I wanted to do serious painting. I wanted to paint something real and enduring . . . something that mattered. I started doing Christmas cards to make money. Now I'm stuck with them. I'll never paint anything except these silly greeting cards that are here today and gone tomorrow.

KIM: But that's where you're wrong, Mr. Tyler. There's nothing silly about Christmas greetings, and they're not here today and gone tomorrow. The people love and remember them. Oh, I know I'm just a stupid high school girl who can't even do shorthand, but I know that much.

JEFF: Do you need a brick wall to fall on you, Uncle Jeff, after all that's happened here today?

MR. TYLER: Maybe I've been a stupid idiot, Jeff. That Mrs. Martinka and the others . . . the cards did mean something to them.

KIM: And to millions of others, Mr. Tyler. Believe me, I know. This afternoon and yesterday, I wanted time off. Do you know why?

MR. TYLER: Well . . . er, Christmas shopping, I suppose.

KIM: No, Mr. Tyler. I've been helping with the Christmas party at the Children's Hospital. If you want to know how much your cards really mean, you should go down there and see the children. They watch for every mail.

MR. TYLER: You know, Kim, maybe I shouldn't have fired you after all. You may not be much on shorthand, but you're great on spirit.

KIM: Oh, Mr. Tyler, would you give me another chance?

MR. TYLER: I should ask you to give me another chance, Kim. Something tells me I've been a pretty crummy employer.

JEFF: Gee, Kim. He means it! Unpack your things and stay a while. (*He makes a grab for the suit-box, the string breaks and out falls a Santa Claus suit with mask.*)

MR. TYLER *and* MR. CANFIELD (*As they pick up the pieces*): What's this?

KIM: Oh, dear! I knew that string wouldn't hold! It's the Santa Claus suit for the Children's party.

MR. TYLER: Who's going to wear it?

KIM: One of the interns usually takes the part.

MR. TYLER (*Trying on coat*): Do you think I have the figure for the job?

MR. CANFIELD: A bit on the skinny side, I should say.

JEFF: Not bad, Uncle Josh, not bad at all!

MR. TYLER (*Holding up empty pack*): But this pack is in a sad state of emptiness. Maybe we'd have time to fill it up on our way downtown. What time is that party, Kim?

KIM: Not until . . . oh, Mr. Tyler, would you really do it? The children would love you.

MR. TYLER: Kim, I have a feeling I know where my lost Christmas spirit is at this very minute. If I put on this suit and go down to that party with you, I believe those children could help me find it. Is it a deal?

KIM: It's a deal, sir, a wonderful deal!

MR. CANFIELD: But, Josh, what about our deadline?

MR. TYLER: See me next week, old man, and if I don't have the warmest, cheeriest, jolliest set of drawings you've ever seen, you can hang me on your Christmas tree next year. (*To* KIM *and* JEFF) Now come on, you two, let's get going. (*A knock at the door is heard, and* JIM, *the elevator boy, enters.*)

JIM: Excuse me, sir. I just heard about your trouble . . . losin' your Christmas spirit, and all, and I was wonderin' if there'd be anything I could do to help.

MR. TYLER: That's mighty good of you, Jim, but . . .

JIM: You see, sir, when I first came here, I felt just about the way you do now. My Christmas spirit was clean down to the last drop. Only the folks here in the apartment house helped me get it back in no time. Yes, sir, they just took me right in. That very first year, the cage of my elevator was filled with Christmas cards. You'd have thought I'd been here all my life. Then the next thing I knew, they had me puttin' up a tree in the lobby, and hangin' the greens, and fixin' the lights . . . till, well, I just sort of got the idea that the whole Christmas depended right on me. And you know something? That did it. By the time I made Christmas for everybody else, my own Christmas spirit was right back where it belonged and it's stayed there ever since. So, well, sir, when I heard about you, I thought maybe I could help you find yours, same as I found mine.

MR. TYLER: What do you have in mind, Jim?

JIM: Well, sir, that tree down in the lobby is a puny lookin' sight this year. The ladies have been so busy fussin' over the color scheme, they plumb got it schemed all out of kilter. I thought maybe—you bein' an artist and all—you might take a look at it, and see what could be done.

MR. TYLER: I'll do just that, Jim, if you think the ladies would take my advice.

JIM: Oh, they'll take your advice sure enough, sir. That sure will be a relief off of my mind.

MR. TYLER: Glad to help out, Jim, and now there's something else you can do for me.

JIM: Anything at all, sir.

MR. TYLER: I'd like you to post a notice on the bulletin board. Kim, get your shorthand pad.

KIM: Right away, sir.

JEFF: You'd better not take any more chances, Uncle Josh. Let her write it down in longhand.

KIM: I won't make any mistakes this time, sir.

MR. TYLER: Head it "*Lost and Found:* This is to inform you that the Unknown Artist in Apartment 9 has found his lost Christmas spirit."

JIM: Say, that's great, Mr. Tyler. That's just great.

MR. TYLER (*Continuing as* KIM *writes*): "And since so many people in this apartment house have helped me find it, you all have a claim to the reward offered. Therefore, all residents are invited to a Christmas Party tomorrow night at eight o'clock. Bring the children. Signed: Gratefully yours, Joshua Tyler."

JEFF: Gee, that's wonderful, Uncle Josh.

KIM (*Giving note to* JIM): Here you are, Jim.

JIM: I'll post this right away, sir.

MR. TYLER: One thing more, Jim, if three young gentlemen are still using your furnace room as a practice hall, tell them I'll be joining them in time for the carols.

JIM: Boy, oh boy, Mr. Tyler, you really did find that Christmas spirit.

JEFF: Actually, Uncle Josh, I don't think it was lost at all. Just temporarily mislaid.

MR. CANFIELD: If someone would just be kind enough to explain to me what all this is about! What's the story on Josh losing his Christmas spirit, anyway?

MR. TYLER: It's too long to tell now, old friend. But on the way downtown, Kim can write you a memo in shorthand. (*Picking up trumpet*) Here we go! All set for a merry Christmas! Forward, march! (MR. TYLER *leads off with a Christmas tune on the trumpet as the rest follow, single file,* JIM *last. As they are about to exit,* JIM *turns, faces the audience and says with a broad grin*)

JIM: That Mr. Tyler man sure has got the merriest Christmas spirit ever! (*Curtain*)

THE END

The Master of the Strait

by Helen E. Waite and Elbert M. Hoppenstedt

Characters

MARY ARDEN, *wife of the keeper of Bear's Head Light*
MARTHA SIMMS, *a neighbor from the mainland*
WILLIAM ARDEN, *keeper of the Light*
WARREN
GEORGE
RUTH
RICHARD } *carolers*

TIME: *Christmas Eve.*

SETTING: *The kitchen of the Bear's Head Lighthouse, in the 1890's.*

AT RISE: MARY *is removing the last of the supper dishes from the table. Having carried them away, she spreads a red cloth on the table, places a few books at one side, and her sewing basket at the other, and a lighted kerosene lamp between. As she finishes, a knock is heard on outer door and* MARY *crosses room to open it.* MARTHA SIMMS *enters.*)

MARTHA: Merry Christmas to the Ardens!

MARY: Merry Christmas. Here, let me have your coat. (MARTHA *turns, and* MARY *takes her coat, shaking off the snow which powders it.*)

MARTHA (*Placing her basket on table*): Here's just a bit of Christmas cheer for you and William.

MARY: How dear you are, Martha. There's never been a Christmas since we've been stationed here at Bear's Head Light which hasn't brought a visit from the Simms.

MARTHA: And why not? Would Christmas be the time to forget friends—especially those who spend so many lonely hours to protect the lives of other folk? (*She settles herself in nearest chair, and* MARY *takes another.*)

MARY (*Sighs*): Aye, lonely hours they are indeed. Sometimes the days are more than long. One stretches out like the next, with only the monotonous thunder of the waves and the sweep of the tides to mark the hours. Listen! The surf is fierce tonight, and the wind is rising. William will be tending the light half the night. The strait is doubly dangerous in such a storm.

MARTHA: But it can be said, truly, that while William Arden tends Bear's Head Light, no ship is in peril passing through this strait. There has been no wreck here since—(*She stops in consternation, biting her lips.*)

MARY (*Speaking without emotion*): You need not fear, Martha. The wound left by that wreck has long since healed in my heart. It is William's which is still heavy and sore.

MARTHA: Yes, you can see William never forgets.

MARY: Not even for a day. And Christmas Eve is hardest of all. It was ten years ago tonight, you know, when—

MARTHA (*Shuddering*): Yes, I know. Yet *I* stood on shore, and you—

MARY: We were on board the *Western Seas*. William and Philip and I Philip was so gay and excited about Christmas. Everyone on board was. Even Captain Sylvester was so intent on reaching home quickly that he wouldn't listen to William's warnings about the dangerous places in this strait.

MARTHA: He never was so careless again. That wreck made

him the best captain in these parts. And the next year the Government built this Lighthouse.

MARY: Yes. I was glad when they asked William to be the keeper. I thought saving other ships which carried boys —but nothing makes up for losing Philip. He loved him so dearly. I can see the longing for him in William's eyes—and sometimes, I—I've thought—I saw something else—

MARTHA: Something else? I don't understand what you mean, Mary.

MARY: I'm not sure I understand it either. But it comes when he meets Captain Sylvester—or hears he is bringing a ship up the strait.

MARTHA: You mean William holds Captain Sylvester responsible for Philip's death? Oh, no. William's not a man to do that! He knows there was no Light here, and that the *Western Seas* was old and unseaworthy—

MARY: And that her Captain was careless. But I do not blame him or anyone tonight—not on Christ's birthday. (*Speaks in a brighter tone*) How foolish of me not to have opened your Christmas basket! (*Unwraps basket, revealing oranges, apples, figs, etc.*) How lovely they look! You always remember how fond William is of apples, and I of figs! May I have one now?

MARTHA: Why, yes, of course! What a foolish question.

MARY: No, I'll wait for William, after all.

MARTHA (*Rising*): I must be going. The snow is very thick, and the wind really bitter.

MARY (*Also rising*): You came in the sleigh?

MARTHA: Yes, and my brother is waiting below. (*She crosses to window and peers out*) The waves are white-crested tonight as they rush for shore. Always the sea here at Bear's Head! Sometimes I wish I could run away from it. It is the sea which has been the cause of heartaches in every household in Bear's Head.

MARY (*Bringing* MARTHA'S *coat*): But deep within you, you know none of us would live away from the sea. We all love it. Yes, it has taken its fee, it has robbed us all of those we loved, but it's a part of us.

MARTHA (*Taking one final look from window*): Perhaps. (*She turns toward door, and, at the same moment* WILLIAM ARDEN *enters room from right*) Oh, there you are, William! I was afraid you were busy with the Light, and that I'd miss saying "Merry Christmas" to you. Nights like this must keep you busy. (WILLIAM ARDEN *is a slow, quiet man, who moves and speaks with precision. His voice is almost toneless, but he greets* MARTHA *with grave courtesy.*)

WILLIAM: Good evening to you, Mrs. Simms. This is no weather for you to be out.

MARTHA: Now, William, do you think I'd let a Christmas Eve pass without bringing a basket to the Ardens? I'd defy a worse storm than this to make my Christmas call! But it *is* a wretched night. And Captain Sylvester is bringing his son Jim home aboard the *Half Moon* tonight. (*She watches* WILLIAM'S *face closely for the effect of her words, but there is none.* WILLIAM *seems politely indifferent.*)

WILLIAM: Is that so? Jim must be getting to be quite a boy, now.

MARTHA: Yes. He's fifteen. . . . Well, I'd better be hurrying if I don't want to spend the night in an open sleigh!

WILLIAM: Let me take you down to the sleigh.

MARTHA: Thanks, but it is only a few steps. It wouldn't be worth your while to come out. (*Opens door*) Good night—and—Merry Christmas!

MARY *and* WILLIAM: Merry Christmas! (*As the door closes,* WILLIAM *stands with down-bent head in the center of room.* MARY *watches nervously. Then she moves to table.*)

MARY: Martha brought this basket of fruit, William.

WILLIAM: It was very good of her. (MARY *selects a bright, large apple, and holds it out.*)

MARY: Just the kind you like. (WILLIAM *takes the proffered apple, but he looks neither at it nor at* MARY.)

WILLIAM: You heard what Mrs. Simms said, Mary . . . about Captain Sylvester . . . and . . . Jim . . . ?

MARY (*Breathlessly*): Yes, William . . .

WILLIAM: Coming up the strait . . . tonight . . . on Christmas Eve . . . ten years ago another boy was coming up the strait . . . Jim is fifteen. The other boy would have been fifteen, too. Just growing into manhood, with light hair, and blue eyes, eyes that twinkled as the moon twinkles on the blue waves . . .

MARY (*Responding to his mood*): More like the sun striking the waves, William. Philip's eyes were too alive to be like the moonlight. That gleam in his eyes was like the rising sun above the water—

WILLIAM (*Shaking his head slowly*): No, Mary. It will always seem like the flash and ripple of the moon on a dark sea, to me. There's something wistful, something inexplicable in moonlight on the water. Philip had that something in his eyes. (*His voice is rough and hurried.*) And one man's carelessness took from us what nothing on earth can give back. I can't keep that from my thoughts. Day and night it haunts me. I've got to do something about it, Mary. Tonight.

MARY (*In a whisper*): You've found something—to comfort you—to—night?

WILLIAM: Yes, I have found it. (*He speaks evenly*) Tonight Sylvester brings his son up the strait. Suppose the oil supply for the lamp is gone?

MARY (*Gasping*): You don't—mean—that!

WILLIAM: No?

MARY: There is a greater Lighthouse than this which

guides all our ships, William. The Keeper gives light to those who do good and to those who do not. His mercy is to all. Tonight we celebrate His birthday. Was He born in vain that you cannot see His great light?

WILLIAM (*Harshly*): I have lost my faith in that Light. (*He goes to table, and from a drawer takes out a candle and candle-holder*) This is the light which shall gleam upon the sea tonight—in memory of little Philip.

MARY: Would he be proud of you? (WILLIAM *moves to window without comment.*) Jim Sylvester was his best friend. And what will you do this night in memory of the Child born the first Christmas Eve? His message was to love those who wronged you. . . .

WILLIAM: You may say what you will, but nothing will change my mind. (*He places candle in window, strikes a match, but candle refuses to light. Tries a second match, with the same result, and gives an impatient exclamation, then stands in a listening attitude. There is a faint sound of music.*) What's that? I thought I heard —singing?

MARY (*Joining him at window*): Singing? . . . I don't . . . (*The sound is plainer, and her voice shows her quick relief and joy*) Oh! Yes, yes! It's the children from the mainland coming to sing their Christmas carols for us. I didn't dare hope they'd venture out here on such a wild night.

WILLIAM: I wish they had remained at home. I do not wish to see children.

MARY: Oh—William!

WILLIAM: Why should they come, anyway?

MARY: Because they are grateful to you for the way you've kept the Light. Because they admire you . . . (*Singing has come very near*) Quick, William, bring the cookie jar from the pantry. (*There is a knock at the door*) I'll open the door. (*She goes to door and admits* GEORGE,

WARREN, RUTH, RICHARD, *and as many other children as may be desired. They wear heavy wraps, and are covered with snow. Faces are vividly red.*)

GEORGE: Merry Christmas to you, Mrs. Arden.

MARY (*A suspicious catch in her voice*): Merry Christmas to you all.

WARREN (*Who is the youngest*): We've come to sing to you! Do you want to hear us?

MARY: Indeed I do! Come in, near the fire. You must be half frozen. It was very brave of you to come out to us this stormy night.

RUTH: Oh, we couldn't miss coming to the Lighthouse on Christmas Eve— Why, Christmas wouldn't be Christmas unless we sang for you and Mr. Arden!

MARY: You are dear to say so. Our Christmas would be very bleak if you forgot us.

RUTH: But we couldn't forget! You and Mr. Arden are so wonder— Hello, Mr. Arden! Merry Christmas! (WILLIAM *has entered with the cookie jar, which he places upon table. He returns* RUTH'S *greeting in a stiff, lifeless tone.*)

WILLIAM: Merry Christmas. (*He walks to the window, staring out at the dark. The children glance first at him, and then at one another, uncertainly.*)

MARY (*Hastily*): Won't you sing your carols for us, please?

GEORGE: All right. What shall we sing first?

MARY: My favorite carol is "Silent Night." (*Children sing "Silent Night," followed by two or three other carols.* MARY *wipes her eyes, and* WILLIAM, *still by window, twists his hands behind his back. At conclusion of songs,* MARY *breaks the short silence.*)

MARY: Oh, you sing beautifully, children! You—you can't know how lovely it was to hear you again. The days are so long and silent when the two of us are here by ourselves. (*Briskly*) And now you must have some of my

Christmas cookies! (*She passes jar*) I baked them especially for you. Sit down, all of you. How will you get back to the mainland through this storm?

RICHARD: My father lent us his horse and sleigh.

MARY: I see. That was kind of him.

RICHARD: My mother and my father both said we mustn't miss coming here if we could possibly help it. My mother says you and Mr. Arden are the best people we have in Bear's Head.

MARY (*In choked voice*): How sweet of her!

RUTH (*Eagerly*): My mother says the same thing. She says Mr. Arden is the best keeper a lighthouse ever had. Every time she looks out her window and sees this lighthouse, she is comforted, because she knows that as long as Mr. Arden is here the menfolk of Bear's Head will bring the fishing boats through the strait safely, no matter what the weather.

MARY (*Choking*): That—that is very kind—(*She looks at* WILLIAM, *still standing by the window. He has turned toward the room now, but his eyes are upon the floor, and he is thoughtfully stroking the back of his left hand with the finger of his right.*)

GEORGE: Well, I guess if anybody is grateful to Mr. Arden, it's our family. Dad wouldn't be with us now if anything had gone wrong with the Light when our boat was caught in that storm last month! As things were, her sails were almost hitting the water. And if she'd gone on those rocks—

MARY (*Huskily*): Bless you, every one, for saying such wonderful things about Mr. Arden. Keeping the Light is a lonely task, and it does us good to know others are grateful. (*Brightly*) Will anyone have more cookies? You have a long trip back to town. (*There are shouts of "Um-m-m!" "I will!" "Sure thing!" as* MARY *passes cookies again*) There now, everyone satisfied?

GEORGE: You make the best cookies of anyone in the world, Mrs. Arden!

MARY: I do? You must come get them more often.

RICHARD: I think we ought to be getting back home. The snow's growing deeper every minute. (*He stands, and others follow his example.*)

WARREN: I'll bet Captain Sylvester will be glad you're here tonight, Mr. Arden. (WILLIAM *makes no response.*)

MARY (*Unsteadily*): Why, dear?

WARREN: Because he's bringing his son Jim back from his school to spend Christmas here, and the strait is so dangerous in a storm. But they'll make it all right with Mr. Arden at the Light to guide them. I like Jim! I can hardly wait till he gets here! He wrote me he was bringing me Christmas presents from the city. What do you think they'll be, Mrs. Arden?

MARY (*Having difficulty with her voice*): I—I don't know, Warren, I'm sure.

WARREN: I hope it's ice skates— You know what, Mr. Arden? It must be great to have so many people trusting you to bring them home safely! Most of the kids want to be captains, like Captain Sylvester, but I don't! I'm going to be a lighthouse keeper, when I grow up, and have a record just like yours, Mr. Arden—not a single ship lost! (*At last* WILLIAM *looks at the boy. He is startled, unnerved, and when he speaks, it is in a queer, croaking voice.*)

WILLIAM: Now—how old are you, son?

WARREN: Ten. I know I'll have to wait a long time.

WILLIAM: Ten years . . . old. Ten . . . years. Why do you want to be like me?

WARREN: Because everyone says you're the grandest keeper a lighthouse ever had. Everybody who comes up this coast knows they'll get through the strait safely just because you're here, keeping watch. You know, Mr.

Arden, I guess Christmas is a Lighthouse. It's Christ's way of telling us each year that He's still with us, and guiding us, no matter what happens. And *you're* something like Jesus: He never fails, and neither do you. That's why I'm going to be a keeper of a light—and try to be just like you!

WILLIAM (*Huskily*): A keeper—like *me!* Better think twice, son. The lives of so many people depend upon a Lighthouse, and it is so easy for a keeper to make a mistake!

WARREN (*Confidentially*): I know it's hard, but I *am* going to be keeper of a light, and when the hard times come, I'll remember about you—and Jesus.

RUTH: My mother feels just the same way about you, Mr. Arden. We always look toward the Lighthouse the last thing at night, and then sometimes we sing the hymn about God's Lighthouse—you know!

WILLIAM (*With emotion*): Yes—I know. Would you—sing it for me—now?

RUTH (*Glancing at others*): All right.

(*Children sing*)

"Brightly beams our Father's mercy
From His Lighthouse evermore.
But to us He gives the keeping
Of the lights along the shore.
Let the lower lights be burning,
Send a gleam across the waves!
Some poor fainting, struggling seaman
You may rescue, you may save.
Trim your feeble lamps, my brother;
Some poor sailor, tempest-tossed,
Trying now to make the harbour
In the darkness may be lost."

RICHARD: Now we really must go!

ALL: Good night—Merry Christmas!

MARY and WILLIAM: Merry Christmas! (*There is a moment of deep silence after door closes. Then* WILLIAM *speaks very slowly.*)

WILLIAM: He is . . . ten . . . years . . . old. And he said I was . . . like Christ . . . because . . . I never failed. (*He shudders*) Oh, dear God, what was I thinking? What was I planning to do before he came?

MARY (*Hurrying to him*): It's over now, William. You didn't fail his trust, and—you never will. Tell me, how do you feel within?

WILLIAM: As if . . . as if I had suddenly been released from chains which held me down all these years. I have only one regret—

MARY: Yes?

WILLIAM: That I needed a little child to teach me—

MARY (*Crying out eagerly*): Oh, no, William, don't regret that! It was a Child who taught us all to love and forgive! Now light the candle in the window, for now you can light it without shame!

WILLIAM: That I will! (*He hurries to window, strikes a match, applies it to wick. The candle glows brightly*) To Philip, wherever he may be, and to a lad like him, who tonight saved me from a horrible sin. (*Looking at* MARY) You know, Mary, we are all Lighthouse Keepers, every one of us. Some good—some bad—

MARY: We take our light from the Great Lighthouse Keeper, Christ. Nineteen hundred years ago He lit His Light, and it has never failed—and it never will.

WILLIAM: Two lights burn from this Lighthouse tonight. One to show the faith Warren restored to me, the other to assure safe passage to *all* who sail up the strait.

THE END

MIDDLE GRADES

O Little Town of Bethlehem

by Olive J. Morley

Characters

MARY	DANIEL	*shepherd boys*
JOSEPH	SAMUEL	
REUBEN, *an Innkeeper*	SIMON	
REBECCA, *his wife*	BENJAMIN	
DAVID, *his son*	GABRIEL	
RACHEL, *his daughter*	A CROWD	

SCENE 1

SETTING: *A Village Street in Bethlehem. Before the rise of the curtain the carol, "O Little Town of Bethlehem" is sung. As the voices softly fade on the last line, they are superseded by a great noise of shouting, jostling, etc.*

AT RISE: *A great number of people are crossing the stage, chattering volubly, carrying packages, etc. Amongst these are* DAVID *and* RACHEL, *two bright-eyed children. Enter* MARY *and* JOSEPH. *They are carrying packages, and look overcome with fatigue.*

JOSEPH: I had thought there might have been a chance in this street, but it seems just as crowded as the others we tried.

MARY: I am sure there will be some rooms here. Let us ask that little boy. (*Pointing to* DAVID)

JOSEPH: Come here a minute, son. (DAVID *approaches*

them.) Do you know of any place where we could lodge for the night?

DAVID (*Whistling*): You've asked for something! Everybody's been trying to get rooms the whole day long, and the village is packed. It's been good fun, I can tell you! Rachel and I—Rachel's my sister, you know—(*Indicating* RACHEL, *who has now stepped up to them*) have been earning pennies all day carrying packages for people, and running messages. I wish Caesar would have an enrolment every year. We should see some life then. People from all over the country, and from over the sea too, even as far as Rome. The languages we've heard! My father keeps the inn here, so we've had a busy time.

JOSEPH (*Looking across at the inn door*): Is that it?

DAVID (*Nodding*): M-m-m.

JOSEPH: Then run and ask him if he can put up just two more travellers, son. My wife here is nearly dying of fatigue.

RACHEL: We'll ask him, but I don't think there's much hope.

DAVID (*Crossing to* MARY, *and looking up at her curiously*): Do you come a long way from here?

MARY (*Smiling down at him*): Yes, a long way. We come from a place much further north.

DAVID: I thought you didn't come from these parts. You don't look or talk like the people around here. (*Impulsively putting his hand in hers*) I should like you to stay with us. I *like* you.

MARY (*Gently*): Do you?

DAVID: Yes. You're sort of quiet—my father and mother are always so busy.

MARY: We're busy, too, when we're at home, you know.

DAVID: Yes, but you don't look as if you'd get *fretted* about it, like most. You've got a kind of *still* look, like I imagine the angels that guard the Ark in the Temple must have . . . Well, I'll go and see if they've got a room. (*Runs off.* RACHEL *follows*)

JOSEPH: The Ark in the Temple! Strange he should say that.

MARY: Children sometimes see what is hidden from others. (*With a quiet serenity, looking out in front of her*) But I have been given something much greater to guard than even the Ark in the Temple. (*Re-enter* DAVID *with* REUBEN, *the Innkeeper. They are arguing heatedly.*)

REUBEN: No, I can't put up another single person.

DAVID: But Father—

REUBEN: I tell you I can't.

DAVID: Father, do! Come and see them anyway. Look, they're over here. (*They continue to argue, as* DAVID *leads* REUBEN *over to* MARY *and* JOSEPH.)

JOSEPH (*Coming forward*): We wondered whether you might perhaps have a room to spare for my wife and myself.

REUBEN: Room? Did you say *room?* People have been asking me for rooms since dawn this morning! I tell you I haven't an inch to spare in the house. I'm afraid you've no chance of putting up here. (MARY *sways.* JOSEPH *puts an arm round her.*)

JOSEPH: But we've been travelling all day, and my wife is almost faint with weariness.

REUBEN (*Grudgingly sympathetic*): Well, I'm sorry—very sorry. But I can't stretch the house, you know. Perhaps you'd like to come in and rest awhile, and then go on to the next village.

MARY: I can go—no further—tonight.

REUBEN: Honestly, I've not an inch to spare. Unless (*Jocularly*) you'd like to sleep in the stable! (JOSEPH *turns to her hopelessly.*)

MARY: Why not the stable?

JOSEPH: But my dear—that is no fitting place.

MARY (*Quietly*): Let us not worry about what is fitting, if that is what God offers us.

JOSEPH: Well, we'll go to the stable, if you've no other place.

REUBEN (*Pointing left*): It's just down over yonder—it's really a cave in the hillside. My son here will show you the way.

DAVID (*Running to* MARY): Come on, I'll show you. And then I'll come back and bring you some supper. May I, Father?

REUBEN: Ay. I'll tell the wife to get something ready.

MARY (*Graciously*): Thank you.

DAVID: I'm sorry it's only the stable.

MARY: Never mind. I'm thankful for anything tonight. (*Enter, from behind,* REBECCA, *the* INNKEEPER'S *wife*)

DAVID: But I'll bring you *such* a nice supper. Come on. (*They move off left,* JOSEPH *supporting* MARY *on one side and* DAVID *leading her by the hand on the other.*)

REBECCA (*Sharply*): Who was that?

REUBEN: Oh, some couple who wanted a room for the night. The lad's taken them down to the stable.

REBECCA: Where do they come from?

REUBEN: I don't know. Somewhere up north, the lad said.

REBECCA (*With conviction*): They come from farther than that.

REUBEN: What makes you say so?

REBECCA: I don't know. She'd a look about her, and it was different from anyone I've seen from this country—or any country, for that matter.

REUBEN: What do you mean, wife?

REBECCA: I don't know what I mean. I only know she'd that look about her—well, queer, I call it.

REUBEN: They seemed a simple, homely enough pair to me.

REBECCA: Simple, they may be, but not homely. (*Looking*

offstage) Only look how she bears herself, tired though she is, poor girl. Why she might be a queen!

REUBEN: They must be natives of these parts, or they'd never have come here for the enrolling. And their clothes are just rough homespun.

REBECCA: So they may be, but look how they wear them. I'll cook them a nice meal, but I'm glad they're not sleeping under our roof.

REUBEN: How do you mean?

REBECCA: Well, I've no fancy to entertain royalty!

CURTAIN

* * *

SCENE 2

SETTING: *The hillsides near Bethlehem. The carol "While Shepherds Watched" is sung. It is night, and the stage is in semi-darkness.*

AT RISE: *Enter right,* DANIEL, SIMON, SAMUEL *and* BENJAMIN. DANIEL *appears to be the leader of the four.* BENJAMIN *is the smallest shepherd boy, and has a wistful, lovable face and manner.*

BENJAMIN: I wonder where he's gone.

DANIEL: He can't be very far. (*Looking around*) Perhaps he's behind those rocks. (*He points to some of the boulders, and they all make a thorough search.*)

BENJAMIN: I don't see him . . . (*Continues search*) Oh, Daniel, suppose he's fallen down the ravine and hurt himself! P'raps he's killed! What shall I do without my little lamb? I must find him. I must! (*Runs all over stage, calling frantically*) Fleecy, Fleecy, where are you? It's Benjamin calling!

THE OTHERS: Fleecy! . . . Fleecy! . . . Fleecy!

BENJAMIN (*Returning disconsolately from his search*): I believe he's dead. Oh, Fleecy, Fleecy! (*He sinks down on the open ground in the center, and begins to cry.*) I said I wouldn't give you up for all the world, and now you're lost!

DANIEL: Don't be silly, Benjy. (*Comforting him*) We'll find him.

SAMUEL (*From a boulder on the extreme left*): Look, what's that?

BENJAMIN (*Running to peer over*): He's there! It's my little lamb! (*Scrambles over the rocks and emerges with the lamb in his arms*) Oh, Daniel, look! He's hurt! His little leg! (*The others gathered round.*)

SIMON: Here, let's bind it up. (*Tears off a strip from his coat and binds up the lamb's leg*)

BENJAMIN (*Cuddling the lamb*): There, there, Fleecy! There, there! I'll keep you warm.

DANIEL: Come on, Benjamin. We must get back to Father and the others.

BENJAMIN: But it is so long and dark. Couldn't we stay here a bit? We might not find the way. I don't mind staying out here all night now that I've found my Fleecy.

DANIEL (*Doubtfully*): Perhaps we'd better stay a bit and rest. It *is* a long way.

SAMUEL: Let's sit down here and eat some of Mother's loaves.

SIMON: And we could light a fire!

THE OTHERS: Yes! Let's! (*They go round looking for sticks and brushwood.* SAMUEL *rubs two flints together and appears to light a fire. From pouches attached to their girdles, loaves are produced. They munch happily.* BENJAMIN *gives little bits to the lamb. At this moment, a faint brightness spreads across the stage.*)

BENJAMIN: It's getting brighter now.

DANIEL: So it is.

SIMON (*Looking off left*): Why, Benjamin, I can see miles and miles—right over to Bethlehem.

SAMUEL (*Getting up and standing back, as he looks off left, shading his eyes*): Why, yes—look, all the houses seem lit up.

DANIEL: It's that bright star over there in the sky—do you see?—there. (*Pointing left*) It seems to have a light all round it.

BENJAMIN: And the light's spreading! (*There is the sound of far-off singing.*) Listen!

ALL (*In hushed voices*): Who can it be?

BENJAMIN: Daniel! I can see something in the sky. Look! Hundreds and hundreds of bright things! (*The children have all risen by now, and are looking and pointing excitedly.*)

SAMUEL: They look like people.

SIMON: Not quite like people. Something strange . . . (*The singing grows louder*) Listen!

ANGEL VOICES (*Off*): Glory to God! Glory to God! Glory to God in the Highest!

ALL: What can it mean? (*There is suddenly a brilliant light coming from the left. In this* GABRIEL *appears, a radiant figure in white. The children cry out, half falling to the ground, and shading their eyes.*)

GABRIEL (*With arm outstretched and raised*) : Fear not, for behold, I bring you good tidings of great joy, which shall be to all people. For unto you is born this day, in the city of David, a Saviour, which is Christ the Lord. And this shall be a sign unto you: Ye shall find the Babe wrapped in swaddling clothes, lying in a manger.

ANGELS (*Off*): Glory to God! Glory to God! Glory to God in the Highest! (*The voices swell to triumphant cre-

scendo, and GABRIEL *vanishes. Instantly the light dims, though it is still brighter than at the beginning of the scene.*)

BENJAMIN: He said—"a Saviour—"

SIMON: "Which is Christ the Lord!"

SAMUEL: He said, "Ye shall find the Babe—" How shall we find Him, if we don't go there?

DANIEL: Then we must go there!

BENJAMIN: But if it's the Christ, He will be a King!

DANIEL: And we have nothing to bring Him!

BENJAMIN: Nothing. (*He turns away, and seems to wrestle with himself.*)

DANIEL (*In a low voice*): We *have* got something. We've all got *one* thing we could give Him.

SIMON: I could give Him my crook—look, it's a lovely one. Father gave it to me the first night I went out with him to watch the sheep.

DANIEL: And I could give Him this coat that Sarah worked—

ALL: But you'll be cold, Daniel.

DANIEL: I don't mind. I should be proud for the Christ to have it. (*They all speak, eagerly, gathering in a little knot.* BENJAMIN *is still apart, making his big decision.*)

BENJAMIN (*Turning and joining them*): I could give Him —Fleecy. (*Exclamations from the others*)

DANIEL: But you'd never give *him* up, Benjy. You said you wouldn't for all the world!

BENJAMIN (*Simply*): But Christ the Lord *is* all the world! (*They turn, walking round the stage in file,* DANIEL *leading,* SIMON *and* SAMUEL *following behind, and* BENJAMIN *bringing up the rear with* FLEECY, *whom he frequently kisses as he walks. They sing the carol "Come, gentle shepherds, leave your flocks," and continue it off stage as the curtain slowly falls.)*

CURTAIN

* * *

SCENE 3

SETTING: *The stable at Bethlehem. The "Adeste Fideles" is sung.*

AT RISE: MARY *sits beside the manger center, in which lies the* HOLY CHILD. JOSEPH *stands on her right.*

JOSEPH: I am sorry it is such a poor place, Mary.

MARY: What does the place matter? If it is God's will that His Son should be born in a stable, who are we to question it?

JOSEPH: I should have liked you to have had a golden palace, and rich hangings of silk for the King of Kings.

MARY: Golden palaces and rich hangings of silk are for earthly kings. My Baby is King of men's hearts.

JOSEPH: But there is the smell of the farm beasts here.

MARY: God loves the farm beasts, Joseph. And tonight He has done them a great honour. His Son has come down in all His glory and been born amongst them.

JOSEPH: But this place is so cold and draughty for you, my Mary. (*Places his hand gently but reverently on her shoulder, and then pulls across one of the curtains of homespun at the side of the stage*)

MARY: What matter the cold and the draughts? (*She lifts up the* BABY, *and gazes at Him tenderly.*) My Baby Jesus is kept warm with His Mother's love. (*Looking out to the audience, as if speaking to the world*) and the love of all the little children who will learn to love Him in days to come. (*Enter, left,* GABRIEL, *followed by the* CHILDREN. *The poem, "How Far is it to Bethlehem?" could be recited here by* GABRIEL *and the* CHILDREN, *the latter miming the actions of tiptoeing in, gently touching the* BABY'S *hand, offering their gifts, which* MARY *silently accepts, placing them beside the manger.*)

DANIEL: Is this the Baby?

GABRIEL: This is the Baby. (*The* CHILDREN *stand in an awed group. Then they come forward in turn, tiptoeing, and peeping in the manger.*)

DANIEL: I have brought Him my coat.

MARY (*Taking it with a sweet smile and placing it at the foot of the manger*): That will keep Him warm.

SIMON: I have brought him my crook.

MARY: He will love a crook when He goes up on the hills. (*Places it by the manger*)

SAMUEL: I have brought Him my belt.

MARY: What a beautiful belt! How grand He will look when He wears His first tunic, with that to gird it! (*Places it beside the crook*)

BENJAMIN: I have brought Him—my lamb. (*Shyly he offers it*)

MARY: A little lamb! How Jesus will love it! He is rather like a little lamb, Himself, isn't He?

BENJAMIN (*Who has gone up to* MARY, *and now nestles lovingly against her*): Ye-es. (*More confident*) I lost him, and then I found him, and now I've brought him to Jesus.

MARY: Jesus will be so kind to the little lost lamb. He will guard it so tenderly, so that it will never stray again. (*Places the lamb in the straw of the manger*) There! Now he's safe.

BENJAMIN: There, Fleecy, now—you're safe with Jesus!

MARY: You must come and play with him sometimes, and see Jesus.

BEN (*Ecstatically, yet with awe*): And see Jesus! (*All instinctively kneel. The carol "Silent Night" is begun, as the curtain slowly falls. When it rises, the children are lying asleep round the manger, and only* MARY, JOSEPH *and* GABRIEL *keep watch as the carol is finished.*)

THE END

Sing the Songs of Christmas

by Aileen Fisher

Characters

MASTER OF CEREMONIES
PEASANT
2 WOODCARVERS
APPRENTICE WOODCARVER
FRANCIS OF ASSISI
3 SHEPHERDS
JEANETTE
ISABELLA
CHILDREN
MARTIN LUTHER
CATHERINE LUTHER
LUTHER'S SONS
LUTHER'S DAUGHTER
WAITS, *roving singers*
3 INDIAN BRAVES
3 INDIAN CHIEFS
ISAAC WATTS
JOSEPH MOHR
FRANZ GRUBER
PHILLIPS BROOKS
LEWIS REDNER
CHORUS

SETTING: *The stage is decorated gaily for Christmas.*

AT RISE: *The* CHORUS *stands upstage.* MASTER OF CEREMONIES *comes in briskly, carrying a script, and goes to a reading stand at one side.*

M.C. (*To audience*): Merry Christmas! (*To* CHORUS) Merry Christmas!

BOY IN CHORUS: In French, it's *Joyeux Noël.*

GIRL: In China, it's *Tin Hao Nian.*

BOY: In Italy, it's *Bono Natale.*

GIRL: In Germany, it's *Froeliche Weinachten.*

BOY: In Sweden, it's *God Jul.*

GIRL: In Mexico, it's *Felices Pascuas.*

M.C.: But wherever you are, however you say it, it means the same thing: Merry Christmas!

ALL: Merry Christmas! (CHORUS *begins to march around gaily, singing the first two stanzas of "Deck the Halls." As they march they throw sprigs of fir or small red paper bells around the stage. At the end of the second stanza,* M.C. *stops them.*)

M.C.: Wait a minute! Wait a minute! I'm afraid you're starting at the wrong place. "Deck the Halls" shouldn't come at the beginning of the program. You'll be getting everybody all mixed up. (*All* CHORUS *members, except one* GIRL, *go back to their places.*)

GIRL: But it's such a merry song, and we were just talking about a Merry Christmas! (*She does a little jig as she sings.*) "Fa-la-la-la-la, la-la, la-la."

M.C.: Merry, yes, but we have to have some order here, not just a jumble of carols. (*Thumbs through script*) "Deck the Halls" doesn't come until page ten.

GIRL (*Jigging again merrily*): Fa-la-la-la-la, la-la, la-la.

M.C. (*Back at stand, ignoring* GIRL): Ladies and gentlemen, a great deal of obscurity surrounds the origin of many of our favorite Christmas carols, but we are going to do our best to put them in their places. (GIRL *begins to jig again.* M.C. *gently but firmly puts her back in her place in* CHORUS, *then returns to stand.*) In the first place, people have been singing Christmas carols for hundreds and hundreds of years. Let's go back to 1223 A.D., more than seven hundred years ago. It is Christmastide in Assisi, a town in central Italy. The day is cool, but fair, with a gleaming jewel of sun in a clear sky. A peasant approaches, carrying a queer wooden box and a bundle of hay. (PEASANT *enters with box and hay, looks around curiously, puts down box and shrugs.*) Something is obviously wrong. He doesn't seem to know what he is here for. Well, here comes a woodcarver. Perhaps he will know. (1st Woodcarver *enters. He carries wooden figures of animals. He looks around.*)

1st Woodcarver: Is this the place?

Peasant (*Shrugging*): Each man has his own place, so they say. What place do you mean?

1st Woodcarver: I was told to come to the edge of town near a certain olive tree.

Peasant: Here's an olive tree, that's certain. What have you there?

1st Woodcarver: An ox, an ass and three sheep, carved of wood and painted according to instructions.

Peasant: You, too, had instructions?

1st Woodcarver (*Nodding*): From Brother Francis. (*Looks at* Peasant's *box and hay*) But I am afraid I do not perceive the meaning of *your* instructions. A box of hay?

Peasant: Box, indeed! Have you never seen a manger?

1st Woodcarver: Oh, a manger. *One* manger for an ox, an ass, and three sheep? I do not understand.

M.C.: Now, a second woodcarver approaches. He recognizes the first. (2nd Woodcarver *comes in briskly, carrying wooden figures.*)

2nd Woodcarver: Good morrow to you. Where is Brother Francis?

1st Woodcarver: Who can say?

2nd Woodcarver: I can say I'd like to know the meaning of all this. Hay. A wooden box. Animals of wood. And my carved figures.

Peasant: What figures?

2nd Woodcarver: A middle-aged man, a young mother, and a child. At first I hesitated to carve the child. "Such a child as the Christ Child might have been," Brother Francis instructed me. How could I carve such a child? How would a stern Judge who fills us with fear and awe look as a child, I wondered. Ah, it was as if Brother Francis read my thoughts.

1st Woodcarver: How's that?

2nd Woodcarver: "Not a Judge!" he told me. "People think of Christ wrongly. I must show them they are mistaken. He is not a dreaded Judge. He is a friendly, loving child. Can you carve him so?" (Apprentice Woodcarver, *carrying other figures, enters, and stands listening.*) So I carved a smiling child, like my own son in the cradle! So! (*Holds up figure. Sees* Apprentice Woodcarver.) Who are you?

Apprentice Woodcarver: I am an apprentice woodcarver. My master is ill. He was unable to bring the three kings to the appointed place. (*Puts kings down, takes angels from pocket*) And the angels. (*Somewhat embarrassed*) Brother Francis asked me, a mere apprentice, if I could carve angels. Are they all right?

1st Woodcarver (*Appraisingly*): A little small, I should say.

2nd Woodcarver: On the contrary, not small enough.

Peasant: Here comes Brother Francis. He will know what is large enough and small enough! (Francis of Assisi *enters joyously.*)

Francis: So you are all here, brothers. Ah! I see you have brought what I asked. Now I can teach the people what they must be taught, and in a simple way. I can teach that Christ is not a stern Judge, but a little Child to be loved. (*Bends over box*) The manger is just as I wanted it—not too fine and fancy. (*Puts in some hay*)

Peasant (*Awed*): The Christ is not to be feared, you say?

Francis: No, no. He is to be loved. Here you see the whole story. (*Gestures at manger and figures*) We shall carry the story into the church and light it with candles, so everyone in Assisi can see.

1st Woodcarver: See what, Brother Francis?

FRANCIS (*Laughing*): You do not understand? Then watch me. (*He begins to set up the creche.*) Here is the manger in Bethlehem, the city of David, where Joseph, who was of the house of David, went to be taxed. Here, brothers, are the humble, friendly beasts in the stable, giving of their warmth that winter night so long ago. (*Places animals around the manger*) This is the little donkey Mary rode from Nazareth, she being great with child. Blessed Mary! (*Places her near the manger*) "And she brought forth her first-born son, and wrapped him in swaddling clothes, and laid him in a manger, because there was no room for them in the inn."

PEASANT: Now I see the need for the manger! And hay for the bed!

FRANCIS: "And there were shepherds in the same district living in the fields and keeping watch over their flock by night." (*To* 1ST WOODCARVER) Your cloak will make an excellent field, brother, being of such a good earthy color. (*Puts cloak to one side, places shepherds on it*) "And behold, an angel of the Lord stood by them . . ."

APPRENTICE (*Holding out angel*): Here is the angel, Brother Francis. Is it too small? Or too large, perhaps?

FRANCIS: Just right, my boy! (*Places angel near shepherds*) "And the glory of the Lord shone round about them."

2ND WOODCARVER: The candles in the church are like the glory of the Lord.

APPRENTICE WOODCARVER (*Intent on the story*): The shepherds were afraid. But the angel told them not to fear, didn't he, Brother Francis?

FRANCIS (*Nodding*): "Behold," he said. "I bring you news of great joy, which shall be to all people. For today in the town of David a Saviour has been born to you, who is Christ the Lord. You shall find Him wrapped in swaddling clothes, lying in a manger."

PEASANT: Aye, a manger.

FRANCIS: "And suddenly, there was with the angel, a multitude of the heavenly host praising God . . ." Come, brothers, we must praise God. We must circle around the manger of God's Son and sing our praises. Christmas is a time of joy, brothers! Christmas is a time for singing. Come, join hands, and sing for the Christ Child in the manger on the holy eve of Christmas. Sing with joy! (*They join hands and circle around the creche singing "Angels We Have Heard on High."*)

PEASANT, WOODCARVERS, FRANCIS: "Angels we have heard on high,
Sweetly singing o'er the plains," etc.

CHORUS (*Joining in*): "Gloria," etc.

PEASANT, WOODCARVERS, FRANCIS (*Circling the creche as they sing*): "Shepherds, why this jubilee," etc.

CHORUS: "Gloria," etc. (PEASANT, WOODCARVERS *and* FRANCIS *begin to move the creche to back center stage where it will be out of sight behind* CHORUS. CHORUS *parts, standing on both sides temporarily.*) "Come to Bethlehem and see
Him whose birth the angels sing"; etc. (*If the creche has not been completely moved by the end of the third stanza,* CHORUS *sings fourth stanza, "See Him in a manger laid."* PEASANT, WOODCARVERS *and* FRANCIS *exit behind* CHORUS.)

M.C.: That was the beginning of Christmas caroling, more than seven hundred years ago—the singing for joy around the first creche of St. Francis of Assisi! That was the beginning. After St. Francis made religion more human by his little drama of the story of the nativity, special Christmas songs sprang up among the people. In many places in Italy, peasants and shepherds came down out of the hills at Christmas time, to sing and play their pipes in the villages. Townsfolk who wished to celebrate Christmas would place a wooden spoon outside their door as a signal. (BOY *from* CHORUS *puts out a wooden spoon. In a moment* THREE SHEPHERDS, *rather frightened, come running in.*)

1ST SHEPHERD: What a woman!

2ND SHEPHERD: Chasing us down the road like that with a stick!

3RD SHEPHERD: Wake her baby, indeed! With our singing? As if her baby wouldn't be lulled to sleep by our singing!

1ST SHEPHERD: Aye. (*Sees spoon*) Look, a spoon. (*Looks back toward wings*) Is it safe? Has she gone? (*Picks up spoon, uses it for baton*) Come, lads, let's give them a song of rejoicing. "O Come, O Come, Emmanuel."

THREE SHEPHERDS: O come, O come, Emmanuel,
And ransom captive Israel," etc.
(SHEPHERDS *move out at the end of two or three stanzas, taking the spoon with them.*)

M.C.: Rejoice! Rejoice in other countries, too, as well as in Italy. In France, too, songs were being sung to celebrate the Christ Child's birthday. Noël, they called it. Noël for the Christmas birthday! Joyeux Noël! And we still sing one of the shepherd carols of medieval France, "The First Nowell."

BOYS IN CHORUS: "The first Nowell the angel did say," etc.

CHORUS: "Nowell, Nowell," etc.

BOYS IN CHORUS: "Then let us all with one accord," etc.

CHORUS: "Nowell, Nowell," etc. (*All five stanzas of "The First Nowell" may be used if desired. During the last chorus, several* CHILDREN *carrying flashlight torches hurry across the stage.*)

M.C.: What was that? Lights? Torches? Yes, of course. We are still in France in the middle ages. We are in Provence, in southeastern France, at Christmas time. There must be a creche for Christmas Eve in Provence. (CHORUS *parts, so creche shows.*)

GIRL IN CHORUS (*Calling out*): "Torches here, Jeanette, Isabella! Torches here to His cradle run!" (JEANETTE *and* ISABELLA, *followed by other* CHILDREN, *come running in again with lights. They stand near the creche to light it while singing "Bring a Torch, Jeanette, Isabella."*)

GIRL IN CHORUS: "This is Jesus, good folk of the village, Christ is born, 'tis Mary calling."

JEANETTE, ISABELLA *and* CHORUS (*Loudly, crowding to look*): "Ah! Ah! What a lovely mother! Ah! Ah! What a lovely Child!"

GIRL IN CHORUS (*Shushing them*): "Wrong it is, when the Baby is sleeping,
Wrong it is to shout so loud."
(OTHERS, *chagrined, shrink back*)

GIRL IN CHORUS: "Now you there, and you others, be quiet!
For at a sound our Jesus wakens."

JEANETTE: Hush!

ISABELLA: Hush!

CHORUS: "He is sleeping so soundly.
Hush! Hush! Hush! Do but see Him sleep!"
(*All look at the creche. Softly* CHORUS *begins to sing the stanza beginning "Softly now in the narrow stable . . ."* JEANETTE, ISABELLA *and* CHILDREN *who followed them take a final look, then tiptoe out with their torches as* CHORUS *finishes the song. A* GIRL *comes back quietly and stands looking at creche, her curiosity mixed with awe. She begins to sing "What Child Is This?"*)

GIRL: "What Child is this, who, laid to rest,
On Mary's lap is sleeping?
Whom angels greet with anthems sweet,
While shepherds watch are keeping?"

CHORUS: "This, this is Christ the King," etc.

GIRL: "Why lies He in such mean estate,
Where ox and ass are feeding?"

CHORUS: "Good Christian, fear," etc.

GIRL (*Speaking*): The Babe, the Son of Mary!

CHORUS: "So bring Him incense, gold and myrrh," etc. (GIRL *goes out behind* CHORUS *as* CHORUS *closes in front of creche.*)

M.C.: "Joy, joy, for Christ is born!" Joy—and rejoice—those are the words for Christmas, over and over again. Good Christian men, rejoice! That takes us to Germany. "Good Christian Men, Rejoice" is a German carol of the middle ages. At that time, half of it was written in German and half in Latin, but for more than four hundred years we have been singing it in English. Rejoice, good Christian men, at Christmas time!

CHORUS: "Good Christian men, rejoice
With heart and soul and voice," etc. (*At least two stanzas more if desired*)

M.C.: Good Christian men in Germany were the first to rejoice around a Christmas tree, as the Italians were the first to rejoice around a creche. It may be just a legend, but a famous German pastor, Martin Luther, is credited with bringing home the first Christmas tree. He also wrote several Christmas songs. (CHORUS *begins to hum very softly, "Away in a Manger" as background.*) It is a snowy Christmas Eve in the 1530's. Martin Luther is walking home through the woods, thinking of the comfort of home ahead, yet not unmindful of the beauty around him. He sees stars caught in the branches of the fir trees. He thinks of the star that shone down on a stable in Bethlehem on just such a sparkling night many years ago. Why, he thought, can we not bring some of the light into a home on Christmas Eve? Eagerly, he cuts a small fir tree by the roadside and hurries home.

(LUTHER *comes in with fir tree.* CHORUS *stops humming.*)

LUTHER: Wife! Wife! My dear Catherine, see here!

CATHERINE (*Stepping from* CHORUS): Sh, Martin. You will wake the children.

LUTHER: Wake the children! Yes, indeed by all means, I will wake the children, so they may see, too.

CATHERINE: See what?

LUTHER: The glory of Christmas Eve! The light of the star! The light of the Christ Child! (*He sets the tree in a pot or stand.*) Have you some small candles, my dear Catherine, so we can bring the starry heavens right into the house?

CATHERINE: Candles for stars? Why, yes. I made some little candles from the last beeswax.

LUTHER: Let us tie them to the tree! (CATHERINE *starts out for candles.*) And one candle larger than the rest, even as the star of Bethlehem dominated the heavens that night. (*She goes, he admires the tree. She returns with a string of white lights.* LUTHER *and* CATHERINE *put the lights on the tree, with one larger light near the top.*) Under the tree we must arrange the manger scene. Stars above to light the heavens, and Jesus below to light the world!

CATHERINE (*Excited*): How did you ever think of it?

LUTHER: Walking through the woods, meditating on the nativity. (*They finish lights, then arrange the manger scene.* CHORUS *parts so they can arrange it.*) Now call the children, Catherine! (*He continues to work on the creche while* CATHERINE *goes to get their* SONS *and* DAUGHTER, *who are very sleepy. They are awed by the lighted tree, and are quickly awake.*)

1ST SON: Where did the shining tree come from?

DAUGHTER: What is it, Father?

2ND SON: It shines like stars in the night.

LUTHER: Do you hear, Catherine? Like stars in the night.

1st Son (*Looking at manger scene*): I know. You have brought in the stars to shine above the Christ Child's head on his birthday!

Daughter: A birthday tree.

1st Son: A Christmas tree. (*They join hands and circle around the tree singing "The Christmas Tree."*)

Daughter: Now we must sing your song, Father, the one you wrote for us. (*She begins to sing "From Heaven High."*)

"From heaven high I come to you
To bring you tidings strange and true.

Sons (*Joining in*): "Glad tidings of great joy I bring
Whereof I now will say and sing."

Luther *and* Catherine (*Joining in*): "To you this night is born a child
Of Mary, chosen Mother mild," etc.

(Chorus *joins in, marching slowly around stage to give the* Luthers *a chance to replace creche and go out with the Christmas tree.*)

Chorus: "Glory to God in highest heaven,
Who unto us His Son hath given!" (Chorus *may repeat a stanza to give plenty of time for* Luthers *to exit.* Catherine *rejoins* Chorus.)

M.C.: Carols from Italy, carols from England, carols from France and Germany. (Girl *steps out from* Chorus.)

Girl: What about America? Didn't we make up any carols of our own?

M.C.: Yes, but first we must go back to England.

Girl: Back to England?

M.C.: We must go back to Elizabethan England, always remembering that England gave us most of our Christmas carols.

Girl (*Jigging*): "Fa-la-la-la-la, la-la, la-la."

M.C.: As a matter of fact, "Deck the Halls" is an old Welsh carol, full of the spirit of England under the first

Queen Elizabeth. In England, as time went on, Christmas became more and more a great festival of merry-making. The halls of the lords were decked with holly.

CHORUS (*Singing*): "Deck the halls with boughs of holly," etc., to end of first stanza. (GIRL *jigs on the refrain*)

M.C.: Elizabethan England was gay with feasting and singing and games and wassailing at Christmas time. Masked actors called *mummers* presented pantomimes. Roving bands of singers called *waits* went about the streets singing Christmas carols, and hoping to be paid for their efforts. (*A group of* WAITS *come in. They are gaily singing "Wassail Song." They turn toward the audience.*)

WAITS: "Here we go a-wassailing
Among the leaves of green," etc. (*Turning to* CHORUS, *holding out little leather purses*)
"We have got a little purse
Of stretching leather skin," etc. (WAITS *gather a few coins and replace purses.*)
"Bring us out a table,
And spread it with a cloth," etc. (*They pantomime hungrily.*)
"Good Master and Good Mistress,
While you sit by the fire," etc. (WAITS *go out, annoyed that they haven't been treated better.*)

M.C.: Christmas in old England! The Yule log—roast goose—plum pudding—singers in the streets—holly and ivy!

GIRL: *Now* do we go to America? To jolly young America?

M.C.: Just a minute! In the early days Christmas was anything but jolly in America.

GIRL: Anything but jolly?

M.C.: The Puritans were opposed to such frivolous sport as singing carols. Early New England colonists even forbade the celebration of Christmas. In 1644, the Puritans declared December 25th to be a market day instead of a holiday, and forbade anyone to have plum pudding or mince pie. Later, they even fined anyone who stopped work or feasted on Christmas Day.

GIRL: So we didn't have any carols in the early days? Or any holiday? Or any mince pie?

M.C.: That's right. But strangely enough, about that very time, the first American carol was born. Not in New England. In New France. The time is around 1640. Father Jean de Brebeuf, Jesuit missionary to the Huron Indians on the neck of land between Lake Huron, Lake Erie, and Lake Ontario, is rehearsing a group of Indians for the celebration of Christmas just a few days off. He has composed a carol for them in their own language. But he has no organ. The Indians have only tom-toms and rattles. So Father Brebeuf used words that would fit a tom-tom accompaniment. Here is the English translation. (*Several members of the* CHORUS *begin to beat muted drums to the rhythm of "God Rest You Merry, Gentlemen." A* BOY *who has slipped on an Indian headdress steps from* CHORUS *to chant words of the carol.*)

BOY: " 'Twas in the moon of wintertime,
When all the birds had fled,
That mighty Gitchi Manitou
Sent angel choirs instead.
Before their light the stars grew dim,
And hunters heard the hymn:

CHORUS (*Joining chant*): "Jesus, your King, is born;
Jesus is born,
In Excelsis Gloria!" (*Several* INDIAN BRAVES *with bows and arrows come in from wings. They kneel in reverence.*)

1ST INDIAN BRAVE: "In the lodge of broken bark
The tender babe was found;

A ragged robe of rabbit skin
Enwrapped his beauty round.
And as the hunter braves drew nigh,
The angel song rang high:

CHORUS (*Joining chant*): "Jesus, your King, is born;
Jesus is born,
In Excelsis Gloria!" (3 INDIAN CHIEFS *come in from wings. They carry pelts, and kneel and offer their gifts.*)

2ND INDIAN BRAVE: "Earliest moon of wintertime
Is not so round and fair
As was the ring of glory
On the helpless infant there,
While chiefs from far before him knelt
With gifts of beaver pelt."

CHORUS: "Jesus, your King, is born," etc.

3RD INDIAN BRAVE: "The children of the forest free,
O sons of Manitou,
The Holy Child of earth and heaven
Is born today for you.
Come kneel before the radiant boy
Who brings you peace and joy:

CHORUS: "Jesus, your King, is born;
Jesus is born,
In Excelsis Gloria!" (CHORUS *repeats chorus as* INDIANS *exit.*)

M.C.: The first American Christmas carol! Few of us have ever heard it sung. The Christ Child in a bark lodge instead of in a manger! Wrapped in a rabbit skin instead of swaddling clothes! Wandering hunters instead of shepherds hearing the angel choir! Indian chiefs coming from afar with their gifts of fox and beaver skins, instead of three Wise Men with gold, frankincense and myrrh! Christmas in the New World!

As America was settled, of course, the Puritans were

outvoted. Carols from the "old country" came over with the settlers, and Christmas became a joyous occasion up and down the Atlantic seaboard.

Meanwhile, the English produced another famous Christmas carol. It was written by the great English hymn writer of the eighteenth century, Isaac Watts. He was working on a book, telling the psalms of David in his own words, when his inspiration came. He was reading the 98th Psalm. (ISAAC WATTS *enters with Bible, reads aloud.*)

WATTS: "Make a joyful noise unto the Lord, all the earth: make a loud noise, and rejoice, and sing praise. Sing unto the Lord with the harp; with the harp, and the voice of a psalm. For he cometh to judge the earth; with righteousness shall he judge the world, and the people with equity." (*Looks up*) Make a joyful noise, for he cometh! What a test for a song! A Christmas song of joy. (*Hums*) Joy to the world! The Lord is come—

CHORUS (*Taking up carol, "Joy to the World"*): "Let earth receive her King," etc.

WATTS (*Singing second stanza as solo*): "Joy to the world! The Saviour reigns," etc.

CHORUS (*Singing third stanza as* WATTS *goes out*): "He rules the world with truth and grace," etc.

M.C.: Carols from Italy, carols from France, carols from England and Germany! But we have to go to Austria for one of the most beloved carols of all. (GIRL *steps out from* CHORUS *and starts to jig.*)

GIRL: To Austria we go! Fa-la-la-la-la, la-la, la-la. (*Others pull her back.*)

M.C.: We go to the little town of Obendorf in the Austrian Alps. It is a sparkling cold night, just before Christmas, 1818. The mountains are covered with snow, the air is clear, almost brittle, the sky bright with stars. Joseph Mohr, 26-year-old vicar of the little church, is hurrying down the village street to call on his friend Franz Gruber, the schoolmaster, who plays the organ at church. Father Mohr has a piece of paper in his pocket to show the schoolmaster-organist. Now he is at his friend's door. Now he is ushered into the house, to warm himself at the stove. (FATHER MOHR *and* FRANZ GRUBER *enter*.)

GRUBER: A cold night to be abroad, Father.

MOHR: But calm and bright. I was struck by the brightness when I returned to my room after meeting with the children of the parish. (*Smiles*) The same children you know and teach, my dear Franz.

GRUBER: Ach, and their minds full of nothing but Christmas!

MOHR: I am afraid that is the state of my mind, too. Soon we shall be celebrating the nativity. My thoughts were full of it as I walked home. I wished for some new way to celebrate, something a little different for the boys to sing in church on Christmas eve. (*He takes the paper from his pocket, thrusts it at* GRUBER.) Here, tell me what you think, Franz, as a schoolmaster and organist, not as a friend who might be prejudiced.

GRUBER (*Reading aloud*): "Silent night! Holy night!
All is calm, all is bright . . ." (*He reads in silence for a moment, then looks up excitedly.*) Why, it is beautiful, Father. Where did it come from?

MOHR: I—well, I wrote it. Do you think the words could make a song, Franz?

GRUBER: Yes, yes. Indeed, yes. (*Looks at words, beats time to imaginary tune.*)

MOHR (*Urgently*): Can you do it, Franz? You can play the organ, you have instruction in music. Can you set it to music right away, for the Christmas celebration? I know there is little time, but will you try?

GRUBER: I will try. (*Looks at words again, becomes absorbed.* FATHER MOHR *smiles and tiptoes out.*)

M.C.: Franz Gruber, the 29-year-old schoolmaster, wrote music for the vicar's words, but when he went to try the song on the organ, the organ refused to play. It was old and there were mice in it! Still, Father Mohr must have his new song for the Christmas festivities. So the schoolmaster taught the children to sing the song with only a guitar for accompaniment. (GRUBER *turns to* CHORUS *and directs the singing of "Silent Night," either a capella or with only a guitar accompaniment.*)

SOLO BOY: "Silent night, holy night,
All is calm, all is bright
Round yon Virgin Mother and Child,

CHORUS (*Softly*): "Holy Infant so tender and mild,
Sleep in heavenly peace,
Sleep in heavenly peace."

(*Second and third stanzas also should be sung with solo parts and* CHORUS. *During the last chorus,* GRUBER *exits.*)

M.C.: Gradually, Father Mohr's wonderful song spread through Austria and Germany. It became popular wherever it was heard. In 1833, twenty-five years after it was written, "Silent Night" was sung at a Christmas concert in Leipzig. From that time its fame was assured. Now it belongs to the world!

Carols have come from Christians of all nationalities and races—from the Czechs, the Chinese, the Croatians; from the Scandinavians, the Sicilians, the Poles; from the Puerto Ricans, the Russians, and even from Negro slaves in the United States before the Civil War. Here is one of the carols the slaves gave us:

BOY (*Swinging into "Rise Up, Shepherd, and Follow"*):
"There's a star in the East on Christmas morn,"

CHORUS: "Rise up, shepherd, and follow." (*Throughout*

the spiritual, CHORUS *comes in only on "Rise up, shepherd, and follow."* BOY *carries the other lines.*)

M.C.: And now here is a strange coincidence. In Austria, Father Mohr and his church organist produced "Silent Night" as something different for the children of the parish to sing for Christmas. Fifty years later, an Episcopalian rector in Philadelphia and his organist composed a new carol for the children of *their* Sunday School to sing as something different. The song was as speedily written and as speedily set to music as was "Silent Night." It, too, became world famous. The American rector's name was Phillips Brooks; his organist was Lewis Redner. (BROOKS *and* REDNER *enter.*)

REDNER: A cold night to be abroad, isn't it, sir?

BROOKS: But calm and bright, Redner. As I walked home from the meeting at the church, I was struck by the brightness. On just such a night three years ago, I was in the Holy Land. I will never forget it. I was riding horseback from Jerusalem to Bethlehem, following the stars.

REDNER: How does Bethlehem look by starlight? I've often wondered.

BROOKS: It's on a hill, you know. Just five miles from Jerusalem. By day it isn't much of a town, but at night —(*Takes paper from pocket*) Redner, you know I have been wishing for some new way to celebrate Christmas this year, something a little different for the children to sing. (*Holds out paper*) Here, tell me what you think of this. Do you see anything in it?

REDNER (*Taking paper, reading aloud*):

"O little town of Bethlehem,
How still we see thee lie!
Above thy deep and dreamless sleep
The silent stars go by;
Yet in thy dark streets shineth

The everlasting Light . . ." (*Looks up*) Where did you you find it?

BROOKS: I wrote it. Perhaps I should say it wrote itself, out of my memories. Do you think it would make a song?

REDNER: I should say it would! (*Studies words, drumming rhythm*)

BROOKS: Will you do it, Redner? Will you set it to music right away? I know there isn't much time. This is Saturday evening. Tomorrow is the last day of Sunday School before Christmas.

REDNER: I will try. A tune is opening up already. (*He is engrossed with the paper.* BROOKS *smiles and tiptoes out.*)

M.C.: Sure enough, the church organist had his rector's words set to music in time for Sunday School the next morning, and the song has been heard at Christmas time ever since. (REDNER *directs* CHORUS *in "O Little Town of Bethlehem," all four stanzas if desired. At the end of the song, he joins* CHORUS.) Hundreds of Christmas songs and carols have been written over the centuries. We couldn't begin to sing them all on one program, but we still have time for one of the oldest and most famous of all Christmas songs. The tune is attributed to St. Bonaventura, who lived in the thirteenth century. The song has been translated into more than a hundred languages and dialects, and every year it is sung in Christian churches throughout the world. "Adeste Fidelis—O Come All Ye Faithful."

CHORUS: "O come, all ye faithful, joyful and triumphant"; etc. (M.C. *gestures for audience to join in.* CHORUS *and audience sing at least two stanzas.*)

THE END

Holiday for Santa

by Jessie Nicholson

Characters

SANTA CLAUS
MRS. CLAUS
SANTA CLAUS' HELPERS
WHOLE WIDE WORLD
BOYS *and* GIRLS

SCENE 1

TIME: *Christmas Eve.*

SETTING: SANTA CLAUS' *shop, which consists of nothing more than a backdrop upon which are painted shelves filled with toys and a clock with the hands pointing to midnight. In the center of the drop is a pot-bellied stove.*

AT RISE: SANTA CLAUS *is taking his ease in a rocking chair, pipe in mouth, red-and-white-stockinged feet resting on the side fender of the stove.* MRS. CLAUS, *who is plump and pink-cheeked with pretty white hair, is busily sweeping the floor.*

SANTA CLAUS (*Wriggling his toes*): Ho, hum! My poor old feet are almost numb. I fear that the cold up here at the North Pole is getting too much for my ancient bones! (MRS. CLAUS *regards him unsympathetically over the top of her spectacles.*)

MRS. CLAUS: Tish, tush! The same old gush. I hear it

straight through from dawn till dusk. Right before Christmas you begin feeling sorry for yourself. If it isn't one thing, it's another you're complaining of. Cold feet, stiff neck, cramps in your legs, ringing in your ears. It's a blessed wonder you don't try to tell me the reindeer are laid up with the stomach-ache!

SANTA CLAUS: As a matter of fact, my dear, Donder did refuse his breakfast this morning, and Blitzen—

MRS. CLAUS: Stop right there! I've heard enough. Excuses, excuses, excuses. Anything to get out of your job on Christmas Eve, or so you pretend, just because you like to have something to grumble about, you old sly boots. (*Smiling at him indulgently*) Why, you know you wouldn't miss making your rounds for all the warm fires and rocking chairs in the whole wide world.

SANTA CLAUS (*Grumpily*): That's what you think. Why, if I had my way, I'd take a long winter's nap like the grizzly bear and not wake up till spring! (*Rubbing his back*) Oh, my aches and pains! (*He groans.*)

MRS. CLAUS: A pretty kettle of fish that would be, I must say. What would the children all over the world do without you?

SANTA CLAUS (*Eagerly*): That's just the point. I have so many helpers these days, I'd never be missed. They're on every street corner and in every department store.

MRS. CLAUS (*Severely*): Not one of them has been trained to go up and down chimneys! You never would let anyone do that but yourself.

SANTA CLAUS (*Virtuously*): I didn't want any of them to get hurt.

MRS. CLAUS: You mean it's a secret you can't bear to part with.

SANTA CLAUS (*Uneasily*): Well, no matter—the children won't care, as long as they get their presents, whether

Santa comes down the chimney or through the cellar window.

MRS. CLAUS (*Sadly*): Do you really believe that?

SANTA CLAUS (*Bluffly*): I certainly do, my dear, and this is as good a year as any to prove it. Hurrah for all my jolly helpers! In fact (*Chuckling*), I think I'll write a letter to them myself and tell them what I would like to find in *my* stocking. Please fetch me a pen and paper, Mama. I feel too old and feeble to even rise from my chair. (*Shaking her head,* MRS. CLAUS *exits right.* SANTA CLAUS *begins to whistle "Jingle Bells," jumps up from his chair and does a little jig in his stockinged feet. He hastily resumes his seat again as* MRS. CLAUS *returns with the writing materials. She continues her sweeping with short, impatient whisks of the broom, watching* SANTA CLAUS *out of the corner of her eye. He has moved his chair forward, facing audience.*) Hm! Now let's see! Shall I address this letter to my helpers, or to myself, or just *to whom it may concern?*

MRS. CLAUS (*Crossly*): It concerns the whole wide world when Santa Claus lies down on his job.

SANTA CLAUS: I'm not lying down on the job, Mama. I'm just in need of a well-earned rest. Which gives me an idea! (*He writes, reading aloud as he progresses.*) "Dear Whole Wide World, How about giving Santa a break? I have been filling your stockings for so many years, while mine always remain empty—except for my feet, of course. I shan't ask for much, just a nice little trip to Florida this Christmas Eve."

MRS. CLAUS (*Shocked*): A trip to Florida on Christmas Eve!

SANTA CLAUS (*Firmly*): "A trip to Florida on Christmas Eve and a new bathing suit, size—size—(*Looking down at his girth*) size five by five should do it, I guess."

MRS. CLAUS: Santa Claus in a bathing suit! Ridiculous!

SANTA CLAUS: "And, dear Whole Wide World, that is just about all I want (*Slyly*), unless you might add a few bathing beauties along the beach—just to improve the scenery, of course!"

MRS. CLAUS (*Indignantly*): Well, I never! (*Then muttering*) This is the last straw—bathing beauties, indeed! I see I shall have to take things into my own hands. (*She reaches into wings at right downstage, as if into a closet, and draws out first a shawl and then a bonnet which she dons hurriedly. She exits left with a flounce.*)

SANTA CLAUS (*Beginning to sing dreamily*): By the sea, by the sea, by the beautiful sea—(*His head nods and he dozes off, noisily. Enter his* HELPERS, *with their packs slung over their shoulders.*)

1ST HELPER (*Dismayed*): Look at him! Here it is time to start, and he's sound asleep!

2ND HELPER: Don't just look! Listen! (SANTA CLAUS *snores loudly.*)

3RD HELPER: It sounds like the trumpeting of an elephant in the jungle!

4TH HELPER: And you know how hard it is to awaken a sleeping elephant.

5TH HELPER: If Mrs. Claus were here, she'd make short work of it.

6TH HELPER: Here's a note in his hand. Let's see what it has to say. (*He takes letter out of* SANTA CLAUS' *hand. Everybody tries to have a look at it over his shoulder.*)

1ST HELPER: It's addressed to Whole Wide World. It's not polite to read other people's mail.

6TH HELPER (*Loftily*): This is an emergency, and in an emergency one is entitled to be nosey. (*He proceeds to read letter aloud hurriedly before anyone can stop him.*)

1ST HELPER: A trip to Florida!

2ND HELPER: A new bathing suit!

3RD HELPER: Bathing beauties!

4TH HELPER: Oh, no, he doesn't want much—not much!

6TH HELPER: It's no affair of ours. After all, the letter *is* addressed to the Whole Wide World.

1ST HELPER (*Reminding him*): But this is an emergency! We *must* do something about it. I'll just give Whole Wide World a buzz and then we can go into conference. (*He leans out into wings, left.*) Hey, you out there! Whole Wide World! Can you pop in for a minute? We have a letter for you.

2ND HELPER (*Looking over his shoulder anxiously*): Do you think he can make it?

1ST HELPER: You go outside and push, and I'll pull. (2ND HELPER *exits and after a bit of a struggle they get* WHOLE WIDE WORLD *on stage. He is outfitted in a pair of huge, round placards, front and back, with a map of the world encircling them.*)

WHOLE WIDE WORLD (*Huffing and puffing*): Oh, my states and counties! That was a close shave! (*Peering down at himself*) You fellows very nearly squeezed Florida right off the map!

3RD HELPER: We could have called it The Great Orange Squeeze! (*Laughing uproariously at his own joke.*)

WHOLE WIDE WORLD (*Grumpily*): It is no laughing matter. After all, where do you think all the oranges come from that Santa Claus puts in good children's stockings?

1ST HELPER: With Florida off the map, our problem would be solved, anyway. Santa would have had to stay at the North Pole and attend to business. (*He hands the letter to* WHOLE WIDE WORLD *who reads it to himself with growing alarm.*)

WHOLE WIDE WORLD (*Sputtering*): Why, this is outrageous, fantastic, ridiculous, monstrous, silly and—and—(*Weakly*) just can't be done.

HELPERS (*Cheering*): Hurrah! Can't be done!

WHOLE WIDE WORLD (*Glowering at them*): What do you mean—can't be done? It has to be done. If old Claus doesn't get what he asks for, he may not believe in the Christmas Spirit any more!

2ND HELPER (*Shocked*): Not believe in the Christmas Spirit!

3RD HELPER: Why, that's practically the same thing as not believing in Santa Claus!

4TH HELPER: You know what he thinks about children who say they don't believe in him.

5TH HELPER: And grown-ups, too!

6TH HELPER (*Anxiously*): This could upset the whole wide world!

WHOLE WIDE WORLD (*Wiping away a tear*): Every year I am refreshed and renewed by the Christmas Spirit. Without it, I would become cold and bleak and a selfish place in which to live.

1ST HELPER (*Firmly*): At all costs we must prevent Whole Wide World from becoming cold and bleak and a selfish place in which to live. Santa Claus *must* have his trip to Florida.

2ND HELPER (*Bravely*): We must carry on for him as he would expect us to. Up and down chimneys, over snow-covered roofs, through the midnight sky on wings of night!

3RD HELPER (*Sarcastically*): In Santa's sleigh, don't you mean?

2ND HELPER: Do you think the reindeer will do our bidding?

4TH HELPER (*Quoting*): "Now Dasher, now Dancer!
Now Prancer and Vixen!
On Comet, on Cupid!
On Donder and Blitzen!

5TH HELPER (*Excitedly*): To the top of the porch!
To the top of the wall!

Now dash away! Dash away!
Dash away all!"

6TH HELPER: It quite takes my breath away just thinking about it!

1ST HELPER (*Dubiously*): There is only one thing that is troubling me. Going down the chimney is all very well, but how does one get back up again? Santa Claus would never tell us his secret method. (*Wrinkling his brow*) I can't figure out whether it is a problem in algebra or geometry.

2ND HELPER: Or maybe even in trigonometry.

WHOLE WIDE WORLD: Pooh, pooh, pooh! Your problems are nothing compared to mine. Number one—transportation for Santa Claus. With that weight on my back (*Pointing to* SANTA CLAUS) I'd never make it as far as Connecticut. Number two—where am I ever going to find a bathing suit big enough to fit him? Now there is a real mathematical problem!

3RD HELPER: Besides that, he's likely to catch his death of cold, changing from his red woollies in the middle of winter!

4TH HELPER (*Disgustedly*): This discussion could go on all night. We'd better do something about it, and do it fast.

5TH HELPER: Let's go into a huddle. That's the way football players solve all their problems. (HELPERS *hurriedly form a huddle near exit* MRS. CLAUS *has taken.* WHOLE WIDE WORLD *hops about anxiously, unable to squeeze in. When huddle breaks,* MRS. CLAUS *is discovered standing in the center, straightening her shawl and setting her bonnet aright. She carries a large knitting bag.*)

WHOLE WIDE WORLD (*Scratching his head in bewilderment*): So this is what happens in huddles. I never did understand how they worked.

1ST HELPER: Hurrah for Mrs. Claus!

2ND HELPER: She'll get us out of our muddle in short order.

MRS. CLAUS (*In great annoyance*): What's all this talk of huddles and muddles? Why aren't you busy getting the sleigh filled, instead of playing at games? (HELPERS *hustle about, pretending to fill their packs from shelves on backdrop.*)

WHOLE WIDE WORLD (*Tearing his hair*): What about me? Where do I come in?

MRS. CLAUS (*Severely*): You don't come in. You go out. I shall attend to Santa Claus' needs myself.

1ST HELPER (*Pausing in his work*): Without upsetting Whole Wide World? (MRS. CLAUS *has removed her bonnet and shawl and put them back in the same way that she got them, from wings, right, downstage.*)

MRS. CLAUS: Without upsetting anybody but me. I've had a lot of trouble, I can tell you. (*She leans out into the wings and calls.*) Come in, children. (*A group of laughing* BOYS *and* GIRLS *come on stage, pushing a backdrop across stage in front of previous scene, children standing at either end supporting it, as* HELPERS *scuttle out of the way. On the drop is painted a sandy beach, blue sky and water with a bright sun shining and a couple of palm trees in the background. All crowd around admiring it.*)

WHOLE WIDE WORLD: Oh, my canals and waterways! It's as real as real! Santa Claus will surely be fooled. (SANTA CLAUS *continues to sleep soundly.*)

1ST HELPER: He can take a sun bath without getting a sunburn!

2ND HELPER: He can go in for a swim without getting wet!

3RD HELPER: He's in no danger of getting his toe bitten by a crab!

4TH HELPER: There'll never be any sand in *his* picnic lunch!

5TH HELPER: A delightful way of spending a holiday.

(*Thoughtfully*) I must tell my wife about it. (MRS. CLAUS *draws out a very large red bathing suit trimmed in white fur from her knitting bag and holds it up.*)

MRS. CLAUS: You see, I've even knitted him a nice warm bathing suit so that he won't catch cold. (*Hangs it over back of* SANTA CLAUS' *chair.*)

6TH HELPER (*Hesitantly*): There's just one thing that seems to have been forgotten.

MRS. CLAUS (*Crisply*): I think that the children from Public School Number 5 did a very thorough job. I'm sure that there is nothing missing.

6TH HELPER (*Insistently*): Just one little teeny thing. (*In a loud stage whisper*) Bathing beauties!

MRS. CLAUS (*Disapprovingly*): Only little boys who have been good all year get *everything* they ask for, and Santa Claus never remembers to wipe his boots after going down chimneys. No. (*Shaking her head*) No bathing beauties! Now, get along with you. I've work to do. (*She resumes her sweeping again.*)

WHOLE WIDE WORLD (*Mopping his brow*): That is one big load off my longitude and latitude! Hey, fellows, how about giving me a hand? (*Waddling over to wings, left.*) And mind you don't go squeezing Florida off the map! (*Wagging his finger at them*) There's nothing like finding a good Florida orange in your stocking.

3RD HELPER: Unless it's finding a California one! (*Laughing. All help to push* WHOLE WIDE WORLD *offstage.*)

CURTAIN

* * *

SCENE 2

TIME: *A little later.*

SETTING: *Florida beach backdrop.*

AT RISE: SANTA CLAUS, *in his red bathing suit, is sitting in the rocking chair. His regular suit hangs over the back of the chair.*

SANTA CLAUS: Oh, this is the life for me, tra, la,
Sun-bathing by the sea, tra, la,
With never a worry to crease my brow,
Or the good wife calling, "Get busy, *now!*" (*Shading his eyes with one hand, he scans the beach up and down.*) There's only one thing missing—bathing beauties! I am sure I asked for some in my letter. I suppose the demand was greater than the supply. (MRS. CLAUS *enters right, busily engaged in sweeping "sand" towards the beach.*) Why, however did you get here, Mama?

MRS. CLAUS (*Carelessly*): Oh, I rode in on the tail of a comet!

SANTA CLAUS: You *what?*

MRS. CLAUS: Never mind, dear. I'm here. Aren't you glad to see me?

SANTA CLAUS (*Hastily*): Oh, yes, of course, Mama. I was just thinking how nice it would be to hear your voice again.

MRS. CLAUS: That's good because I have quite a few things to say to you.

SANTA CLAUS (*Heartily*): Why don't you put down your broom and take a sun bath? No need for all that hustle and bustle down here!

MRS. CLAUS (*Sweeping harder than ever*): I declare, this sand gets into every crack and crevice! It keeps me busy all the time, I can tell you, just sweeping it out from underfoot.

SANTA CLAUS (*In exasperation*): Mama, it's meant to be underfoot! Can't you just enjoy it, as I am? Feel that warm sunshine (*Holding his face up towards the sun*) and smell the salt water (*Taking deep breaths*) and bask in the breeze from those palm trees. (*Lying back contentedly in his chair*)

MRS. CLAUS (*Pointedly*): I'd much prefer to be trimming Christmas trees, thank you.

SANTA CLAUS: You know my helpers are taking care of all that, my dear. They'll come through with flying colors.

MRS. CLAUS (*Ominously*): Not through the chimneys, they won't. They're getting stuck, left and right.

SANTA CLAUS (*Looking startled*): What are they doing in chimneys? That's my specialty. No one goes up and down chimneys but Santa Claus himself!

MRS. CLAUS: What would you have? Wee Willie Wilson nearly yelled his head off from fright when he saw one of your helpers coming in through a window. He thought it was a burglar. Bobby Baxter chased another out of the coal cellar when he caught him hiding behind the furnace. He was so covered with coal dust he mistook him for a tramp!

SANTA CLAUS (*Outraged*): They can't do this to me!

MRS. CLAUS: That's not all. They were chased by policemen and bitten by watchdogs. Finally, in self defense, they took to the chimneys and then they got into more trouble. One came down much faster than he intended and landed on his pack of toys, smashing everything in the bag.

SANTA CLAUS (*Distressed*): Not those beautiful walkie-talkie dolls I have been perfecting all year? (MRS. CLAUS *nods emphatically and* SANTA CLAUS *groans.*)

MRS. CLAUS: Another got quite badly singed. He hadn't learned that it isn't wise to go into a chimney with a fire still burning below!

SANTA CLAUS: Of all the idiotic nincompoops!

MRS. CLAUS: As for the rest of them, they got stuck in chimneys and are there still!

SANTA CLAUS: This is a catastrophe! A national catastrophe! A whole wide world catastrophe! I should never have left the North Pole.

MRS. CLAUS (*Airily*): Oh, well, you said the children wouldn't know the difference. I expect they'll get along somehow.

SANTA CLAUS (*Indignantly*): Not know the difference between my fine touch and that of these clumsy, blundering fellows? (*Reproachfully*) How can you say such a thing, Mama? Why, this may do irreparable damage to the Christmas Spirit all over the whole wide world!

MRS. CLAUS: But you said you needed a holiday. Remember your aches and pains. Think what this warm sunshine and salt air and gentle breezes are doing for your constitution.

SANTA CLAUS: Confidentially, Mama, this Florida vacation doesn't anywhere near come up to my expectations. That sun isn't as hot as it looks—in fact I'm positively chilly. (*Shivering*) And though you may not believe it, that salt air doesn't really smell any different from the air at home. I'll tell you something else—I can't even feel the breeze from those palm trees. Silly looking things, aren't they?

MRS. CLAUS: Not to people who live in Florida, I expect.

SANTA CLAUS: They can have them. My constitution calls for a more rugged climate. And goodness knows how long I'll be stuck here, with all those poor, neglected children having their faith in Santa Claus brought to such a pass. If I just had a magic wishing rug, I would hop onto it this very minute and wish myself back at the North Pole.

MRS. CLAUS: And you wouldn't ever complain of cold feet, stiff neck, cramps in your legs, ringing in your ears again?

SANTA CLAUS (*Solemnly, with right hand raised*): No more

aches and pains—ever. And the only ringing I want to hear in my ears is the ringing of sleigh bells!

MRS. CLAUS: Now, that's a coincidence! Do you hear what I hear? (*There is the sound of sleigh bells ringing merrily offstage, followed by the clop-clop-clop of reindeer hoofs.*)

SANTA CLAUS: I can't believe my ears! It sounds like—like —(*Rushing to wings, left, and looking out*) Why, it is! My reindeer, my good old faithful reindeer! (MRS. CLAUS *beckons to children to enter from right wing, upstage. They tiptoe in and remove Florida backdrop, revealing original backdrop, while* SANTA CLAUS *is jumping up and down in excitement. As he shouts to reindeer,* MRS. CLAUS *and children exit.*)

"Now Dasher, now Dancer!
Now Prancer and Vixen!
On Comet, on Cupid!
On Donder and Blitzen!"

Come and look, Mama. Do you suppose they have followed me all the way to Florida? (SANTA CLAUS *turns around and then begins to rub his eyes in bewilderment.*) Why, I must have fallen asleep and had a bad dream. (*Glancing at the clock on the backdrop*) Thank goodness it is only midnight! I still have time to visit all the little children all over the world. My, what a silly dream that was! Ha, ha, ha! Ho, ho, ho! As if Santa Claus would ever think of taking a holiday on Christmas Eve! I must tell this one to Mama. She will have a good laugh. (*He hurriedly steps into his* SANTA CLAUS *suit, claps his hat on his head and slings his pack over his back, humming cheerfully as he does so. He calls out to audience as he leaves stage.*) "Happy Christmas to all, and to all a good night!"

THE END

Adobe Christmas

by Mary Nygaard Peterson

Characters

PAPA LOPEZ
MAMA LOPEZ
ROSA } *their children*
PEDRO }
MR. RIVERA
MRS. RIVERA

TIME: *Christmas Eve.*

SETTING: *The main room of the Lopez home, near Santa Fe, New Mexico.*

AT RISE: PAPA *is putting on heavy outdoor wraps.* MAMA *is helping him, and the children,* ROSA *and* PEDRO, *look on, handing him gloves, cap, and scarf as he needs them.*

MAMA: Do you think you should go out on a night like this? I am sure there will be a storm. (*She looks out window.*) It is beginning to snow already.

PAPA: Don't worry, Mama. I can find my way to the city and back blindfolded. If it is a stormy night, so much the better. People in Santa Fe will be needing wood—both for their fireplaces and for their beacon lights.

ROSA (*Taking one of her father's hands in both of hers*): Papa, if you sell all your wood will you bring us something from Santa Fe?

PAPA (*Smiling at her*): What would you like to have, Rosa?

ROSA (*Clasping her hands and looking upward dreamily*): Would there be enough money, do you think, for a doll? One of those that says "Mama?"

PAPA (*Soberly*): I don't think so, little one. Dolls cost a lot of money. Even with three burros carrying wood, I don't think I would have so much money.

PEDRO (*Giving a tug to* PAPA'S *other hand*): Would you have enough money to buy some candy and nuts for us, Papa?

PAPA: I think I can promise you that, son. St. Nicholas is probably in Santa Fe right now, and he always sees that we have something for our piñata.

PEDRO (*Jumping and clapping*): Oh, goody. Be sure to find the good saint, Father.

PAPA: If he is there, I will find him.

PEDRO: I know you will, Papa. And then, when all the candy is in the piñata, *bang,* I will break it with my stick, and all the good things will come falling down on me. (*He makes a gesture with arms curved over his head and descending upon his shoulders.*)

PAPA (*Laughing*): What a shower of blessings that will be!

PEDRO (*Looking around seriously*): But they will be for everyone—for Rosa, and Mama, and you, not just for me.

PAPA: That's a good boy. Now I must hurry along so that I will be back when the Christ Child comes to bless our home.

ROSA: We'll keep the beacon fires burning so the Christ Child will be sure to find the house.

MAMA: The fires will help guide you safely home, too, Papa.

PAPA (*Going to door and opening it*): That will be fine, Mama. I will look for the light of the fires.

CHILDREN: Goodbye, Papa.

PAPA: Goodbye, for a little while. (*He exits.*)

ROSA (*Turning from door*): It already seems lonesome without Papa.

MAMA (*Busy putting on her wraps*): Keep busy and the time will go faster.

PEDRO (*Alarmed*): Where are you going, Mamacita? Aren't you going to stay here with us?

MAMA (*Laughing and patting his shoulder*): Of course, I'm going to stay with you, son. But I must gather wood for our fires—a great deal of wood. We don't want the fires to go out before Papa gets back. (*She opens the door.*) Be good children, now. Rosa, you are in charge. No mischief! (*Exits*)

PEDRO (*Half whining*): Now it *is* lonesome. I wish Mama didn't have to go out.

ROSA (*Practically*): She does have to, though. How else could we keep our fires burning?

PEDRO: I don't care whether the fires burn or not. I want Mama to stay here.

ROSA (*Shocked*): You don't care about the fires? Don't you care if the Christ Child can't find our house?

PEDRO (*Cautiously*): Couldn't He find it anyway?

ROSA: He might, or He might not. Our house is built of adobe, you know, and it is hard to find. From a distance, it looks just like the hillside. The Christ Child might pass it by. Lots of other travelers do.

PEDRO (*Undecided*): Maybe so.

ROSA: And even if the Holy Child could find the house, don't you want the fires to light Papa home?

PEDRO (*Nodding*): Yes, I do. But I wish Mama would come in soon. (*He goes to window.*) It's snowing hard now, Rosa. I can't see anything. Do you think the Christ Child is out in this storm?

ROSA: I suppose He is. He has to bless all the houses this

night. But I'm sure He is all right. Come, help me with the manger scene. It'll make the time pass faster.

PEDRO: May I hold the Baby Jesus when you make the manger ready for Him?

ROSA (*Picking up the doll tenderly*): If you will hold Him carefully. He is very precious, you know. (*She holds the doll lovingly to her cheek before putting it into* PEDRO's *outstretched arms.*)

PEDRO (*Cradling the doll lovingly and rocking Him in his arms*): Rosa—

ROSA: What is it, Pedro?

PEDRO: Why is the Christ Child coming here tonight—the real One, I mean?

ROSA (*Impatiently*): To bless the house, of course. Then we won't have any sorrow or trouble all next year.

PEDRO: Oh.

ROSA (*Giving a final pat to the interior of the manger*): Let me have the Precious Baby now, Pedro. His bed is ready for Him. (*She takes the doll, holds it lovingly a moment, and then places it in the manger.*)

PEDRO (*Sad again*): Mama's been gone an awfully long time.

ROSA (*Importantly*): Now don't be a baby. I'll find you a cracker, if you like. Will that make you feel better? (PEDRO *nods. He munches the cracker* ROSA *gives him.* MAMA *enters, covered with snow.*)

MAMA (*Gasping as she forces the door shut*): My! What a wind!

PEDRO (*Brushing off the snow*): You're covered with snow, Mama. Are you cold?

MAMA (*Shaking snow off her wraps and hanging them up*): Very cold, my pet, but I'll soon be warm now that I'm indoors. (*She blows on her fingers and rubs her cheeks to bring warmth into them. She looks around.*) Have you been good children?

PEDRO (*Proudly*): Rosa let me hold the Baby Jesus.

MAMA (*Affectionately*): That was nice. (*She sits near fireplace.*)

ROSA: Did you get enough wood to last the night, or will you have to go out again?

MAMA: I hope it will last. Will you please see if the fires are still burning? The wind may have blown them out before they got started. (ROSA *and* PEDRO *peer out the windows.*)

PEDRO: They're still burning, Mama. They look pretty.

ROSA (*Excited*): Mama! Mama, come, look!

MAMA (*Rising*): What's the matter, Rosa? What do you see?

ROSA: Look! Is that a burro, with a woman on its back? Is it?

MAMA (*Wonderingly*): Yes, Rosa, it is. There is a burro with a woman on its back, and a man walking beside.

ROSA: Mama, is it—do you think it is the Holy Family?

MAMA (*Briskly*): Whoever it is, they will need shelter and warmth this cold night. (*She goes to door, opens it, and stands looking out. Then she calls.*) Come in. Come in, friends, and get warm. (MR. *and* MRS. RIVERA *enter.* MRS. RIVERA *carries a large doll, wrapped in a blanket.*)

MR. RIVERA (*Bowing*): Thank you, Señora. I turned my burro into your shed. Was that all right?

MAMA: That was exactly right, Señor. Come in and warm yourself. (*She begins helping* MRS. RIVERA *with her wraps.*) What a lovely child!

MRS. RIVERA: Thank you. He is a good boy, and no worse for the cold, thank goodness.

MAMA (*Placing chairs and making the guests comfortable*): We didn't expect to see anyone out this stormy night.

PEDRO (*Seriously*): Except the Christ Child. We built fires to guide Him to our house.

MRS. RIVERA (*Smiling at him*): We were glad to follow

your beacons. I am afraid we might have been lost without them.

MR. RIVERA: It was clear and calm when we left Santa Fe. We could see the stars shining low overhead, and very bright.

MRS. RIVERA: That is why we decided to visit Mr. Rivera's father (*She indicates that her husband is* MR. RIVERA.) He lives in a cabin farther up the mountain. We thought he might be lonely this Christmas Eve.

MAMA: I didn't know that anyone lived farther up the mountain. It must be very stormy up there. (*She goes to look out the window.*) I am glad you saw our lights and stopped here. You must stay until you are sure you can find your way.

MRS. RIVERA: Thank you. We will do that. (ROSA *has approached and has been watching the baby.*)

ROSA: Doesn't the baby cry?

MRS. RIVERA (*Smiling*): Not very often. He is a good baby. (*There is a stamping outside the door.* PAPA *enters.*)

ROSA *and* PEDRO (*Excitedly*): Papa!

PAPA: Here I am. (*He removes his wraps and shakes the snow from them.*) It's a good night to be home. I was glad to follow the light from your bonfires, Mama. (*He looks at her, and then questioningly at the strangers.*)

MAMA: These are the Riveras, Papa.

PAPA (*Bowing to them politely*): Our house is your house.

MR. RIVERA: Thank you. Your beacons led us to safety.

ROSA (*Taking her father's hand*): Did you bring me a dolly from Santa Fe, Papa?

PEDRO (*At his other hand*): Did you bring some candies and nuts?

PAPA: Yes, to both of you. Here is your dolly, Rosa. (*He hands her a package. She turns it over and a doll says "Mama."*) Don't peek inside yet—not until I say so.

MAMA: But Papa, could you afford it?

PAPA: It was on sale, Mama, marked 'way down. (*He puts other small packages on table.*)

PEDRO (*Jumping up and down*): The candy, Papa? The nuts? (*He tries to feel the packages.*)

PAPA (*Laughing and pulling him back*): Just a minute. Just a minute. We must put them in the piñata.

PEDRO (*Hopping with excitement*): Did the good saint give them to us, Papa? Did he? Did he?

PAPA (*Laughing*): How else do you suppose I got them? (*He stuffs small gifts and candies into the piñata, a strong tissue bag shaped and colored to represent some bird, animal or figure.* ROSA *and* PEDRO *watch him.*) How about a piece of that string, Rosa? (*He indicates the package he has given her.*)

ROSA: All right, Papa. (*She removes the string and hands it to him.*) I'll put my dolly on the table until it is time. (*She squeezes the box and puts it on the table.*)

PAPA (*Holding the piñata up by the string*): Now we'll see if this will hold.

PEDRO: It'll hold, Papa. It'll hold. Hang it up, Papa, and let me hit it. I bet I can break it.

PAPA (*Hanging it up*): We'll soon see. Mama, this boy thinks he can break the piñata. Do you have a blindfold?

MAMA: Right here, Papa. All ready. (*She hands him a kerchief.*)

PAPA: Hold still. (*He ties kerchief over* PEDRO'S *eyes.*) Here's your stick. (*He picks one up from beside the fireplace.*) Remember, now, strike just once. Then it will be Rosa's turn.

ROSA (*Jumping up and down*): Oh, I hope he misses it. I hope he misses. (PEDRO *makes a wild swing and misses.*)

ROSA (*Jumping up and down*): You missed! You missed! It's my turn now.

PAPA: Hold still, then. (*He puts blindfold on her.*)

PEDRO (*Peering up at her eyes*): She can see. She's peeking!

ROSA (*Vigorously*): I can't, either.

PAPA: Just one swing now, Rosita. (*He gives her the stick.* ROSA *swings deliberately and misses.*)

PEDRO: My turn. My turn. This time I'll break it.

PAPA: All right, son. Surely someone in this house will break the piñata and give us a lucky year.

PEDRO: I will. I will. I'll break it this time. Give me the stick, Papa.

PAPA: Just a minute. Let me check your eyes. (PEDRO *strikes the piñata and breaks it.*)

PEDRO (*Ripping the blindfold off*): I did it! We'll have a lucky year! Come on, Rosa! Come on, everyone! (*He makes an all-inclusive gesture. The children scramble to pick up goodies and gifts while the older folks smile at them and at each other. Impulsively*) I'm going to give some of my gifts to the Baby Jesus. (*He tucks one or two into the manger.*) Here, these are for you.

ROSA: And I would like to give some to the real baby. (*To* MRS. RIVERA) Could I give the baby some of the little gifts?

MRS. RIVERA (*Smiling*): One. I will keep it for him, since you are so kind as to offer it. You keep the others.

PEDRO (*Not to be outdone*): I want to give the baby *two* presents.

MRS. RIVERA (*Smiling at him*): Since you wish it, you may. I will keep them for him. Thank you.

PAPA (*Handing* PEDRO *a package*): Here is something else for you, Son. Rosa has her doll, you may have this.

PEDRO (*Ripping off a paper*): A truck! A dump truck! (*Seeing* PEDRO *open his gift,* ROSA *unwraps her doll at a nod from* PAPA. *She cradles it to her cheek immediately.*)

PAPA: A dump truck is a good thing to have. Now you can haul clay and build pueblos and adobe houses wherever you wish. (*He looks at* ROSA.) How's the new baby, Rosita?

ROSA: She's wonderful, Papa, Mama. Thank you! (*She smiles happily at both, and they at her.*)

PEDRO: Thank you, Papa. (*He begins wheeling the truck on the floor.*)

MR. RIVERA (*After looking out the window*): This is such a happy place, but the storm is over. Do you think we had better go on, Maria?

MRS. RIVERA (*Graciously*): Whatever you think, José. (*She rises immediately.*)

MAMA: I will help you with your wraps. Thank you for visiting our home. (MR. RIVERA *opens the door.* MRS. RIVERA *bows and exits.* MR. RIVERA *turns back.*)

MR. RIVERA: Thank you for your shelter and warmth. (PAPA *and* MAMA *bow.*)

PAPA: You have honored our house. (*The door closes behind the* RIVERAS.)

MAMA: I never knew there was any house farther up the mountainside than ours.

PAPA: If there is, I have never seen it, or heard of it, and I have been all over the mountainside.

ROSA (*With awe*): Do you think, maybe, it was the Holy Family?

MAMA: Who are we to think about such things? It is our duty to help those who need help, to shelter those who need shelter. It is not right for us to ask who they are.

PAPA (*Gently*): Yet, the Holy One Himself once said, "As ye give it unto the least of these, my brethren, ye give it unto Me."

THE END

Touchstone

by Helen V. Runnette

Characters

ALCHEMIST
SERVANT

Knights
SIR COLIN
SIR PHILIP
SIR FRANCIS
SIR DAVID
SIR CUTHBERT

DAME JUDY
LADY JANE

Minstrels
CHARLES
ROBIN
STEPHEN
KENNETH
WILLIAM

Waits
GERALD
ROBERT
GRINNELL

MASTER
MISTRESS

Apprentices
PETER
TERENCE
DEREK
GEORGE
JOHN
PUFFIN
LUKE
NOBBY

CHILDREN
WAITS

NOTE: *Many of the parts in this play may be taken by either boys or girls.*

Scene 1

TIME: *A Christmas Eve, during the late medieval period.*

SETTING: *The interior of an alchemist's workroom. Bottles, alembics, retorts, crucibles, a brazier, bellows, tongs, etc., are scattered about on benches and tables.*

AT RISE: ALCHEMIST *is deeply absorbed in his work.* SERVANT *helps but is not paying close attention.*

SERVANT (*Handing tool to* ALCHEMIST): 'Tis Christmas Eve, my master. (ALCHEMIST *does not hear.* SERVANT *sighs; speaks louder.*) It doth distress me, master, to break in upon thy thought, but, sir, 'tis Christmas Eve! (*A bit louder*) Waits will come to sing at our door. We have no wassail to serve them. Nor have we gold to give them. (*Sighs again, since* ALCHEMIST *is too engrossed to hear*) Not even pennies have we. What shall I do? (*He looks around, but sees only darkness shrouding the place, its retorts and alembics. He hears knocking at the door and despairingly goes to open it. A gay band of waits, standing in doorway, bursts into song.*)

WAITS (*Singing to tune of "In Joseph's Lovely Garden"*):
As Joseph was a-walking
He heard an angel sing,
This night shall be the birthnight
Of Christ our Heavenly King.

Then be ye glad, good people,
This night of all the year,
And light ye up your candles,
For His star shineth clear.

SERVANT (*In despair at having nothing to give, and fearful of the disturbance to his master, starts to shoo them away. This they resent. He suddenly hears the word "candles" and hastily gets four or five, gives them to the leading waits and presses the door closed, heaving a sigh of relief.* ALCHEMIST *has heard and seen nothing.* SERVANT *then busies self in attending to master's needs. Another knocking—quite loud—is heard*): Master, again there is knocking at the door.

ALCHEMIST: I would not be interrupted. (*Knocking becomes louder; cries of "Open! Open!" are heard.*)

SERVANT: What shall I do, master? (ALCHEMIST, *engrossed, makes no reply. Door bursts open, and* SIR COLIN, SIR PHILIP, SIR FRANCIS, SIR DAVID *and* SIR CUTHBERT *enter.*)

SIR COLIN: Why didst thou not open, Alchemist?

SIR PHILIP: Little use thy asking, Colin. The Alchemist hears nothing when he is absorbed in work.

SIR FRANCIS: This fellow (*Points to* SERVANT) could have heard, methinks.

SIR COLIN (*Going close to* SERVANT, *bellowing*): Canst hear this?

SERVANT: Oh, sir, disturb not the master, pray.

SIR COLIN: And wherefore not? Is his work more important than we are?

SERVANT: He was about to find the answer!

SIR DAVID: Answer to what?

SIR COLIN (*Excitedly*): Can he change base metal into gold?

SERVANT: He hath promised so.

SIR FRANCIS (*Watching* ALCHEMIST): Indeed, he worketh mightily. (ALCHEMIST *pours stuff from one retort to another; holds it up to light.*)

SIR COLIN: Is it gold? Is it gold?

ALCHEMIST: I know not. When it cools, I will apply it to the touchstone.

SIR CUTHBERT: Show us the touchstone. (ALCHEMIST *does so.*)

SIR PHILIP: This black stone? Can this determine what is gold?

ALCHEMIST: Aye. Make a line upon its surface with the metal; that will show gold or silver.

SIR FRANCIS: Or—base metal still.

ALCHEMIST: True.

SIR PHILIP: It seemeth a little thing to hold so much power.

ALCHEMIST: 'Tis ever so. Small things be often great.

SIR DAVID: But while thy metal cooleth, tell us of thy struggles. Dost thou truly change base metals into gold and silver?

ALCHEMIST: I try to. No one hath succeeded yet.

SIR CUTHBERT: Why keep trying?

ALCHEMIST: 'Tis part of the endless struggle of life. (*Goes over to retort to test it, but it is still too hot*)

SIR FRANCIS: I have often wondered why 'tis that gold is so all-powerful.

SIR PHILIP: And that men should spend their lives in dingy rooms like this, searching for what must really be impossible to discover.

ALCHEMIST: Is it all impossible? Methinks searching for gold makes one value gold—not for itself but for its truth.

SIR COLIN: So-o-o-o! 'Tis truth we seek now—distilled from—what?

ALCHEMIST: Patience, perhaps, and humility.

SERVANT: From love of beauty too.

ALCHEMIST: From all beautiful things and thoughts.

SIR PHILIP: Methinks, Sir Alchemist, we wander far from gold. Gold that we can see—

SIR DAVID: And feel. (*Gloatingly*) Ah, could I but get my hands on gold—piles of gold.

SIR PHILIP: Thou hast been commissioned to make such gold, O Alchemist. Wherefore now talk of gold that is not gold?

SIR DAVID: Gold that filleth not our pockets.

ALCHEMIST: Ah, but is there not a gold that can fill our hearts?

ALL (*Blankly*): Hearts?

ALCHEMIST: Aye. List ye. There be two kinds of gold: that which I seek to create from baser metal—

SIR CUTHBERT: And wherefore not?

ALCHEMIST: And that which is more precious—golden thought.

SIR DAVID: But golden thought can purchase nothing.

SIR FRANCIS: If the King requireth me to send gold for a ransom for his son, will "golden thought" be welcome?

ALCHEMIST: If golden thought were in all hearts, would ransoms be required?

SIR COLIN: Thou talkest like a fool. "Golden thought"!

SERVANT: Oh, sir, he talketh wisely. There is pure gold in kindness—such as he hath shown to me.

SIR FRANCIS: Well, lad, I do bethink me thou dost pay him back in loyalty.

SIR PHILIP: Bless me! That is gold, too!

SIR CUTHBERT: The fellow hath a pretty thought, in truth.

SIR PHILIP: But is not thy metal cooled enough to put it to the touch? (ALCHEMIST *goes to table, takes up piece of metal; tests it on touchstone as all eagerly watch.*)

SIR DAVID: Alas! Thou hast failed!

SERVANT: Oh, master, thou canst surely do it next time!

ALCHEMIST: Nay, nay, there will be no next time.

SIR COLIN: What meanest thou—"There will be no next time"?

ALCHEMIST: I have failed again. Two thousand times I have made this effort, concentrating on it all my skill, to the exclusion of all else. Now, at last, I know that no base metal can be transmuted into gold.

SIR PHILIP: None at all?

SIR CUTHBERT: How then shall we find gold?

SERVANT: What shall I do, without thee to serve?

ALCHEMIST: Thou shalt accompany me in my search for gold.

SIR FRANCIS: Whither wilt thou go?

SIR DAVID: May we also accompany thee? Truly, I must find gold.

ALCHEMIST (*Thoughtfully*): To find this kind of alchemy in the world, look not in crucibles and alembics and retorts.

SIR PHILIP: Where?

ALCHEMIST: In people's hearts, as I have said.

SIR CUTHBERT: But that filleth not our pockets. What good does it do?

ALCHEMIST: It transmutes base thoughts to golden ones.

SIR DAVID: But what good is that to us? Truly I do need gold.

ALCHEMIST: If all hearts were noble, would there be fighting through the land?

SIR COLIN (*Delightedly*): And if there were no fighting, then we would not have so great a need for gold!

SIR CUTHBERT: Fewer armies to maintain . . .

SIR PHILIP: More people could raise food, and there would be less want, less need to fight.

SIR FRANCIS: Granted that the gold of noble thoughts and deeds may be desirable, how and where do we search for it?

ALCHEMIST: In people's hearts, I said.

SIR COLIN: We go around with a touchstone, saying, "Sir, let me scratch your heart on this black stone, to see if it be golden"?

SERVANT: I think the touchstone, too, is in our hearts.

SIR COLIN: I feel no stone in mine.

SERVANT: Ah, sir, make not a mock of this!

SIR FRANCIS (*Perplexedly*): Still do I not see how we can find such gold.

ALCHEMIST: Sirs, ye wished for gold. Ye commissioned me

to search for it in base metals. Will ye now commission me to search for this other gold, a gold that is more true, more lasting?

SIR COLIN: But how find such a gold?

ALCHEMIST: I propose our going on a crusade.

SIR PHILIP: To the Holy Land? I have but just returned.

ALCHEMIST: To a new holy land—to a holy land of peace and good will.

SIR CUTHBERT (*Disappointedly*): Thou dost sound like the Bishop on a Christmas Eve.

SERVANT: Truly, masters, *'tis* Christmas Eve, when angels sang of peace on earth!

SIR DAVID: 'Tis true this is the time of all the year when hearts are open wide.

SIR FRANCIS: Why, so it is the Holy Night—Good will to men, the angel said.

ALCHEMIST: Then go we through the town, to discover how the alchemy of Christmas may change leaden thoughts to gold! On this night of nights, in baron's hall or townsman's dwelling, there surely shall we find the gold of loving-kindness.

SIR COLIN: But will it fill our purses?

ALCHEMIST: Alas, no alchemy may change such selfishness to gold. 'Tis only sharing, not keeping, that increases one's golden hoard.

SIR DAVID: Shall we take a touchstone?

ALCHEMIST: God giveth to each his own peculiar touchstone whereby he knoweth what is truly gold.

SERVANT: Methinks pity is gold, and understanding; joy and laughter are part of it; beauty and truth are its core.

ALCHEMIST: Yea, truly. Test everything in such crucibles. Ere midnight falls, bring back your tale of gold, to scatter before all people, so they may win gold too.

SIR DAVID: May I not keep some of it, for mine own?

ALCHEMIST: 'Tis a strange thing: he who findeth gold and shareth it, doth give himself much gold. I do not understand it, but 'tis true. (SIR DAVID *opens his pouch; looks perplexedly from it to the* ALCHEMIST. *All exit.* ALCHEMIST *is in the lead;* SERVANT *brings up rear, staying a second to bank the fire and see that all is safe.*)

SERVANT (*Taking up a candle, holding it high*): Peace—on earth. Good will to men!

CURTAIN

* * *

SCENE 2

TIME: *Several minutes later.*

SETTING: *A kitchen.*

AT RISE: ALCHEMIST *and* SERVANT *watch from one side, unnoticed.* DAME JUDY *is busy getting pies in oven. She drops one and is angry.* CHILDREN *are playing on the floor.*

DAME: There! Again I drop a pie and ruin it! I'll never get them all baked, at this rate. Her ladyship ought to come to the kitchen and see what troubles I have. Instead she just orders more pies—more work—more everything. Let her try to do any work, with so many children around, always underfoot, or singing or laughing.

CHILDREN (*Singing to tune of "I Saw Three Ships"*):
Dame, get up and bake your pies, and bake your pies, and bake your pies.
Dame, get up and bake your pies
On Christmas Day in the morning. (*They break off and retreat as* DAME *advances toward them.*)

DAME: Such insolence! I'll teach you to laugh at your elders. (*Starts toward them with a broom*)

CHILD: 'Tis Christmas Eve, Dame!

DAME: Christmas Eve or no Christmas Eve, I want no laughing where I do my work.

ALCHEMIST (*From side*): No laughing, Dame? Laughter helps one work.

DAME (*Looking up, but not placing the sound, she busily resumes work*): Laughter? 'Twas an echo I heard. Laughter, is it? Laughter, laughter, laughter. But there's work, work, work to be done. (CHILDREN *who have been playing fairly silently, bubble up in laughter.*)

DAME (*Holding head*): Will no one rid me of these laughing children?

ALCHEMIST (*From side*): A world without children, Dame? Would that be a happy world?

DAME: Why should I care for happiness? Whatever put that thought into my head? Oh, 'tis addled I am with work—work—work—and all the while these bothersome children underfoot. (*She wipes a tear of self-pity from her eye.*) Now, you, child, (*Pointing*) bring hither the kettle. Look out! (CHILD *drops kettle and scuttles away, frightened.* DAME *is stooping to clean up floor when* LADY JANE *enters.*)

LADY JANE (*Ignoring the fact of spilled stew*): Such ravishing odors, Dame! Thou hast done well.

DAME: Small thanks to the children, always laughing and bothering me.

LADY JANE: Laughter—is that a bother, Dame? Where should we be without laughter? Look! 'Tis Christmas! Here is a cap and bells for thee, my child, and a riband for thee, and a sweetmeat for each one! Come, let us play together. (DAME *wipes up floor, but watches* LADY JANE *and* CHILDREN.) Leave thy work for a bit, Dame; join in our fun! (*She gathers* CHILDREN *into a circle.*)

ALCHEMIST: Play with them, Dame! Mix thy work with fun! 'Tis a rich pudding, so. (LADY JANE *and* CHILDREN *sing "I Saw Three Ships Come Sailing In."* CHILDREN *make room for* DAME, *who joins them as if in a dream.*)

DAME (*To* LADY JANE): Methinks my heart is lighter. What has happened to me?

LADY JANE: Children, help Dame Judy now. Go ye to pick up nuts for puddings she will bake. (CHILDREN *exit.*) Seest thou, Dame Judy, fun and laughter are a part of work? No one can work all the time without a little laughter. 'Tis Christmas cheer thou dost bake in a Christmas pie.

Without the door let sorrow lie,
And if for cold it hap to die,
We'll bury it in a Christmas pie
And evermore be merry! (*They exit,* DAME *following rather dazedly but with an expectant look on her face.*)

SERVANT (*To* ALCHEMIST): Lead is changing into gold, master.

ALCHEMIST: Laughter is a solution, I ween, that transmutes base fretfulness into joy.

SERVANT: May joy come from God above
To all those who Christmas love.

SCENE 3

TIME: *Same as Scene 2.*

SETTING: *A street. Upstage left is a doorway to a house. There is a cathedral door upstage center.*

AT RISE: SIR COLIN *and* SIR PHILIP *pause before doorway to house.*

SIR COLIN: Belike some good-hearted merchant doth dwell here. Let us collect the gold that the alchemist assures us is in all hearts.

SIR PHILIP: Alas! I have great need of real gold, but I fear me none will be forthcoming here. (SIR COLIN *starts to knock, but stands aside as a band of minstrels, including* CHARLES, ROBIN, STEPHEN, KENNETH, *and* WILLIAM, *comes gaily down the street, some leaping and springing, some plucking strings. They halt before door.*)

CHARLES: This is a goodly door. Methinks a rich man dwelleth here.

ROBIN: Let us knock long and loud. He will have much to give us.

STEPHEN: Good coins! Wassail!

KENNETH: Plenty to fill our pouches with!

WILLIAM: Why wait we? (*Knocks, but receives no answer. A ragged band of waits, led by* ROBERT, GERALD *and* GRINNELL, *enter from other side of stage.*)

CHARLES: What have we here? Ragged rascals! Away with you—away!

GRINNELL: Nay!

ROBIN: *I* say begone! *We* came here *first!*

CHARLES: We want no beggars such as ye.

KENNETH: Covered with filthy rags!

STEPHEN: Your faces evil, pock-marked, black with dirt!

ROBERT: We are as good as ye!

WILLIAM: Push them away! We'll have no truck with them!

KENNETH: They're not our kind. Away! Away!

ROBIN (*Seizing knocker and banging it*): What ho, within!

STEPHEN: In sooth we'll have no wassail, bring we not the master to the door.

CHARLES: Let not *these* partake of what will be given *us.* (*They try to rush waits off.*)

SIR PHILIP (*Coming forward*): Oh, pity 'tis to show no brotherhood! They be lads like yourselves in all but clothing.

SIR COLIN: Their voices are the same. Why not all sing together, and stir the master of this house, to give us golden welcome! (*The waits and minstrels are startled by* SIR COLIN'S *words. They nod in agreement, come together and sing, "Here We Come A-Wassailing."* SIR PHILIP *and* SIR COLIN *join the singing.*)

MASTER (*Coming to door, gruffly*): What means this noise?

MINSTRELS, WAITS *and* KNIGHTS:

God bless the master of this house,
Likewise the mistress, too,
And all the little children
That round the table go. (*Etc.*)

MASTER: Ye need not think ye will be given wassail in my house. Begone!

SIR COLIN: What? All? Even Sir Philip and *me,* Sir Colin?

MASTER: Yea. I want none of ye, knights, or minstrels, or ragged waits.

SIR COLIN: Forsooth, that is no way to greet a gentleman.

CHARLES: Certes, that is no way to greet a townsman.

GERALD: In truth, that is no way to greet a beggar.

MISTRESS (*Coming to door*): Shame on thee, James, to drive any from our door. Bid them enter.

MASTER: And who will feed them, beggars all?

MISTRESS: There is enough to share. Welcome, all!

MASTER: There is not room enough in this house for all of these.

MISTRESS: Then let them dance and sing here in the street. (MINSTRELS, WAITS *and* KNIGHTS *sing "Deck the Halls."*) Now will I set the wassail bowl down yonder, and ye may come to drink of it. (*Singers smile.*)

MASTER: Why, truly, thou wilt have us beggars if thou dost give our food to these.

MISTRESS: 'Tis given us to share. Oh, James, take heed! Shall we be like the innkeeper who found no room for wayfarers on that first Christmas Eve? Shall not our hearts and homes be open wide to help all in distress?

Say thou wilt give—and give—and give to all who knock upon our door!

GRINNELL: Why, lady, thou shalt win many blessings on thy head.

MISTRESS: On his head, too,—on all our heads, this Christmastide. O, James, prithee soften thy heart to show kindness to the poor!

MASTER (*Grudgingly*): Thou shalt have thy way.

MISTRESS: The Christmas way! (*Opens door*) Enter, all! (*The* MINSTRELS *and* WAITS *begin to enter.*)

SIR PHILIP (*To* SIR COLIN): The master is base lead—

SIR COLIN: But the mistress is pure gold—

SIR PHILIP: We have used the touchstone!

SIR COLIN: Let us go tell the Alchemist! (*They exit.*)

CURTAIN

* * *

SCENE 4

TIME: *A few minutes later.*

SETTING: *The same as Scene 3. There is a table at right of cathedral door.*

AT RISE: *A group of apprentices, including* PETER, TERENCE, DEREK, GEORGE, JOHN, PUFFIN, LUKE *and* NOBBY, *stands at left of cathedral arguing in pantomime.* SIR DAVID, SIR CUTHBERT *and* SIR FRANCIS *enter. They do not see the apprentices at first.*

SIR DAVID: Surely we shall find gold in the cathedral.

SIR CUTHBERT (*Sadly*): None that we may take away.

SIR FRANCIS: Out upon thee, Cuthbert! We were to seek gold, and tell the Alchemist where 'twas found.

SIR DAVID: So we could scatter more gold. Mind you what he said was gold?

SIR FRANCIS: Beauty, he said, and truth.

SIR DAVID: Here methinks will be both beauty and truth.

SIR CUTHBERT: These apprentices I hear arguing—are they beautiful, or even truthful? (*At this, the wrangling of apprentices in corner becomes loud.*)

PETER: Mine is the best!

TERENCE: I finished mine first!

DEREK: Ye are both wrong. *Mine* is best; *mine* was finished first.

GEORGE: But *I* came here first; *ye* may all go home.

JOHN: First or last, it matters not. *Mine* will be chosen. The Bishop said so.

PUFFIN: He had no right to choose thine, before he had seen ours!

LUKE: I will ask him if thou hast said the truth!

NOBBY (*Looking at designs*): Methinks they all are lovely.

ALL (*In varying tones*): But mine is the *most* beautiful!

NOBBY: 'Tis true each deems his own the best. Did not each work to create the best design? To carry it out with the most skillful art? Then all are good. 'Twould not surprise me if our Bishop found that all could be worked together into one window in the Cathedral!

SIR FRANCIS (*Coming forward*): We would fain see these designs, my lads. (*Eagerly they show him, thrusting them at him.*) Nay, not so fast—I must have time to appreciate each one.

TERENCE: But thou art not the Bishop, to choose the design.

SIR CUTHBERT: Not one of us is bishop.

SIR DAVID: Yet know we which designs are pleasing.

ALL: Mine! Mine! Mine!

SIR CUTHBERT: Nay, I see no devotion in them.

TERENCE (*Showing his design*): See you not the Magi offering gifts?

LUKE (*Pointing to his design*): Regard how shepherds kneel before the Child.

GEORGE (*Indicating his own*): Angels praise Him from on high!

PETER: How say you that the windows lack devotion? Each is a story of devotion. See how I placed the sheep, the ox and ass, the doves?

JOHN: Surely the Bishop will decide that my pattern of the Holy Night is much the best. Though methinks thou'rt right, Nobby. Each pattern has its own loveliness.

NOBBY (*Who has started to arrange all together in a framework on a table upstage center near door*): Come, lads, let us see if we can fit our designs together. Belike the sum of all the parts will add a harmony not visible before.

PUFFIN: 'Tis amazing! Each one adds beauty to the whole!

SIR CUTHBERT (*Looking at window*): True is that word. Each design is good in itself; all work together to the glory of God—not to the glory of men. See that ye remember.

DEREK: Glory to God—peace and good will to men! 'Tis what the angels sang. (*All apprentices continue to work on the window till end.*)

SIR FRANCIS (*To* SIR DAVID *and* SIR CUTHBERT): Think ye that yon apprentice tried to turn the lads' base metal of selfishness to the gold of cooperation?

SIR DAVID: Now see I what the Alchemist did mean! Let us tell him of the gold we found: that men can work together, if they will. (*Enter from opposite directions,* ALCHEMIST *and* SERVANT, SIR PHILIP *and* SIR COLIN.)

ALCHEMIST: Found ye any gold?

SIR FRANCIS (*Eagerly*): Yea, truly.

SIR COLIN (*Wonderingly*): With the touchstone of understanding.

SIR CUTHBERT (*Factually*): Much base metal was there—

SIR PHILIP (*Enthusiastically*): But it turned to gold.

SIR DAVID: A wealth of gold beyond my dreams.

SERVANT: In people's hearts, as he said.

ALCHEMIST: Belike ye found the solvent to turn base metal into gold?

SIR COLIN: Nay—tell us, pray.

ALCHEMIST: The solvent of devotion. There is no gold without it.

SIR DAVID: Look ye. Yon workmen found it, in working together, instead of each for self. (*Points to them; they gather round to inspect window*)

SIR COLIN: Some townsmen found it in treating men like brothers.

SERVANT: And others found a generous heart with which to share life's blessings.

ALCHEMIST: And ye, yourselves?

SIR CUTHBERT: Why, so did we discover gold.

SIR FRANCIS: By changing greedy hands—

SIR DAVID: To sharing hearts—even mine.

SIR PHILIP (*To* ALCHEMIST): Thou art indeed an alchemist!

ALCHEMIST (*Pointing to window, which at this moment is illuminated from behind*): Not I, my friends; not I. (*They enter cathedral, followed by all characters from preceding scenes, all singing "Adeste Fidelis."*)

THE END

The First Christmas Tree

by Loretta Camp Capell

Characters

JOHANN, *who works for his mother and sisters*
ELSA *and* FRIEDA, *his sisters*
MOTHER, *a poor peasant woman*
CHRISTMAS CAROLERS
THE CHILD
CHRISTMAS TREE SPIRITS

SCENE 1

TIME: *Long ago, on Christmas Eve.*
SETTING: *In the woods.*
AT RISE: *It is very cold and the wind is blowing hard. Children pass along the path and greet each other with a "Merry Christmas." Some boys drag a log along through the snow. A group of carolers enter, singing "Oh, Tannenbaum." They meet* JOHANN *as he trudges along with several packages under his arm.*

1ST CAROLER: Come along, now, it is very cold. We must hurry!
2ND CAROLER: Oh, here is Johann. Perhaps he will come with us, too.
3RD CAROLER: Come with us, Johann. We are going to sing carols in the village. We need you to help us sing.

JOHANN (*Returning their greeting*): I should like to, but I must go home now. I have been working since early morning, and I am tired.

1ST CAROLER: Poor Johann, he does work hard. I guess he is hungry, too!

2ND CAROLER: What do you have there, Johann, Christmas gifts?

JOHANN: Yes, I just bought them in the village. (*Smiling*) And I have spent all of my money for them. This is a warm pair of gloves for Mother. These are woolen stockings for Elsa, and this is a bright scarf for Frieda. She loves pretty things!

2ND CAROLER: What fine presents! And how happy they will be!

JOHANN: They deserve to be happy! I have the very best mother and sisters in the world, I think! All day my mother works in the great castle on the hill to earn food and clothing for us. And all day my sisters work hard tidying the cottage and cooking the meals. I am glad that now I am big enough to help, too! (*Starts to go*) But I must hurry home, supper will be ready. I am so cold that I can hardly wait to be by the warm fire again!

3RD CAROLER: It *is* cold, indeed! Well, we must hurry on to the village! Good night, Johann, and a merry Christmas to you!

1ST CAROLER: You will surely have a merry Christmas yourself, when you have planned such fine presents for the others!

JOHANN (*As he goes along*): Merry Christmas to you all! Good night. (*The* CAROLERS *pass on, singing. The wind blows and a few snowflakes fall.* JOHANN *trudges on, slowly. He turns up his collar against the cold. A soft wail is heard.* JOHANN *stops and looks around. Then he shakes his head and goes on again. Again the cry sounds softly but plainly.* JOHANN *stops again. To himself*)

What can that be? It sounds almost like a child or an animal lost in the snow. But it seems so far away. . . . I am so tired. . . . Perhaps it is only the wind. I must get on to the cottage or I will freeze!

CURTAIN

* * *

SCENE 2

SETTING: *The interior of* JOHANN'S *cottage.*

AT RISE: *A bright fire is burning in the fireplace.* MOTHER *is bending over the kettle stirring the soup.* FRIEDA *and* ELSA *are helping about the room, setting the table, etc. As* JOHANN *pushes open the door,* FRIEDA *and* ELSA *run to him, take his hands and dance him around the room.*

FRIEDA: Oh, Johann, we're so glad you have come!

ELSA: But how cold you are! Come dance a bit with us and you will soon be warmer. (*To the tune of an old folk dance the children dance.* MOTHER *watches, smiling.*)

FRIEDA (*Picking up the packages dropped in the dance*): Oh, oh! Packages!

JOHANN: Be careful! It isn't time for you to see those yet. (*He gathers up the packages and puts them up on shelf.*)

FRIEDA: Oh, Johann, you should see the pudding! Such a big one! And it smells so good!

ELSA (*Leading him to the cupboard*): And see my cakes. They are all ready and a real surprise to Mother! I made them better than ever this year! We will have a real Christmas feast!

JOHANN: They look fine! They make me hungry! When will we have supper?

MOTHER: Supper will be ready soon. And a nice bowl of soup will warm you. Come, take off your heavy coat and sit by the fire. (*She unties his muffler and helps him off with his coat.*) You were such a good boy to get in all the fire wood this summer, so now we shall be warm and happy by the fire this Christmas time, no matter how cold the winds may blow! And I have a surprise for you, too! We will have a fat goose for our Christmas dinner tomorrow!

JOHANN: A goose, Mother? Really? A goose?

MOTHER: I made a little extra money and was able to get a good one in the market. We shall start cooking it now, so it will be fine and tender.

FRIEDA: Oh, I will help turn it! (MOTHER *and the girls bustle about, getting the goose before the fire, finishing supper, etc.* JOHANN *sits on a little stool by the fire and warms his hands. Outside the wind blows louder. He sits quietly for a while, and then remembers the cry he heard out in the woods.*)

JOHANN (*Jumping to his feet*): Mother! I must go out again! I think there is someone out in the storm crying for help! (MOTHER *and sisters stop their work and look at him in surprise.*)

MOTHER: I hear nothing, Johann. Come, sit down and warm yourself. You must be chilled through. It is only the wind you hear. My boy mustn't be thinking of sorrow when it is Christmas Eve and everyone should be happy. Soon the Christ Child will be abroad with the presents. (JOHANN *sits down again, but he is restless and listens for the cry again. He thinks he hears it.*)

JOHANN: Mother, there *is* someone calling! I must go out again! I heard it before I reached home, just as I was coming out of the woods.

FRIEDA (*Listening*): We hear nothing, Johann.

ELSA: It is only the wind.

JOHANN (*Putting on his scarf and coat*): I *do* hear it—I

do! I must go. Someone is out in the storm! (*As he opens the door a gust of wind blows in. He goes out.*)

* * *

Scene 3

SETTING: *In the woods.*

AT RISE: *A tiny figure is huddled, nearly covered in the snow, near center, back.* JOHANN *enters, struggling along against the wind.*

JOHANN: I don't hear it now. But it was in this direction. I have come far but I have found nothing. Oh, how cold it is! (*Sees figure*) But what is this? A little boy! Asleep! Oh, he must be nearly frozen! Can I lift him, I wonder? I will try. . . . I will try! (*He struggles to lift the child. Finally he manages to swing him on to his shoulder and staggers out.*)

* * *

Scene 4

SETTING: *Inside* JOHANN's *cottage.*

AT RISE: MOTHER *is sitting by the fire, paring apples. The girls are at the window. As they see* JOHANN, *they rush to the door.*

FRIEDA: Here comes Johann.

ELSA: He is carrying something. Something heavy.

FRIEDA: What can it be? (JOHANN *staggers through the door. They close it after him.*)

GIRLS: Oh Johann, what have you found?

MOTHER: Why, it is a child! Nearly frozen from the cold! Bring him here Johann. Here, by the fire. (*The* CHILD *is carried to the big chair by the fire.*)

FRIEDA: Oh let me rub his poor little feet! They are so cold! (*She takes off* CHILD's *shoes and stockings and warms his feet.*)

ELSA: And his little hands are like ice . . . poor child! (*She rubs his hands.*)

MOTHER: I will get him a bowl of soup . . . that will warm him. (*She brings the soup and forces some between his lips.*) Drink this, little one. (*The* CHILD *opens his eyes and drinks. Then he looks around him.*)

ELSA (*Laughing a little*): See, he is awake, now. He doesn't know where he is! I wonder where he has come from!

FRIEDA (*Still rubbing the little feet*): His feet are warmer now. We must find him some shoes and stockings. I believe my new ones will do. (*She runs to get the shoes and stockings and puts them on him*) See, they are a little large, but how fine they look!

JOHANN: He should have a warm coat. I think the suit that Mother made for me would do. It will be big for him, but no matter! It will keep him warm. (*He gets the coat and puts it around the* CHILD.)

FRIEDA: I will get my warm mittens for his poor little hands. (*She brings the mittens for him. The* CHILD *looks all around the room, but says nothing.*)

MOTHER: Come, Frieda, we are forgetting the goose! If you don't keep turning it, it will cook only on one side! (FRIEDA *goes to the spit;* ELSA *finishes setting the table.* JOHANN *puts more wood on the fire. They are laughing and happy. As they pass the* CHILD, *they pat his curls.*) Now the soup is ready. We will not eat much tonight, for we must save room for the goose, tomorrow! Come, children. (*They gather around the table, helping the* CHILD *to a place. Then they bow their heads for a moment, and eat.*)

FRIEDA (*As she finishes her soup*): And now for the presents! We always have them on Christmas eve.

ELSA (*Glancing at the* CHILD): Sh . . . sh. Come here! (*The three children talk together*) We must have presents for *him*. Johann, you can give him the present you bought for me! I will wait for mine until next Christmas.

FRIEDA: Yes, and mine, too.

JOHANN: And you can give him the ones you planned for *me*.

GIRLS: All right, that will be fine! (*The children go to bring the presents.*)

CHILDREN: Now for the presents! These are for you. For you. For you! (*The* CHILD *smiles as the packages are put in his arms. He says "thank you" and holds the bundles close. Then he looks at each one, pats it, but does not open it. He holds them close in his arms.*)

JOHANN (*Whispering*): He looks as if he never had a present before!

ELSA: But oh, how he loves them!

FRIEDA: It is good to see him so happy. (MOTHER *has been clearing away the dishes. Now she pulls up her chair before the fire. The children gather around her.*)

ELSA: Tell us a story, Mother, do.

MOTHER (*Taking the* CHILD *upon her lap*): Come here, little one. I will hold you.

FRIEDA: Tell us about the Christ Child, Mother. It is Christmas Eve and time to hear about Him again.

MOTHER (*Very slowly, as though seeing the picture*): He is dressed in white robes, sometimes, and sometimes He comes as a poor child, instead. (*She smiles at the* CHILD *in her arms*) Around his head there is a light that looks like gold. His smile is sweeter than the smile of angels. He comes on Christmas Eve and brings presents to all of the good people in the world. Sometimes folks can see Him, but one never knows where He can be seen or when He is coming. Those who have seen Him say He is so beautiful and sweet that there is great love in their hearts ever after. He gives love to all.

ELSA: Oh, how I wish *we* could see the little Christ Child . . . the dear little Christ Child! Has the great lady at the castle ever seen Him, Mother?

MOTHER: No, she has not seen Him. She told me only yesterday that she has seen many things and has been in many places in the world, but she has never seen the Christ Child. (*The* CHILD *puts his head against the* MOTHER's *breast and sleeps.*)

MOTHER: The poor child is sleeping. He must go to bed, but where can he sleep? We have no extra bed.

JOHANN: Put him on my bed, Mother. I will sleep on the hearth. (MOTHER *carries out the* CHILD. *Then she makes up a bed on the hearth for* JOHANN. *The girls go out with "good nights."* JOHANN *curls up by the fire to sleep and all is still. After a little, the* CHILD *comes back through the door. He smiles as he goes over to* JOHANN *and touches him.* JOHANN *opens his eyes and sits up.*) Why . . . Child! Child!

CHILD: I must go . . . I must be on my way.

JOHANN: But it is cold! The snow is deep! You will be lost!

CHILD: No, I am never lost where there are warm and loving hearts. It is only among the careless who forget me, that I am lost. (*Slowly He goes to the door, opens it, and goes out.*)

JOHANN (*Fully awake now*): Mother! Frieda! Elsa! (*Jumps up*) The little boy has gone out into the cold! We must go and bring him back! (*The others come to the door. He starts to put on his coat. Then all stand in amazement as the* CHRIST CHILD *opens the door again. He comes slowly up to them, carrying a small pine tree.*)

CHRIST CHILD: See . . . I bring you this. It is the tree of life. Every year at Christmas time it will bloom for you. (*He goes to the hearth and puts the tree before it*) Watch the tree closely and you will see it grow. You will see on its branches bits of the blue, blue sky that looked down over Bethlehem. You will see the beams of starlight that gleamed over the lowly stable so long ago. And the sparkling stars themselves that shone that night to guide the Wise Men on their way. You brought me in out of the cold, Johann and gave me your bed. Though the path was dark, you kept on. And you (*Turning to the others*) warmed me and fed me and gave me your presents. And now I give you this Christmas tree. It will come to you every year, and to all children with loving hearts. (*They watch in amazement as He slowly walks to the door and out into the night. The lights are focused on the tree. Then, in slow and graceful rhythm, the tree spirits enter and trim the tree.*)

THE END

The Christmas Sampler

by Eleanor D. Leuser

Characters

PATTY CROCKER
HENRY CROCKER, *her father*
JOHN } *her brothers*
WILLIAM }
DEBBY, *her small sister*
MISTRESS MALTBY, *the Mayor's wife*
SUSY MALTBY, *her daughter*
CAPTAIN HALE, *a British officer*
PRIVATE MARGROVE } *Redcoats*
PRIVATE SUTTON }
VILLAGERS

TIME: *A Christmas Eve during the Revolutionary War.*
SETTING: *A kitchen in a little Massachusetts village.*
AT RISE: PATTY *is working on her sampler.* DEBBY *and* SUSY *are playing on the floor with their rag dolls.* JOHN *is polishing a wooden bowl.* MISTRESS MALTBY *is arranging some Christmas greens around the room.*

MISTRESS MALTBY (*Looking at her arrangement*): Well, that looks more cheerful, doesn't it? I'm glad I thought of bringing those greens over. I declare it's a shame for you children to have your mother away sick on Christmas Eve and your father driving that stagecoach back and forth from Boston over those dangerous roads.

JOHN (*Looking up*): The British always search his coach too, to see if he's carrying anything they've forbidden.

PATTY: They never find anything, though. Father's too clever for that. The British think he's harmless because he's lame. He's just an ordinary stagecoach driver to them.

MISTRESS MALTBY: I hope they keep on feeling that way. I've heard he's bringing more than passengers this time. I hope he gets through.

JOHN: He's bringing guns and ammunition for the village, he is.

PATTY (*Putting her hand over* JOHN'S *mouth*): Hush, John! That's a secret.

MISTRESS MALTBY: I know about it. I've heard the Mayor and your father planning. The village just has to get some more guns to replace all those that the British took away from them.

JOHN: This village wouldn't be under the British any more then I bet. We'd surprise those two guards they left and Bang! Bang! (*He shoots an imaginary gun.*)

MISTRESS MALTBY (*Sighing*): If they ever found out that your father was bringing them in—oh, we'd better not talk about it.

DEBBY (*Coming over*): I'd rather talk about Christmas, Mistress Maltby. Do you know Patty's helping us with it?

JOHN: We're all making presents for Mother, too. I'm making this bowl for her porridge.

MISTRESS MALTBY (*Looking at it*): That's nice work, John. Your mother will like it.

PATTY: I'm making her this sampler. It's almost finished. Mother will be so surprised because she knows how I hate to sew.

MISTRESS MALTBY (*Looking at it closely*): That's as good as I could do myself, Patty. For gracious sakes, isn't that our old red barn up in the corner?

PATTY: Yes, it is. I sketched it myself then drew it on the sampler. I drew Father's stagecoach too.

MISTRESS MALTBY: I like your motto, child. "The way to a friend's house is never long." It fits right in with the stagecoach. I'll be bound your mother will be proud of that sampler.

DEBBY: Please, Patty, can I tell the Mayor's wife one more thing?

MISTRESS MALTBY: What is it, little Debby?

DEBBY (*Excitedly*): Patty is going to let us hang our stockings tonight even if Mother is sick and not home.

MISTRESS MALTBY (*Patting* DEBBY): Patty is a good sister to all of you. But I must be going. Come, Susy. We have to get ready for Christmas at our house, too.

SUSY: Oh, Mother, please can't I stay a little longer?

DEBBY: Please let her stay, Mistress Maltby. Patty's going to help us sing carols and Susy wants to sing too.

PATTY: We'll see she gets home, Ma'am. One of the boys will bring her right after carol singing. Debby's set her heart on having Susy stay.

MISTRESS MALTBY: Well, don't let her be too late, Patty. These are war times. Anything can happen. (*She goes to door, putting her shawl around her.*) Be good now, Susy. I hope your father gets home safely, children.

PATTY: Oh, I hope so, too. The stagecoach is due tonight. (*Going to door*) Good night, Mistress Maltby. Thank you for letting Susy stay.

MISTRESS MALTBY: Good night and a good Christmas for you all. (*She goes out. The children go on with what they were doing. After a few moments' work on her sampler,* PATTY *puts it down with a sigh of relief.*)

PATTY: There! The sampler's all finished. It will be ready

to give Mother if she comes home tomorrow. Let's practice our carols before William comes. (*The children gather around* PATTY *and she leads them in "Hark, the Herald Angels." The door bursts open and* WILLIAM *rushes in. The children stop and stare at him.*) Goodness, William, whatever is the matter?

WILLIAM (*Breathlessly*): I saw Father driving toward town about an hour ago. I was going to go to the inn and wait for him when he turned off on a side road and whipped the horses up like all get-out.

PATTY: Was someone following him?

WILLIAM: I'm afraid so. A few minutes later a British officer came riding past. He went right on to the inn. I heard him asking about Father and the stagecoach. Then he talked to the two Redcoats on duty in the village. He told them to search all the houses to see if any of the people had guns again. I left him waiting for the coach.

JOHN: Phew! I bet Father was bringing guns in and they suspect him. If they ever catch him—

WILLIAM: That's what I'm afraid of. Better get the hiding cupboard ready, Patty, in case Father comes to the house. (PATTY *opens a door and pushes some things aside.*)

PATTY: This cupboard has helped more people. Nobody ever guesses there's an extra room back of it. Yes, it's all ready but Father will never be able to bring his guns here now if they're watching for him. (*The door opens suddenly and* HENRY CROCKER *limps in.*)

ALL: Father!

HENRY: Listen, children! The British suspect something. They searched the coach in Boston before I left. But they never found the false bottom to the floor. Still, one of their officers followed me all the way here. I gave him the slip right outside the village.

WILLIAM: Are the guns still in the coach?

HENRY: No, I have them hidden. But Patty you'll have to get word to the Mayor where they are so he can give them out. The British will never suspect a girl of carrying a message.

PATTY: I'll get word to the Mayor, Father. But you must hide or the British will make you prisoner. William heard them say so. The cupboard is all ready.

HENRY (*Going toward cupboard*): Go at once, Patty. The villagers must get those guns before the British find them. Then we can free ourselves from British rule.

WILLIAM: Hide, Father. I think I hear someone coming! (HENRY *steps into cupboard.*)

PATTY (*Rushing after him*): Father, you didn't tell me where they are hidden. Where? (*He bends down and whispers in her ear.* PATTY *has just time to close the cupboard door as footsteps are heard. She hastily sits down and picks up her sampler. Each of the children busies himself silently as the door opens and two British soldiers and a Captain enter.*)

PRIVATE MARGROVE: This is the home of the stagecoach driver, Henry Crocker, Captain Hale. These are his children. His wife is away ill.

CAPTAIN HALE (*To* PATTY *who has risen*): Has your father come in, little girl? I wish to speak to him.

PATTY (*Curtseying*): I believe he's not due, sir, for another half hour.

CAPTAIN HALE: His coach is here for we found it. But he is missing. We want him for questioning.

WILLIAM: He sometimes stops at the inn, sir, to chat with his friends.

CAPTAIN HALE: He did not stop there today. (*To soldiers*) It is a curious thing how often we have searched that coach and found nothing. Yet I have a feeling that this stagecoach driver is putting something over on us. Today the armory is short a supply of guns and the watchman swears he saw a man limping about among them. I think we will take away the pass of this Henry Crocker and see that he does not leave the village. Perhaps even put him in gaol. (*The children look at each other.*)

PRIVATE MARGROVE: This village has given us no trouble, sir, ever since the British took it over and made the people give up all their arms.

CAPTAIN HALE (*Thoughtfully*): That in itself is a bad sign. It is not like these colonists to take capture by the enemy so easily. 'Tis true their young men are away with Washington, but I think these villagers are planning something. When I have talked with this Henry Crocker I shall go back and order more guards sent here at once. (*He walks up and down restlessly.*)

PATTY: If you are planning to stay here till my father comes, sir, perhaps you wouldn't mind if we sang a few carols. It's Christmas Eve, and Susy wanted to hear them before we took her home. She's been spending the day with us.

CAPTAIN HALE: Go ahead and sing. But none of you must leave the house. You might warn your father for all I know. Yes, sing, I'd forgotten it was so near Christmas. (PATTY *starts singing and the children join in, then the two soldiers.*)

PRIVATE MARGROVE: Reminds me of home, Captain.

SUSY (*Running over to* PATTY): Patty, I want to go home.

PATTY (*To* CAPTAIN): Couldn't I just take this little girl home, sir? Her mother is expecting her. I was planning to take this Christmas present to her mother, too.

CAPTAIN HALE (*Sharply*): What is the present?

PATTY: Just this sampler, sir. I just have two or three stitches to put in.

CAPTAIN HALE (*Looking at it*): A pretty thing! My sister makes samplers, too. You say it's a Christmas present?

PATTY: Yes, for Susy's mother.

DEBBY: But Patty, I thought—

PATTY (*Silencing* DEBBY): Little girls should be seen and not heard, Debby. Yes, it's for Susy's mother. Couldn't I please walk home with Susy and take it?

CAPTAIN: No, it's best not. But I tell you what I'll do since it's Christmas Eve. Private Margrove can take Susy home and deliver your present, while we wait for your father.

PATTY (*Hurriedly picking up sampler and putting in a few stitches*): Thank you, Captain. There, it's finished. Go with the soldier, Susy. Please, will you carry the sampler carefully, sir. Give it to Mistress Maltby and tell her I'm sorry not to be able to deliver it myself. Be sure to tell her it's my Christmas present to her and to look for the latest kind of stitch I put in. (*She puts a shawl around* SUSY.)

PRIVATE MARGROVE: I'll do my best, Miss. Come, Susy. (*They exit.*)

CAPTAIN HALE: Sutton, you keep watch at the back of the house in case Crocker decides to enter that way. (SUTTON *salutes and goes out.*)

PATTY (*Who has been busy with some cakes*): Won't you have a little refreshment while you wait? My father should not be long now.

CAPTAIN HALE (*Taking a cake*): Thank you, you are a thoughtful little girl. (*To* DEBBY) Could you sing a Christmas song for me, little lady?

DEBBY: Can I, Patty?

PATTY: Of course, Debby. You know "Away in a Manger." Sing that. (DEBBY *sings.*) The boys know "There Were Three Kings." (*The boys start to refuse but* PATTY *motions to them and they realize she is trying to hold the* CAPTAIN'S *attention. They sing.*)

CAPTAIN HALE: Now how about you, Miss Patty?

PATTY: Oh, I don't sing alone but we could all sing together for you. (*The children have sung several carols when a commotion is heard outside. The* CAPTAIN *rises hastily but before he can get his hand on his sword the door opens and he is surrounded by* VILLAGERS *with guns.* PATTY *opens the cupboard door.*) You can come out now, Father. (*As* CROCKER *appears the British officer stares in astonishment.*)

CAPTAIN HALE: So you had me fooled all along the line, Crocker. You did manage to get some guns in after all. You must have hid them somewhere and reached here before me.

HENRY: That stagecoach was specially constructed, Captain. That's how we brought the guns in under your nose. But I nearly missed getting word to the people that they were here. It must have been Patty here and your soldier that did it.

CAPTAIN HALE: What? Margrove a traitor?

HENRY: Oh, no! I'm sure he didn't know what he was doing. You'll have to get Patty to explain it to you. I couldn't see what was going on. I just heard you send Margrove with Susy so I knew Patty must be sending a message.

CAPTAIN HALE (*To* PATTY): I should like to know how I was outwitted by a little girl.

PATTY: It was the sampler, sir.

CAPTAIN HALE: The sampler?

PATTY: Yes, when you wouldn't let me go with Susy to give the message myself I thought of the sampler. So I made it tell the hiding place.

CAPTAIN HALE: But I saw that sampler myself. I could swear there was no message there.

PATTY: Well, I knew the Mayor's wife would think it odd for me to be giving the sampler to her. For only this afternoon I'd told her it was a gift for my mother.

CAPTAIN HALE: But how did it tell where the guns were hidden?

PATTY: When I said I was finishing it, I stitched in a little black arrow over the red barn. You never noticed it. But I knew Mrs. Maltby would for I'll wager there never was a black arrow on a sampler before and it was new since she'd seen it all finished earlier today. I just prayed she'd guess the reason I'd put it there.

CAPTAIN HALE: So she did. And that's how the villagers got their guns. Well, if the British must lose to the enemy I'm glad it's because of a quick-witted little girl like you. Crocker, I give my sword to a brave man and his daughter. I see the village is once more in colonists' hands.

HENRY (*Taking sword as the* VILLAGERS *free the* CAPTAIN): Right, sir. We can all be proud of Patty, there. But I knew she'd think up some way to get the message through.

WILLIAM, JOHN *and* DEBBY: Hurrah for our Patty!

VILLAGERS: Hurrah for Patty Crocker!

THE END

Keeping Christmas

by Mary Peacock

Characters

EDNA ARNOLD	GERDA	neighbors
ALAN, *her brother*	HENDRIK	
MRS. ARNOLD	KAREN	
MR. ARNOLD	SUSIE	
	KARL	

TIME: *Christmas Eve, 1843.*

SETTING: *The living room of the Arnold home in Bethlehem, Penna.*

AT RISE: MR. ARNOLD *is seated by a table reading, and* MRS. ARNOLD *sits near him knitting.* EDNA *and* ALAN *are peering out a window at right.*

EDNA (*Excitedly*): Oh, look, Alan—you can see the Beidlemans decorating their Christmas tree!

ALAN (*Peering closer*): There's Karl, handing something to his father.

EDNA: It's a star—a big golden star—and his father is standing on a chair to reach the very top!

ALAN: There! He's fastened it on. Oh, isn't it pretty, Edna?

MOTHER (*Turning her head*): *What* is so pretty, children?

FATHER (*Looking up from his book*): Yes, I've been wondering why you've kept your noses glued to the window for so long!

EDNA (*Turning from the window*): We've been watching the Beidlemans decorating their Christmas tree.

ALAN: You should see the things they're putting on it! Shiny silver strings . . .

EDNA: And apples and oranges—

ALAN: And a big gold star on top!

EDNA (*Standing by her mother's chair*): I wish *we* had a Christmas tree!

ALAN: So do I. Everyone else around here keeps Christmas. I don't see why *we*—

FATHER (*Sternly*): Now Alan, you know very well that New England folk don't hold to any such nonsense.

MOTHER: Why, when *my* mother was a little girl in Massachusetts, there was even a law forbidding anyone to celebrate Christmas.

EDNA: But that was so long ago, Mother—and so far away, too. It is different here, in Pennsylvania.

ALAN: Hendrik's mother has been baking for weeks—all sorts of special sweets.

EDNA: At Gerda's house, they've been busy for days, making little fancy cookies—Christmas cakes, they call them.

ALAN: And Susie Meriweather is going to hang up her stocking tonight. She says all the boys and girls do, down in Georgia, where she used to live.

EDNA: Then St. Nicholas comes after they're fast asleep, and fills the stockings with presents. That is, if they've been *good,* of course.

ALAN: But if they *haven't* been good, Susie says St. Nicholas leaves a pack of switches. Wouldn't it be dreadful to find a stocking full of switches on Christmas morning?

MOTHER (*Briskly*): Well, there's no need to worry about what St. Nicholas leaves here, for he will find no stockings to fill!

FATHER: I should say not! Never in all my life did I hear of such foolishness!

EDNA (*Wistfully*): All the same, I *do* think it would be fun.

ALAN (*Pleadingly*): Couldn't we keep Christmas just this once?

MOTHER: Don't tease, Alan. Your father and I never even *thought* of such things when we were your age.

FATHER: And what was good enough for us is good enough for our children. (*A knock sounds on door.*)

ALAN (*Turning away*): Shall I see who's at the door? (*Runs to door and flings it open*) Oh—it's Gerda! Come in!

GERDA (*Entering*): Hello, Alan and Edna—and good evening to you, Mr. and Mrs. Arnold! We were on our way to the Love Feast at our Church, and Mother asked me to stop in and give you this. (*She hands a basket to* MRS. ARNOLD.)

EDNA (*Peering into the basket curiously*): What is in it, Gerda? (MRS. ARNOLD *lifts napkin, and takes out a star-shaped cookie.*)

GERDA: It's a basket of our Moravian Christmas cakes. We thought you might like to sample them.

ALAN (*Reaching in for a cookie*): I should say we would!

MOTHER: Why thank you, Gerda! Please tell your mother that we are very grateful.

ALAN (*Nibbling*): Mmm—they're good!

EDNA (*Tasting cookie*): So crisp and crunchy and sweet!

GERDA: Mother will be pleased that you like them. But I must hurry along.

MOTHER: So soon, child? Can't you stay for a minute?

GERDA: Oh no! I might be late for the Love Feast, and then it wouldn't seem like Christmas Eve at all. So goodnight, everybody—and Merry Christmas!

ALL: Goodnight! (GERDA *goes out, turning at door to wave.*)

MOTHER: What delicious little cakes!

FATHER (*Holding one up*): And what curious shapes! Stars, birds, leaves—(*Another knock is heard at door*)

EDNA (*Running to door*): May I answer this time? (*Opening door*) It's Hendrik! Come in, come in!

HENDRIK (*Entering with bundles*): A pleasant evening to you! My mother sends her greetings, and a loaf of stollen, fresh from the oven. It's to help you celebrate Christmas!

MOTHER: Why thank you, Hendrik. Your mother is most kind.

FATHER (*Sniffing*): And what *is* stollen, pray?

HENDRIK: A kind of sweet bread that all German housewives bake at Christmas time. It has lots of currants in the dough—and sugar is sprinkled on top.

ALAN: Doesn't it smell good, Edna?

HENDRIK: Oh! I almost forgot the sack of winter apples my father sent. (*He puts the sack on floor, and* EDNA *reaches in for one.*)

EDNA: Did you ever see such rosy ones!

HENDRIK: I must be getting home now, or Pelznickel might miss me when he comes for his visit.

ALAN (*Puzzled*): Pelznickel? Who is he?

HENDRIK (*Laughing*): That's just another name we Pennsylvania German folk have for old St. Nicholas. Well, goodnight, everybody—and a happy Christmas to you!

EDNA *and* ALAN: Happy Christmas! (*Exit* HENDRIK)

EDNA: My! I almost feel as if *we* were keeping Christmas, too!

ALAN (*Looking out window*): Edna, look! There's Karen coming up the walk!

EDNA (*Running to window*): With another package, too! (*She throws door open*) Welcome, Karen!

KAREN: My mother sends greetings to your parents. Here is a bit of our lut-fisk, to add to your Christmas dinner.

MOTHER (*Accepting gift*): How thoughtful of your mother!

FATHER: And what is lut-fisk, child?

KAREN: The most delicious smoked fish you ever ate, made

from an old Swedish recipe. We *do* hope you will enjoy it.

MOTHER: I am sure we will. If it tastes as good as it looks—

KAREN: Oh, it does, Mrs. Arnold, really it does!

EDNA: Can't you stay and visit, Karen?

KAREN: Not tonight, Edna. I must hurry home to set out a dish of sweets for the Tomtar.

EDNA: What are *they?* I never heard of them!

KAREN: Oh, they are little elf men who creep in at night and help about the house. Sometimes they leave gifts for my sister and me, and I am quite sure they will tonight, on Christmas Eve! Goodnight, all—may your Christmas be bright!

ALL: Goodnight. (*Exit* KAREN)

EDNA (*Standing with door ajar*): Oh Alan, here comes Susie Meriweather!

ALAN: Is *she* bringing a present, too?

EDNA: I think she is—at least, there's a package in her arms. Hello, Susie! Come in.

SUSIE (*Entering*): I can't stay but a minute. Mother wanted you to have one of her Southern fruit cakes, Mrs. Arnold, and Granny sent popcorn balls for Edna and Alan, too.

MOTHER (*Taking gift*): How good everyone is to us!

FATHER: Christmas Eve in New England was never like this!

EDNA: Isn't it wonderful? Now if we only had a tree. (*Enter* KARL, *dragging a small tree.*)

KARL: Did I hear someone say something about a tree?

ALAN: Karl, you brought one!

KARL: Since you are so new here, I was afraid your father wouldn't know what woods were best for cutting, Alan. So I cut one for you myself. There! (*He sets the tree up straight, slightly to left of table.*)

EDNA: There's even some mistletoe in the branches—and

you brought a bunch of holly, too! Oh, thank you, Karl!

KARL: I hope you have fun trimming it. Well, I must be on my way. The relatives will be coming to see *our* tree lighted, and to sing carols.

ALAN: We watched you decorating it through the window tonight.

EDNA: And we wished for one just like it, didn't we, Alan?

SUSIE: Then your wish came true just like in a fairy story. I'll walk along with Karl, for it's time I was going. Goodnight, everybody!

KARL: And a Merry Christmas to you!

EDNA *and* ALAN: The same to you!

MOTHER (*Calling*): And thank you, thank you both! (*Door closes on* SUSIE *and* KARL.)

EDNA (*Skipping back to her mother*): Now we just *have* to keep Christmas, don't we?

MOTHER (*Turning to* FATHER): Well?

FATHER (*Smiling*): It looks as if the Arnolds are keeping Christmas in spite of themselves!

EDNA (*Excitedly*): The tree—we must decorate that first.

MOTHER: Perhaps we could run strings through Gerda's cookies, and hang them on the branches.

ALAN: And the popcorn balls that Susie's Granny sent.

FATHER: And how would some nice red apples look, bobbing about? I'll fasten strings to the stems. (*They all set to work.*)

MOTHER: Now *why* did the neighbors send all these lovely things, I wonder?

EDNA: Perhaps it was because Alan and I told them that we didn't keep Christmas at our house.

ALAN: And they wanted to show us how much fun it could be. (MOTHER *turns away and stands very still.*)

FATHER: Why, what's the matter, Mother? Aren't you going to help?

MOTHER: Oh, dear! I've only finished one pair of stockings,

instead of two. (*She picks up the red stockings from the table.*) But then they only need one apiece, don't they? Why of course! I never thought of that!

EDNA (*Running to her mother*): Mother! Do you mean we can hang up our stockings, too—for St. Nicholas to fill?

ALAN: How will he know where to find us?

FATHER: St. Nicholas will find his way to every home tonight where families keep Christmas together. I am very sure of that, my boy.

MOTHER: Here, Edna. (*Handing her a stocking*) Here, Alan. (*Handing the other one to him*) Hang them by the hearth. Then we will finish decorating our tree. (*Children hang up stockings.*)

EDNA: There! Oh, isn't it fun—keeping Christmas? And to think, there are so many different ways of doing it!

ALAN: Yes—Gerda's way and Karl's way, Karen's way and Susie's way.

MOTHER: And Hendrik's way, too. But after all, aren't they very much alike?

FATHER: And don't forget *our* way. Somehow I think *that's* going to be the best way of all!

EDNA: Merry Christmas, everybody!

ALL (*Joining and facing audience*): Merry Christmas!

THE END

The Way

by Helen V. Runnette

Characters

INNKEEPER
AMERICANS
DUTCH
FRENCH
MEXICANS
PERUVIANS
ENGLISH
SWEDISH
GERMANS

} *families consisting of men, women and children*

TIME: *Christmas Eve.*

SETTING: *Interior of an inn.*

AT RISE: INNKEEPER *is placing candle at window, near outer door.*

INNKEEPER: 'Tis Christmas Eve. I'll put a light in the window in honor of the Christ Child. Perhaps it will lead some wanderer to the Inn. Ah! Someone is coming. (*He goes to door.*) Welcome! Welcome, sir!

AMERICAN FATHER (*Complainingly*): We've come so far—all the way from America. We're lost, I think. Here I am with all my family, and I haven't any idea which way to go!

INNKEEPER (*Heartily*): Well, now, you don't need to go anywhere tonight. Stop right here and rest yourself—and you too, good lady, and all the children.

AMERICAN MOTHER: That's kind of you, sir. I'll gladly rest a bit—and as for the children, they're tired and hungry and would be crosser than two sticks if it weren't Christmas Eve.

AMER. FATHER: Christmas Eve or no Christmas Eve, I just want to find my way. I'm lost, I tell you. It's like being in a thick forest—too much of everything in the way.

INNKEEPER: Then that's the time to stop and rest, and then take account of yourself and see where you want to go.

1ST AMER. CHILD: I want to go find Santa Claus.

AMER. FATHER: Don't bother the Innkeeper, son.

AMER. MOTHER: Oh, John, the children have to have their Christmas Eve!

INNKEEPER: So they shall. So they shall. (*To child*) What do you want to do?

1ST AMER. CHILD: I want to hang up my stocking.

2ND AMER. CHILD: I want to put my presents under the Christmas tree—(*Lowers voice so only* INNKEEPER *will hear*) for Daddy and Mommy and Tommy, you know.

INNKEEPER: That's just fine. Now show me where you want to hang your stockings. (*Child runs to fireplace to hang stocking.*)

2ND AMER. CHILD: Daddy, don't forget the Christmas tree!

AMER. FATHER (*To himself*): Ah yes, the tree. Now how shall I manage that?

INNKEEPER (*To children*): And so Santa Claus comes down all the chimneys in America and fills all the stockings?

AMER. CHILDREN: Yes! Yes!

AMER. MOTHER: But you must be asleep or he'll never come.

INNKEEPER: I'll show you your room. (*Starts off*—AMER. FATHER *detains him.*)

AMER. FATHER: Innkeeper, I *must* find a tree for the children.

INNKEEPER: I'll be back. I'll help you if I can. (*Exits*)

AMER. FATHER: I don't know what country this is, but surely there must be some kind of tree or bush or something.

INNKEEPER (*Returning. There is loud and repeated knocking at door*): What's that? More guests? (*Opens door.*) Why, bless my soul! 'Tis people from Holland! Come in! Come in!

DUTCH MOTHER (*Stomping with wooden shoes*): Such a state as we are in! We have come so far, and we're very tired, and I'm afraid the children will track in a lot of dirt. Children, take off your shoes before you come into the Inn. (*While they do so she goes to fireplace to warm self.*)

INNKEEPER (*In mock puzzlement*): Now where will I find room for all these pairs of wooden shoes?

1ST DUTCH CHILD: By the fireplace, please, sir.

INNKEEPER: Oh—you want them to get dry?

1ST DUTCH CHILD: Oh, no, sir. We want St. Nicholas to fill them with goodies.

INNKEEPER: So it's St. Nicholas who comes to you?

1ST DUTCH CHILD: If we're good, sir.

2ND DUTCH CHILD: Do you think he'll find us here?

DUTCH MOTHER: You'd better go to bed now to dream of the morrow. St. Nicholas likes obedient children. He will put a switch in your shoe if you're not good. (*Exit* INNKEEPER *followed by* DUTCH MOTHER *and* CHILDREN.)

AMER. FATHER (*To* DUTCH FATHER): Santa Claus and St. Nicholas seem very much alike. Your saint fills shoes and ours fills stockings.

DUTCH FATHER: To be sure. Good saints—good children.

INNKEEPER (*Returning*): Good parents, too. (*Knocking at door.* AMERICAN *and* DUTCH MOTHERS *return.*) Bless my soul! I do believe that's another knock I hear. (*Goes to door and peers out. A troop of French children with lanterns, singing "Un Flambeau," enter gaily, followed by parents.*)

1ST FRENCH CHILD: But where is the *berceau?* I do not see the cradle of the Christ-Child!

FRENCH FATHER (*Explaining*): In France, we always make—

FRENCH MOTHER (*Interrupting*): Where is the creche? Without the creche, where is Christmas?

INNKEEPER: Oh. So there is something more than getting gifts.

2ND FRENCH CHILD: Of course.

3RD FRENCH CHILD: But certainly!

AMER. FATHER (*To* DUTCH *and* FRENCH FATHERS): Sometimes it seems as if there's too much thought about getting gifts. I mean, the way our stores are crammed full of things, and so many people buy gifts for people they don't care for, just because it's the thing to do.

DUTCH FATHER: You mean they've lost sight of the real spirit of Christmas? There's no love in the giving?

FRENCH MOTHER: The creche—that is Christmas, of a truth.

DUTCH MOTHER: What, then, is a creche?

FRENCH MOTHER: You do not know? That is astonishing.

1ST FRENCH CHILD: Tell her.

FRENCH FATHER: In our fair land of France, we make the little figures of La Mere et petit Jesus, of St. Joseph, the ox and ass and sheep—

2ND FRENCH CHILD (*Interrupting*): The shepherds and the Wise Men, and the angels.

FRENCH FATHER: We place them round the manger where they can worship the Babe. And we sing Noëls.

FRENCH MOTHER: Come and let us make a creche—(*Fetch straw, etc.*)

AMER. FATHER: In our country, we often have a manger scene in church—in our homes, too; and we sing "O Little Town of Bethlehem." (*They sing softly.*)

INNKEEPER: Then you do know part of the way?

AMER. FATHER: What? What did you say? (*Knock*)

INNKEEPER (*Peering out of window*): Here come some other Americans.

AMER. FATHER: Oh, they look like *South* Americans.

INNKEEPER: You, then, are *North* Americans?

AMER. FATHER: Well, ye--es, I suppose you might call us that.

INNKEEPER: Go, welcome them. You may be host in my place. (*Enter* MEXICANS *and* PERUVIANS.)

MEXICAN FATHER: Buenas noches, amigos!

AMER. MOTHER: Oh, John, why don't we know any Spanish words!

AMER. FATHER: Let's see—I know a Spanish word. *Adios! Adios!*

PERUVIAN FATHER: But we have just *come* from Peru!

INNKEEPER: 'Twas the only word he knew. Come in, my friends. Here's food and shelter for the night.

MEXICAN MOTHER: *We* come from Mexico. Have you any room for our ninos?

INNKEEPER: How many?

MEX. FATHER: Nine.

AMER. FATHER: Whew!

INNKEEPER: On this night I turn no one away.

MEX. FATHER: You know it is the Holy Night? The Three Kings will ride this way?

1ST MEX. CHILD: Please say they'll find us here!

MEX. FATHER: If you are good and kind, they will find you, wherever you are.

2ND MEX. CHILD: In the whole world?

MEX. MOTHER: In the whole wide world. Come, let us say our prayer and go to bed. (*Gives each a candle*) But first

I will put the little Lord in the manger. (*Children exit.*)

PERUV. FATHER: And I will prepare the piñata.

DUTCH MOTHER: Tell us what a pin—piñata is.

PERUV. FATHER: 'Tis for the children's Christmas. See this fat jug I have, this so-lovely bird? I have carried it all the time so carefully—

MEX. FATHER: So it will not break, you see.

AMER. MOTHER: Wouldn't it look more like Christmas if it were red and green?

PERUV. FATHER: Ah! But 'tis the Christmas *inside* it!

MEX. FATHER: We stuff it full of goodies for the children!

FRENCH FATHER: But how do the children get the bonbons?

PERUV. FATHER: 'Tis a game! (*He hangs piñata in doorway.*)

MEX. FATHER: We blindfold a little one—so. (*He seizes his wife's shawl and blindfolds* AMER. MOTHER'S *eyes.*)

PERUV. FATHER: We put a stick in the hand—(*Does so*)

MEX. FATHER: And give a push toward the big fat bird—(*Does so*)

PERUV. FATHER: And she will try to break it with the stick. (AMER. MOTHER *enters into spirit of game and brandishes stick wildly, almost reaching the piñata.*)

FRENCH FATHER (*Excitedly*): Non! Non! She will break it!

MEX. FATHER (*Guiding* AMER. MOTHER *and removing blindfold*): She is the good child. She learns quickly.

PERUV. FATHER (*Taking stick*): So, she shall have a goody! (*He takes the shawl and presents it with a bow.*)

AMER. MOTHER: Oh, thank you! That was fun!

AMER. FATHER (*Musingly*): Christmas *is* fun. I had almost forgotten. (*Enter Swedish family. They are gay and ready to dance and sing. They bring the* INNKEEPER *a basket of good things.*)

SWEDISH FATHER: Here is thy Christmas, Innkeeper. Be merry all! We have been serenading.

MEX. FATHER: Will you serenade us? That will be good.

SWEDISH FATHER: But here, first, is a Yule gift for everyone.

AMER. FATHER: For me, too?

SWEDISH FATHER: Why not? Yuletime is a love-your-neighbor time.

DUTCH FATHER: Neighbor? Americans live so far from Sweden. Are they neighbors?

SWEDISH FATHER: Assuredly. We all are neighbors in this world—and see, here is a sheaf of wheat for the birds.

INNKEEPER: There is a post outside to fasten it on. (SWED. FATHER *goes out and returns.*)

AMER. FATHER: You even give the birds a Christmas?

SWEDISH FATHER: Aye, give—and give—and give! (*Knocking is again heard.*)

ENG. FATHER (*Entering with three or four of his family*): This is jolly good of you, Innkeeper, to welcome so many guests this Christmas Eve. To tell the truth, we were a little puzzled as to the route we should take.

AMER. FATHER: Welcome, cousin!

ENG. FATHER (*Looking around*): Christmas gifts here? And a creche? Stockings hung up, wooden shoes by the fireside? It looks to me as if good old Father Christmas should put in an appearance.

INNKEEPER: Did you bring no Yule log with you, the Yule log that burns out the memory of old wrongs, and brings happiness and cheer? An English Christmas without a Yule log—

AMER. MOTHER: An American one without a tree—oh, John, the children must have a tree.

AMER. FATHER: Yes, yes. I was going to ask the Innkeeper if there's a sprig of something—anything—we can decorate for a tree.

ENG. FATHER: What say I go outdoors to find a Yule log

and some evergreen branches? (*Exit with two or three children, one a very small child.*)

PERUV. FATHER: Tell us about your tree.

AMER. MOTHER: We hang pretty, shiny, tinsel balls on it—

AMER. FATHER: And we string colored electric lights all over it—

SWEDISH FATHER: *We* light candles and sing and dance.

AMER. MOTHER: Under the tree, we place gifts, all gaily wrapped in colored paper. (*To* SWEDISH FATHER) It's sort of like your Yule basket, isn't it?

PERUV. FATHER: Or like our piñata.

MEX. FATHER: Or the Gifts of the Magi. (*Enter* ENG. FATHER *dragging Yule log, small child astride it; other children carry garlands.*)

ENG. FATHER: We found a Yule log! Now for the garlands. Here are some evergreens. Come on, everyone! Help us hang them! (*They sing "Deck the Halls."*)

AMER. FATHER: It seems as if Christmas has really come to this Inn.

DUTCH FATHER: All kinds of people making Christmas together. That is good.

INNKEEPER: I must open the door once more. Who is this, I pray? (*Enter* GERMANS, *carrying tree.*)

GERMAN FATHER: Pray give us lodging for the night. We Germans have wandered far. The night is cold and dark and we have no place to rest. Pray take us in.

ENG. FATHER (*To* INNKEEPER): How can you take even one more person in?

INNKEEPER: The doors of this house are open wide to all who wish to enter.

AMER. FATHER: I begin to think it is a special kind of house, Innkeeper—a kind of *world*-house.

GERMAN FATHER (*Eagerly*): With room to trim the Christmas tree?

AMER. MOTHER: The Christmas tree!

AMER FATHER: The Christmas tree? You brought a Christmas tree?

GERMAN FATHER: Don't you remember that it is we Germans who have given the Christmas tree to all the world? It is the symbol of eternal life. (*They sing "O Tannenbaum."*)

ENG. FATHER (*Thoughtfully*): Every country gives something special to Christmas.

INNKEEPER: But who gave most?

MEX. FATHER: And who gave first?

FRENCH FATHER: 'Tis the manger that draws us all together!

AMER. FATHER (*Slowly as if thinking it out*): And shows us the way.

PERUV. FATHER: Let us go to the cathedral . . .

SWED. FATHER: With love for all God's creatures!

DUTCH FATHER: We'll praise the Lord, the King . . .

INNKEEPER: Who shows us the way! (*All exit singing "O Come All Ye Faithful."*)

THE END

The Chosen One

by Lucille M. Duvall

Characters

NARRATOR
PÈRE MICHAUD, *a sheep herder*
MISÉ MICHAUD, *his wife*
FELIX MICHAUD, *their son*
PÈRE REYNOULD, *a neighbor*
COUNT BERNARD, *a nobleman*
LADY ELINOR, *his daughter*
PHILIP, *a little crippled lad*
PIERRE, *leader of carolers*
GIRL CAROLER
OTHER CAROLERS
MEMBERS OF THE PROCESSION
FIGURES OF NATIVITY SCENE
CHOIR
READER OF BIBLE STORY

PROLOGUE

NARRATOR:

In far Sur Vane, in northern France,
This Christmas tale is told
And though it's passed from son to son
It never has grown old.

It tells about a peasant poor
Who tended to his sheep
Through summer's sun and winter wind
Yet barely earned his keep.

He had a son, Felix, by name,
Who loved to carve at night
Exquisite figurines and molds
That filled him with delight.

His father felt the time ill spent
Throughout most of the year,
But let him work to make a crèche
When Christmas time drew near.

For then in every single home
A miniature town was made
Amid toy beasts in stable bed
A tiny Christ Child laid.

With tender care the good folk carved
Each little house and tree.
The animals, the manger scene,
Were there for all to see.

To such a home we take you now,
A peasant's cottage bare.
It's the day before Christmas, early morn,
And all the family's there.

Scene 1

Time: *Long, long ago. Early morning, the day before Christmas.*

Setting: *A humble French peasant's cottage. A crèche occupies a prominent position in the room.*

AT RISE: MISÉ MICHAUD *bustles back and forth between table and hearth, preparing the Christmas cakes and humming happily all the while.* PÈRE MICHAUD *sits near table, lacing his boots.*

PÈRE MICHAUD: Mmmmm! Your cakes smell as fine as ever, my dear.

MISÉ MICHAUD: No one in Sur Vane is fonder of his pompou and fougasse at Christmas time than my Père Michaud. And such fine cakes they are this year! (*Displaying cakes proudly*) See how grand they are. (PÈRE MICHAUD *sniffs appreciatively.*) We shall sup well tonight. Let visitors come and be welcome. There is enough for all.

PÈRE MICHAUD (*Grumbling*): A feast tonight and a famine tomorrow. It's all a poor shepherd can do to get bread for his family and keep the wolf from the door—and you talk of feeding the neighbors with the best in the house.

MISÉ MICHAUD: Christmas is a gracious season, and we shall keep it so, if there's no more than a crust of bread to bless and share with others. (*A knock at the door is heard.*)

PÈRE MICHAUD (*As he goes to the door*): That will be Père Reynould. We're to go together to the woods for our Yule logs. Come in, good friend—you look half frozen.

PÈRE REYNOULD (*Entering and stamping his feet with cold*): It turns bitter cold and will worsen before the midnight hour, I fear. Greetings, Misé Michaud, and the best of the season's joy to you.

MISÉ MICHAUD: And to you, good friend. What tidings do you bring?

PÈRE REYNOULD: Good tidings about the festival. The cathedral is decorated and ready. The choir is even now practicing and pilgrims from far and near have gathered for the service tonight. But the roads, I fear, are blocked with snow and it comes down thicker by the moment. But where's my young friend, Felix?

MISÉ MICHAUD: With Beppo, his lamb, in the sheepfold there. (*Nods in direction of inner door*) I declare, the boy has hardly slept or eaten these last few days—what with combing, washing, and brushing that lamb of his and working on his figures for the crèche.

PÈRE REYNOULD (*Crossing to the crèche and examining it closely*): It is a fine crèche. I've seen all in the village and there's not one can hold a candle to this one the lad's carved. One would swear the sheep are grazing on that grass and the cows chewing their cuds in contentment. This is no common lad, Michaud. The boy has talent that should not be wasted here in a sheep herder's cottage.

PÈRE MICHAUD: Let there be no more of such talk lest the boy hear you. There are enough foolish notions in his head now. For days and nights now he has been carving on a little figure he carries in his pocket and will show no one. There's no time for such foolery in a sheep herder's life. Let the boy build his crèche at Christmas, then let him put his knife away until the next season. I tell you he's too occupied with carving. I like it not.

PÈRE REYNOULD: Why not let him be a wood carver if he likes it so well?

PÈRE MICHAUD: And starve to death? It's little enough a carver can make unless he studies under a master, and I've no money for that. No, he shall be a sheep herder just as his father and his father's father, and his great-grandfather before him. Then, at least, there will be loaves of bread to feed the family when I am grown too old and feeble to work any more.

PÈRE REYNOULD: And may it be a long day before that comes to pass, good friend. (*Raises voice*) Felix, Felix, come talk to your old friend and stop wasting time on those old sheep.

FELIX (*Entering from sheepfold*): Good morning, Père Reynould, I didn't hear you come in. I have to comb and brush little Beppo. Oh, I hope he will be chosen!

MISÉ MICHAUD: Don't set your heart on it, little one. There will be so many there.

FELIX: You know lambs well, Père Reynould—do you think Beppo has a chance? I have washed him and brushed him until he is as beautiful as an angel. And I have trained him to lie quietly so he will not disturb the beauty of the manger scene when the time of offering comes. Do you think he will be chosen?

PÈRE REYNOULD: So goes the talk in the village. I have heard none who felt other lambs could measure up to your Beppo.

PÈRE MICHAUD: Come, Reynould, let us be on our way. Felix, be sure to hang out some sheaves for the hungry birds.

MISÉ MICHAUD: And I have promised the good sisters that I would look in on poor sick Misé Matin and try to make her day a little happier. (*Takes shawl from wall and wraps up some of the Christmas cakes to take with her*) Be a good boy, Felix, and finish your crèche. 'Twill be late evening before your father and I get back. Keep the fire going and watch the last of the cakes that are in the oven. When you get hungry, help yourself. There is plenty prepared.

PÈRE MICHAUD: Yes, lad, and see that you don't stir outside the door. The snow falls fast and it's no fit day for little ones to be abroad alone. Come, Mother, Reynould and I will see you to Misé Matin's on our way to the big woods.

PÈRE REYNOULD: Au revoir then, for now, little Felix. I

shall see you tonight in all your glory when Beppo becomes the chosen one, is it not so?

FELIX: I hope so. Au revoir, Père Reynould. Au revoir, Mama and Papa. I shall do exactly as you say. I've much work to do before midnight, too. (*He touches his jacket pocket lovingly as the three exit. He busies himself about the kitchen for a few minutes, then sits down and taking a figurine of the Christ Child from his pocket, becomes completely absorbed in his carving. He is aroused by the sound of laughing and singing outside and goes to the door. There is much loud stamping and confusion. Voices call, "Felix, Felix, where are you?"*) Here, good friends, come in. (*A troop of youngsters enter with much jostling and laughing.*)

PIERRE: We've been to the woods and gathered laurel and evergreens. Now we're on our way to sing carols to the shut-ins. Can you come with us?

FELIX: Not today, Pierre. Papa has gone for the Yule log and Mama has gone to help poor Misé Matin. So I must stay here and watch the cakes and keep the fire going.

GIRL CAROLER: Oh, what a shame! (*In sudden delight*) But Felix, then you are a shut-in. We should carol for you.

CAROLERS: Yes, let's.

FELIX (*Laughing*): That will be wonderful! And when you have finished singing, I shall give each one of you one of Mama's Christmas cakes. (*Takes them from oven*) See, they are fresh from the oven.

PIERRE: It's a bargain. Come, let's sing! (CAROLERS *sing while* FELIX *listens appreciatively. When they have finished he applauds vigorously.*)

FELIX: Bravo! Bravo! You are in fine voice today. Now here are your cakes. (*Passes cakes to the group*)

PIERRE: Many thanks, Felix, and thank your good mother,

too. Tell her we know now it's no idle boast that Misé Michaud's Christmas cakes are the best in the village. (*Group murmurs appreciatively*) But before we go, may we see Beppo?

FELIX: You shall see him tonight for sure. Now he is resting and I would rather not disturb him.

PIERRE: Well then, Felix, until tonight. We shall see you at service. (FELIX *sees them to the door and is about to return to his carving when* PHILIP, *one of the littlest carolers who walks with a decided limp, slips back into the room*)

PHILIP: Felix?

FELIX (*Starts suddenly and hides his carving*): Philip, I thought you had gone with the others.

PHILIP: It's hard for me to walk in the snow and I would only hold the others back. My brother Brian's sled is just outside and I shall ride home with him. But before I go, Felix, may I take one little peep at Beppo? The snow may be too thick for me to come to the midnight service and I shall not see him chosen. I've never seen the service.

FELIX: Sit here, Philip, by the fire. But suppose Beppo is not the chosen one?

PHILIP: But he will be. Everyone says so. Aren't you proud of him, Felix?

FELIX: There are but two things I want of life, Philip, and that is one of them. I love little Beppo as I have never loved anything before. Of course I shall be proud if he is chosen. (*Sighs softly, then speaks in a hushed and reverent voice*) I wish you could see the service, Philip. It is so beautiful that it would make you cry; the soft music, the quiet, and the lighted candles making a pattern in the dark. And there kneeling are rows and rows of people with their eyes fixed on the altar.

PHILIP: Mama told me about that. And on the altar are Mary and Joseph and the Baby Jesus.

FELIX: Yes. Then at midnight there is a peal of bells and the cathedral doors are opened and the great procession enters.

PHILIP: Tell me about the procession, Felix. You've seen it, haven't you?

FELIX: Yes, last year. First there come four peasants with their flutes and flageolets. They sing the song good King René made up three hundred years ago for this very ceremony. Behind them walk ten shepherds, two by two. The first carries a staff and a bowl of fruit, the second a pair of pigeons. All the others carry lighted candles. Last of all comes the offering for the Christ Child, the chosen lamb.

PHILIP: Carried by his owner, my mama says. She told me it was the greatest honor that can come to anyone in Sur Vane to have his lamb chosen.

FELIX: That is why I have worked so hard on my Beppo. Stay here, by the fire, Philip, and I'll bring him to you. (*He goes out. There is a moment of silence, then* FELIX'*s voice is heard, puzzled at first but gradually rising in fear and apprehension.*) Beppo! Beppo! Where are you, little one? (*In panic*) The door—it's open! (*Fading off into the distance*) Beppo! Beppo! Where are you, Beppo?

PHILIP (*Hobbling to the sheepfold door*): Felix, what happened? Felix, Felix, please come back. You will be lost in the snow. Your coat, Felix, you will freeze to death without your coat. (*Crosses back to outside door, crying as curtain closes*) He will surely be lost. Oh, what shall I do?

CURTAIN

* * *

Scene 2

Time: *Late afternoon of the same day.*

Setting: *Same as Scene 1.*

At Rise: *The room is deserted as the curtain opens. The silence is broken by a knock at the door, then another and another. Finally the door opens to admit* Count Bernard *and his daughter,* Elinor.

Elinor: There is no one here, Papa. Perhaps we should not come in like this.

Count Bernard: The good people of Sur Vane are noted for their hospitality. Not one of them would turn us from his door on a day like this. We shall wait here for a while and perhaps the owner of the cottage will return. There's little hope of getting our horses out of that snowdrift unless I can find help. Besides you are much too tired and cold to go on further without a little rest.

Elinor (*Throwing off her coat and looking around*): The heat will revive me. I feel better already. This is a curious room, isn't it?

Count Bernard (*Laughing*): Because your home is a castle, must everyone else live in one, too?

Elinor: Oh, no, Papa. I don't mean that. This is much more home-like than the big cold rooms of the castle. It looks so lived in and cozy. (*Notices crèche*) Look, they even have a crèche.

Count Bernard: Of course! Every family in France, rich or poor, has a crèche for the Christmas season. (*Crossing to the fireplace*) The good folk of the cottage must have been out overlong. The fire grows low. I'll replenish it. (*Puts another log on the fire*)

Elinor: Do come and look at the crèche, Papa. It is such a beautiful one. I've never seen its like.

COUNT BERNARD: Come now. After all the money I've spent to make yours the finest available. Such ingratitude!

ELINOR: Oh, I'm truly grateful, Papa. But do look at these figures. Are they not beautiful?

COUNT BERNARD (*Examining them carefully*): They are the work of a great master. How came they in such a humble cottage, I wonder? They must be priceless.

ELINOR: All of them are of the same fine workmanship. See. There are the sheep, the donkeys, and all of the other animals. How proudly Joseph stands, and how lovely Mary looks. (*Exclaims in surprise*) There's no Christ Child in the manger. I wonder why. (*Before the* COUNT *can answer, the door to the sheepfold opens and* FELIX *comes sadly in, cold, tired, and wet. He goes to the fireplace and leans his head on the mantel, so preoccupied with his grief that he does not notice the strangers at the crèche. The* COUNT *goes quietly to the bereaved lad and lays his hand gently on his shoulder. As* FELIX *looks up in alarm, he speaks compassionately.*)

COUNT BERNARD: I'm sorry, lad. I didn't mean to startle you.

FELIX (*Regaining his composure with difficulty*): That's all right, sir. I didn't see you. I was thinking of my poor Beppo.

COUNT BERNARD: Your Beppo?

FELIX: My little lamb. He ran away from me this morning and though I've searched everywhere, I cannot find him.

ELINOR: Oh, what a shame! Papa, can't we give the little boy another lamb?

FELIX: Thank you, but I—I don't want another lamb.

COUNT BERNARD: Of course. We understand. This is my daughter, Elinor. I am Count Bernard of Bois Varne. We came for the festival tonight but were delayed by the storm. Our carriage is stuck in a snowdrift just down the road and I thought I might find help here.

FELIX: I am Felix Michaud. My father and mother have both gone out, but I will be happy to help you.

COUNT BERNARD: You are in a sad state, little one, and I think you'd better get yourself warm and dried out before the family returns. I'll go on to the next house and see if I can find help there. But may my Lady Elinor stay by the fire until the carriage is ready to take her to the inn?

FELIX: I shall be very happy to have her stay, sir.

COUNT BERNARD (*Patting his little daughter on the head*): I'll not be long. Be careful now that you do not talk poor Felix to death. And mind now, no questions.

ELINOR (*Indulgently*): Oh, Papa! (*She regards* FELIX *intently as her* FATHER *leaves. He seems ill at ease under her scrutiny and she speaks as if to dispel his embarrassment*) Have you any brothers or sisters, Felix?

FELIX: Nay. There were three but all died save me.

ELINOR: I, too, am the only one. So you see we are very much alike. But you have a mama, haven't you?

FELIX: Of course. Everyone has a mama.

ELINOR: I haven't. At least not any more. My mama went to live in heaven when I was very young. But see, I have a picture of her. (*She opens the locket she wears around her neck and shows it to* FELIX)

FELIX: She was very beautiful.

ELINOR: Yes. And my papa says she was as kind as she was beautiful. Everyone loved her. Even the servants cry when her name is mentioned.

FELIX (*Awed*): You have servants?

ELINOR: So many I cannot count them. But I am very lonesome for my mama. You cannot guess how very sad it is to lose someone you love very much.

FELIX: But I can. That is how I feel about my Beppo.

ELINOR: A lamb! But there are so many lambs. You can always get another lamb.

FELIX: But Beppo was different. He was the most beautiful lamb in all Sur Vane. Everyone said so.

ELINOR: I am so sorry that you lost him, Felix.

FELIX: Tonight at the festival he would have been chosen as the offered lamb. I know he would. I've prayed for it so long and I felt so certain.

ELINOR: We would have seen him chosen, for that is why we came to Sur Vane—to see the great festival. Papa has often told me about the procession of the chosen lamb and now I am to see it at last. (*As* FELIX *appears about to cry again*) Don't be sad, Felix. Come, I will help you look for the lamb.

FELIX: Nay. 'Tis no use. I have scoured the hills and woods this livelong day. If Beppo were still alive he would have come when he heard me call.

ELINOR: I do not believe he is dead. For surely the good Saviour watches over his lambs, even the littlest of them. (*Attempting to rouse him from his apathy*) This is such a beautiful crèche. Did you help to set it up?

FELIX: It is mine alone. I made every bit of it with my own fingers.

ELINOR (*Incredulously*): You made the figures, Felix? All of them?

FELIX: Yes. I love to carve. My father has but little patience with me and scolds me when he finds me working at it. But at night when my work is done, I slip back down by the fire and carve as long as I can keep my eyes open.

ELINOR: I can't believe you really made them. Papa says they are the work of a master.

FELIX: But surely he jests. I am but a boy and have no training.

ELINOR: No. Papa meant it. And he would know because even Père Verduin says there is no judge as good as Papa.

FELIX: Père Verduin! The master carver! You know him?

ELINOR: He lives with us. He and Papa grew up together. They are like brothers. That is why I am sure that Papa knows about the figures.

FELIX: I have always dreamed about some day meeting Père Verduin. He carved the portals on the great cathedral. Whenever I am sad or unhappy I go to see the master carver's work. And to think that you know him!

ELINOR: He is a nice man. The very nicest man I know—next to Papa. You will like him, Felix.

FELIX: Like him! Why, it would be the greatest honor of my life even to see Père Verduin.

ELINOR: I know he would like your work if he could but see it.

FELIX: That will never be. Besides I would not dare to show my figures to the great master. I have only this old knife to carve with and there is so much I must learn.

ELINOR: Well, I think they are beautiful, Felix. And even though I have some that Père Verduin carved for me, I would give almost anything to have one like yours.

FELIX: Would you put this in your crèche? (*Holds figure of Christ Child out to her.*)

ELINOR: The Christ Child? But it is for your crèche. (*As* FELIX *continues to hold it out to her*) It is so very, very beautiful. How could you bear the thought of parting with it? It must be the most beautiful thing in the world.

FELIX: Please take it. I want you to have it. It makes me feel better about Beppo, somehow or other. I think I would have died of losing him if you had not told me about the Saviour and the lambs. (*Beseechingly*) You do believe he watches over them? (*At* ELINOR'*s silent nod of assent*) If I could have my Beppo back I'd never, never be vain or want too much again. (*As* ELINOR *is about to answer there is an excited shout and* PHILIP *bursts into the room carrying a bundle in his arms.*)

PHILIP: I've found him, Felix! I've found him!

FELIX: Not Beppo? Not my Beppo?

PHILIP: Yes, it's Beppo. I found him in Brother Brian's wolf trap. Something has been bothering our sheep lately so Brian has set a trap for him.

FELIX (*Taking the lamb from* PHILIP *and cradling it gently in his arms*): My poor Beppo! My poor little one!

PHILIP: He's not hurt, Felix. He's just cold and frightened.

ELINOR: But how did you know he was in the trap?

PHILIP: I didn't, but I felt so badly about Felix losing his Beppo that I decided to help him. I'm too crippled to go a long way, especially in a storm. So I looked everywhere I could think of in the neighborhood. Somehow I felt that Beppo couldn't have gone far alone. The trap was the last place I looked and there he was.

FELIX: Bless you, Philip. I can never repay you for finding him.

PHILIP: I shall be paid back when I see him in the procession tonight.

FELIX: But he will not be in the procession.

PHILIP *and* ELINOR (*In unison*): Not in the procession!

FELIX: I promised that if I got my Beppo back I should not again be vain and proud. I shall wash and brush him as carefully as ever but he shall stay safely at home.

PHILIP: Oh, Felix.

ELINOR: I think you are the bravest boy I ever met, Felix. Papa has read me stories about how knights win a token from their ladies after doing a brave deed. I shall be your lady, Felix, and this token shall bring you good luck. (*Takes ribbon from her hair and pins it on* FELIX)

PHILIP (*Who has wandered to the window*): The snow has stopped. It will be a good night after all.

CURTAIN

* * *

SCENE 3

TIME: *Just before midnight.*
SETTING: *Outdoors, in front of the cathedral.*
[NOTE: *This scene may be played before the curtain.*]
BEFORE RISE: FELIX *appears before the curtain, a sad and lonely figure. Children jostle past him, calling him, but he does not hear them. Various groups move back and forth and there is a growing feeling of excitement as the procession begins to gather. Suddenly,* ELINOR *slips out of the shadows and joins* FELIX.

FELIX: Elinor, what are you doing here? Why aren't you in the procession?

ELINOR: I couldn't find you although I looked everywhere. Suddenly I remembered what you had said about coming to gaze at the carvings on the portals when you felt sad and lonely. You are sad and lonely, aren't you, Felix?

FELIX: Yes, but it is wicked to feel so. I wanted only my Beppo back and I should be happy that he is safe at home, instead of grieving because he cannot be the chosen one.

ELINOR: Felix, I have some glad news for you. Perhaps it will lighten your heart. Papa took your Christ Child to Père Verduin. He said you had the touch of an artist.

FELIX: Père Verduin? But he is not here.

ELINOR: Yes, he is. That was my surprise. But I dared not tell you for fear it would prove to be another disappointment. He came to the festival, too.

FELIX: Père Verduin here in Sur Vane! And he liked my work? I cannot believe it.

ELINOR: And you are to go back home with us and study with him. He says you will be a greater master than he.

FELIX: Oh, that could never be . . . besides, Papa would never let me go.

ELINOR: Oh, but he will. My father has already talked to him and made all the arrangements.

PHILIP (*Running up to him as fast as his crippled leg will carry him*): Felix! Felix! Come quick! The procession is forming and you are to carry Beppo. He has been chosen.

FELIX: But—but he couldn't. I left him home. He is not here.

PHILIP: You must forgive me, Felix, but I brought him after you had gone. I could not believe the good Saviour helped me to find him only to have him left in the sheepfold. I must have been right, for he was chosen. Oh, hurry, Felix, the procession waits.

FELIX: Both my wishes come true. I cannot believe it. (*Feels of the ribbon on his lapel*) The token—it must have brought me good luck. (*The children pull the bewildered* FELIX *with them toward the outer door of the assembly room where the procession has been forming. There is a sudden silence and then as the bells peal the hour of midnight the curtains slowly part to reveal the interior of the cathedral chancel. The Nativity is depicted by Mary and Joseph and the Christ Child. Two tiny angels kneel on either side of the manger. As the* CHOIR *sings softly, the procession enters the church and groups itself about the tableau of the Nativity. At the end of the procession comes* FELIX *with Beppo in his arms. As the* CHOIR *sings softly, he lays the lamb reverently before the manger and then kneels with bowed head. The singing dies away and from the darkness behind the manger scene come the beautiful words of the Christmas story, St. Luke II:1-16. The* CHOIR *sings softly as the curtain falls.*)

THE END

Nine Cheers for Christmas

by Aileen Fisher

Characters

John	4th Boy
Jane	1st Girl
1st Boy	2nd Girl
2nd Boy	3rd Girl
3rd Boy	4th Girl

Nine Children, *representing the nine letters which spell* CHRISTMAS.

Time: *The present.*
Setting: *Bare stage.*
At Rise: *The* Chorus *is lined up in two rows at the back of the stage.* Jane *and* John *step out and come to the front at the right side of the stage.*

John: We went through the village
And knocked at each door;
Jane: We asked everybody
What Christmas was for.
John: And one said . . .
1st Boy: For getting a trinket or toy!
Jane: And some said . . .
1st Girl: For giving.
2nd Boy: For peace.

2ND GIRL: And for joy.

JOHN: We asked every stranger
And person we knew.

JANE: We said, "What's the meaning
Of Christmas to *you?*"

JOHN: And one said . . .

3RD BOY: For feasting!

JANE: And one said . . .

3RD GIRL: For mirth.

JOHN: And one said . . .

4TH BOY: For singing.

4TH GIRL: For gladness on earth.

JOHN: And so we wrote Christmas
A letter, saying, "Please . . .

JANE: "Just *what* do you stand for,
Since no one agrees?"

JOHN: "Just *what* is your meaning?"
And Christmas replied,
(*He takes out a letter; they both look at it, and read slowly.*)

JANE AND JOHN: "Each letter means something.
I'm sending a guide.
I don't stand for *one* thing,
I stand for a lot.
Just follow my spelling
To know what is what."
(JOHN *puts letter back in pocket.*)

1ST BOY: Each letter means something!

1ST GIRL: And CHRISTMAS . . . let's see . . .
(*Counts on fingers*)
Has nine different letters.

2ND BOY: Nine things it must be!

JANE: We've asked all the letters
To come and explain.

JOHN: They should have arrived
On the six-o'clock train!
2ND GIRL (*Pointing to wings at left*):
Oh, look! They are coming.
3RD BOY (*Peering toward wings*):
The letters, all nine,
With "C" as a leader,
Are waiting in line.
JANE (*Tiptoeing back to* CHORUS):
Now if we keep quiet . . .
JOHN (*Tiptoeing back to* CHORUS):
And listen with care . . .
CHORUS: We'll learn why each letter
In Christmas is there.

(*A* GIRL *with a large letter* C *on her headband comes skipping in gaily from left. Eight other children are ready in the wings to come in, each with a bright cardboard letter on headband.*)

C: I am C!
I stand for Carols.
I bring you joy—
Just barrels and barrels.
(*Curtsies joyfully*)
My music sounds
Across the snow;
It loops the globe
By radio;
And during Christmas
Holidays,
I'm sure to be
In lots of plays!
(*Looks around, sees* CHORUS)
I stand for songs of Christmas cheer . . .
Haven't I some helpers here?

CHORUS (*Eagerly*): Yes. Yes!

(*With* C *leading them, they sing a joyful carol, such as "There's a Song in the Air," or "Joy to the World!" or "Hark! the Herald Angels Sing." At the end of the carol,* C *sits down on the floor in front of the* CHORUS, *at the far right of the stage.* H *comes in with a holly wreath.* NOTE: *any evergreen wreath with red ribbon will do.*)

H: H is for Holly—
The colors of Christmas
From pole to pole
And from gulf to isthmus.
Colors of red
And green together,
For light and life
In winter weather.
Hang up the wreath!
(*Goes to hang it near* CHORUS)
And all those near it
Soon feel the tingle
Of Christmas spirit!

CHORUS (*Looking at wreath and calling merrily*):
Merry Christmas! Merry Christmas!
(H *sits down next to* C, *as* R*—a boy—comes prancing in from left.*)

R: R is for Reindeer Santa Claus drives.
On Christmas, we have the time of our lives! (*Prances around*)
We're very unusual; we race through the sky
And never fall down . . . though you mustn't ask why!
You know what we are? The fun and frolic
Of Christmas Eve . . . so away we rollick!
(R *prances to his place next to* H, *and* I *comes in softly and slowly from left.*)

I: I stands for Infant
Born in a manger,

In a land that was strange,
On a night that was stranger.
At an hour that was silent,
A place that was lowly,
An infant was born,
And his birthday is holy.

(*The* CHORUS *sings softly "Away in a Manger" as* I *tiptoes to her place next to* R. *When the song is over,* S *comes in, carrying a sack of toys over his shoulder.*)

S: S is for Santa—a jolly good fellow,
With a smile as broad as a violoncello! (*Makes a big gesture.*)
With a heart as kind and full of devotion
As there are drops in a great big ocean!
With a sack full of gifts, for—as you're living—
Santa Claus means the spirit of giving.

(S *opens sack and distributes miscellaneous gifts to the* CHORUS, *amidst their "Oh's," "Ah's," and "Thank You's." Then* S *takes her place next to* I. T *comes in with a small Christmas tree on a stand, which he places left center. The tree is sparsely trimmed with bright balls and tinsel, leaving room for the stars which the letter* S *brings in later.*)

T: T is for Tree:
The spruce, or fir,
Fragrant and frankincense
And myrrh,
Its branches green as snow is white,
Its speartop pointing toward the light.
Out of the cold
We bring the tree,
And set it here
Where all can see
Its sun-like balls and tinsel-rays,

That brighten up our holidays.
(CHORUS *sings "O Tannenbaum" in English as* T *takes his place next to* S. M *comes in with a handful of Christmas cards.*)

M: M is for Message;
I am starred
On every tag and Christmas card.
(*Begins to look through cards and distribute them to* CHORUS.)
Message of joy.
Message of cheer.
Message of hope throughout the year.
I bring you merry words—just dozens—
From aunts and uncles and friends and cousins!
(*Children in the* CHORUS *look at their cards and read out messages, one at a time.*)

JANE: May Christmas happiness and cheer
Be yours throughout the coming year.

1ST BOY: Merry Christmas! Hip, hooray!
And here's to fun on New Year's day!

1ST GIRL: This lighted candle that you see
Is flashing joy to you from me.

2ND BOY: The ocean's not so full of fishes
As this card is of Christmas wishes!

2ND GIRL: I hope your Christmas will be glad—
In fact, the best you've ever had.

3RD BOY: My fondest wish I now divulge:
I hope your Christmas sock will *bulge*.

3RD GIRL: Words are much too small and few
For all the things I wish for you.

4TH BOY: I'm making tracks, as you can see,
To wish you Christmas jollity.

4TH GIRL: I hope your Christmas will be bright
As tree lights twinkling in the night.

JOHN (*Looking at audience*):
Christmas greetings to you all—
Young and old, and big and small.
(M *takes place next to* T, *while* A *comes in slowly.*)

A: A is for Angel
Who dazzled the sight
Of shepherds who watched
In the cold of the night—
An Angel with tidings
Of peace and good will,
On a night that was holy
And wondrous and still.

CHORUS (*Recites slowly, in the manner of choral reading, Luke,* 2:8-12, *while* A *quietly takes her place next to* M):

"And there were in the same country shepherds abiding in the field, keeping watch over their flocks by night.

And, lo, the angel of the Lord came upon them, and the glory of the Lord shone round about them: and they were sore afraid.

And the angel said unto them, Fear not: for, behold, I bring you good tidings of great joy, which shall be to all people.

For unto you is born this day in the city of David a Saviour, which is Christ the Lord."

(S *comes in, carrying some tinsel stars.*)

S: S is for Star
In the eastern sky,
Which wise men saw
And were guided by.
(*He goes to the tree and puts on stars.*)
And S is for stars
That we all see
Shining each year

On our Christmas tree.

(S *sits down next to* A. *The* LETTERS *should now be sitting across the stage so* CHRISTMAS *is spelled out for the audience.* JOHN *and* JANE *come forward to stand at extreme downright corners of the stage.*)

JANE: We went through the village
And knocked at each door;

JOHN: We asked everybody
What Christmas was for.

JANE: And one said for that thing,
And one said for this;

JOHN: And here we see nine things
That no one should miss!

CHORUS: Nine cheers for Christmas—
A cheer for each letter!
Three cheers are usual,
But *nine* cheers are better!

JANE: The letters in Christmas
Are needed, each one.

JOHN: They stand for its spirit . . .
(H *for Holly, and* T *for Tree stand up.*)

1ST BOY: Its story . . .
(I *for Infant,* A *for Angel, and* S *for Star stand up.*)

1ST GIRL: Its fun!
(R *for Reindeer stands.*)

2ND BOY: They stand for its message . . .
(M *for Message stands.*)

2ND GIRL: Its gifts . . .
(S *for Santa stands.*)

3RD BOY: And its song.
(C *for Carols stands.*)

CHORUS: We need all the letters,
And we did right along!

JANE: And now that we're certain

We have them all right,
Let's sing one more carol;
Let's sing "Silent Night."
(*Everyone on the stage joins in singing "Silent Night," as the curtain falls.*)

THE END

The Twelve Days of Christmas

by Doris G. Wright

Characters

THE KING
THE QUEEN
COURT JESTER
HERALD
LADY ELSPETH
COURTIERS
PAGES
LADIES IN WAITING
LORDS
MAIDS
MILKMAIDS
PIPERS
DRUMMERS
CHORUS

BEFORE THE CURTAIN: *The* KING *enters with a paper and pen in his hand. He paces up and down, looks at what he has written on the paper, shakes his head and scratches it out, heaving deep sighs. The* JESTER *peers in, then slips in unobserved and squats on the floor in a corner. The* KING *continues his pacing and the* JESTER *chuckles. The* KING *turns, startled at this intrusion.*

KING: Knave, why dost thou presume to laugh when thy lord is greatly troubled?

JESTER: Sire, I have a riddle which perchance may divert the King's mind. When is a door not a door?

KING: Bah! Any idiot knows that—when it is ajar.

JESTER (*Crestfallen that his joke has fallen flat*): Forsooth. I have one that I'll wager that thou dost not know.

What is it that when we catch it, we throw it away, but if we do not catch it we keep?

KING (*Stops his pacing to think. Unable to guess he becomes angry with the* JESTER): How should I guess thy silly riddles when I have a far more difficult one to solve? Tell me the answer or I shall give you a lashing.

JESTER: Sire, it is a flea. (*Suddenly he frowns and scratches his back.*) Yea, truly, a flea.

KING (*Scornfully*): A flea. (*Suddenly he begins scratching.*) You and your silly riddles. Now you solve *my* riddle.

JESTER: Certainly, Sire, tell me what it is.

KING: Come and I will make it known to you. (*He pulls the* JESTER *by the ear. The* JESTER *pulls away and leaps nimbly across the stage where he sits cross-legged as far away as possible from the* KING.) The Yule season approacheth— (JESTER *rises and approaches* KING.)

JESTER (*Interrupting*): A time to make merry, to eat (*Smacks his lips, rubs his stomach*), to receive gifts. (*The* KING *strikes at him and the* JESTER, *drawing away from the blow, loses his balance and falls back. The* KING *laughs heartily. The* JESTER *is now the sulky one and gets up rubbing his aching anatomy and putting on his cap which has fallen off.*)

KING (*Beginning all over again*): The Yule season approacheth when every heart *is,* or *should be* joyous. Fain would I give my Queen, the fair Lynette, a gift worthy of her beauty. Alas, she hath jewels, silken gowns without number, a harp of gold to play when she wearies of thy foolish jokes. Alack, what is there in all my kingdom that is not already hers?

JESTER: Sire, leave this matter to me. I have ideas on the subject.

KING: Mind now, the gift must be worthy of the Queen.

JESTER: And if I succeed, do I go unrewarded for my labors?

KING: Have I ever yet not paid my debts?

JESTER: Nay, Sire, not even a lashing when I needed it.

KING: Go, then, and if the Queen is pleased, your reward shall be handsome. But delay not for it lacks but a few days for the merry-making to begin. (*They exit together.*)

* * *

SETTING: *The throne room.*

AT RISE: *The* KING *and* QUEEN *are seated on thrones at one side, the* JESTER *on the steps to the thrones, and the court seated around the room. The* HERALD *enters and blows a fanfare on his trumpet.*

HERALD: His majesty the King hath proclaimed twelve days of rejoicing, when all in his kingdom shall feast and give and receive gifts to celebrate the Yule season. Let joy be unrestrained. (*He goes to one side. A small* CHORUS *sings the first verse of the carol "The Twelve Days of Christmas" and as they finish a* COURTIER *approaches, bows to the* QUEEN *and presents a "partridge in a pear tree." Offstage someone may whistle the partridge's song.*)

QUEEN: Truly, my Lord, this sweet bird is most welcome. When I hear his cheery note I will forget the snow and the chill of winter winds. (*The* KING *smiles and bows in acknowledgment of her pleasure.*)

HERALD (*Coming forward*): The second day of Christmas. (*He retires to one side and the* CHORUS *sings the second verse. At its close, two* COURTIERS *appear with two turtle doves. The doves' cooing may come from offstage.*)

QUEEN (*Smiling at the* KING): The cooing of these doves is music to my ears.

KING: Yes, my love. (*The* JESTER *clears his throat signifi-*

cantly as if to remind the KING *that he is to receive the praise but the* KING *pays no attention to him.*)

HERALD (*Coming forward*): The third day of Christmas. (*As before, the* CHORUS *sings the verse. They sing another verse each time the* HERALD *announces another day. At the close of this verse, three* COURTIERS *appear with three fat hens, each with a bow of ribbon around its neck.*)

QUEEN: These hens, while not so graceful as the doves and the partridge, shall be no less welcome, as each day they shall lay an egg. *One* shall be for my breakfast . . .

KING: And two for mine!

JESTER (*Springs up frowning and attempts to speak to the* KING): Hath the King forgotten his promise of reward . . . (*The* KING *does not allow him to finish his speech.*)

KING: On second thought, the third egg shall go to the Jester. He is a good-natured soul, even though he is a knave. (*The* JESTER *sinks down on the steps, momentarily appeased.*)

HERALD: The fourth day of Christmas. (*This time two* MAIDS *and two* PAGES *bring in four blackbirds, singing. Offstage someone may blow a toy musical instrument.*)

LADY ELSPETH: Before my Lady e'er dreamed of being a queen we roamed the fields, two happy girls together, and in the spring the blackbirds' song did tell of golden weather.

QUEEN: 'Tis true, Lady Elspeth, and my heart turns over in my breast for joy at their sweet notes. Ne'er have I received such gifts as these. My Lord hath outdone himself, for fair. (*The* KING *smiles complacently, but his joy is short-lived as the* JESTER *rises and starts to tell him he is the clever fellow. The* KING *pushes the* JESTER *down on the steps and whispers in his ear. This silences the* JESTER, *but the* KING *glances at him uneasily from time to time.*)

HERALD: The fifth day of Christmas. (*Five* MAIDS *skip in rolling five gold hoops. The* QUEEN *is so delighted that she flips her train over her arm and descends from the throne.*)

QUEEN: I pray thee, may I join in thy sport? (*One of the* MAIDS *relinquishes her hoop, and the* QUEEN *and the other four trip gaily around the stage. Then the* QUEEN *returns the hoop and mounts the throne.*) For the moment I quite forgot that I am now a queen and must conduct myself with the dignity befitting that rank.

KING (*Anxiously*): Dost thou regret those carefree, girlish days?

QUEEN: Nay, my Lord. But even the happiest queen likes to throw off the cloak of dignity at times, to be a girl again.

HERALD: The sixth day of Christmas. (*Six* COURTIERS *enter bringing six geese.*)

JESTER (*Springs up and turns a cartwheel*): With six geese a-laying, the cooks can make omelettes, custards, cakes, sweet pastries, pies, meringues . . .

KING: Greedy pig, thou dost forget thyself.

JESTER: Sire, it is thou who dost forget that I am to receive a reward for—

KING: Silence! Did I not promise thee a new-laid hen egg for thy breakfast every morning?

JESTER: Yea, but one small egg is small reward for all of my hard work.

KING: Thou shalt have thy share of all the goodies and a handsome reward as well, only be not so forward in claiming it.

HERALD: The seventh day of Christmas. (*Seven swans in a simulated pool are pushed on the stage.*)

ALL: Oh, how lovely—how beautiful.

HERALD: The eighth day of Christmas. (*Eight* MILKMAIDS *enter with pails and stools.*)

A COURTIER (*Sings*): Where are you going, my pretty maids?

MAIDS (*Sing*): We're going a-milking, sire, they said. (*They finish the song.*)

JESTER: Now we shall have milk punch, creamy eggnog—

KING: Hold thy tongue, thou glutton. Thinkest thou of nothing but thy stomach and what goes in it?

JESTER: Yea, sire, of my reward. (*He ducks as the* KING *slaps him.*)

HERALD: The ninth day of Christmas. (*Nine* DRUMMERS *march around the stage. The* JESTER *jumps up and follows after them, imitating them.*)

KING: Something other than food hath at last stirred thy knavish heart. (*All laugh.*)

HERALD: The tenth day of Christmas. (*Ten* PIPERS *parade around.*) The eleventh day of Christmas. (*Eleven* LADIES *enter and dance a minuet.*) The twelfth day of Christmas. (*Twelve* LORDS *dance. At the conclusion of the dance, the* KING *rises, deciding he can no longer pretend he has thought of these gifts and is resigned to giving the* JESTER *his due.*)

KING: It is plain to all that not only is my Queen pleased with her gifts, but that they have given pleasure to all. It is now time to reward him who hath assembled them, so now I bestow this purse and robe upon the Jester, who shall no longer be a Jester but shall become one of my wise counsellors. It shall be his first duty to find a new Court Jester. (*The* JESTER *is completely taken by surprise. As its full import dawns on him he becomes highly elated and springs up, immediately tripping and falling over the cumbersome robe which the* KING *has just placed on his shoulders. All laugh heartily, thinking the* JESTER *has tripped on purpose. The more injured and sulky the* JESTER *becomes, the more they laugh. Sud-*

denly the JESTER *turns to the* KING, *and throwing off the robe he dons his cap and bells again.*)

JESTER: Sire, thy praise and the gratitude of thy fair Queen are full reward for my labors. 'Twould be a burden to be serious and wise so long have I cut capers. Now I cannot change. If it please thee, I'll keep the purse and claim the fresh-laid egg for breakfast, but return this cloak and be a jester 'til I die. (*Advancing to the front of the stage, he speaks to the audience.*) "I would do what I pleased, and doing what I pleased, I should have my will, and having my will, I should be contented." (*As the curtains close slowly, the whole cast sings a verse of the carol.*)

THE END

LOWER GRADES

The Legend of the Christmas Rose

by Eleanore Leuser

Characters

MADELON, *a shepherd girl*
ESTEBAN, *her older brother*
ALDERAN, *her younger brother*
JOSEF, *her youngest brother*
ANDRES, *a neighbor boy*
MICHELA, *a neighbor girl*
THE THREE WISE MEN
THE ANGEL
OTHER ANGELS

TIME: *The first Christmas.*

SETTING: *A snow-covered road near the field where Madelon tends her sheep. There is a well at left, and a large rock near center stage.*

AT RISE: ESTEBAN *runs in breathlessly as though looking for someone.*

ESTEBAN (*Calling*): Madelon—Madelon—where are you?

MADELON (*Entering. She carries a crook.*): I am here, Esteban, looking after my sheep. What is it?

ESTEBAN: Three most noble strangers have just now alighted at our door and are coming down the road for a drink of water at the well.

MADELON: Why so excited, my brother? We have surely seen strangers before.

ESTEBAN: Not like these! They are richly dressed and bearing gifts. They say they are going to a place of great importance not far from here.

MADELON: Bearing gifts—to a place not far from here. That is indeed strange. Why and for whom? Surely you found out more. . . .

ESTEBAN: They were so thirsty and weary I had not the heart. See, here they come. Perhaps you can ask them, sister, after you have given them water. (*The* THREE WISE MEN *carrying caskets enter and come to the well.*)

1ST WISE MAN: May we have a drink of water from your well? We have traveled far and would quench our thirst.

MADELON (*Stoops and fills a cup from the well. She hands it to each in turn as she refills it.*): Gladly! All travelers like our water. Do you still have far to go?

2ND WISE MAN: We think not, for we have been following the Star, and now it moves slowly—very slowly. Soon it must stop.

MADELON: What seek you? Whom would you find?

3RD WISE MAN (*Who has been sitting on the rock*): We seek the Holy Babe—He that was born in a manger. We bring Him royal gifts, for we have heard that He is to be King and Saviour of all mankind. We would worship Him.

MADELON: What a wondrous tale! I, too, would see this Babe.

1ST WISE MAN: You? A little girl? Had you not better stay close to home this frosty night?

2ND WISE MAN: My brother is right. (*Kindly*) Besides, one must have a gift to bring the Holy Babe. (MADELON *looks crestfallen.*) Would you like to see the treasures we are carrying to Him?

MADELON (*Eagerly*): Oh, yes, if I only might! (2ND WISE

MAN *opens his casket.* MADELON *and* ESTEBAN *peek inside, overcome with wonder.*) Ooooh—it's gold, rich yellow gold!

ESTEBAN: See all the jewels!

1ST WISE MAN: We must be on our way, my brothers, lest the Babe be moved and we do not find Him. Come. (2ND WISE MAN *closes casket.* 1ST *and* 2ND WISE MEN *start offstage.* 3RD WISE MAN *notices that* MADELON *and* ESTEBAN *look disheartened and lets his brothers go off ahead.*)

3RD WISE MAN: Do not look so sad. All gifts need not be rich and magnificent.

MADELON: You mean that even humble shepherds like us might bring gifts?

3RD WISE MAN: Yes. No matter how humble the gift or the giver, the Babe will rejoice. If the giver has wrought the gift himself or put something of himself into it, I think it will be as welcomed and as blessed as all the gold and jewels of kings and princes. (*He hurries off to join the others.*)

ESTEBAN: How wonderful of him to tell us that! I wish I could go and see this Babe.

MADELON: Why not, Esteban? If this King or Prince or Wise Man has spoken truly, why not go? Take our little red cockerel that we raised together. Then go at once, eldest son of our father, and find the Babe.

ESTEBAN: A thousand thanks, my sister. I shall go. (*He hurries out.*)

MADELON (*Sitting on rock*): How wonderful! A Holy Babe born in a manger and a star to lead people to Him.

ALDERAN (*Running in*): Our brother has told me of the Babe in the manger. He is going to find Him. I wish I could go, too.

MADELON: Go then, Alderan. Take the gray goose with you. It belongs to all of us, after all. Did we not save it from dying of cold and of hunger? Is it not a pet of our house?

ALDERAN: I'll take it gladly and be on my way. (*Runs off-stage*)

MADELON: I hope there will be many people going to worship this Babe. (JOSEF *enters and goes up to* MADELON. *He is sobbing.*)

JOSEF: Sister, sister, both my brothers are going to see this newborn Babe. But I cannot go with them, for I have no gift.

MADELON: Do not fret, little Josef. I will think of something.

JOSEF: They are taking the red cockerel and the gray goose. There is nothing left for me.

MADELON: Look, I will give you my little pet lamb.

JOSEF: He is all yours. He follows you everywhere with his wobbling legs. You love him dearly.

MADELON: We all love him, little Josef. Take him. He will be a fitting gift for the new Babe.

JOSEF: Thank you, Madelon, thank you! (*He runs off as the two* NEIGHBOR CHILDREN *come in.*)

MADELON: Greetings, Andres! Greetings, Michela! Are you two going on a journey?

ANDRES: Indeed we are! We have been hearing about the Royal Babe who lies near here in a manger. We are off to worship Him and rejoice.

MICHELA: We have heard that we do not have to offer Him rich gifts but something that we ourselves treasure.

ANDRES: So I am taking Him this shepherd's flute. You know how many hours I spent fashioning it from a reed. It is the best I ever made.

MICHELA: I have put some honey in this basket I wove myself. Do you remember how you helped me with it—how slow I was at learning? Yet you said it was good when I was finished.

MADELON: Indeed you have woven it beautifully, Michela.

MICHELA: We stopped to see if you would not come with us, Madelon. Truly nothing so wonderful has ever happened before.

MADELON: I would love to see this Babe better than anything on earth but I cannot leave my sheep. You two go on and be sure to stop and tell me everything about Him when you return.

ANDRES: That we will, Madelon. Come, Michela, we must hurry. (*He takes* MICHELA*'s hand and hurries her out.* MADELON *sits sadly on the rock. An* ANGEL *appears with a wand tipped with a lily. She touches* MADELON *gently with it.*)

ANGEL: What is the matter, Madelon?

MADELON (*Looks up and starts*): An Angel in my Father's fields! Indeed strange things are happening.

ANGEL: Why are you sad, Madelon?

MADELON: Indeed, I should not be. Everyone is going to see the newborn Babe . . . He that is to be a King and Saviour of mankind. I should be filled with happiness that He is born, but—but I should like to see Him, myself.

ANGEL: Why do you not go, Madelon?

MADELON: I could not leave my sheep.

ANGEL: I will guard them for you, Madelon, for you have sent your brothers, thinking not of yourself. This is a Holy Night. Now will you go?

MADELON: An Angel guarding my sheep! That would indeed be wonderful, but still I cannot go. I have no gift to take.

ANGEL: Are you certain, Madelon?

MADELON: Most certain! The red cockerel and the gray goose that we owned together I sent with my older brothers. To little Josef I gave my pet lamb. I cannot carve a flute like Andres, and Michela is taking honey in the basket I taught her how to weave. Gladly I saw these things go, but I have nothing I could offer.

ANGEL: Think, Madelon, think! Is there nothing else that you have worked over and put your whole heart into?

MADELON: I can think of nothing.

ANGEL: Think again! What did you do here in the spring? Your back ached. You worked from dawn till dusk. You carried water to them, and the whole neighborhood shared in their loveliness.

MADELON: Why, I had forgotten. I made a little garden here by the well, and tended it. It grew fair for all to see and I gathered many flowers and sent them round about to people who had none. But it is winter now and the blossoms all have died and the snow has covered them.

ANGEL: The blossoms have not died, Madelon. They wait for you to gather them to take to the Holy Babe! See! (*She touches the ground by the well with her wand.*)

MADELON: It cannot be possible! A rose in winter! (*She stoops down and picks it.*)

ANGEL: From now on there will always bloom a white rose in the middle of winter to show that one shepherd girl thought of others besides herself. Go—it is a fitting gift for this Child who was born in a manger.

MADELON (*Stooping and picking more roses*): I shall go, kind Angel. I go and rejoice and worship the Holy Babe. (*The* ANGEL *stands watching* MADELON *as she goes offstage. Then she turns and beckons and a group of* OTHER ANGELS *join her and sing "Silent Night" as the curtain closes.*)

THE END

Granny Goodman's Christmas

by Rowena Bennett

Characters

VAGABOND
GRANNY GOODMAN
HOUSEWIVES, *three*
SMALL BOY
SMALL GIRL
WOODMAN
COBBLER
TAILOR
ELF-MEN, *two*
NEIGHBORS
CHILDREN

TIME: *A few days before Christmas.*
SETTING: *Granny Goodman's kitchen.*
AT RISE: GRANNY GOODMAN *sits at the kitchen table, sobbing, her handkerchief to her eyes, while around her lies the ruin of her Christmas cooking. Broken dishes, upset tins, stray cookies and cake crumbs are scattered over table, chairs, shelves and floor. Outside there is a sound of singing.*

VAGABOND (*Singing offstage, to tune of "Yankee Doodle"*):
I'm on my way to Granny's house
  To have some Christmas puddin'—
There's no cook in all the world
  Like good old Granny Goodman.

Granny Goodman keeps it up,
  Granny Goodman, darling,

Gives the hungry food and sup
  And does not charge a farthin'.

(VAGABOND *sticks his head in at the window, right, calling jovially.*)

Good morning, Granny Goodman,
  I bring you Christmas wishes . . .

(*He sees poor* GRANNY *and the ruin all around her. Gives an astonished whistle*)

Good grief! Whatever happened here?
No wonder that you shed a tear!
  Who was it broke your dishes?
Alackaday! Alackaday!
  Such food! And so delicious!

(*He takes a bright bandanna handkerchief from his pocket and mops his brow mournfully. He shakes his head, then turns and calls offstage.*) Come, neighbors near! Come, neighbors far!
  Come, tailor, cobbler, woodman—
Come see what's happened to the house
  Of neat old Granny Goodman.

(*His head disappears from the window and he enters at the door, left.* GRANNY *looks up at him, points with a sweeping gesture to her disheveled room, then buries her face in her arms on the table sobbing again loudly. The* VAGABOND *goes over to her and puts a friendly hand on her shoulder. As the sobs diminish, the neighbors begin to arrive. Some of them look in at the window. Some come in through the door. There are little people and big, a few with their wraps thrown on hastily, and many carrying tools or utensils to indicate the various occupations they left in their haste. They speak rapidly, almost talking at the same time.*)

ALL (*As they enter*): OOOOH!
  Alackaday! Alackaday!
  Who threw this precious food away?

CHILDREN (*Running around, almost in tears, looking over and under scattered tins or plates*): What's happened to
our Christmas cakes
That dear old Granny always bakes
Just for us . . .

1ST HOUSEWIFE (*Looking at floor*): Oh, what a muss!

SMALL BOY (*Picking up an empty cooky tin*): Where is the
gingerbread man
She used to bake me in this pan?

SMALL GIRL (*Carrying doll*):
Where are the scones and apple tarts
She sends to me, all shaped like hearts?

2ND HOUSEWIFE (*Opening a cupboard and looking in*):
Her Christmas cookies, where are they?
She always bakes so many!
I saw them only yesterday
And now there are not any . . .

(*From time to time everyone looks at* GRANNY *for explanation, but she keeps her head buried in her arms.*)

WOODMAN (*Picking up a few forlorn leaves from the floor*):
And all her pretty Christmas greens
She bought for decoration
Have disappeared. (*He goes over to* GRANNY *and pats her on the shoulder.*)
Oh, I, for *one*
Would like some explanation!

GRANNY (*Wiping her eyes and straightening her little cap*):
It all began on yester-night
Before I blew the candlelight:
I set a trap for nosey rats.
(*She points to cage-like trap in corner.*)
I baited it with cheese and sprats.
I didn't want any goodies nibbled,
My cookies crumbled, candies dribbled.

ALL: Of course you didn't. We know *that!*
But did you catch a mouse or rat?
GRANNY: Oh, no! Oh, no! Much worse than that!
I caught an *elf-man* in my cage!
ALL (*Aghast*): AN ELF-MAN?
GRANNY (*Nodding*): Yes, and what a rage
That elf was in! I can't begin
To tell you of the noise and din
That wakened me this morning early.
ALL (*Curiously*): You let him out?
GRANNY: Of course.
ALL: But he's still mad, no doubt.
GRANNY (*Weeping*): He warned me with a dreadful shout—
Then tossed my goodies all about.
He made my house an ugly mess,
And he'll come back again, I guess.
(*She sobs wildly.*)
ALL: What *can* we do? What *can* we do?
To make that elfin chap
Believe it was a bad mistake—
The setting of that trap!
VAGABOND: I know! I know! I have a plan!
Let's all give gifts to that small man.
What if the rat trap *did* displease him?
The Christmas spirit will appease him.
GRANNY (*Excitedly*): He'll know I never meant to tease him.
ALL: Yes, Christmas presents ought to please him.
WOODMAN (*Holding up an evergreen spray*): Here is a branch I chanced to cut,
When I was working near my hut.
Since elfin men are very wee,
This branch would make his Christmas tree. (*He stands it up, center.*)

ALL (*Enthusiastically*): An elf-man's tiny Christmas tree!

CHILDREN: Oh, leave the trimming to the boys
And girls, for we have brought some toys! (*They set to work trimming tree with lights, balls and tinsel.*)

COBBLER (*Taking a scrap of leather from his pocket*): I'll make for him a pair of shoes—
The *dancing* kind that elf-men use.

3RD HOUSEWIFE (*Getting out her knitting*): These socks I knitted for a baby,
But they will fit an elf-man, maybe.
(*She holds them up and then puts them under the tree and sits down to knit more.*)

TAILOR (*Holding up a scrap of bright green cloth*): What elf man would not like *this* shade?
He'll have a coat that's tailor-made.
(*He gets out his scissors and begins to cut.*)

GRANNY (*Taking up her broom and starting to sweep*):
Now I had better sweep and dust
And clean a room that's badly mussed.

NEIGHBORS (*Who are not occupied*): We will help you make things clean,
And hang a bit of Christmas green.
(*All sing "Jingle Bells" as they work.*)

GRANNY (*As all finish work and song*): It must be almost eventide
We'll light the candles, then we'll hide.

ALL: Yes, we must hurry. We must hide. (*They light candles and find hiding places about the room. They peek out now and then—here and there. After a few moments two* ELF-MEN *enter, tiptoeing.*)

1ST ELF-MAN (*To* 2ND, *in stage whisper*): Now, I'll show you what I did:
Broke her pot and cracked the lid,
Strewed things here and flung things there,

Tossed her dishes everywhere. (*He waves his arms, bursts into laughter.*)

2ND ELF-MAN (*Looking about in astonishment*): Strewed things here? Flung things there?

Where, you stupid? Tell me *where?*

1ST ELF-MAN (*Looking about, puzzled*): Well! I can't believe my eyes!

This is surely a surprise! (*He almost bumps into the Christmas tree as he wanders about eyeing things. Suddenly he sees the tree and his eyes all but pop out.*)

What is this? This lovely thing

Standing where the shadows cling?

2ND ELF-MAN (*Running over to look*): What is that? Oh, deary me!

A Christmas tree! A Christmas tree!

(*The tree all at once bursts into light.*)

ELF-MEN (*In awe and pleasure*): Oh!

1ST ELF-MAN: I scarcely can believe my eyes!

See! The tree is *elfin* size.

There are presents on it, too—

A coat for me and shoes for you.

(*He picks them off tree and the two* ELVES *dress up as they talk.*)

1ST ELF-MAN: See the playthings and the toys—

Everything an elf enjoys. (*They play with them.*)

2ND ELF-MAN: Granny is the best of friends.

You had better make amends.

1ST ELF-MAN: I will bake and so will you.

We will bake and we will brew.

(*He begins to get out pans and bowls.*)

2ND ELF-MAN (*Dancing about delightedly*): We will boil and we will stew.

(*He, also, begins to get out cooking materials.*)

ELF-MEN: It's the least that we can do.

1st Elf-Man: First of all, let's chop some wood
For the oven.

2nd Elf-Man: Yes, we should!
Everyone must have some fuel
When he bakes the cakes of Yule.
(*They help themselves to a hatchet and a saw as they talk. Then off they go skipping merrily. As soon as they disappear* Granny Goodman *and neighbors come out of hiding.* Granny *gazes after the departing* Elves *and smiles. Her neighbors rush in and surround her.*)

All: Hurrah for Granny Goodman!
She'll nevermore feel tragic.
Her Christmas cakes and cookies
Will all be baked by *magic.*

Granny: But that's because of old friends,
Of tried friends and true.
I would not have a feast to *share*
If it were not for *you.* (*She throws them kisses.*)

All: Hurrah for Granny Goodman! (*They join hands and circle around her singing "Auld Lang Syne."*)

THE END

Twinkle

by Claribel Spamer

Characters

TWINKLE
GLITTER
SPARKLE
THE STAR OF BETHLEHEM
OTHER STARS
SANTA CLAUS
NED } *Santa's helpers*
TED }

SETTING: *The sky.*

AT RISE: NED *and* TED *enter excitedly, skipping and jumping as they talk. They carry brushes and cloths.*

NED: Santa has left Santa Land and will be coming through as soon as it is dark. I wish the stars would hurry up and come out. There is so much to be done.

TED: Yes, yes! I get so excited when Christmas Eve finally comes. There won't be much time for polishing.

NED: We shined the stars up pretty well last night, but of course they must be *extra* bright tonight. (*Looks offstage*) They ought to start coming out.

TED: A quick dusting will do, I think. After all, we want to watch Santa from the edge of the sky. The brushes will take off any new tarnish spots in a hurry. (GLITTER *enters from right.*)

NED: Starlight, star bright, first star I've seen tonight—

TED: Wish I may, wish I might, have the wish I wish tonight.

GLITTER: You said that last night.

NED: But last night wasn't Christmas!

TED: Christmas needs an extra special wish.

NED: Yes—a wish that it will be the best Christmas yet. That's a good wish. (TWINKLE *enters from left.*)

TWINKLE: I heard you. Can stars wish too? There is something I want very much.

TED (*Scratching his head*): I don't think so. After all—

TWINKLE: Why not? Glitter is the first star *I've* seen tonight.

NED: You're sure you haven't looked in a mirror?

TWINKLE: No, no. I never see myself, except once in a great while, when the ponds and lakes down below are unusually calm.

TED: I guess it's all right.

GLITTER (*Glancing offstage to left and right*): Hurry, because here come the others.

TWINKLE (*Quickly*): Starlight, star bright, first star I've seen tonight. Wish I may, wish I might, have the wish I wish tonight. (*Sighs*) There! I hope it works. (SPARKLE, STAR OF BETHLEHEM, *and other* STARS *enter from right and left.*)

NED: Oh, Bethlehem, you are beautiful tonight! Just a tiny speck of tarnish, perhaps—(*Whisks at him with his brush*)

TED (*Waving his cloth at him*): Or in case there's the least bit of dust.

STAR OF BETHLEHEM (*Drawing away from them*): I am perfect. This is my night. (NED *and* TED *busy themselves cleaning up the other stars.*)

SPARKLE: I wish I were as bright as you.

ANOTHER STAR: I wish I had guided the Wise Men to the infant Christ.

GLITTER: Cheer up! Tonight we shall *all* shine brightly.

TWINKLE: We'll help Santa see his way to the world.

ANOTHER STAR: Let's look down and see the people. (*They all go to the benches and, sitting or kneeling, look over them and downward.*)

SPARKLE: There's a house right below.

NED: An old couple lives there. They wrote Santa and told him not to stop because they didn't need anything.

TED: They don't have very much, but they said Santa should spend his time visiting the children. They know he doesn't have much time.

TWINKLE: That's where my tree is, too!

STAR OF BETHLEHEM: *Your* tree!

TWINKLE: The tree I call mine. The big fir tree in their yard. Isn't it a beauty?

GLITTER: It's a nice enough tree, but hardly much for that poor old couple to own. I understand they have very little, just enough to get along on. (*Sleighbells are heard offstage at right.*) Here comes Santa! (*They all jump up and run toward right.* SANTA *enters.*)

SANTA: Merry Christmas! I'm on my way through, and stopped to see if you are all in Christmas dress. (*Bells keep tinkling offstage at right.*)

STAR OF BETHLEHEM: We are. (*He turns around to show himself to* SANTA.)

SANTA (*Nodding approval*): Fine. (*All the stars turn, and* SANTA *nods again.*) Very good. You will light my way very well. Now I must be going. The reindeer are impatient.

TWINKLE (*Stepping toward him*): Santa—

SANTA: Well?

TWINKLE: Would you grant me a favor as a Christmas present? I made a wish tonight.

NED: Don't tell it, or it won't come true.

TWINKLE: You told. You said you wished it would be the nicest Christmas.

NED: No, I didn't. I said that would be a good wish but I didn't say whether or not I wished it.

TWINKLE: I don't care. I want it so much, Santa, will you take me with you?

SANTA: Twinkle, I can't. I have a full load already.

TWINKLE (*Sadly*): I suppose I must stay up here and shine with the others. But I've always wished I could be like the Star of Bethlehem and shine very brightly for an extra special reason.

STAR OF BETHLEHEM: You're too small.

TWINKLE: Not for—

TED (*Interrupting*): Santa, the old couple's house is right below. Are you going there?

SANTA: I'd like to, but if I am to see all the children in the world, there isn't much time. Since they understand so well, I'm sure they'll have a wonderful Christmas anyway, knowing how generous they've been with my time. I must hurry. Goodbye. (*Moves toward right, waving.* STARS *and* NED *and* TED *wave. He exits right. Bells tinkle loudly and then recede, dying out completely.* STARS *and* NED *and* TED *return to the benches and look down again, all except* TWINKLE, *who stands wistfully near center front.*)

TWINKLE: I wished on Glitter, I asked Santa—

NED: Come on over and watch, Twinkle. We can see Santa in his sleigh.

TWINKLE: I'm afraid my wish won't come true. There isn't much time.

TED: It's only a game anyway, wishing on stars. Forget it.

TWINKLE: A game? Then wishing is no use, really?

NED: Not really. If you want something you must do it yourself.

TWINKLE: Yes, I guess I must. Santa couldn't do it because he is too busy doing the things he has to do *him*self. The old couple make Christmas for *them*selves. And I'll do this for *my*self.

TED: What?

TWINKLE (*Speaking rapidly*): Go to my tree. Shine on the top of it for all the forest creatures and the old couple to see. Make a beautiful star just for them alone. Like the Star of Bethlehem did for the Wise Men and those who went to see Jesus. (*Ecstatically*) Goodbye! (*Rushes offstage at left. All others peer intently over benches.*)

SPARKLE: She dived out of the sky!

ANOTHER STAR: She is a shooting star for all the world to see!

STAR OF BETHLEHEM: She is landing on the top of the old couple's fir tree!

NED: Isn't she beautiful!

TED: Listen. (*Silence, while they all strain to hear.*) The old couple have come out of the house and are gazing at the tree and Twinkle. They are singing carols.

NED: That was Twinkle's wish, that she could sit on that tree.

TED: For the old couple.

STAR OF BETHLEHEM: Tonight is Twinkle's night. Mine was long ago. (*All sing "Twinkle, Twinkle Little Star" or a Christmas carol as curtain closes.*)

THE END

A White Christmas

by June Barr

Characters

SNOW KING
SNOW QUEEN
TEN SNOWFLAKES
JACK FROST
NORTH WIND
EAST WIND

SETTING: *A cloud.*

AT RISE: KING *and* QUEEN *are seated on thrones.* QUEEN *is adjusting the beret on the* 7TH SNOWFLAKE. *The other* SNOWFLAKES *are dancing around, bouncing up and down, etc.* 2ND SNOWFLAKE *teases the girls, pushing, chasing, etc.* 10TH SNOWFLAKE *moves dreamily around on the edges of the group.*

1ST SNOWFLAKE (*Jumping in excitement*):
It's here at last! It's Christmas Eve!
Oh, Snow Queen, is it time to leave? (*Runs over to her.*)

9TH SNOWFLAKE (*In superior tone*): 'Course not, be still, you silly boy!

3RD SNOWFLAKE (*Eagerly*):
But Christmas is a time for joy!

QUEEN: The King will tell you when to go.

KING: We're waiting for Jack Frost and the Winds, you know.

8TH SNOWFLAKE: Won't it be *fun!* I can scarcely wait!

1ST SNOWFLAKE: Maybe we should start, so we won't be late! (*Starts for edge of the cloud*)

QUEEN: You'd better calm down, you're far too excited.

1ST SNOWFLAKE: But—Christmas!! And *snow!!!* Won't the folks be delighted?

7TH SNOWFLAKE (*Starting to cry*): Oh, I'm afraid to fly through the air! (QUEEN *puts arm around her.*)

5TH SNOWFLAKE (*With authority*): Just close your eyes, and you'll soon be there!

4TH SNOWFLAKE (*Boasting confidently*): *I'm* not afraid! I shall dance and whirl! (*Dances and whirls.*)

2ND SNOWFLAKE (*Teasing*): Look at him! Ha! He's as pretty as a girl! (4TH SNOWFLAKE *stops, makes face at* 2ND)

6TH SNOWFLAKE (*Giggling*): *I'll* have fun, too! Oh, how nice it will be! (*Does a little dance step, holding out skirt.*)

10TH SNOWFLAKE (*Dreamily puts arm around* 7TH SNOWFLAKE, *as* QUEEN *smiles*): You won't be afraid if you stay close to me. . . .

1ST SNOWFLAKE (*Yelling with excitement*): Oh, here's the North Wind coming in! (NORTH WIND *enters, huffing and puffing, followed by* EAST WIND *and then* JACK FROST, *who grins broadly all the time.*)

3RD SNOWFLAKE (*Eagerly*): And East Wind and Jack Frost! Now we can begin! (*Dashes toward door, with* 1ST SNOWFLAKE *on his heels.*)

KING: Wait a minute! Come back, you two! (*They reluctantly turn back.*)

NORTH WIND (*He has come to bow before* KING *and* QUEEN, *followed by* EAST WIND *and* JACK FROST): Oh, King, we have come to report to you.

KING (*Motioning them to rise*):
Yes, how are things in the world below?
QUEEN: Are the people eager to have it snow?
NORTH WIND: Oh, yes, your Majesties, everyone's singing
Of glistening trees—
EAST WIND:
And sleigh bells ringing . . .
(KING *and* QUEEN *exchange smiles,* SNOWFLAKES *dance up and down.*)
KING: Did you give them a hint?
JACK FROST: I nipped their toes!
NORTH WIND:
There's simply no counting the puddles I froze!
EAST WIND:
I whistled and moaned, and I heard people say,
"We'll surely have snow for Christmas Day!"
(1ST SNOWFLAKE *has been jumping up and down, running back and forth, clapping softly, etc., and now he stops and looks dismayed and frightened.*)
1ST SNOWFLAKE:
What has happened? What's that I felt?
Oh, dear Snow Queen! I'm starting to melt!!
QUEEN:
You will get excited! Now stand still, do, please.
NORTH WIND (*Laughing with the others at* 1ST SNOWFLAKE's *chagrin*):
Come stand close to me, I'm so cold you will freeze!
(1ST SNOWFLAKE *goes close to him, and wherever the* NORTH WIND *moves, he goes with him.*)
QUEEN:
Well, they've all done their duty, everything is set.
KING (*Standing up*):
A White Christmas they want, and a White Christmas they'll get!
Is everyone ready?

3RD SNOWFLAKE (*Dashing for doorway*): I am!

4TH SNOWFLAKE: I, too!

7TH SNOWFLAKE (*Fearfully*): Oh, dear!

KING (*Stepping down from throne, followed by* QUEEN): Now, Snowflakes, you know what to do!

1ST SNOWFLAKE (*Excited again*): We fly down to earth . . .

5TH SNOWFLAKE: And we cover the ground!

2ND SNOWFLAKE: We steal down in the night.

8TH SNOWFLAKE: We don't make a sound.

10TH SNOWFLAKE: Some of us drift.

6TH SNOWFLAKE (*Giggling*): And some of us are whirled.

3RD SNOWFLAKE (*Eagerly. Leans out door as though leaning over edge of cloud*):
Oh, I see lights! I see down to the world!
Ooohhhhhh! (*Exits tumbling, as though he fell over the edge.*)

9TH SNOWFLAKE: He's gone! (*All rush to door to look after him.*)

2ND SNOWFLAKE: He fell over!

1ST SNOWFLAKE: Oh, I see him! Look there!

7TH SNOWFLAKE:
Why, how softly and gently he floats through the air!
Come, let us try it . . . (*Turns to* 10TH SNOWFLAKE, *who looks at* KING.)

KING (*Nodding*): Go ahead, and goodbye. . . .
(10TH SNOWFLAKE *takes* 7TH SNOWFLAKE'S *hand, and they step out door as though stepping off edge of cloud.*)

1ST SNOWFLAKE (*Excited as usual*):
Come on then, let's all go, we'll fill the whole sky!
(*He jumps off, others glance to* KING *and* QUEEN *and they nod.*)

4TH SNOWFLAKE:
I shall whirl round and round. (*Exits.*)

2ND SNOWFLAKE:
I shall spin as I go! (*Exits.*)

9TH SNOWFLAKE (*Smoothing dress*): *I* shall float daintily. (*Exits.*)

5TH SNOWFLAKE:
Look out below! (*Exits.*)

8TH SNOWFLAKE (*To* 6TH SNOWFLAKE):
Come along, let's follow, for we are the last!

6TH SNOWFLAKE (*Giggling*):
Hurry, or we'll be late!

NORTH WIND:
I'll blow you down fast!
(*The last two* SNOWFLAKES *exit, with* NORTH WIND *blowing along after them.*)

EAST WIND:
I'd better come, too! (*Exits.*)

JACK FROST:
And I! They'll be lost
Without the cold pictures of happy Jack Frost!
(*He exits, with a goodbye wave to* KING *and* QUEEN, *who smile at each other and then turn back to their thrones.*)

QUEEN (*Sighing*):
Weren't they nice? So twinkly and sparkling and bright!

KING:
Yes, earth will have its White Christmas all right!

THE END

Candles for Christmas

by Helen L. Howard

Characters

THE CANDLE MAKER
PETER, *his grandson*
STRANGER
FREDRICK, JUDITH, SYLVIA } *Village Children*

TIME: *On Christmas Eve.*
SETTING: *In the Candle Maker's Shop.*
AT RISE: *The* CANDLE MAKER *is dipping candles, while his grandson,* PETER, *is stirring the kettle hanging in the fireplace.*

PETER: Grandfather, what tall candles you are making!

CANDLE MAKER: These are the church candles for this Christmas Eve.

PETER: I am anxious to see the church and all your beautiful candles! And the crèche with the Christ Child and the animals about it. Do you know what I wish for, Grandfather?

CANDLE MAKER: What, Peter?

PETER: A lamb! I wish I had a lamb like the one Elan, the shepherd boy, brought to the Christ Child. How I should love a little lamb to hold and feed.

CANDLE MAKER: Ah, Peter, we have no sheep here, and I have no money to buy one from the shepherds.

PETER (*Runs to him*): Oh, no, Grandfather! I am sorry I said that I wanted a lamb! It just came out without my meaning to say so. (*The bell over the door rings and the three children enter.*)

FREDRICK: Come, Peter, it is time to go to the forest to get the Christmas greens for the church.

JUDITH: What beautiful candles you are making, sir.

SYLVIA: Christmas candles are so much prettier than everyday candles!

CANDLE MAKER: More love goes into them. That's why.

PETER: Grandfather, may I go with them to get the Christmas greens?

CANDLE MAKER: Why, of course, Peter. The candles are all dipped now.

PETER: I'll bring some extra greens for the shop window. Goodbye, Grandfather. Thank you for letting me go. (*Children exit.*)

CANDLE MAKER (*Watches the children through the window and then turns back to his work table*): A lamb! A little white lamb like the one the shepherd boy brought to the Christ Child. (*The* CANDLE MAKER *goes to the fireplace and removes the kettle of left-over candle drippings. He pours the warm wax into a jar. Suddenly he stops and looks at the warm white wax.*) The wax! When it is warm, it is soft. Perhaps I could mold a lamb from the wax. A little white lamb from the wax. (*Begins to mold the wax into a little lamb*) With a bit of wick placed just so it will be a candle. It will look like the little white lamb Elan, the shepherd boy, brought to the Christ Child. (*While the* CANDLE MAKER *is working the* STRANGER *enters followed by* PETER *and the three children.*)

PETER: Here, sir, is the Candle Maker. Grandfather, we

met this gentleman on our way to the woods. He has lost his way and we told him you could help him.

CANDLE MAKER: Welcome, good sir. I hope you will stop with me and rest awhile.

STRANGER: Thank you, Candle Maker. I would like to watch you work.

PETER: Oh, Grandfather, what is this? (*Picks up the lamb*)

JUDITH: It's a real little lamb!

SYLVIA: Just what you wanted, Peter.

FREDRICK: Let me hold him. (*Touches the lamb as* PETER *holds it out to him*) Why, it's wax! Just like a candle!

CANDLE MAKER: It is the lamb you wanted, Peter.

JUDITH: How I would like one!

SYLVIA: So would I! Look, he even has a little black nose.

FREDRICK: Perhaps my father would order one!

CANDLE MAKER: I'll make one for each of you if I can get the wax.

STRANGER (*Stepping forward*): This little lamb is beautifully made. Can you make candles into other figures as well?

CANDLE MAKER: To be sure I could. I could make other sheep and a shepherd as well. And angels and choir boys in their robes!

PETER: And Christmas trees! And Elan, the shepherd boy, holding the lamb, his gift to the Christ Child.

CANDLE MAKER: If I only had the wax!

STRANGER: You shall have all the wax you need, Candle Maker. I shall furnish the wax. (*Gives* CANDLE MAKER *a bag*) I shall pay you now for one hundred candles to be ready by next Christmas.

CANDLE MAKER (*Opens bag*): A bag of gold pieces! Oh, sir, this is too much.

STRANGER: It is little enough for your artistic work. I order them for your king.

CANDLE MAKER: My candles for the king!

CHILDREN: Candles for the palace!

STRANGER: And each year, hereafter, we should like you to make many candles such as these, for the palace. I shall send the wax at once and the drippings you may use to make lambs for the village children.

CANDLE MAKER (*Bows*): Oh, thank you, sir. An order like this for each year. Oh, Peter, we're rich! Tomorrow you shall have a real live lamb for your Christmas!

PETER: Just as I dreamed of having! What a merry, merry Christmas it is, Grandfather.

CANDLE MAKER: My candles will bring Christmas happiness to many people. The little figures will remind us of that first Christmas, and the candlelight will brighten our homes and welcome weary travellers to our doors. Every year my candles will say "Merry Christmas" to the world!

THE END

Merry Christmas Customs

by Mildred Hark and Noel McQueen

Characters

BOY
GIRL
SANTA CLAUS
MARTIN LUTHER
DRUID
SIR HENRY COLE
ITALIAN BOY
FRENCH GIRL
GERMAN BOY
OTHER CAROLERS
SHEPHERD

TIME: *Late Christmas Eve.*

SETTING: *A living room decorated for Christmas. There is a fireplace in the right wall and a large, decorated Christmas tree at left. Two stockings hang on the fireplace and there are Christmas cards on the mantel. A large sprig of mistletoe hangs over the door at center. The stage is dimly lighted.*

AT RISE: BOY *and* GIRL *tiptoe into room.*

BOY (*Looking around*): I guess Mama and Papa have gone to bed all right.

GIRL: Yes, and that's where we ought to be.

BOY: I couldn't sleep.

GIRL: It's hard to sleep on Christmas Eve.

BOY: Besides, I wanted to have one more look at everything.

GIRL: So did I. (BOY *goes to wall and pushes light switch.*

Christmas tree lights come on and rest of stage is lighted. GIRL *sighs and looks around.*) Christmas is so beautiful and happy!

BOY: Of course. That's why everybody says, "Merry Christmas."

GIRL: So many wonderful things happen at Christmas time. I wonder how all the different customs got started. Why do we have Christmas trees and hang up our stockings?

BOY: Why do we send Christmas cards and put mistletoe over the door?

GIRL: What about Santa Claus? Why, he must have been coming every Christmas Eve for hundreds of years. I wonder why he started doing it.

BOY: I don't know. (*He sits in chair and yawns.*) I guess I'm too tired to think about it now.

GIRL (*Sitting in chair and yawning*): I'm getting sleepy, too, but the tree's so beautiful, so bright and shiny. (*Sleepily*) I just want to sit and look at it for a while. (*They lean back in chairs. Their heads nod forward. There is a pause. The sound of sleigh bells is heard offstage.*)

BOY (*Looking up*): Sleigh bells!

GIRL: It's Santa Claus coming now. (*She jumps up and starts left.*) We'd better go!

BOY (*Rising*): No. It's someone at the front door. You know Papa always hangs those old sleigh bells out for Christmas, to ring instead of the doorbell.

GIRL (*Turning*): That's right, but who'd be coming in the middle of the night? Let's see who it is. (*They tiptoe to door, and* BOY *opens it. Both jump back in surprise, as they see* SANTA CLAUS *standing in the doorway. He has a large bag over his shoulder.*)

BOY *and* GIRL: Santa Claus!

SANTA CLAUS (*Coming in and closing door*): Of course it's

Santa Claus! Who did you expect on Christmas Eve? Merry Christmas! Merry Christmas!

BOY *and* GIRL: Merry Christmas! (*They back downstage and sit again in the chairs.*)

SANTA CLAUS: I must get to work. (*He puts his bag down near the fireplace and takes out small toys, fruit, and candy.*) Seems to me I heard you talking about me just before I rang your bell.

BOY: Yes, we were.

GIRL: I was wondering how you ever started bringing presents to children at Christmas time.

SANTA CLAUS: I don't blame you for wondering. It all started so long ago I can hardly remember myself. You see, I'm really a saint. I'm Saint Nicholas, the patron saint of children, so I started going around every Christmas with gifts for the good children and switches for the bad ones.

BOY: Switches? Do you still have them?

SANTA CLAUS (*Laughing*): Ho, ho, ho! No, I gave that up. Seems most boys and girls go out of their way to be good around Christmas time.

GIRL: If you're really Saint Nicholas, why do we call you Santa Claus?

SANTA CLAUS (*As he fills the stockings*): The Dutch children started changing my name. First they called me San Nicolaas and then that became Sankt Klaus and finally Santa Claus. The Dutch and German children started this business of the stockings, too.

BOY: You mean they were the first ones to hang them on the fireplace for you to fill?

SANTA CLAUS: No, they didn't hang stockings. They put their wooden shoes in a row in front of the fireplace. Then, after some of their people moved to America, the children didn't use wooden shoes any more, so they hung up stockings instead. (*He finishes with last stocking.*)

Much more convenient, too. I don't have to lean over so much. (*He picks up bag and goes left to tree, takes out packages and puts them under tree.*)

GIRL: How did giving presents start, Santa?

SANTA CLAUS: That goes way back to the old Romans and their god, Saturn. He was a god of peace and happiness and contentment. They celebrated by giving gifts. They did it at the same time of year that we celebrate Christmas, so we took over the custom.

BOY: Did they have Christmas trees, too?

SANTA CLAUS: In a way they did. They didn't call them Christmas trees, of course, but they did decorate trees with trinkets.

GIRL: With lights, too?

SANTA CLAUS: No, not lights. Would you like to meet the man who first put lights on a tree?

BOY *and* GIRL: Yes, where is he?

SANTA CLAUS: Just a minute. (*He starts for door.*) You've probably heard of Martin Luther, the great religious leader. He's the man. (*Opening door*) Mr. Luther, won't you come in? (MARTIN LUTHER, *wearing a dark robe, enters.*)

LUTHER: Why, thank you, Saint Nicholas.

SANTA CLAUS (*Closing door*): You see? Mr. Luther goes way back. He still calls me by my old name. (*To* LUTHER) I was telling these children that you were the first one to put lights on a tree. Isn't that right?

LUTHER: Why, yes, it is. I had the idea of decorating an evergreen tree for Christmas. I put candles on it to represent the star above Bethlehem on the first Christmas Eve, and that was probably the first Christmas tree.

GIRL: Mr. Luther, I'm so glad you started Christmas trees.

LUTHER: Thank you, my dear. I certainly had no idea that I was starting something that was going to last so long and spread to so many countries.

BOY: Did you begin the custom of hanging mistletoe, too?

LUTHER: No, that was started long before my time by the ancient Druids who lived in what is now France and the British Isles. There is a member of that ancient tribe outside right now. (*Starting for door*) Shall I ask him to come in?

SANTA CLAUS: By all means. He'll be welcome.

LUTHER (*Opens door and beckons with his arm*): Come in, come in. (*A* DRUID, *dressed in a light-colored robe, enters.* LUTHER *closes door.*)

DRUID: Thank you. A merry Christmas season to all.

SANTA CLAUS (*Pointing*): We've been wondering about the mistletoe you see hanging over the door. Do you know how the custom was started?

DRUID: Yes, I can tell you. In olden times, mistletoe was an emblem of peace. After wars, enemies would stand under some mistletoe and embrace to show they were friends. It became a very popular custom.

GIRL: It's still popular. Papa always kisses Mama under the mistletoe.

DRUID: Kissing under the mistletoe has been going on for thousands of years.

GIRL: What about sending Christmas cards? Have people been doing that for a long time, too?

DRUID: No, no, that's a modern custom. It's only a little over a hundred years old. It was started by a man named Cole.

SANTA CLAUS: That's right. Sir Henry Cole. (*Starting for door*) I'll call him in. (*Opening door, calling*) Sir Henry, Sir Henry, won't you come in? (SIR HENRY COLE *enters.*)

SIR HENRY (*As he enters*): A happy Christmas to everyone. What can I do for you?

SANTA CLAUS (*As he closes door*): Tell us about your Christmas cards. When did you start making them?

SIR HENRY: That was in the year 1846, in my little art shop

in London. I had an artist design a card with a picture of a merry family celebrating Christmas.

BOY: How many cards did you make, Sir Henry?

SIR HENRY: Only a thousand, but that was a big job because they all had to be colored by hand. Today millions of Christmas cards are sent out each year. (*There is the sound of carolers singing off.*)

GIRL: Listen! Carolers are coming.

BOY: Who can they be? It's so late.

SANTA CLAUS: You don't know them, but for many years they've followed me as I make my rounds. (*He starts for door.*) They are from different countries all over the world. (*He opens door.*) Come in, come in, all of you! (CAROLERS *enter wearing costumes of different countries. They are singing a Christmas carol.* SANTA CLAUS *closes door and then goes upstage left with* SIR HENRY. LUTHER *and* DRUID *move upstage right.* CAROLERS *are at stage center. As* CAROLERS *finish singing*) Ho, ho, ho, we're having a fine Christmas Eve celebration. (*To* BOY *and* GIRL) Have you learned enough about Christmas customs?

BOY: We've learned a lot, but tell us about singing carols.

SANTA CLAUS: That's an old custom. Maybe some of these folks can tell us about it.

ITALIAN BOY: In Italy, we don't call them carols. We call them *pastorelles*.

FRENCH GIRL: In France, the Christmas songs are called *noels*.

GERMAN BOY: The custom started in Germany. People sang carols while they danced around a crib in a church. Later on they walked about from house to house singing. (*Some of the* CAROLERS *move left, some right.*)

SANTA CLAUS: There, you see, all your questions have been answered. You've found out how our Christmas customs started. (*Sleigh bells on door ring.*) Still more guests!

(*Going to door and opening it. A* SHEPHERD *stands in the doorway.*)

SHEPHERD: Good evening, Saint Nicholas. I am a shepherd. May I come in?

SANTA CLAUS: Of course, you'll be welcome. (*He closes door.*) There were shepherds watching their flocks by night on the first Christmas Eve.

SHEPHERD: I was one of them. I've been listening to all that you've been saying about Christmas customs. They are all related in some way to that night in Bethlehem. (*He goes to stage center and indicates* SANTA CLAUS *and various objects as he speaks.*) The message we received was "Peace on earth, good will toward men." You show that spirit of good will, Saint Nicholas. So do the gifts and cards we give. The mistletoe is an emblem of peace. The tree, the shining decorations, the bright-colored lights—all are things of beauty to remind us of that glorious time when our Lord came on earth. The songs we sing are sung because of Him, like the song we heard as we watched our flocks by night. (CAROLERS *begin to sing "Glory to God in the Highest." All except* BOY *and* GIRL *join in the singing.* BOY *and* GIRL *nod their heads forward, asleep as the curtain falls.*)

THE END

Little Chip's Christmas Tree

by Lucille M. Duvall

Characters

GRANDFATHER
CHIP
PUCK, TWINK, SLIP, FLICK, PUDGY, SAUCY — *elves*
TWO GUARD ELVES
NINE CAROLERS

TIME: *Long, long ago.*

SETTING: *The interior of a poor cabin in Ireland. There is a fireplace at center back with a large window to the right of it. A tall evergreen stands at left of fireplace.*

AT RISE: GRANDFATHER *is stirring up the fire.* CHIP *stands at window, looking out.*

GRANDFATHER: It's a cold wind that's blowing out there. I'm after thinking it's going to be a bitter night.

CHIP: I'm afraid so, Grandfather. The Little People will be needing the warmth of the fire tonight to cheer them up.

GRANDFATHER: Aye, it's been a hard winter for them. For us, too.

CHIP: You mustn't feel sad, Grandfather. Soon I will be big enough to help you chop wood. Then we shall have enough money to have a fine feast to celebrate the Christ Child's birthday.

GRANDFATHER: This year we have only a crust of bread. You are only a little boy, Chip, and Christmas should be a happy time.

CHIP: It will be. This is the first year that I have been old enough to go caroling with the village children. Besides, you told me yourself that it is more precious to give than to receive.

GRANDFATHER: What do we have to give, little one?

CHIP (*Pointing to tree*): We gave shelter to the Little People during the cold winter nights. The extra fuel did not cost us much, and think how happy it must have made them.

GRANDFATHER: Perhaps you're right. I must be going now to chop wood. Be sure to wrap up warmly if you go caroling.

CHIP: I will, Grandfather, but I still wish that you would let me help you with the Yule log for the big house.

GRANDFATHER: Not this year. The log is too big and you are still too small. Next year you can help me. (*As he goes toward door*) Listen, I hear your friends now. (*Offstage sound of children's voices singing a carol becomes stronger.* GRANDFATHER *and* CHIP *stand quietly and listen. As the music stops,* GRANDFATHER *exits left. There is an offstage chorus of greetings between* CAROLERS *and* GRANDFATHER, *then* CAROLERS *burst into the room.*)

1ST CAROLER: Come, Chip, not ready yet?

2ND CAROLER: Hurry, the villagers will think we are not coming.

3RD CAROLER (*Looking around as* CHIP *takes down his outer wraps from a nail on the wall and begins to put them on*): I say, what's this? (*Points to tree*)

4TH CAROLER: A tree! What are you doing with a tree in the house? (*They all laugh.*)

CHIP: It's for the Little People. They live in trees, you know.

5TH CAROLER: The Little People?

6TH CAROLER: I know. They're elves—little elf men. My great-granny told me about them. They live in the branches of evergreen trees. Why did you bring the tree into the house, Chip?

CHIP: It's been such a cold and stormy winter. I worried about the Little People out there in all kinds of weather. So Grandfather said I might bring their tree in where it will be warm for them.

7TH CAROLER: How do you know they come into the house?

CHIP: I often hear them after I'm in bed at night. They sing and dance all night long.

8TH CAROLER: Do you ever watch them?

CHIP: No, you must never do that. If you see an elf, the spell is broken and they will never come back again.

9TH CAROLER: The villagers will go without their caroling if we don't get started soon.

CHIP: I'm ready. (*As* CAROLERS *exit*) Wait just a minute until I open the window a little so the elves can get in. (*Opens window, then rushes out after* CAROLERS. *Voices can be heard caroling, then gradually fading out into the distance. The mischievous face of* PUCK *appears at the window. He looks around the room, then climbs in, followed by a throng of little elves.*)

PUCK: Hurray! We're safe. They're both gone.

SAUCY: Let's hurry. We don't want them to get back before we finish.

PUCK: Don't be in such a rush! We've loads of time and this heat feels good to me. (*Holds hands out to fire*)

SLIP: We didn't come here to relax, Puck. We've enjoyed a warm place to sleep all winter, thanks to little Chip. Now it's our time to help him.

PUDGY (*Returning from an exploratory trip offstage right*): I've looked in the cupboard. There's nothing to eat but a crust of bread.

PUCK: Poor Pudgy! This is no place for you, is it?

PUDGY (*Indignantly*): I was thinking of little Chip. Remember how he went out in the snow to gather nuts and berries for us so we wouldn't go hungry in winter?

FLICK: We must pay him back somehow. Can't you help us with some magic, Twink?

TWINK: I'll try! (*Goes to right exit, waves hands, chants mysteriously*)

Hippy, hoppy,
Empty shelves.
Shame on you,
Now fill yourselves.

PUDGY (*Who has followed* TWINK, *jumps up and down in excitement*): Look, look, they're full of food.

TWINK: The best part is they'll always be that way. That's part of the magic. (*To* PUDGY *who is pacing up and down the room deep in thought*) Now, shall we go?

PUCK: No, wait. That's not enough to repay Little Chip all his kindness to us. (*Looks around the room*) What else could we do?

SAUCY: I know. Let's dress up the tree.

SLIP: Dress up the tree?

SAUCY: Yes, make it beautiful. Then the whole room will shine. Remember the way he hung nuts and berries on it for us? Let's hang our treasures on it.

FLICK: We're taking them to the Fairy Queen.

SAUCY: We could make her some more tonight.

PUCK: The very thing. Why didn't I think of that? (*Goes to window and calls*) Ho, guards, bring in the treasures. (*Two* GUARD ELVES *carrying sacks over their shoulders clamber into the room.*) Here, spread them out on the table. (GUARDS *empty sacks of brilliant Christmas decorations on table. There are "Oh's" and "Ah's" of admiration from all.*)

SLIP: Let's hurry. It will take us all night to make more treasures for the queen. (*All bustle, and to the strains of "Let's Trim the Christmas Tree," they proceed to decorate the tree with the ornaments. There is much laughter and excited talking.* GUARDS *make a trip outside and return with greens to decorate the mantel. Some of the others find candles for either end. When they finish, they stand back and admire their handiwork, then show their joy by capering around the stage to the tune of the music.*)

PUCK: Sh-h! Quiet! I think I hear the carolers. (*There is complete silence and the* CAROLERS' *song can be heard faintly, as if from a distance.*)

SLIP: Hurry. We mustn't be caught here. (*They all exit gleefully through the window with the exception of* PUDGY *who can't quite make it and sticks in the window.*)

PUDGY (*Frantically*): Help me! Help me! I'm stuck. (*There is a sound of muffled laughter from the elves and then* PUDGY *disappears through the window just as the* CAROLERS *burst in through the door.*)

1ST CAROLER: It feels good in here! It's nice and warm.

2ND CAROLER (*With teeth chattering*): I'm so cold I don't know what to do. (*All crowd up to fireplace so intent on getting warm they do not notice tree or decorations.*)

3RD CAROLER: And hungry! I could eat most anything.

CHIP: I'm sorry. We have only a crust of bread and I must save that for Grandfather.

GRANDFATHER (*Entering at door*): Share it with your friends, Chip. It's not much, but it's all we have to offer.

CHIP (*Going offstage right*): Grandfather, look! The cupboard is full of food.

4TH CAROLER (*Starting to go to* CHIP, *but stopping suddenly when he notices the tree*): Chip, what's this? Look, your tree is full of beautiful ornaments. (*All gather around examining and exclaiming over tree*)

CHIP (*Bewildered*): Grandfather, what is this? What can it mean? Who has filled our cupboard with food and trimmed our tree with treasures?

GRANDFATHER: It could be no one but the Little People. Once when I was a child I saw a sample of their work. It was like this.

6TH CAROLER: But Great-Granny said the Little People were mischievous elves who loved to play tricks on people.

GRANDFATHER: That's true, but they are said to never forget a favor, and Chip has been their friend.

CHIP: I can't wait until tonight to thank them.

GRANDFATHER: I'm afraid that's impossible, Chip. Once they give you a gift, you will never see them again.

6TH CAROLER: But they say if the Little People visit you, luck will go with you the rest of your days.

CHIP: How can I ever thank them for being so kind to me?

7TH CAROLER: There must be some way that you can show them how much you appreciate their kindness.

8TH CAROLER: The tree!

CHIP: The tree?

8TH CAROLER: Why not bring in a tree each Christmas Eve and trim it with these treasures in memory of the elves and what they did for you? Then they will know you have not forgotten them.

CHIP: A Christmas tree! That's a wonderful idea.

9TH CAROLER: Let's all do it. It sounds like fun.

1ST CAROLER: Come on. What are we waiting for? We still have time to get a tree tonight.

CHIP (*As they start to exit*): Wait—there's food now.

3RD CAROLER: That can wait. We've a lot to do. (CAROLERS *exit. Their voices can be heard raised in song.* GRANDFATHER *and* CHIP *listen until the sound dies out in the distance.*)

CHIP: Grandfather, what a wonderful night this is.

GRANDFATHER: All because you thought of others more than you did of yourself. Come, let's have our feast. There's plenty of food now, thanks to your little friends. (CHIP *and* GRANDFATHER *exit as curtain closes slowly.*)

THE END

Old King Cole's Christmas

by Marguerite Atherton

Characters

KING COLE
QUEEN COLETTE
FIDDLE-DEE-DEE } *the Fiddlers Three*
FIDDLE-DEE-DO
FIDDLE-DEE-DUM
NITA } *maids*
RITA
LITA
SIR ALGERNON GRUMPY, *Prime Minister*
FLIP, *the King's page boy*
FATHER, *Flip's father*
SERVANTS
COURT ATTENDANTS
VILLAGERS

TIME: *Two days before Christmas.*
SETTING: *Throne Room of King Cole's Castle.*
AT RISE: FIDDLE-DEE-DEE *is seated on a stool, head in hands, looking dejected.* FIDDLE-DEE-DO *is standing at right.* FIDDLE-DEE-DUM *paces up and down at left.*

FIDDLE-DEE-DEE (*Sighs*): What a gloomy place this court has become! No one ever laughs or smiles—or even says anything cheerful. We all go around with long faces.

FIDDLE-DEE-DO: All except Flip, the King's page boy. Sometimes I think he is the only one who hasn't forgotten how to smile. He's always happy. (*Crosses to* FIDDLE-DEE-DEE) But what has happened to the rest of us?

FIDDLE-DEE-DEE (*Shaking his head sadly*): I don't know, unless we all follow the pattern set by his Majesty, King Cole.

FIDDLE-DEE-DUM (*Joining others*): Do you remember the good old days when this court was the happiest and most carefree in the whole world, and everyone sang:
Old King Cole was a merry old soul,
And a merry old soul was he, (*All forget to be sad.*)

FIDDLE-DEE-DO (*Gaily*): He called for his pipe,
He called for his bowl,

FIDDLE-DEE-DEE: And he called for his Fiddlers Three.

FIDDLE-DEE-DO *and* FIDDLE-DEE-DUM (*Pointing to* FIDDLE-DEE-DEE): Fiddle-Dee-Dee.

FIDDLE-DEE-DEE (*Bowing*): At your service!

FIDDLE-DEE-DEE *and* FIDDLE-DEE-DUM (*Pointing to* FIDDLE-DEE-DO): Fiddle-Dee-Do.

FIDDLE-DEE-DO (*Bowing*): At your service!

FIDDLE-DEE-DEE *and* FIDDLE-DEE-DO (*Pointing to* FIDDLE-DEE-DUM): Fiddle-Dee-Dum.

FIDDLE-DEE-DUM (*Bowing*): At your service!

FIDDLERS THREE (*Together*): He called for his Fiddlers Three. (*Bowing*) At your service!

FIDDLE-DEE-DUM: Those were happy times, and now (*Looking around*) look at this place! Here it is, only two days until Christmas, and not a sign of Christmas anywhere. No wreaths, no holly, no mistletoe, and (*Shaking head sadly*) worst of all, no preparations for Christmas dinner.

FIDDLE-DEE-DO: I wish I were home helping to put up the Christmas tree.

FIDDLE-DEE-DUM: Smelling the mince pies and good things my mother and sisters are making. (*Rubbing stomach*) Yum, yum! The very thought of it makes me hungry! What's wrong here, anyway?

FIDDLE-DEE-DEE: I'll tell you what's wrong! It's that old Sir Algernon Grumpy! The trouble all started when he became Prime Minister and Adviser to the King.

FIDDLE-DEE-DO: Perhaps you're right. The King used to call for us every day, but now we never see him. (RITA, NITA *and* LITA *enter from backstage and stand listening.*)

FIDDLE-DEE-DEE: We know Sir Algernon doesn't like us.

RITA, NITA *and* LITA (*Together*): Hi, Fiddlers Three!

FIDDLERS THREE (*Together*): Hi, Maidens Three!

RITA: We heard that last remark and you are certainly right.

LITA: Old Sir Algernon gets meaner every day.

NITA: Nobody likes him, and he is as jealous of you as he can be.

FIDDLERS THREE (*Together*): Jealous of us! Why?

LITA: He knows the King likes you.

RITA: Come on, we'd better get to work.

FIDDLE-DEE-DEE: We'd better be on our way. (FIDDLERS *move to exit.*)

NITA: Remember what we said and watch out for Sir Algernon.

FIDDLERS THREE (*Turning as they reach exit, and making deep bows*): Goodbye.

RITA, NITA *and* LITA (*Waving feather dusters and curtsying*): Bye-bye.

LITA: How I wish we could hear some of their jolly tunes again!

NITA: That's what everyone in the court wishes; that is,

everyone except Sir Algernon. They say each time King Cole asks for the Fiddlers Three, old Sir Algernon makes some excuse to keep them apart.

LITA: Let's get our work done. (*They busy themselves dusting thrones, remove stool to wings, and flick dust from other parts of room.*)

RITA (*Stopping her dusting and listening*): I hear the King coming!

NITA: Quick, let's go! (*They run out left, as* KING *and* QUEEN *enter right, followed by* COURT ATTENDANTS. KING *and* QUEEN *sit on thrones.*)

KING (*Looking about*): Where is my Prime Minister? (SIR ALGERNON *enters*) There you are, Sir Algernon. Today we wish to see the Fiddlers Three.

SIR ALGERNON: Your Majesty, your Adviser feels it would not be wise.

KING (*Slightly impatient*): Why not?

SIR ALGERNON: Their gay, silly tunes would keep us from doing our important work, Your Majesty.

KING: Piffle! We wish to hear some of their gay tunes instead of your sad talk.

SIR ALGERNON: My lord!

KING: Not another word! Begone, and do as I say!

SIR ALGERNON: Yes, Your Majesty. (*Bows and exits*)

KING (*Wearily*): The rest of you may go. We are tired of being surrounded by sad faces. We want merriment and happiness. Go, all of you, except Flip. It seems my Queen and Flip have the only cheerful faces in the whole court. (COURT ATTENDANTS *exit.*) Come closer, Flip.

FLIP (*Advancing to throne*): Yes, Your Majesty.

KING: Tell me, boy, why do you look so happy?

FLIP: I suppose, Your Majesty, because I am happy inside. (*Touching heart*)

KING (*Sighs*): I wish I were. Where do you live, Flip?

FLIP: I live in the village, Sire, with my mother and father and eight brothers and sisters.

QUEEN: Are they all as happy as you?

FLIP: Yes, Your Majesty. They are all very happy, especially now that Christmas is almost here.

KING: Christmas? (*Thoughtfully*) Why, I had forgotten all about Christmas. Tell me, what does your father do?

FLIP: He is a shoemaker, Your Majesty, and a very wise man.

KING: A wise man—(*Pondering*) He must be a wise man to make so many people happy. Is he wealthy?

FLIP: No, Sire, we are poor; but we have a roof over our heads and, since my brothers and I are old enough to work, we always have something to eat. We all help as much as we can and this year will have a very merry Christmas.

KING (*Slowly*): Christmas—and you are all happy. (*Leaning forward.*) If your father is such a wise man that he can make ten people happy on the little he earns, perhaps he can help me.

FLIP: I am sure he can, Your Majesty.

KING: Go, bring him to me, Flip.

FLIP: Yes, Your Majesty. (*He bows and exits.*)

QUEEN: It will be wonderful if we can all be happy again, my lord.

KING: I wonder what the secret can be. (SIR ALGERNON *enters.*)

SIR ALGERNON (*Bowing low*): I am deeply sorry, Sire, that I am the bearer of unhappy news.

KING: Out with it, whatever it is.

SIR ALGERNON: The ungrateful Fiddlers Three have departed from Your Majesty's Court.

QUEEN: What! How terrible!

KING (*Surprised*): My beloved Fiddlers Three *gone*. Without even a farewell to their King! Why did they go?

SIR ALGERNON: I know not, Sire. (*Enter* FLIP *and* FATHER.)

KING: That will do. You may go. (SIR ALGERNON *hesitates.*) Go, I say! (SIR ALGERNON *bows, reluctantly exits.* KING *turns to* FLIP) So this is your father, Flip. Come, my good man, and speak to your King. (FLIP *and* FATHER *advance to throne.* FATHER *kneels.*) Rise, my good fellow. (FATHER *rises.*) Your son tells me you have a happy family.

FATHER: A very happy family, Your Majesty.

KING: What makes them so happy?

FATHER: I suppose, Sire, because each one helps the others to be happy.

KING: Do you think I could be happy?

FATHER: I am sure Your Majesty could be most happy.

KING: Tell me how.

FATHER (*Slowly*): By helping others.

KING: Whom could I help? (FATHER *hesitates.*) Don't be afraid, answer my question.

FATHER: Sire, if you would only take the same interest in your people that you used to, it would not only bring happiness to them but to yourself as well.

KING: I do take the same interest in my people that I always have. Every day some of them used to come for an audience with me. Now they no longer come.

FATHER: Many still come, Your Majesty, but they are always sent away. For days they have been coming with Christmas gifts for Your Majesty, and all are told to go home and take their gifts with them.

KING: Who dares send them away?

FATHER: It is said, Your Majesty, that Sir Algernon Grumpy gives the orders.

FLIP: Yes, Your Majesty, and on the road here we met the Fiddlers Three and they were very sad because Sir Algernon had told them to leave the court and never return.

KING (*Rising and speaking angrily*): What! That scoundrel sent away my beloved Fiddlers Three! He shall pay for this! (*Claps hands and servants enter*) Quick! Send messengers in all directions, find the Fiddlers Three, tell them their King desires their immediate return to court. Send Sir Algernon Grumpy here. Make haste.

SERVANTS: Yes, Your Majesty. (*Bow, exit hurriedly.*)

QUEEN: I hope you will soon find another Prime Minister, who can smile and have the people like him.

KING: I have already found such a one. (SIR ALGERNON *enters.*)

SIR ALGERNON: You sent for your Prime Minister, Sire?

KING: I sent for you, but you are no longer my Prime Minister. For your plans to separate me from the Fiddlers Three and from my people, I hereby banish you from the court. (*To* SERVANTS) Take off his robe of office and decorations, and place them upon Flip's father, our new Prime Minister! (SERVANTS *take robe and decorations from* SIR ALGERNON *and place them on* FLIP'S FATHER.)

QUEEN (*Excitedly*): Three cheers for the new Prime Minister!

ALL (*Led by* QUEEN): RAH! RAH! RAH!

KING (*Pointing to* SIR ALGERNON): Take him away. (SERVANTS *take* SIR ALGERNON *out.*)

QUEEN: Now we'll be happy once more! Decorate the halls with holly and mistletoe; tell the cook to make preparations for the biggest and best Christmas dinner we have ever had!

KING: Send forth a proclamation to my people that their King will welcome them to the palace any time they wish to come. Now, I call for my pipe, my bowl and my Fiddlers Three. (*Two* SERVANTS *enter. One carries a cushion on which rests a long-stemmed pipe, the other carries a tray on which is a bowl. Behind them come the*

FIDDLERS THREE, *carrying fiddles. They are followed by* COURT ATTENDANTS *and* VILLAGERS *who range themselves about the stage.* FIRST SERVANT *kneels before the* KING *who takes the pipe.* SECOND SERVANT *places bowl on table beside the* KING, *who rises and extends his hands in welcome*) Welcome, thrice welcome, my beloved Fiddlers Three! The same to all my friends here.

FIDDLERS THREE (*Bowing*): Thank you, Your Majesty.

KING: How about a jolly tune? Play my favorite. (*If the* FIDDLERS THREE *cannot play the violins, they pretend to play, while a recording of "Old King Cole" is played offstage. All join in singing as the* KING, *smiling and using his pipe as a baton, keeps time.*)

QUEEN: Let's begin our Christmas celebration now!

KING: A splendid idea, my love! But first (*Rising and speaking to audience, making a sweeping gesture*) may we wish each one of you a very Merry Christmas!

ALL: Merry Christmas! Merry Christmas! (*As music continues, those on stage dance and sing; some call "Merry Christmas" and throw confetti. The* KING *sits on the throne watching with a pleased expression, smoking his pipe, as the curtain falls.*)

THE END

The Talking Christmas Tree

by Margaret Georgia Fawcett

Characters

PINE TREE
SNOW FAIRY
TINSEL FAIRY
JINGLE BELL FAIRY
BRIGHT BALL FAIRY
MARK
SALLY

TIME: *Christmas Eve.*
SETTING: *A clearing in the woods.*
AT RISE: PINE TREE *is alone in the center of the stage. The* SNOW FAIRY *comes running onto the scene, from the left.*

PINE TREE: Hello! Who are you?
SNOW FAIRY: I'm one of the Snow Fairies.
PINE TREE (*Disappointed*): I hoped you were someone else.
SNOW FAIRY: Why?
PINE TREE: I have special reasons.
SNOW FAIRY: If I make you white with snow, to keep you warm all night, won't you be glad? (*She scatters artificial snow all over him.* PINE TREE *shakes himself, trying to shake it off.*)

PINE TREE: I don't want to be all white. I want to be bright with tinsel and shiny balls, like other pine trees, on Christmas Eve.

SNOW FAIRY: You have to be chopped down to be a Christmas tree!

PINE TREE: Being chopped down isn't much fun, of course. It's better when people bring along a shovel and dig us up by the roots.

SNOW FAIRY: And plant you by the garden gate?

PINE TREE: No, in a bucket in the warm living room, with my lights all lit, and my branches full of presents. That must be fun!

SNOW FAIRY: How do you know? You've always lived in the forest.

PINE TREE: Every pine tree knows it's fun to be a Christmas tree! Children clap their hands when they see you and grown-ups smile. Everyone is happier when you're around. That's worth all the trouble it takes to grow to be a tree. (*He looks offstage, as laughter and the jingle of bells are heard.*) Who's this coming through the woods?

SNOW FAIRY (*Peering offstage*): It looks like the Christmas tree fairies. I'll call them to come here. (*She waves her wand.*) This is their busy night. (BRIGHT BALL FAIRY, TINSEL FAIRY, *and* JINGLE BELL FAIRY *run onstage.*)

TINSEL FAIRY: I should say it is our busy night! We've been here, there, and *everywhere!* We're still on our way.

BRIGHT BALL FAIRY: There's a new magic polish this year, that makes the balls shine brighter than ever. You should see them sparkling on all the Christmas trees! (*The* PINE TREE *groans and sighs.*)

JINGLE BELL FAIRY: What's the matter with him?

SNOW FAIRY: He doesn't want to *see* a Christmas tree—he wants to *be* one.

TINSEL FAIRY: Why isn't he, then? Was he naughty?

PINE TREE: I was not! Perhaps it's because I'm too small.

BRIGHT BALL FAIRY: We polished balls on a lot of *small* trees.

PINE TREE: Then maybe I'm too *large*.

TINSEL FAIRY: There are plenty of big grandfather trees, with tinsel stars touching the ceiling.

JINGLE BELL FAIRY: With bells on every branch. They're so beautiful! (PINE TREE *starts to cry.*)

PINE TREE: Boo hoo hoo! I want to look beautiful, too!

SNOW FAIRY: Poor little Pine Tree, don't cry!

TINSEL FAIRY: I'll tell you what we'll do! We'll trim him, right where he is! (*She starts unwinding tinsel from around her waist.*)

JINGLE BELL FAIRY: Here, in the woods?

BRIGHT BALL FAIRY: Why not? I've plenty of bright balls to spare. (*She takes balls from large bag she carries and starts attaching them to branches of tree.*)

TINSEL FAIRY: Now he'll look bright and beautiful to anyone who may pass by. (*The* FAIRIES *are busy trimming the tree.*)

PINE TREE (*Drying his eyes*): It's no use. Nobody will be passing so late on Christmas Eve.

SNOW FAIRY: Never mind, the rabbits will like it.

PINE TREE: It might scare them to see me dressed up this way.

JINGLE BELL FAIRY: How surprised the birds will be when they wake up at dawn!

PINE TREE: They'll think it's a new new kind of fruit, and start pecking at me.

TINSEL FAIRY (*Finishing winding tinsel on tree*): There, I'm through! (*She waves her wand over the tree*) Sparkle, sparkle! Catch the light!

BRIGHT BALL FAIRY (*Waving her wand*): Shine, shine, red balls and white!

JINGLE BELL FAIRY (*Waves her wand*): Tinkle, tinkle, in the night! (PINE TREE *shakes, and bells jingle.*)

SNOW FAIRY (*Stands to one side, admiring* PINE TREE): Oh, Pine Tree! What a pretty sight!

PINE TREE (*Shakes himself a little, looking pleased*): I must say, I do feel better. (*Looks glum again*) Dear me! I don't want to be ungrateful, of course, but I would like to be in a warm room where there are lots of little children.

SNOW FAIRY (*Looking off right, through the woods*): There are some children in the woods now.

PINE TREE (*Excitedly*): Where are they? Can they see me?

TINSEL FAIRY: They're coming this way! Let's stay and hear what they say.

BRIGHT BALL FAIRY: Yes, they can't see us, but they'll see our trimmings on the tree. (FAIRIES *move upstage left and right.* MARK *and* SALLY *enter.* MARK *is wheeling a wheelbarrow, which has a shovel in it. They do not see* PINE TREE *yet.*)

SALLY: Which way shall we go now? We haven't found any small trees on this path.

MARK: I don't think it makes much difference. I don't know what good it would do to have a tree so late on Christmas Eve, anyway. We haven't anything to trim it with.

SALLY: I found some red ribbon we can tie on the branches, and we have the popcorn I strung this morning.

MARK: Which way shall we go? You choose. Straight ahead?

SALLY: Let's try this way. (*They start towards center stage.* SALLY *stops quickly*) Mark, look! What's that?

MARK: My goodness!

SALLY (*Running over to* PINE TREE): It's a pine tree! A

pine tree all trimmed for Christmas! How beautiful it looks! Mark, quick, let's dig it up.

MARK: Wait a minute! It may belong to somebody!

PINE TREE (*Shaking his head and speaking softly*): Noooo!

MARK (*Looks around puzzled*): What was that? Who said "no"? (FAIRIES *softly giggle to themselves.*)

SALLY: It was the wind, silly! Hurry, here's the shovel. Did you ever see anything so bright and shiny and pretty?

MARK: Sally, I don't think we should take it.

SALLY: Mark, it's for us! I know it is! It's meant for us, to take home to surprise the new baby and all the other children. Mother said that Santa is tired of coming to our house because there are so many of us, but I'm sure he left this here so we could find it. (FAIRIES *laugh again softly.*)

MARK (*Looks around quickly*): What was that?

SALLY: Just the ice crackling in the branches. Please, Mark, do start digging! Don't chop it down. We can plant it after Christmas and maybe it will grow ornaments every year. (*The* PINE TREE *giggles.* MARK *looks surprised again.*)

MARK: More funny noises around here! Let's get away—it's too scary! (*He starts to go.* FAIRIES *crowd around him.*)

SALLY (*Trying not to cry*): No, no! If that tree weren't meant for us, we wouldn't have found it! I can't leave it.

MARK: All right, I'll dig it up for you. Then we'll go away. It's spooky here in the woods. (*He pretends to dig around the tree with his shovel.*)

SALLY: Spooks can't be out on Christmas Eve, but I'm sure the woods are full of Christmas Spirits wanting to make everyone happy. (FAIRIES *smile and giggle to themselves.*)

MARK: Spirits or not, it's strange finding a tree all fixed up this way. There it goes, we've got it now, trimming and all! (*He lifts tree into wheelbarrow.* SALLY *helps.*)

SALLY: Do be careful! We don't want to break any of the pretty balls! I'm so happy and grateful! Come on, quickly, Mark! Let's take the pretty thing home! (*She leads the way through the woods.* MARK *pushes the wheelbarrow.* PINE TREE *waves to* FAIRIES, *who wave back to him and laugh merrily, as they run off in opposite direction. Curtain.*)

THE END

North Pole Confidential

by Stanley C. Jensen

Characters

SANTA-NORTH
MRS. SANTA-NORTH
SANTA-SOUTH
MRS. SANTA-SOUTH
SANTA-EAST
MRS. SANTA-EAST
SANTA-WEST
MRS. SANTA-WEST
SANTA-IN-CHIEF

TIME: *A few days before Christmas.*

SETTING: *Santa's workshop at the North Pole.*

AT RISE: *The four Santas and their wives are sitting at their respective workbenches doing some last minute jobs on Christmas toys.*

SANTA-NORTH: I don't want to brag, fellows, but actually I *do* have the choicest route of all, you know.

MRS. SANTA-NORTH: You be careful what you say, dear. You know that Santa-in-Chief warned us all about boasting.

SANTA-NORTH: I'm not boasting. Why, look here. (*Points to map in his hand*) Siberia, Iceland, Canada, Greenland, Norway, Sweden, Denmark—the most beautiful countries in the world!

SANTA-SOUTH: Hah, what's so beautiful about them? Have you ever covered the southern route? Now there's something really choice! Australia, New Zealand, South

America, the Philippine Islands, the Hawaiian Islands. Palm trees, tropical breezes! Ah, that's the route for me! Eh, wife?

MRS. SANTA-SOUTH: I suppose so, dear. Still, I've been wondering— Do you suppose that children all over the world know that there are actually *four* Santa Clauses who do all the running around for Mr. Santa-in-Chief?

SANTA-WEST: Of course they don't! As far as my youngsters in the United States are concerned there's a Santa on every street corner, ringing a bell. They don't know whether there are one or one thousand Santa Clauses.

MRS. SANTA-WEST: What's the difference? As Santa-in-Chief says: "We do this job for the good of mankind and not for personal glory."

SANTA-EAST: That's right! That's why I say I have the best route of all. Just consider the population of the territory I cover— Arabia, Iran, India, China, Russia, Japan. Why, you fellows don't have a thing!

MRS. SANTA-EAST: You do get awfully tired, dear. Remember last year?

SANTA-NORTH: You see! Now, my route—

SANTA-SOUTH: Ice and snow! You should see Honolulu on Christmas Eve! (SANTA-IN-CHIEF *appears, silently at office door.*)

SANTA-WEST: Honolulu, bah! Now you take Rockefeller Center on Christmas Eve. Boy, oh, boy!

SANTA-IN-CHIEF: Stop it! Stop this bragging and boasting right now. I've heard all I'm going to listen to. You should be ashamed of yourselves!

SANTA-WEST: Chief, we were only comparing notes on our routes.

SANTA-IN-CHIEF: Comparing notes, nonsense! You were glorifying the unimportant, little extras that go with your Christmas routes—the beautiful land, the climate, the population. You're doing exactly the same thing that millions of well-meaning people do every Christmas season, when they think only of tinsel, decorations, Christmas dinner, and forget the whole spirit of the holiday—the brotherhood of man.

SANTA-EAST: We hadn't really forgotten, Chief. We were—

SANTA-IN-CHIEF: You hadn't, eh? Well, I'm going to see to it that you *don't* forget. I'm going to be listening to every word you say from now until Christmas, and I'm going to penalize you for every boastful, bragging statement you make.

SANTA-NORTH: Penalize us, Chief? How?

SANTA-IN-CHIEF: I'm going to leave my office door open. Every time one of you makes a statement that is not in the true Christmas spirit I'll sound my buzzer. When you hear that buzzer you will come into my office bringing your route map with you.

SANTAS: Our route maps?

SANTA-IN-CHIEF: Yes, your route maps. Any time one of you is guilty of a remark that is not in keeping with the character of a Santa Claus, and a gentleman, I'm going to take away part of his territory.

SANTA-SOUTH: Chief, if you took away part of our routes, it would mean that all the boys and girls in those countries wouldn't get to see Santa. Why, they wouldn't have any Christmas! They'd—they'd hate us! (*He sobs.*)

SANTA-IN-CHIEF: That's exactly right, Santa-South. So keep on your toes. It's entirely up to you now. (*He exits into his office. There is a silence of several seconds during which the four* SANTAS *and their wives just look at each other and at their maps.*)

MRS. SANTA-SOUTH: Don't be unhappy, dear. (*She pats his arm.*) Maybe you'll remember not to say anything unworthy of a Santa Claus.

SANTA-WEST: Him, remember? Ho, ho, that's a good one! He forgets his route book half the time. Why, I—(*A buzzer sounds loudly and menacingly. Others all look at* SANTA-WEST *who claps his hand over his mouth, horror-stricken.*) Oh, oh! Here I go. (*He takes his map and enters Santa-in-Chief's office. The others simply sit and stare at the door. He returns in a few seconds with the lower one-fourth of his map cut away.*)

SANTA-SOUTH: What did you lose, Santa-West?

SANTA-WEST: Alabama, Tennessee, North and South Carolina, Florida, Louisiana, Georgia, and *Texas!*

MRS. SANTA-WEST: What shall we do?

SANTA-EAST (*Slyly*): What's so bad about that? You'll get through work that much earlier on Christmas morning. (*Buzzer sounds sharply five or six times.*)

SANTA-WEST: Why, sure! What a fool I am to be unhappy —(*Buzzer sounds again.* SANTA-EAST *and* SANTA-WEST *look guiltily at each other, snatch up their maps, and hurry into the private office.*)

MRS. SANTA-EAST (*Apologetically*): Santa-East didn't really mean that. He knows what it means to folks all over the world to have Santa visit them on Christmas Eve. Why, he's dedicated his whole life to learning to be a good Santa Claus. (SANTA-EAST *and* SANTA-WEST *return, very much subdued and looking extremely penitent.*)

MRS. SANTA-WEST: Well, Santa?

SANTA-WEST (*Holding up his map*): I lost Oregon, Washington, and California.

MRS. SANTA-EAST: And you?

SANTA-EAST: I lost Iran and Arabia, dear.

MRS. SANTA-SOUTH: I think we'd all better get busy putting the finishing touches on these toys. It'll keep us out of mischief, maybe. (*Everyone gets busy at the work-benches, and for several seconds there's no sound except a subdued humming and a few barely-audible mumbles between couples.*)

SANTA-SOUTH: Speaking of mischief, did I tell you about that little boy in Rio de Janeiro?

SANTA-NORTH: I don't believe you did, Santa. What about him?

SANTA-SOUTH: This tyke had decided he was going to stay awake and see Santa, so he put a mouse trap in his stocking figuring that if he did fall asleep, I'd waken him when the trap snapped on my hand.

SANTA-NORTH: Why, the little imp! I'd have left him a pound of cheese if it had been I. (*Buzzer sounds.*)

MRS. SANTA-NORTH: Santa! Why can't you hold your tongue?

SANTA-NORTH: What did I say? What did I do? (*He takes his map and goes into the private office.*)

SANTA-SOUTH: Ho! Ho! Ho! Ho!

SANTA-EAST: What's so funny?

SANTA-SOUTH: I didn't leave that boy a pound of cheese, but I left him something even better. I left a little mouse in his stocking! Ho! Ho! Ho! Ho! (*Buzzer sounds again. Others all turn and point at* SANTA-SOUTH *who picks up his map and heads for the private office. He meets* SANTA-NORTH, *just returning, at the entrance.*)

SANTA-NORTH: You and your Rio de Janeiro! Now I've gone and lost Norway and Denmark—my two favorite countries.

SANTA-SOUTH: I'm sorry, Santa—truly, I am. (*He enters office.*)

SANTA-NORTH: *He's* sorry. I guess he's no sorrier than I am. There's no place in the whole world where Santa has as much fun as in Norway and Denmark.

MRS. SANTA-SOUTH: I do hope Santa-in-Chief doesn't take South America away from us. (SANTA-SOUTH *reappears.*)

SANTA-SOUTH: He did! Central America too! (*He sobs and* MRS. SANTA-SOUTH *trys to comfort him.*)

SANTA-WEST: Some Christmas this is going to be! All because the Chief wants to show his authority. (*Buzzer sounds.*) I'll show him—I won't go! (*Buzzer sounds again and* SANTA-WEST *leaps up and actually runs to the office, map in hand.*)

MRS. SANTA-WEST: This is going to be terrible. If only he hadn't said: "I won't go." Santa-in-Chief will sometimes overlook impudence, but never defiance of authority.

MRS. SANTA-EAST: Maybe Santa-in-Chief didn't hear that part of it, dear. Maybe he—(SANTA-WEST *re-appears, apparently empty handed.*)

MRS. SANTA-WEST: Santa! Where's your map? Did Santa-in-Chief take it all away from you? (SANTA-WEST *shakes his head.*) Well, for heaven's sake, tell us! What do you have left?

SANTA-WEST (*Produces a tiny bit of paper from between thumb and forefinger*): Rhode Island!

MRS. SANTA-WEST: Oh, dear! Oh, dear! Oh, dear!

SANTA-NORTH: Don't be unhappy, Mrs. Santa-West. Maybe we can persuade the Chief to give us back our routes before Christmas Eve.

SANTA-EAST: Hah! Not a chance. You know how he is when he makes up his mind.

SANTA-SOUTH: He'll never relent.

MRS. SANTA-SOUTH: Just think of all those poor, little children in Denmark, South America, and North Carolina, and—(*She dissolves into tears.*)

MRS. SANTA-EAST: It's not fair! He can't do it!

SANTA-NORTH: You're right! I say we should tell Santa-in-Chief what we think of his high-handed methods.

SANTA-EAST: Yes!

SANTA-NORTH: You're right!

SANTA-SOUTH: Let's do it!

SANTA-WEST: WAIT!

OTHERS: What?

SANTA-WEST: I said, "Wait." Don't do anything silly.

SANTA-NORTH: What do you mean? (SANTA-IN-CHIEF *silently appears in the doorway, unseen by anyone.*)

SANTA-WEST: I've lost more than any of you. (*He holds up his little scrap of map.*) I have more reason than anyone here to be resentful. But I'm not.

SANTA-EAST: No. Santa-in-Chief is right—absolutely right! We've behaved very badly, all of us. We deserve the punishment he's inflicted on us.

SANTA-SOUTH: That's all very well and good, but how about all the thousands of innocent children who are being punished too?

MRS. SANTA-SOUTH: Yes, how about them?

SANTA-WEST: Santa-in-Chief doesn't want to punish those children. Don't you suppose it's breaking his heart to think of all those youngsters not having any Christmas? Of course it is.

SANTA-NORTH: Then why is he doing this?

SANTA-WEST: He *has* to do it. We forced him to it. (*They all shake their heads in disagreement.*) Yes, we did. By our own petty, little selves we did it.

SANTA-SOUTH (*Belligerently*): You'd better explain that, Santa-West.

SANTA-WEST: Didn't Santa-in-Chief warn us about our attitude? (*They nod.*) Didn't he explain why our attitude was wrong? (*They nod again.*) And didn't we keep right on in spite of his warning? (*They nod once more.*) Then, we've got no complaint. It isn't as though we didn't know what we were doing.

MRS. SANTA-WEST: Oh, dear, what shall we do?

SANTA-NORTH: Do you think he'll relent before Christmas?

SANTA-WEST: No, I don't—but I've got an idea. (*He beckons them to gather around him.*) Listen: Santa told *me* that I couldn't visit forty-seven of my states on Christmas Eve, didn't he? He didn't tell *you* (*Pointing to* SANTA-NORTH) that you couldn't call there, did he?

SANTA-NORTH: No, of course he didn't. But, I don't get what you're driving at.

SANTA-WEST: He told me that I couldn't call on those forty-seven states, but he didn't say that you couldn't. Also, he told you that you mustn't visit Norway and Denmark on Christmas Eve, but he didn't tell *me* that I couldn't.

SANTA-NORTH: Yes, but—

SANTA-WEST: Don't you see? Santa-in-Chief told us what we *couldn't* call on—not what we *could* call on.

MRS. SANTA-WEST: You mean you could swap routes?

SANTA-WEST: Sure! Why not?

SANTA-EAST: Then Santa-South could swap routes with me, eh? Wonderful! Let's do it!

SANTA-SOUTH: I don't know your route at all, Santa-East. Why, it would take days to cover it.

SANTA-WEST: What's the difference? It would be hard work and we'd probably be all worn out when we finished, but think how happy all those children will be. Maybe we can make it up to the Chief for causing him so much heartache.

SANTA-EAST: Let's do it!

SANTA-NORTH: I'm all for it!

SANTA-WEST: There's just one thing we have to figure out: How to keep Santa from finding out!

SANTA-IN-CHIEF (*Stepping forward*): You won't have to do that. (*They all drop back in alarm.*) He knows all about it already. (*He beckons them together again.*) I was quite angry with all of you a little while ago, but now I'm quite pleased with you. (*They look at him in amazement.*) You should know by now that you can't put anything over on me. I heard everything you said. Your plan was a little bit tricky, but I have to admit it was perfectly legal. Most important, though, is the fact that you were so concerned with the happiness of others that you were willing to do any amount of work to achieve it. I'm touched—truly I am. (*He wipes a tear from his eye.*)

SANTA-WEST: We're sorry we were so stupid, Santa-in-Chief, really we are. (*He glares at the others.*) Aren't we?

SANTA-EAST: Yes!

SANTA-SOUTH: Of course!

SANTA-NORTH: We surely are, Santa!

SANTA-IN-CHIEF: Here's a Christmas present for all of you then. (*He hands out new maps.*) You're all forgiven and here are your own routes.

SANTA-SOUTH: Whoopee!

SANTA-NORTH: Thank you!

SANTA-IN-CHIEF: Merry Christmas! Ho! Ho! Ho! Ho! (*They all join hands, circle around* SANTA-IN-CHIEF *and sing "Jingle Bells."*)

THE END

Mrs. Claus' Christmas Present

by Catherine Urban

Characters

MRS. CLAUS
SANTA CLAUS
CRITZY
FRITZY
MITTENS
FITTENS
} *Santa's helpers*

TIME: *It is almost time for* SANTA *to leave on his trip to earth with his Christmas presents.*

SETTING: *The living room of the Claus home.*

AT RISE: SANTA *is pacing back and forth worriedly.* CRITZY *and* FRITZY *are hiding in back of the large chair, peeking out at* SANTA. SANTA *picks up the clock and looks at it, then puts it back and shakes his head. He touches the rocking chair, pauses, but shakes his head. He goes off stage left, with head down.*

FRITZY (*As he and* CRITZY *come from behind the chair*): Critzy, you see, I was right! Something *is* the matter with Santa!

CRITZY: I do agree with you. He seems most troubled! (MITTENS *and* FITTENS *enter.*)

MITTENS: Who can be troubled on the night before Christmas?

CRITZY: Santa. Haven't you noticed? He just doesn't seem like himself!

FITTENS: We wondered! We passed him just now and he didn't even see us!

FRITZY: What does he have to worry about? My goodness, things have been easier this year than any year I can remember.

FITTENS: That's right. No one has been ill.

MITTENS: No one has been cross.

CRITZY: Everyone has worked well with his partner.

FRITZY: He can't be worried about any of us. All the toys are ready and packed into the big bag. We've surely done our jobs.

FITTENS: The bag is all tucked into the back of the sleigh.

CRITZY: The sleigh simply shines with all the polish I rubbed into it!

MITTENS: I've brushed the reindeer until their coats glisten!

FRITZY: Santa must be worried about something. He's been pacing the floor. (MRS. CLAUS *enters rolling up some yarn which she puts into her knitting bag on the rocking chair.*)

MRS. CLAUS: Why, hello, boys. I understand your work is all finished. I must congratulate you. I've never seen such lovely toys. (*She looks at them carefully.*) You all look so tired and worried. Perhaps you're catching colds. I'd better get the big bottle.

MITZY: Oh, no! We're not sick!

FRITZY: Goodness, we're just as well as can be!

FITTENS: I *never* felt better!

MRS. CLAUS: Something must be wrong!

MITTENS: It's Santa.

MRS. CLAUS: Santa! Surely, nothing has happened to Santa!

FITTENS: No accident! He seems to be worried.

FRITZY: He's been pacing back and forth as if he didn't know what to do about something!

MRS. CLAUS: Don't worry, boys. Every year, right at the last minute, Santa has a problem. But he always solves it very well, indeed. Now, I must get back to the kitchen. I have a few cakes to bake!

FITTENS: A chocolate cake? (MRS. CLAUS *nods, smiling.*)

FRITZY: An angel food? (MRS. CLAUS *nods.*)

CRITZY: You know that I like apple sauce cake?

MRS. CLAUS: Indeed, I do, and I know that Mittens likes caramel cake. Each of you is to have a small cake of the kind he likes best! (*She goes off right, smiling.*)

MITTENS: She's so good to us. We always have such a wonderful Christmas.

FRITZY: That's right! My, I can just taste that turkey! (*Licks his lips*)

FITTENS: It won't be so happy even with good cakes and roast turkey if Santa is worried! (*Others look depressed.* SANTA *comes in left. He does not seem to see helpers, who move back and line up in front of the rocker.* SANTA *picks up a book, looks at it briefly, then puts it down. He paces back and forth nervously, shaking his head with obvious agitation. Helpers exchange worried looks.*)

CRITZY: Santa?

SANTA (*Somewhat crossly as he stops and looks at them*): What do you want?

CRITZY: Isn't everything all right, Santa? Aren't the toys the way you want them?

SANTA: Yes, yes! The toys are well done.

FITTENS: Aren't they packed the way you like them?

SANTA: They are packed very well.

FRITZY: Doesn't the sleigh shine bright enough?

SANTA: The sleigh has never looked better.

MITTENS: Then it must be the reindeer, and I *did* brush them, Santa!

SANTA (*Impatiently*): Goodness me! The reindeer look very sleek! I do wish you wouldn't bother me so!

CRITZY: This isn't like you. Are you sick?

SANTA: No, I'm not sick! The trouble is—well, maybe *you* can help me!

FRITZY: Of course, we'll try!

SANTA: The trouble is, I can't think of anything to give Mrs. Claus for Christmas! She has practically everything in the world and in toyland—and I just—(*Shakes his head*)

HELPERS: Ohhhhhh!

SANTA: I've racked my brain, but I can't think of anything new for Mrs. Claus!

CRITZY: I'm giving her a new cup and saucer for her collection. I designed it myself, and decorated it, too.

FRITZY: I made a three-quart copper kettle for her. I heard her say she would like to have one.

FITTENS: I'm giving her some new green place mats that I wove on my loom.

MITTENS: I'm giving her a pair of fine leather house slippers. Once I heard her say that her feet got very tired in regular shoes.

SANTA: That's just it! You can each do many clever and magic things but I can only drive a team of reindeer through the sky, and give a jolly laugh or two after I've delivered the gifts!

FRITZY: We ought to be able to think of something!

FITTENS: What about a clock?

SANTA: I gave her the one on the mantel last year.

CRITZY: A new rocking chair?

SANTA: That was the year before's gift, and it is just as

good as new! Anyway, I'd like to give her something that *I* made—something different.

MITTENS: In a magic place like this, where things never wear out, it is very hard to think of a Christmas gift!

SANTA: She always gives me a fine new sweater and some socks that she has made herself. (*Paces with head bowed*)

FRITZY: Goodness, you'll get your deliveries all mixed up if you go off like this.

FITTENS: We could ask Mrs. Claus what she wants.

SANTA: Then, she wouldn't be surprised.

CRITZY: I know, you hide behind the chair, Santa, and we'll get her in here and ask her what she wants.

MITTENS: That's it. Then she'll still be surprised when she gets the present, because she'll think you thought of it!

SANTA: It doesn't seem quite right, but it's the only way. I must be off in just a few minutes. Go get her. (SANTA *hides behind the chair and* MITTENS *exits right to get* MRS. CLAUS. (*Helpers line up in front of the chair, thus helping to hide* SANTA. MRS. CLAUS *enters with* MITTENS, *wiping her hands on her apron.*)

MRS. CLAUS: Boys, what is it?

FRITZY: We were wondering what we should get Santa for Christmas?

MRS. CLAUS: Now, Fritzy, I know you have your present for Santa all wrapped up. Don't you remember you showed me that lovely—

FRITZY (*Hurriedly*): Yes, that's right.

MRS. CLAUS: I'm sure he'll be very happy to get it. And I know each of you has a gift all ready for him! There's something else you want to know. Now, what is it, because I'm sure *you* don't want my cakes to fail! (*They shake their heads and look at each other.*)

MITTENS: What we really wanted to know is what *you* want for Christmas.

MRS. CLAUS (*Laughs*): You boys always give me lovely gifts, but Santa always gives me the most wonderful gift of all!

FRITZY: You mean like the clock?

MRS. CLAUS: The clock? That is very nice, but it isn't the most wonderful gift I'll get from Santa. (*Helpers look puzzled and* SANTA *leans out to listen.*)

CRITZY: You mean the rocking chair?

MRS. CLAUS: The chair? That was a fine gift, too, but not the most marvelous gift of all! (SANTA *leans so far out that he falls over on the floor. Helpers jump away and* MRS. CLAUS *sees* SANTA.) Why, Santa *Claus*, you were listening in!

SANTA: I'm sorry, but I *must* find out what you mean? What is this marvelous gift that I give you each Christmas?

FITTENS (*As* MRS. CLAUS *hesitates*): Please, tell us. Santa is so worried about your gift that we're afraid he'll get the toys mixed up and deliver them to the wrong people!

SANTA: Please, tell me.

MRS. CLAUS (*Smiles*): All right. Of course, I liked the clock and the rocking chair and all the other things you've given me, but the best of all is *yourself!*

SANTA: Myself! But you always have me!

MRS. CLAUS: Not to myself, especially at this season of the year! The nearer it gets to Christmas, the less I see of you! You are so busy supervising all the workers, and *they* are so busy, that I don't see much of them, either.

SANTA: Why, I guess that's true! I know. I've hardly had time to eat these past few days.

MRS. CLAUS: And no time to read to me, or to talk at night.

MITTENS: That's right. We haven't played any games together for months!

MRS. CLAUS: That's right. Christmas Day is a wonderful day, but to me, the most wonderful gifts of all are the days *after* Christmas when we can all settle back and talk together, play all the new games, and read all the new books. What I like best is to have Santa read the latest books to me as I sit knitting beside the fire, with all you little helpers sitting on the floor playing jacks or dominoes or some other game.

HELPERS (*Ad lib*): We like that best, too. That's the best gift of all. That's our favorite thing! (*Etc.*)

SANTA: I like it, too! Still, you should have another gift as well, to unwrap tomorrow morning.

MRS. CLAUS: What I would like is lots and lots of fine Scottish yarn, so that I can knit during the wonderful happy evenings that we will be having!

SANTA: You will have it, my dear! I'll stop on my way back from delivering the toys, and fill the sleigh with your yarn!

HELPERS (*Ad lib, excitedly*): Hooray for Christmas! Hooray for all the wonderful days after Christmas! Hooray! Hooray! (*Etc. Curtain*)

THE END

CHRISTMAS CLASSICS

Dramatizations of famous stories
for round-the-table reading
or microphone performance

Editor's Note

The dramatizations of Christmas stories in this section will serve as an excellent introduction to favorite classics. These scripts may be used as microphone plays; broadcast over a public-address system; or tape-recorded for later replay. They may also be performed as round-the-table reading plays in classroom or assembly, requiring no memorization and a minimum of rehearsal. And they may be successfully used as part of the remedial or developmental reading curriculum.

With only slight modification, these adaptations may also be effectively staged as easy-to-put-on "spotlight plays," with or without scenery or special costumes.

A Christmas Carol

by Charles Dickens

Adapted by Lewy Olfson

Characters

FRED
EBENEZER SCROOGE
BOB CRATCHIT
A GENTLEMAN
GHOST OF JACOB MARLEY
GHOST OF CHRISTMAS PAST
LITTLE FAN
OLD FEZZIWIG
BELLE
GHOST OF CHRISTMAS PRESENT
MRS. CRATCHIT
CRATCHIT BOY
CRATCHIT GIRL
MARTHA CRATCHIT
TINY TIM
A YOUNG COCKNEY

MUSIC: *A gay Christmas carol, in and under.*

SOUND: *Slam of door.*

FRED (*Robust and happy, fading on*): A merry Christmas, Uncle! God save you!

SCROOGE (*A mean old man*): Bah! Humbug!

FRED (*Gaily*): Christmas a humbug, Uncle Scrooge? You don't mean that, I'm sure.

SCROOGE: I do. Merry Christmas! What right have you to be merry? What reason? You're poor enough!

FRED: Come then, what right have you to be dismal, what reason to be morose? You're rich enough!

SCROOGE: Bah! Humbug! What's Christmas time to you

but a time for paying bills without money? A time for finding yourself a year older, but not an hour richer?

FRED: Though it has never put a scrap of gold or silver in my pocket, I believe that Christmas *has* done me good, and *will* do me good; and I say, God bless it!

CRATCHIT (*Applauding, off mike*): Very well said, Mr. Fred!

SCROOGE: And *you,* Bob Cratchit, my fine young clerk. One more sound out of you, and you'll keep Christmas by losing your situation.

CRATCHIT (*Subdued, off mike*): Beg pardon, Mr. Scrooge.

SCROOGE: If I could work my will, Fred, every idiot who goes about with "Merry Christmas" on his lips would be boiled with his own pudding, and buried with a stake of holly through his heart.

FRED: Uncle!

SCROOGE: Nephew! Keep Christmas in your own way, and let me keep it in mine!

FRED: *Keep* it? But you *don't* keep it!

SCROOGE: Let me leave it alone, then. Good afternoon.

FRED: Don't be angry, Uncle. Come! Dine with us tomorrow!

SCROOGE: Good afternoon!

FRED: I am sorry with all my heart to find you so resolute, Uncle. Merry Christmas!

SCROOGE: Good afternoon!

FRED (*Fading*): And to you, too, Cratchit!

CRATCHIT (*Off mike*): Thank you, sir.

FRED: And a happy New Year!

SOUND: *Door slamming shut.*

SCROOGE (*Muttering*): Christmas, indeed! Humbug! Bah!

SOUND: *Doorbell ringing.*

SCROOGE: Well, Cratchit. See who's at the door!

CRATCHIT (*Fading*): Very good, sir.

SOUND: *Door being opened.*

SCROOGE: And who are you?

GENTLEMAN (*Fading on*): Scrooge and Marley's, I believe. Have I the pleasure of addressing Mr. Scrooge or Mr. Marley?

SCROOGE: Mr. Marley has been dead these seven years. He died seven years ago this very night.

GENTLEMAN: I have no doubt his liberality is well represented by his surviving partner.

SCROOGE (*Suspiciously*): Liberality?

GENTLEMAN: At this festive season of the year, Mr. Scrooge, it is more than usually desirable that we should make some slight provision for the poor and destitute, who suffer greatly at the present time.

SCROOGE: Are there no prisons?

GENTLEMAN: Oh, plenty of prisons.

SCROOGE: And the Union workhouses? Are they still in operation?

GENTLEMAN: They are. Still, I wish I could say they were not.

SCROOGE: Oh! I was afraid from what you said at first, that something had occurred to stop them in their useful course. Let those who are badly off go to the institutions I have just mentioned.

GENTLEMAN: Many can't go there; and many would rather die.

SCROOGE: Let them do it, then, and decrease the surplus population.

GENTLEMAN: Oh, I'm sure you don't mean that, Mr. Scrooge. What shall I put you down for?

SCROOGE: Nothing!

GENTLEMAN: You wish to be anonymous?

SCROOGE: I wish to be left alone. Good day!

GENTLEMAN (*Fading*): I see. Good afternoon, Mr. Scrooge.

SOUND: *Door being shut.*

SCROOGE: Christmas, Christmas, Christmas! A poor excuse

for picking a man's pocket every twenty-fifth of December. And you, Cratchit!

CRATCHIT (*Fading*): Yes, Mr. Scrooge?

SCROOGE: I suppose you'll want all day tomorrow.

CRATCHIT (*Timidly*): If quite convenient, sir.

SCROOGE: It's not convenient and it's not fair! If I were to dock you half a crown for it, you'd think yourself ill-used; and yet you don't think me ill-used for paying a day's wages for no work.

CRATCHIT: It's only once a year, sir . . .

SCROOGE: Bah! But I suppose you must have the whole day off. See that you're here all the earlier next morning. Good night, Cratchit.

CRATCHIT (*Fading*): Oh, I will, Mr. Scrooge. Good night, Mr. Scrooge! (*Beat*) And . . . Mr. Scrooge . . .

SCROOGE: Eh?

CRATCHIT (*Off mike*): A merry Christmas, sir!

SCROOGE: Humbug! That's what it is, humbug!

MUSIC: *Lively theme, then into eerie music, in and under.*

SCROOGE (*Tossing in his sleep*): Mmm . . . can't sleep . . . so tired . . . must get some rest . . .

SOUND: *Clock tolling twelve.*

SCROOGE (*After third peal*): Eh? Twelve midnight already? What's wrong with me? I can't sleep. Something must have upset me. Ah yes! That door knocker downstairs. Strange, that knocker. It looked like Marley's face . . . my old business partner, Jacob Marley. But that's impossible! What are you thinking of, Ebenezer Scrooge? It was the knocker, nothing else! Now get to sleep.

SOUND: *Chains dragging, far off mike, getting closer.*

SCROOGE: Eh? What sound is that? Someone's on the stair. Someone dragging a chain. Humbug! There's no one there. There's that noise again. Chains! It's humbug still! I won't believe it! He can't get in here; I locked the door before getting into bed. He can't get in here! But

. . . wait! He's coming . . . *through* the door! It's Marley, that's who it is. Marley! I know him; it's Marley's Ghost! (*Louder*) What do you want with me?

MARLEY (*An unearthly voice*): Much.

SCROOGE: Who . . . who are you?

MARLEY: Ask me who I was.

SCROOGE: Who were you, then? You're a might particular!

MARLEY: In life I was your partner, Jacob Marley.

SCROOGE: Dreadful apparition, why do you trouble me?

MARLEY: It is required of every man that the spirit within him should walk abroad among his fellow men, and travel far and wide. And if that spirit go not forth in life, it is condemned to do so after death.

SCROOGE: You are fettered with chains, Marley. Tell me why?

MARLEY: I wear the chain I forged in life. I made it link by link, and yard by yard. I girded it on of my own free will, and of my own free will I wore it. Do you know the weight and length of your own chain?

SCROOGE: Jacob, old Jacob Marley, speak comfort to me, Jacob!

MARLEY: I have none to give, Ebenezer Scrooge. Hear me; my time is nearly gone.

SCROOGE: I will. But don't be hard upon me, Jacob, pray.

MARLEY: I am here tonight to warn you that you have yet a chance and hope of escaping my fate. You will be haunted by three spirits.

SCROOGE: Is . . . is that the chance and hope you mentioned, Jacob?

MARLEY: It is.

SCROOGE: I—I think I'd rather not.

MARLEY: Without their visits you cannot hope to shun the path I tread. Expect the first tomorrow, when the bell tolls one.

SCROOGE: Couldn't I take 'em all at once?

MARLEY: Expect the second on the next night at the same hour. The third will come the next night, when the last stroke of twelve has ceased to vibrate. Goodbye, Ebenezer Scrooge. (*As his voice fades away*) You will see me no more. Goodbye. . . .

SCROOGE: I'm cold. Humbug, I don't believe it! Ghosts! Ha! Humbug!

SOUND: *Clock tolls one.*

SCROOGE: One! Oh, dear! It's time for him to come, the first spirit. Nonsense, Ebenezer, there's no one coming. It's all humbug! (*Gasps*) Who . . . who are you? Are you the spirit whose coming was foretold to me?

CHRISTMAS PAST (*A kindly but ghost-like voice*): I am.

SCROOGE: Who . . . what are you?

C. PAST: I am the Ghost of Christmas Past.

SCROOGE: Long past?

C. PAST: No, your past. Rise, and walk with me. Come!

SCROOGE: Out the window? But I am a mortal, and liable to fall!

C. PAST: Bear but a touch of my hand upon your heart, and you shall be upheld in more than this.

SOUND: *Slight wind, up and under.*

SCROOGE: Good Heavens, I know this place. I went to school here when I was a boy!

C. PAST: The school is not quite deserted. A solitary child, neglected by his friends, is left there still.

SCROOGE: Poor boy . . . why . . . it's me! And who is that little girl running into the schoolroom?

C. PAST: Do you not recognize her?

SCROOGE: Why, it's my little sister, Fan!

FAN (*A young, girlish voice, off mike*): Ebenezer, dear brother!

SCROOGE: Poor Fan! How I miss her, now that she's dead.

FAN: I have come to bring you home, dear brother. Home,

home! Father is so much kinder than he used to be, that home's like Heaven. We're to be together all the Christmas long, and we'll be happy!

SCROOGE: Pretty little Fan! Fred's mother . . . and I turned Fred from my door.

C. PAST: Come, Ebenezer Scrooge. Another vision spreads before us!

SCROOGE: Why, where is this?

C. PAST: Another Christmas from your past, Ebenezer Scrooge.

SCROOGE: It's the Fezziwigs! Dear old Fezziwig—the best-hearted man there ever was. I worked for him when I was a lad. Old Fezziwig!

FEZZIWIG (*Off mike, a jocular man*): Ho there, Ebenezer! It's Christmas Eve! No more work for the day. It's holiday time! Put up the shutters, my boy. And clear the floor! It's time for the Christmas dance. Come, come, Ebenezer. Hurry! 'Tis Christmas!

SCROOGE (*Laughing*): Bless his heart, old Fezziwig.

C. PAST: Come, Ebenezer Scrooge.

SCROOGE: Oh, let me stay a while longer.

C. PAST: No, another vision appears. You are older still . . . a young man, engaged to be married, I think.

SCROOGE: Yes. And that young lady, there—that was Belle, my intended. Lovely Belle . . .

C. PAST: Listen . . . and remember.

BELLE (*A sweet woman's voice, off mike*): It matters little, Ebenezer. To you, very little. Another idol has displaced me in your heart; and if it can cheer and comfort you in time to come, as I would have tried to do, I have no just cause to grieve. Our engagement is an old one, made when we were both poor. You are changed, Ebenezer. Gold and gain are all that matter to you now. I have no dowry, no fortune. And so I release you from your promise to marry me, with a full heart, for the love of him you once were. May you be happy in the life you have chosen.

SCROOGE: No more, Spirit! Show me no more! Take me home! No more!

C. PAST (*Fading*): So be it . . . Ebenezer Scrooge.

SCROOGE (*In wonder*): Why . . . why, I'm in my room. I'm home . . . and alone! Did I dream it all? No . . . I couldn't have. Belle . . . Fan . . . Fezziwig. Such a lot of memories. But I must sleep, I'm tired. So tired.

SOUND: *Clock tolls one.*

SCROOGE: What? One o'clock? Could I have slept through a whole day?

SOUND: *Bells jingling gaily.*

SCROOGE: But what sound is that? Bells jingling?

CHRISTMAS PRESENT (*Laughs heartily off mike.*)

SCROOGE: Laughter! Someone's in my sitting room! I'll see who . . .

C. PRESENT (*A jovial, vigorous voice, fading on*): Come in! Come in, and know me better, man!

SCROOGE: Who—who are you, fellow?

C. PRESENT: I am the Ghost of Christmas Present. Look upon me!

SCROOGE: What's all this mess you've got in my room? Holly, mistletoe, ivy—turkeys, geese, poultry!

C. PRESENT: And see here! A roaring fire in the chimney, sausages, mince pies, plum puddings, oranges, pears, bowls of punch! A Christmas feast!

SCROOGE: All to teach me a lesson, no doubt. Well, if you have aught to teach me, let me profit by it. Spirit, conduct me where you will.

C. PRESENT: Touch my robe!

SOUND: *Wind, up and under.*

SCROOGE: What house is that, the one with the peeled paint, there?

C. PRESENT: Go to the window, and see. Watch the people who live there; listen to their words.

SCROOGE: It's a poor woman, with several young 'uns by her side. She's talking to them.

C. PRESENT: Listen!

MRS. CRATCHIT: What has got your precious father, then? And your brother, Tiny Tim? And Martha warn't as late last Christmas Day by half an hour!

CRATCHIT BOY: Here comes Martha now, Mother!

MARTHA (*Fading on*): Merry Christmas, Mother, children!

ALL: Merry Christmas, Martha!

CRATCHIT GIRL: Wait till you see the goose, Martha!

MARTHA: I'm sorry I'm late, but there was so much work to be done.

MRS. CRATCHIT: Well, never mind, so long as ye are come. Sit ye down by the fire and have a warm, Lord bless ye!

GIRL: No, no! There's Father coming!

BOY: Hide, Martha, hide! We'll pretend you aren't coming!

MARTHA (*Gaily*): All right!

CRATCHIT (*Fading on*): Merry Christmas, Mother, children!

ALL: Merry Christmas, Father! Merry Christmas, Tiny Tim!

TINY TIM: Merry Christmas! Mmm, the goose smells so good!

CRATCHIT: And how is . . . why, where's our Martha?

MRS. CRATCHIT (*Seriously*): Not coming.

CRATCHIT: Not coming upon Christmas Day?

MARTHA (*Fading on slightly, laughing*): We're only teasing, Father. Here I am. And a merry Christmas to you!

GIRL: Come on, Tiny Tim. Come with us!

BOY (*Fading*): Come listen to the Christmas pudding sing in the copper!

TINY TIM (*Fading*): Oh, yes! Show me!

MRS. CRATCHIT (*Softly*): And how did little Tim behave?

CRATCHIT: As good as gold, and better. Somehow he gets thoughtful, poor little cripple, sitting by himself so much, and thinks the strangest things you ever heard. He told me that he hoped the people in church saw him, because he was a cripple, and it might be pleasant for them to remember, upon Christmas Day, who made lame beggars walk and blind men see.

MRS. CRATCHIT: If only we could do something for him . . . but hush! Here come the children back again!

TINY TIM (*Fading on*): I saw the goose!

BOY (*Fading on*): And we smelled the pudding!

GIRL: It looks delicious!

MARTHA: And it will be delicious, too!

CRATCHIT (*Lustily*): And now—a toast!

AD LIB: A toast! Hurrah! Serve out the punch!

CRATCHIT: Mr. Scrooge! I'll give you Mr. Scrooge, the Founder of the Feast!

MRS. CRATCHIT: The Founder of the Feast, indeed! I wish I had him here. I'd give him a piece of my mind to feast upon, and I hope he'd have a good appetite for it.

CRATCHIT: My dear, the children. Christmas Day!

MRS. CRATCHIT: It should be Christmas Day, I'm sure, on which one drinks the health of such an odious, stingy, hard, unfeeling man as Mr. Scrooge. You know he is, Robert. Nobody knows it better than you do, poor fellow.

CRATCHIT: My dear, Christmas Day!

MRS. CRATCHIT: Very well. I'll drink his health for your sake and the day's, but not for his. Long life to him! A merry Christmas and a happy New Year. He'll be very merry and very happy, I'm sure.

ALL (*Listlessly*): To Mr. Scrooge.

CRATCHIT: And now, a merry Christmas to us all, my dears. God bless us!

ALL: God bless us!

TINY TIM: God bless us, every one.

SCROOGE (*In close*): Spirit, tell me if Tiny Tim will live.

C. PRESENT: I see a vacant seat in the poor chimney corner, and a crutch without an owner, carefully preserved. If these shadows remain unaltered by the Future, the child will die.

SCROOGE: Oh, no, kind Spirit. Say he will be spared!

C. PRESENT: Why worry about crippled Tiny Tim? If he be like to die, he had better do it, and decrease the surplus population. Man—if man you be in heart—remember and repent your words.

SCROOGE (*Miserably*): I do, I do. Oh, take me home, Spirit. Show me no more. Take me home!

C. PRESENT (*Fading, mysteriously*): As you wish, Ebenezer Scrooge!

SOUND: *Wind, up and under.*

SCROOGE: Take me home, home! Why—why I'm in my bed again. In my bed! Was it a dream? No, impossible. And yet—there's no holly, no mistletoe! But it wasn't a dream, I'm sure of it!

SOUND: *Clock tolling twelve.*

SCROOGE (*After the third toll*): Oh, dear, oh, dear, it's midnight! It's time for him to be coming, the Ghost that I fear most of all—the third. The Ghost of Christmas Future. The Ghost of Christmas yet to come.

MUSIC: *Eerie theme, sneak in and under.*

SCROOGE (*Gasps*): It's he—there in the shadows, I see him. A phantom, draped and hooded, coming like the mist! (*More loudly*) I am in the presence of the Ghost of Christmas Yet To Come? You nod. You are about to show me shadows of the things that have not happened, but will happen in the time before us. Is that so, Spirit? Ghost of the Future, I fear you more than any spectre I have seen. But as I know your purpose is to do me good,

I am prepared to bear you company. Lead on! Lead on! The night is waning fast, and it is precious time to me, I know. Lead on, Spirit!

SOUND: *Wind, up and under.*

SCROOGE: What, Spirit? Do you, too, bring me to the home of my clerk, Bob Cratchit? You motion me toward the window. There is Mrs. Cratchit by the fire, with her sewing. And the children—they're so quiet! Still as statues, they are.

MARTHA: Are you crying, Mother?

MRS. CRATCHIT: No, dear, it's—it's the light, it hurts my eyes. They're weak by candlelight, and I wouldn't show weak eyes to your father when he comes, for the whole world. It must be near time for him to come.

MARTHA: Past it, rather.

BOY: He walks a little slower than he used to, these past few evenings, Mother.

MRS. CRATCHIT: I've know him to walk with—I've known him walk with Tiny Tim upon his shoulder, very fast indeed.

GIRL: So have I, Mother.

MARTHA: And so have we all.

MRS. CRATCHIT: But he was very light to carry, and his father loved him so, that it was no trouble. Now, there's your father at the door!

MARTHA: Come here, Father. Sit by the fire.

CRATCHIT (*Slowly, sadly, as he fades on*): Thank you, Martha, my dear.

GIRL: Your tea is ready, Father.

MRS. CRATCHIT: You—you went today, Robert?

CRATCHIT: Yes, my dear. I wish you could have gone. It would have done you good to see how green a place it is. But you'll see it often. I promised him that we would. (*With a break in his voice*) My . . . little child. My . . . Tiny Tim.

SCROOGE: Poor Tiny Tim . . . oh, why did he have to die? You draw me with you, Spirit. This court through which we hurry now—I know this place. This is where my place of occupation is. I see my office. Let me look in. Why . . . why, it's not my office! The furniture has been changed. That man at my desk, who is it? Why, it's my nephew, Fred! What is the meaning of this? Will you answer my questions, Phantom? But no; you draw me on. A churchyard, overrun with weeds and grass, the growth of vegetation's death, not life. What miserable place is this, unkept, uncared for? What wretched souls find their ends beneath this neglected soil? You single out a grave, Spectre. Before I draw nearer to that stone to which you point, answer me one question. Are these the shadows of the things that will be, or are they the shadows of the things that may be? You answer not, but point to a headstone. The stone is decayed—I can't make out the name. I can only feel out the letters. They spell Eb . . . Ebe . . . Ebenezer Scrooge! Then this wretched grave, this dismal end, is mine! No, Spirit, oh, no! Spirit, hear me. I am not the man I was. Why show me this, Spirit? I will change! I will honor Christmas in my heart, and try to keep it all the year. I will live in the Past, the Present, and the Future. The Spirits of all three shall strive within me. Oh, tell me I may sponge away the writing on this stone. Tell me so! Tell me! Tell me!

SOUND: *Clock tolling one.*

SCROOGE (*Whimpering*): Tell me, Spirit! Tell me! Why—why, I'm in my room. I'm home—I'm alive! Oh, Jacob Marley, I will change! Heaven and Christmastime be praised! I say it on my knees, Jacob, on my knees! Oh, I don't know what to do. I'm as light as a feather, as happy as an angel. I'm as merry as a schoolboy! Merry Christmas, old room, old bed curtains! Merry Christmas, old saucepan! But what am I standing here for? I must find out what day it is!

SOUND: *Window being opened.*

SCROOGE: Hallo! Hallo there, what's today, boy?

A YOUNG COCKNEY (*Off mike*): Today? Why, it's Christmas Day!

SCROOGE: Thank heavens! Christmas! Then I haven't missed it. Hallo, my fine fellow!

COCKNEY: Yes, sir?

SCROOGE: Do you know the Poulterers in the next street but one, at the corner? Do you know whether they've sold the prize Turkey that was hanging up there—not the little one, but the great big one?

COCKNEY: It's hanging there now, sir.

SCROOGE: Is it? What an intelligent boy you are! Go and buy it—here's the money, and a half-crown extra for you.

COCKNEY (*Impressed*): Yes, *sir!*

SCROOGE: And have them send it to this address. Merry Christmas!

COCKNEY (*Fading*): Merry Christmas to you, too, sir!

SCROOGE: Ha, ha! I'll send it to Bob Cratchit's! He shan't know who sent it. What a surprise it will be—twice the size of Tiny Tim! But what am I standing here in my nightshirt for? I've things to do, people to see. I must be off. Whee!

MUSIC: *Gay theme, in and under.*

SOUND: *Knock at door; door opens.*

SCROOGE: Fred!

FRED (*Amazed*): Why, who is this I see?

SCROOGE: It's I, your Uncle Scrooge. I've come to dinner, for Christmas, you know. Will you let me in, Fred?

FRED: Let you in! You'll be lucky if I don't shake your hand off! Merry Christmas, Uncle Ebenezer! (*Calling off mike*) Nancy! Look who's here! Set another place at table. It's Uncle Scrooge, for Christmas!

MUSIC: *Delightful theme, in and under.*

SCROOGE: Ah, what a wonderful time that was at Fred's yesterday. What a charming girl his wife is. I really must do something for them! (*In secret glee*) Oho, but here comes Bob Cratchit. I hoped I'd get here to the office ahead of him to surprise him!

SOUND: *Door opening.*

SCROOGE (*Sourly*): Hallo! What do you mean by coming here at this time of day, Cratchit?

CRATCHIT (*Timidly*): I'm very sorry, Mr. Scrooge, sir. It won't happen again, sir, I promise. I was making a bit merry yesterday, and . . .

SCROOGE (*Growling*): Now, I'll tell you what. I'm not going to stand for this sort of thing any more, and therefore I am about to—raise your salary!

CRATCHIT (*Aghast*): Mr. Scrooge!

SCROOGE (*Laughing genially*): A merry Christmas, Bob. A merrier Christmas, my good fellow, than I've given you for many a year. I'll raise your salary—and we must find the best doctor in all of London for that young son of yours.

CRATCHIT: I—I don't know what to say, Mr. Scrooge.

SCROOGE: Don't say anything, Bob, old fellow. This is the happiest Christmas of my life.

CRATCHIT: And of mine. As Tiny Tim observed, God bless us, every one!

MUSIC: *Christmas finale.*

THE END

The Coming of the Prince

by Eugene Field

Adapted by Jane McGowan

Characters

NARRATOR	SEXTON
BARBARA	MAN
WIND	WATCHMAN
SNOWFLAKE	PINE TREE
OLD MAN	VINE
WOMAN CUSTOMER	FIR TREE
CHILD	SNOWDROP
SHOP KEEPER	VOICE
PARTY GUESTS, *five*	CHORUS
WORSHIPPER	CHORAL READING GROUP
CHILD	

SOUND: *The swish and swoosh of a strong wind, as it sets signs and shutters squeaking on a blustery Christmas Eve.*

NARRATOR: Hear that sound? That is the voice of the North Wind as it roars through the streets of an ancient city on Christmas Eve. The wind has come straight from the forest to the city, sweeping everything before it in its gusty path. It tears through the narrow lanes and by-ways with a rush and a roar, turning umbrellas inside and out and driving snow in fitful gusts before it. To little Barbara, trudging lost and alone through the icy streets, it does not seem strange that the Wind should speak in accents she can understand.

WIND: Whirr-r-r! Whirr-r-r! Hold your head up, child. Lift your face from that ragged shawl so I can see who you are.

BARBARA: My name is Barbara. You'll have to excuse me for not lifting my head. The snow blows in my eyes so that I can hardly see. I am almost frozen.

WIND: Whirr-r-r! Whirr-r-r! Why are you out in such a storm? You should be at home by a warm fire with your parents.

BARBARA: I have no home, and no parents either. I . . . Oh, dear! Watch what you're doing. You're blowing a cloud of snow right into that old man's face.

OLD MAN: Out of my way, child. I must get home with these market baskets or my good wife will be angry.

BARBARA: Your baskets look very full and heavy.

OLD MAN: Aye, that they are! Packed to the brim with all the good things for tomorrow's feast.

BARBARA: Oh, dear! I wish . . .

OLD MAN: There, there, Child! Let me pass. Can't you see I'm in a hurry.

BARBARA: Excuse me, sir.

WIND: Whirr-r-r! Oh, there you are! I've brought you some company. A little snowflake. Snowflake, this is Barbara. She's lonely and needs a friend. If you perch there on the edge of her shawl, you two can have a little visit.

BARBARA: But my shawl is almost covered with snowflakes.

WIND: This one is different. You'll find she has quite a personality. Whirr-r-r! But I must be on my way. I'll leave you two to get acquainted.

SOUND: *Roaring of Wind.*

SNOWFLAKE: Did he say your name is Barbara?

BARBARA: Yes, it is. Do you have a name?

SNOWFLAKE: Just Snowflake. But tell me, Barbara, why aren't you in the cathedral? I heard grand music and saw beautiful lights as I floated down from the sky a moment ago.

BARBARA: What's going on? What are they doing in the cathedral?

SNOWFLAKE: Why, haven't you heard? I supposed everybody knew that the Prince is coming tomorrow.

BARBARA: Sure enough. This is Christmas Eve. And the Prince *will* come tomorrow. I had almost forgotten the beautiful stories my mother used to tell me about the Prince; how beautiful and good and kind and gentle he is, and how he loves little children. But now— I have no one to tell me about the Prince and his coming . . . no one at all.

SNOWFLAKE: You still have me, Barbara. Remember?

BARBARA: I should like to see the Prince, little Snowflake. Have you ever seen him?

SNOWFLAKE: No, I have never seen him. But I heard the pines and the fir trees singing about him as I floated over the forest tonight.

BARBARA: Oh, look! Look! Look at the beautiful store windows, ablaze with lights. I wonder if I can get close enough to see the toys.

SNOWFLAKE: Be careful! Be careful! You'll brush me off your shawl in the crowd.

BARBARA: Oh, dear! Excuse me, sir. Excuse me, ma'am.

WOMAN: Who is that rude child pushing and shoving her way in here?

CHILD: I can't see, Mamma. Lift me up. Lift me up. I want to see the pretty toys.

WOMAN: You could see perfectly well if it weren't for this horrid child. Can't you see, you little wretch, that you're blocking my little boy's view. The storekeeper shouldn't permit beggars to take up all the space in front of the toyshop window.

SHOPKEEPER: Ah, good evening, madam. Are you and your little son admiring the pretty toys?

WOMAN: We're trying to see them, Mr. Dolfus, but this miserable child keeps getting in the way . . .

SHOPKEEPER: What? What do you mean, you little beggar! How can the customers see all my fine things if you stand before the window! Be off with you, you little bag of bones.

BARBARA: I'm sorry, sir. I . . . I didn't understand.

NARRATOR: And so Barbara continued to wander through the city. The little Snowflake, jostled from her shawl in the crowd at the toy store, did not reappear, and she felt lonelier and lonelier as she trudged on through the snow. Presently she came to a large house where there seemed to be much mirth and festivity. The shutters were thrown open and through the windows Barbara could see a beautiful Christmas tree in the center of the spacious room . . . a beautiful Christmas tree, ablaze with red and green lights, and heavy with toys and stars, and glass balls and other beautiful things that children love. As Barbara gazed at the beautiful scene before her, the children in the household gathered around the tree, and Barbara could hear their happy voices singing their favorite carol:

SOUND: *Children softly sing two verses of O Christmas Tree (O Tannenbaum).*

BARBARA: This must be the house where the Prince will stop. How I would like to see his face and hear his voice. If only I might go inside.

SOUND: *Horse-drawn sleigh with the tinkle of bells. There is laughter and the sound of children's voices as the carriage stops.*

MARY: This is the place, James. You may drive the horses around to the carriage house.

TOM: And be sure to stop in the kitchen, James, while we're at the party. There will be plenty to eat and drink. Come on, Mary. Be careful, Sally. Easy, Sarah. Watch your footing. It's icy.

BILL: Look at the house. It's lighted from cellar to attic.

SARAH: Hurry, hurry! The party has begun.

SALLY: I don't want to miss a single minute.

MARY: Be careful girls. Don't drop your packages.

BARBARA: Excuse me . . .

SOUND: *Exclamations of fright from girls.*

TOM: Who are you—there in the dark? What do you mean frightening these young ladies?

BARBARA: Oh, dear! I didn't mean to frighten anyone. I only wanted . . .

BILL: We have no alms for beggars.

BARBARA: I do not want money. I only wanted to know if this is the house where the Prince will stop.

MARY: What is she jabbering about? What Prince?

TOM: Don't mind her. It's only a street beggar. You know how they are at this time of year. Hurry along. The wind will blow us off our feet if we aren't careful.

BILL: Let's make a dash up the steps. Here we go!

SOUND: *Laughter and voices followed by rising wind.*

WIND: Whirr-r-r! Whirr-r-r! Oh, there you are again. I've been looking for you all over town.

BARBARA: And you've almost blown me to pieces, Mr. Wind. Where are you going in such a rush?

WIND: To the cathedral. The great people are flocking there and I will have a merry time among them, blowing off their hats, whipping their scarves into their faces, and blinding them with sudden flurries of snow.

BARBARA: It is there that the Prince will surely come. The cathedral is the most beautiful building in the city, and the people will do him homage there. Perhaps I might see him if I join the crowd.

WIND: Then come along and watch me at my pranks. It's just around the corner. Lean on me and I will blow you there in no time. Listen! You can hear the sound of the chimes even above the roar of my voice.

SOUND: *Chimes play softly at first, then swell into "Adeste Fideles."*

BARBARA: Hurry, hurry! I must be on time to greet the Prince.

SOUND: *Chimes up and out.*

NARRATOR: The wind swept Barbara around the corner and almost up the steps of the cathedral, but she was too shy to mingle with the richly dressed throng before the door. She hesitated for a few minutes as the last of the stragglers mounted the steps of the great stone church.

SOUND: *Organ music playing Christmas carols in background.*

WOMAN: This is the most beautiful service of the year . . . in honor of the Prince of Peace.

CHILD: Will we see the Prince, Mamma?

WOMAN: Hush, child. Remember, you must be very quiet and listen to every word. Come along, we must not be late.

MAN: Ah, good evening, sexton, the cathedral is almost filled, I see.

SEXTON: Yes, sir. The biggest crowd of any Christmas Eve since I've been in service here at St. Michael's.

MAN: Ah, yes, indeed. The best people in town come to St. Michael's. What have we here? Who is this little creature on the steps?

SEXTON: Who indeed? She's not one of our parishioners, sir. Where did you come from, child? We want no loitering here.

BARBARA: Please, sir, I am not loitering. I only came to . . .

MAN: Then be on your way. Run along home where you will be out of the cold. Doubtless your parents will be worrying about you.

BARBARA: But I have no parents, sir.

MAN: Then we want no beggars on the church steps. There are charities who will look after you. You had better close the door, sexton. We don't want to waste the warmth in the cathedral, and most of our worshippers have arrived.

SEXTON: Very well, sir.

SOUND: *Organ music fading.*

BARBARA: Please, sir . . .

SEXTON: You heard what the gentleman said. Now be off with you!

BARBARA: Please, may I go and sit inside?

SEXTON: No, indeed. The cathedral is crowded. This is the greatest service of the year.

BARBARA: But I will be ever so good and quiet. Please may I not see the Prince?

SEXTON (*Laughing*): You! See the Prince! And what have you for the Prince or he for you? Out with you and don't be blocking the doorway.

NARRATOR: The sexton was really not a rough man, nor did he mean to shove Barbara quite so hard, but she slipped and fell on the icy steps and it was there that the little Snowflake found her a few minutes later, crouched in the darkness and crying bitterly.

SNOWFLAKE: Dear little Barbara! I thought I had lost you, but our friend, Mr. Wind, guided me back to you. What are you doing here? Have you seen the Prince?

BARBARA (*Tearfully*): No, no! I have not seen him. But what cares the Prince for me? I am a wretched beggar child. There is no room for me in any corner of this hateful city.

SNOWFLAKE: Do not speak so bitterly, little one. Come with me into the forest and you shall see him. The Prince always comes through the forest to the city.

BARBARA: Oh, Snowflake, that is a beautiful idea. I love the forest so much better than the city. The stars are so near and the trees are so big and strong. Perhaps I could hide among the trees and vines and be quite close to the Prince without ever being noticed.

SNOWFLAKE: Then hurry. I will dance along ahead of you and lead the way.

NARRATOR: So Barbara followed the dancing Snowflake through the narrow twisting streets to the city gates. Wrapped in her ragged shawl, her head bent low against the wind, she almost plunged headlong into the stout, kind-hearted watchman who guarded the main gateway.

WATCHMAN: Not so fast! Not so fast! Look where you're going, friend, if you have eyes in your head. Here, stand back a pace, and let me have a look at you under my lantern. (*Pause*) Why, you're only a child . . . a wee mite of a girl. Who are you and where do you think you're going at this hour of the night?

BARBARA: My name is Barbara, and I'm going to the forest.

WATCHMAN: Into the forest? And in such a storm? No, child, you will perish.

BARBARA: But I'm going to see the Prince. I really am.

WATCHMAN: But not in the forest, you silly girl. 'Tis freezing cold out there and by morning the snow will be as high as my boot tops.

BARBARA: They will not let me watch for the Prince in the church, nor in front of the shops, nor in any of the pleasant homes, so I am going into the forest.

WATCHMAN: Now, now, now! Be reasonable. I have a little

maid at home just about your size, and I would never let her go into the forest on a night like this. Now come along with me and . . .

BARBARA (*Wildly*): Let go of me! Let go of me! I'm going into the forest to see the Prince. No one shall stop me.

WATCHMAN (*Calling, his voice getting fainter and fainter*): Come back, child, come back! You will perish in the forest. Come back, come back!

NARRATOR: But Barbara did not heed his cry. The falling snow did not stay her, nor did the cutting blast. On and on she ran, straight into the forest where a little vine clinging close to the frozen ground was talking to a gigantic pine tree.

VINE (*In a small voice*): What do you see up there, O Pine Tree? You lift your head among the clouds tonight and you tremble strangely as if you saw wondrous sights.

PINE TREE: I see only the distant hills and the dark clouds, little Vine. And the Wind sings of the Snow King tonight. To all my questions he says, "Snow, snow, snow," till I'm wearied with his refrain.

VINE: My little neighbor, Snowdrop, says the Prince will surely come tonight. We heard the country folk talking as they went through the forest yesterday. Do you know anything about it?

PINE TREE: Oh, yes, he is coming, but not until the day dawns and it is still all dark in the east.

VINE: Sh! Listen! There is someone coming through the forest.

PINE TREE: Nonsense. No one would venture into our forest at such an hour.

BARBARA (*Bravely*): Indeed! And why not? Will you not let me watch with you for the coming of the Prince?

PINE TREE: How do I know you have not come to chop me down?

BARBARA (*Laughing*): It would take stronger arms than mine to do that, mighty Pine Tree.

VINE: How do we know you won't tear me up by the roots or pluck the blossoms from my little neighbor, Snowdrop. She is so timid she is almost afraid to poke her head above the ground.

BARBARA: I promise I will hurt nothing in the forest. Too many people have hurt me tonight. (*Sobbing*) I have been turned aside by everyone in the city. There is no place for me. I thought if I came to the forest, I might . . .

PINE TREE (*Clearing throat*): There, there, child! No one will harm you here. You may lie at my feet and I will protect you.

VINE: Nestle close to me and I will rub your temples and body and limbs until you are warm. Lie still and our little Snowdrop will sing you the legend of the Christmas Rose.

SOUND: SNOWDROP *softly sings "Lo, How a Rose E'er Blooming."*

BARBARA: That was very beautiful. Thank you, Snowdrop. It is very pleasant here. You are making me feel welcome and glad I came.

VINE: Tell us, Pine Tree, what do you see in the east? Has the Prince entered the forest?

PINE TREE: The east is full of black clouds and the winds that hurry to the hilltop sing of snow.

FIR TREE: But the city is full of brightness. I can see the lights in the cathedral and I can hear wondrous music about the Prince and his coming.

PINE TREE: Keep your head out of my way, Fir Tree. With your constant bobbing around I can scarcely see.

FIR TREE: Never fear. We will all see the Prince when he comes.

VINE: And we will be the *first* to see him because his way leads through the forest.

BARBARA: It is very cold. My hands and feet are like ice.

PINE TREE: Fir Tree and I will shake our branches so that the snow will cover you like a soft blanket.

BARBARA: Oh, thank you, thank you.

VINE: Try to rest while Snowdrop sings her Christmas lullaby.

SOUND: SNOWDROP *sings traditional Christmas lullaby.*

NARRATOR: As Snowdrop sang the Christ Child's lullaby, Barbara fell asleep, the little Snowflake still resting on her shawl. By morning the ground was white with the robe the Storm King had thrown over it, and everything was bright, sparkling and beautiful, for the coming of the Prince was close at hand. A little snowbird flew down from the fir tree's bough, perched upon the vine and caroled the glad tidings in Barbara's ear.

SOUND: *Bird warbling and chirping.*

NARRATOR: But Barbara did not waken. She did not even hear the soft voice of her little friend, the Vine.

VINE: Barbara, Barbara! Wake up! The Prince is coming.

SOUND: *Fanfare softly fading into triumphal music.*

ALL: The Prince is coming!

NARRATOR: A great light shone in the forest as the Prince, clad in royal raiment and wearing a golden crown appeared in the forest with his company of angels. As the trees bowed low and the birds stilled their song, the Prince stopped before the sleeping child. She stirred beneath her blanket of snow as she heard the gentle, beloved voice.

VOICE: Barbara, my little one, waken and come with me.

SOUND: *Music up and under.*

NARRATOR: Then Barbara opened her eyes and beheld the Prince; and it seemed as if a new life had come to her, for there was warmth in her body and a flush upon her cheeks and a light in her eyes that were divine. The Pine Tree and the little Vine spoke in hushed voices:

VINE: Look! Look! She is clothed no longer in rags but in snowy white raiment.

PINE TREE: And in her hair there is a golden crown such as the angels wear.

VINE: And the little Snowflake on her shawl has become a pearl . . . a precious jewel.

NARRATOR: And the Prince took Barbara in his arms and blessed her, and turning round about, returned with the little child into his home, while the forest and the sky and the angels sang a wondrous song:

SOUND: *Chorus singing traditional carol, "Angels We Have Heard on High."*

NARRATOR: The city waited for the Prince, but he did not come. None knew of the glory of the forest that Christmas morning, nor of the new life that came to little Barbara.

SOUND: *Chorus softly hums "O Sanctissima" as* CHORAL READING GROUP *speaks against humming background.*

CHORAL READERS: Come thou, dear Prince, oh come to us this holy Christmas time! Come to the busy marts of earth; the quiet homes, the noisy streets, the humble lanes; come to us all, and with thy love, touch every human heart, that we may know that love, and in its blessed peace, bear charity to all mankind.

SOUND: *Chorus up, singing final stanza of "O Sanctissima."*

THE END

Christmas Every Day

by William Dean Howells

Adapted by Jane McGowan

Characters

ANNOUNCER	GROCER
THE CHRISTMAS FAIRY	MRS. DAVIS
TWO ELVES	TOMMY
TWO BROWNIES	JACK
CHIEF CLERK	ORATOR
MARY	SUE
FATHER	MABEL
BILLY	DICK
MOTHER	RAG MAN
SALLY	BOY

ANNOUNCER: Once upon a time there was a little girl who liked Christmas so much that she wanted it to be Christmas every day in the year. So, as soon as Thanksgiving was over, she began to send post cards to the Christmas Fairy to ask if it might be that way. Year after year she kept sending post cards, and getting no reply, until one year she decided to try something different. This time the Christmas Fairy was impressed.

MUSIC: *Tinkle of music box.*

CHRISTMAS FAIRY: Attention, Elves and Brownies! Something must be done about the little girl who wants Christmas every day.

FIRST ELF: What is her name, Christmas Fairy?

CHRISTMAS FAIRY: She signs herself *Mary X*. I don't know if the X stand for Xmas or a Christmas kiss.

SECOND ELF: Maybe it just stands for "X—the Unknown Quantity." There are millions of Marys in the world.

FIRST BROWNIE: Is this the same little girl who writes to you every year?

CHRISTMAS FAIRY: Yes, but this year she really means business. She always sent post cards before, but now she's written a real letter, sealed and stamped; and what's more she's used her mother's best monogrammed stationery.

SECOND BROWNIE: In that case, I don't see how we can ignore her request.

FIRST ELF: But think what it will mean! Christmas every day! It makes me shudder.

CHRISTMAS FAIRY: Nevertheless, the little girl wants it very badly and she has been ever so polite and persistent. I think . . . I really think we should grant her wish.

SECOND ELF: Not forever, Christmas Fairy. Please, please, not forever.

CHRISTMAS FAIRY: No, not forever. Just for one year. That should give her time to see how she likes it.

FIRST BROWNIE: She'll make up her mind long before that.

CHRISTMAS FAIRY: Don't be too sure. Chief Clerk, take a letter.

CHIEF CLERK: At your service, ma'am.

CHRISTMAS FAIRY: Dear Mary: Your letter of November 30th has been duly received and contents noted. In reply to your request for a Christmas every day, we are happy to inform you that your request has been granted. Beginning on the twenty-fifth of December of this year, every one of the next 365 days shall be Christmas. If, at the end of this trial period, you still wish every day to be Christmas, please notify this department and we will give your request every consideration.

Trusting that you may have a happy holiday season, I am, Sincerely yours, The Christmas Fairy.

MUSIC: *Music box tinkle.*

ANNOUNCER: This letter was delivered to the little girl but in the rush and excitement of preparing for the old-fashioned once-a-year Christmas, she didn't pay too much attention to it, except to keep it to herself as a grand surprise to spring on the rest of the family when Christmas was officially over. And then as the great day actually approached, it slipped out of her mind altogether. She was too excited to think about another thing except Santa Claus. Little Mary went to bed especially early on Christmas Eve in order to give Santa a good chance at the stockings, and in the morning, she was the first one up.

MARY: Merry Christmas! Merry Christmas, everybody! Mother, Daddy! Come on. Get up! It's Christmas morning.

FATHER (*Yawning*): It couldn't be morning. I just crawled into bed.

MARY: Yes, it is! Yes, it is! And here are Sally and Billy, ready to see the tree.

SALLY *and* BILLY: Merry Christmas! Merry Christmas!

MOTHER: And merry Christmas to you, my darlings. Now run along downstairs and look at your stockings. But remember, we don't open our Santa Claus gifts till after breakfast. I'll try to get this sleepy-head Daddy out of bed. Come on, John, it's merry Christmas. (*Sound of snores*) John, wake up, dear! It's Christmas morning. John, John, try to get awake! It's Christmas! Merry Christmas, dear.

FATHER (*Half awake*): And merry Christmas to you! Now go away and let me sleep. (*Sound of snores*)

ANNOUNCER (*Chuckling*): Well, Father really did get up and the whole family had a wonderful Christmas Day. There was a mile-high stack of presents in the living room under the great big tree: Books, and games, and breast pins, and little toy stoves, and scores of handkerchiefs, and ink stands, and skates and snow shovels and boxes of water colors, and stockings, and candy, and pipes and tobacco and dozens of ties for Father. By noon the living room rug was covered with tissue paper and the electric train had jumped the track three times. But after dinner was the very best time of all.

FATHER: I simply couldn't eat another bite. That last helping of plum pudding almost put me under the table.

MOTHER: I do think the turkey was even better than last year. I was worried about the new roaster but everything turned out just fine. Gracious, Billy, what are you eating now?

BILLY: Just a few raisins. I needed them to fill in a hollow place under my left rib.

FATHER: That boy will burst wide open if he doesn't stop eating.

SALLY: How can you be such a pig, Billy?

BILLY: Who's a pig? I saw you pop a chocolate cream in your mouth just a while ago, so there!

MOTHER: Children! Children! Don't argue on Christmas Day. Come over here and sit by me where we can watch the Christmas tree lights and relax. It's been such a lovely day.

SALLY: Such wonderful presents.

MARY (*With a sigh of contentment*): And such a good dinner!

SOUND: BILLY *starts to cry.*

MOTHER: Why, Billy, what's the matter?

BILLY: I don't know! It's either the turkey or the filling! I've got the most awful stomach-ache! (*Loud wails*)

ANNOUNCER: But Christmas wouldn't be Christmas without a stomach-ache or two, and even in spite of that the day ended happily for everybody. Along about seven o'clock Billy revived sufficiently to eat a light supper and the whole family went to bed early, tired and happy, with the strains of Christmas music ringing in their ears.

MUSIC: *"Christmas Comes Again."*

ANNOUNCER: Little Mary slept soundly all night long, and probably would have slept the whole day through, but bright and early she was awakened by happy shouts.

SALLY *and* BILLY: Merry Christmas! Merry Christmas! Merry Christmas!

MARY: What is it? What's the matter?

SALLY: Nothing's the matter! Wake up! It's Christmas Day!

MARY: You can't fool me, silly. Yesterday was Christmas.

BILLY: Who's a silly? You just get out of that bed and come and see. It really *is* Christmas.

MARY: But how could it be? Yesterday was Christmas. Don't you remember? You got a bicycle and a train and a pair of skates . . . and my goodness! You even got a Christmas stomach-ache.

BILLY: I can't help that. It's Christmas today just the same. If you don't believe me, come and look.

SALLY: It's really and truly Christmas, Mary. Put on your slippers and come downstairs. (*Sound of footsteps*) There! You can see for yourself!

MARY: Why, it must be Christmas after all! There are the stockings! Mother's, Dad's, Billy's, Sally's and mine! And there's the tree with all the presents and not a one unwrapped!

SALLY: Isn't it wonderful? Isn't it perfectly marvellous?

Yesterday was Christmas and now we're having it all over again.

BILLY: Will I have a stomach-ache again today?

SALLY: That depends on you. If you make a pig of yourself again today I guess you will.

BILLY: I don't care. It was worth it.

MARY: But I don't understand.

SALLY: Neither do I. Do you suppose we're going to have Christmas every day?

MARY: Oh, my goodness! Oh, my goodness, gracious sakes alive! It can't be . . . and yet it must be the Christmas Fairy!

SALLY: What are you talking about?

MARY: Oh, dear! I don't know! I seem to be all mixed up. Here's Mother. Maybe she can explain it.

BILLY: Look, Mother! It's Christmas all over again.

MOTHER: Yes, I know! And where are we going to put all these new toys and gifts? The house was filled to bursting yesterday.

FATHER: And what about the bills? Now we'll have another set of bills for the tree and the turkey and the presents! Indeed I don't know what will become of us.

BILLY: Don't worry, Dad, Look! Here's another electric train and another set of tracks. Now we can have a race.

SALLY: Don't look so glum, Dad. Here . . . open one of your presents.

FATHER (*Sound of tissue paper being unwrapped*): Just as I expected! Another tie! I'll have enough ties to hang myself if this keeps up!

MUSIC: *Up and out.*

ANNOUNCER: And the worst part of it was that it did keep up. The next day was just the same thing over again. The stockings, the Christmas tree, the presents, the turkey, the cranberry sauce, even the stomach-aches!

Poor Mary began to get frightened keeping the secret all to herself; she wanted to tell her mother, but she didn't dare, and it seemed ungrateful to ask the fairy to take back her gift. And so it went on and on . . .

MUSIC: *"Christmas Comes Again," up and under.*

ANNOUNCER: It was Christmas on St. Valentine's Day!

It was Christmas on George Washington's Birthday!

And even on April Fool's Day!

In the stores and at the markets people were talking like this.

MOTHER: How much are your turkeys today, Mr. Smith?

GROCER: We're getting a thousand dollars apiece for the hens, Mrs. Brown, but I can let you have a fine gobbler for nine hundred dollars!

MOTHER: Why, that's simply outrageous! I'm sure I saw some at the other market for five hundred.

GROCER: If you ask me, ma'am, you'd better be careful. I don't trust this cheap merchandise. Why, they tell me that some of the farmers are passing anything with feathers off on the public in place of genuine turkeys. I even heard that half-grown eagles, chicken hawks and poll parrots are being sold.

MOTHER: Goodness! I wouldn't want to eat a poll parrot. Oh, good morning, Mrs. Davis. Isn't shopping a problem these days?

MRS. DAVIS: It's simply terrible. I've been all over town looking for cranberries. Some of the stores are asking a diamond apiece for them. Indeed, I don't see how poor people are going to live!

MOTHER: I know. It's almost impossible to make ends meet with Christmas coming every day. We've used so much coal to wrap up in the toes of the children's stocking that our winter supply is almost exhausted.

MRS. DAVIS: It's the same way with potatoes at our house. We always wrap up a potato as one of our stocking gifts and now you can hardly get enough to serve at the Christmas dinner table!

MOTHER: And isn't it dreadful about the trees? Whole forests are being cut down. . . . The landscape is getting to be nothing but stumps.

MRS. DAVIS: Well, we've solved the Christmas tree problem at our house.

MOTHER: How?

MRS. DAVIS: We're making ours of rags. I cut a pattern and the children stuffed it. It really doesn't look half bad.

MOTHER: Rags! That's a splendid idea. I think we'll have to try that at our house. That is, if you'd lend us the pattern.

MRS. DAVIS: Oh, I'd be glad to. And rags are so easy to get these days. People are so poor buying presents for one another that they just wear their clothes to tatters.

MOTHER: That's true. I don't remember when things were so bad for so many people.

MRS. DAVIS: Whoever would have thought that Christmas could cause such changes? The only rich people in the country these days are the candy sellers and gift shop keepers!

MOTHER: And the difference it's making in the children's manners! Our youngsters used to take such pains wrapping their presents and making little cards for "Dear Daddy" or "Dear Sister," or "Dear Billy." Now, they just throw the presents at each other and say, "Here, take it, you horrid old thing!" And I can't scold them too much because I feel the same way myself.

MRS. DAVIS: If only we could find out who's responsible. Some people say it's the government . . . but I can hardly believe such a thing.

MOTHER: Yes, I know . . . and some people say. . . .

MUSIC: *Up and out.*

ANNOUNCER: Yes, people were saying all sorts of things and

offering all kinds of explanations for the strange state of affairs. But no matter what they said or what they did, Christmas kept right on coming. One of the most terrible days in the whole year was the Fourth of July. All over America small boys jumped out of bed on the morning of the glorious Fourth and ran downstairs to get their fireworks. And all over America there were the same bitter disappointments.

TOMMY: Hey, Jack, you better hold your ears! I'm gonna smash this torpedo right down on the pavement. There!

SOUND: *A slight thud or slap.*

JACK: I didn't hear anything.

TOMMY: Neither did I! I guess that one was no good. Here, you try one.

JACK: O.K.! Stand back! This one should wake the dead!

SOUND: *Thud or slap.*

JACK: Say, where did you get these? They must all be duds!

TOMMY: Let me look at them. Maybe they got damp or something.

JACK: Well what do you know! Look, Tommy. These aren't torpedoes at all! They're nothing but big fat raisins!

TOMMY: Raisins?

JACK: Yeah! Raisins! It must be this Christmas deal again! Can you beat that? Raisins instead of torpedoes on the Fourth of July!

TOMMY: Say, Jack, if these torpedoes are raisins, what about the rest of our fireworks. Open your box of Roman candles.

JACK: Holy smokes! They're nothing but sugar candles!

TOMMY: And the fire crackers are hard candy painted red.

BOTH: Oh, no! It can't be! It's not another Christmas Day!

ANNOUNCER: And that's how it was all over America. The boys were so angry and so disappointed that they just sat down and cried! And it was all the grown men could do to refrain from joining them, because every time a Fourth of July orator got up to read the Declaration of Independence, instead of this. . . .

ORATOR: "When, in the course of human events, it becomes necessary for one people to dissolve the political bands which have connected them with another. . . ."

ANNOUNCER: The words came out like this—

ORATOR: " 'Twas the night before Christmas when all through the house, Not a creature was stirring, not even a mouse!"

ANNOUNCER: And at all the parades, when the band started to play:

MUSIC: *Opening bars of "Yankee Doodle."*

ANNOUNCER: Without any warning the music changed to this—

MUSIC: *"Christmas Comes Again."*

ANNOUNCER: Oh, I'm telling you, folks, the Fourth of July was like a Christmas nightmare. Everybody agreed things just couldn't get any worse. But they did. And they got very much worse for our little friend, Mary. By the time Thanksgiving Day rolled around Mary was so sick at heart and so worried that she began to talk in her sleep, and before she knew it, her secret was out. First her family and then her friends discovered that *she* was to blame. After that, she had no peace. One by one, her friends turned against her.

SUE: Go away, you horrid girl. It's all your fault we're having Christmas every day!

MABEL: I'm not allowed to play with you any more, and my mother says if she ever catches you in our yard, she'll skin you alive.

DICK: There she is! There's the girl who did it! Come on, let's get her!

MARY: Help! Help! Mother! Mother! They're after me! Make them stop!

MOTHER: Run in the house quickly and slam the door!

SOUND: *Running feet. Door slams. Shouts and cries fade out.*

MARY: Oh, Mother, Mother! What am I going to do?

MOTHER: I wish I could tell you, child, but I don't know what any of us will do if this keeps up much longer. What made you do such a thing?

MARY: I don't know. I guess I was just greedy! Just a Christmas pig! Now I'd give anything in the world to undo it.

MOTHER: Have you written again to the Christmas Fairy?

MARY: I write every day, but she doesn't answer. I've even gone to her house but the maid always says "Not at Home" or "Engaged" or "In Conference," or something like that. Oh, Mother, everybody hates me! Even you don't love me any more.

MOTHER: Nonsense! Of course I love you . . . but we'll all be driven out of our minds celebrating Christmas every day. I thought surely it would stop by now. Just think, tomorrow is Thanksgiving.

MARY: What are we going to have for Thanksgiving dinner?

MOTHER: Why ask such a question? What do we have for *every* dinner? Turkey, or some substitute for turkey, mashed potatoes, sweet potatoes, cranberry sauce, pumpkin pie, plum pudding. . . . You know the menu as well as I do.

MARY: But won't we go to church and give thanks for all our blessings?

MOTHER: We'll try, but there's only one blessing that people want these days . . . and that's to see the last of Christmas.

MUSIC: *Up and out.*

ANNOUNCER: Poor Mary! And poor Mother! And poor everybody! They had to endure 365 solid days of Christmas with no relief in sight! But finally came the old once-a-year Christmas Eve. Mary fell asleep and suddenly she was awakened by the sound of bells. And she could hardly believe her ears! They were *not* Christmas bells. They were church bells and fire bells and school bells, and cow bells and burglar alarms and dinner bells and alarm clocks all ringing in a perfect frenzy!

SOUND: *Clamor of bells up and under.*

MARY: What is it? What is it? What's the matter? Is it the end of the world?

FATHER: No, it's better than that! It's the end of Christmas.

ALL: Hooray! Hooray! It's the end of Christmas!

MOTHER: No more turkey and cranberry sauce.

SALLY: No more presents to wrap and unwrap!

MARY: No more Christmas trees to trim!

BILLY: No more stomach-aches!

FATHER: And no more Christmas bills.

RAG MAN: Old cakes and candies! Bring out your old cakes and candies! Bring out your stale dates and raisins.

BILLY: Look, the old man has a whole cart of candies, nuts and raisins.

FATHER: Why, it's our old Rag Man. Hello, Joe, and Merry . . . I mean . . . hello, Joe . . . and how are you? Where are you going with all that trash?

RAG MAN: Gonna haul it to the river and dump it in!

MOTHER: Aren't you afraid it will make the fish sick?

RAG MAN: Hadn't thought of that, ma'am, but we've gotta get rid of this sweet stuff somehow. All the kids are eating themselves sick. Guess it won't do the fish any harm to take their turn.

MOTHER: Well, meet me at the back door and I'll give you all we have.

BOY (*Running*): Hurry up, Mister Brown. Hurry up!

FATHER: Where are you going, sonny?

BOY: Down to the square for the big bonfire! They're

burning all the Christmas greens and decorations and all the gifts that people don't want. You better hurry or you'll miss all the fun!

BILLY: Come on, let's run.

FATHER: You children go ahead, don't wait for me. I'm going to load up all those neckties and meet you down at the square.

MUSIC: *Up and out.*

ANNOUNCER: Yes, the town ran wild with excitement. People hugged and kissed each other and cried for joy and those bonfires extended the length and breadth of the country, clear up into Canada and Alaska. But while everybody was making merry over their first Non-Christmas in 365 days, our little friend, Mary Brown, went and knocked once more on the Christmas Fairy's door.

SOUND: *Door knocker.*

CHRISTMAS FAIRY: Come in.

MARY: Oh, I'm so glad you're at home today.

CHRISTMAS FAIRY: We've been expecting you, haven't we, Elves and Brownies?

ELVES *and* BROWNIES: We certainly have.

FIRST ELF: And we can hardly wait for your report.

SECOND ELF: How did you like it?

FIRST BROWNIE: Was it as nice as you expected?

SECOND BROWNIE: Did you like having Christmas every day?

MARY: Like it? No! It was horrible. That's why I came here today. First of all, I want to thank you for granting my wish and second, I have another request.

CHRISTMAS FAIRY: Another request?

MARY: Yes. Please see to it that Christmas never never comes again.

CHRISTMAS FAIRY: Are you sure that is your wish?

FIRST ELF: Never any more Christmases?

SECOND ELF: This is a serious decision, my child.

FIRST BROWNIE: It affects the whole world, you know.

SECOND BROWNIE: You'd better think it over carefully.

MARY: Well . . . maybe we could have Christmas once in a thousand years.

CHRISTMAS FAIRY: Are you sure you're not being greedy *this* time too . . . only in reverse? Are you sure that's often enough?

MARY: On second thought, make it once every hundred years.

FIRST ELF: I know a lot of children who won't like this.

SECOND ELF: And a lot of adults too.

FIRST BROWNIE: The world won't be the same, you know.

SECOND BROWNIE: It will be a long time between Christmas carols.

MARY: Oh, well . . . I guess once every ten years wouldn't be too close together, after people got used to the idea again.

CHRISTMAS FAIRY: That means all the children born on this day will be ten years old before they ever taste a turkey leg or see a Christmas tree.

FIRST ELF: And all the boys who are ten years old today will be twenty before they get another pair of Christmas roller skates.

SECOND ELF: And all the six-year-old girls will be sweet sixteen before Santa Claus can bring them a dolly.

CHRISTMAS FAIRY: And think of this, little Mary: the Christmas story of the Baby and the Wise Men and the Star will have to go untold for ten long years.

MARY: Oh, dear me. That would never do!

CHRISTMAS FAIRY: No, it wouldn't do at all. Think of the hope and happiness the Christmas story brings into our lives. Think of what the world would be like if people couldn't be reminded at least once a year of the true meaning of Christmas—peace on earth, good will toward men.

MARY: Now I can't seem to make up my mind at all! I don't know what to do.

CHRISTMAS FAIRY: How about going back to the good old-fashioned way?

MARY: You mean Christmas once a year?

CHRISTMAS FAIRY: After all, that is the good old way which has meant so much to people all over the world ever since Christmas began.

MARY: Then do let's have it that way, Christmas Fairy. And this time, make it forever and ever.

CHRISTMAS FAIRY: That's the best way, Mary, and it shall be as you wish.

ELVES *and* BROWNIES: And we'll all live happily ever after with Christmas once a year!

MUSIC: *"Christmas Comes Again" up and out.*

THE END

The Left-Over Reindeer

by Helen Louise Miller

Characters

FAITH, *an Irish nursemaid*
ROBBIE, SANDY } *her charges*
MR. MARBORO, *the father*
ST. NICHOLAS
JING, JANG } *his helpers*
CHOIR MASTER
VILLAGE CHILDREN
DANCER

MUSIC: *"Jingle Bells" with sleighbell accompaniment up and under.*

ANNOUNCER: If ever you walk past a rambling brick house, set well back from a certain road, in a grove of oak trees, and notice the cast-iron figure of a deer on the south lawn, you'll recognize the spot immediately as the setting of our story; and what's more you'll identify the graceful animal with its wide-spreading antlers as the Left-Over Reindeer. How he happened to be left-over concerns a family who didn't believe in St. Nicholas, and a sensitive reindeer who didn't believe in not believing.

The Christmas that Sandy Marboro was six years old,

a young Irish girl named Faith O'Flannagan made the mistake of filling the child's head with some bits of what his older brother was pleased to call "St. Nicholas Nonsense!"

FAITH (*Reading*):

"The moon on the breast of the new-fallen snow
Gave the lustre of mid-day to objects below,
When what to my wondering eyes should appear,
But a miniature sleigh, and eight tiny reindeer,
With a little old driver, so lively and quick,
I knew in a moment it must be St. Nick."

SANDY: Who is that, Faith? Who is *St. Nick?*

FAITH: Hush now, Sandy, and stop your teasing. You know as well as I do who St. Nick is.

SANDY: But I don't, Faith. Honest! I never heard of him.

FAITH: Sure and every child has heard of St. Nicholas.

SANDY: I'm a "nevery child" and I never heard of him. Tell me about him, please.

FAITH: If I thought you were really in earnest! Well, listen to the story, and you'll learn all about the good old Saint who brings good children all the presents they want most on Christmas Eve.

SANDY: Father brings Robbie and me our presents on Christmas Eve. But they aren't always the things we want most. Last year I wanted a sled and Robbie wanted a train, but we got socks and overcoats instead.

FAITH: Socks and overcoats are very useful and lots of little boys would be grateful for them. You and Robbie can be thankful you were never cold and hungry.

SANDY: We *are* thankful, but what about St. Nicholas? How does he know what children want for Christmas, and how does he get into their houses?

FAITH: Sure and he comes in his sleigh, right over the roof-tops, and down the chimney.

SANDY: How can a sleigh get up on the roof-tops, Faith?

FAITH: Begorra, you're as full of questions as a plum pudding is full of plums! The sleigh is driven by eight tiny reindeer, and if you listen to the story you'll learn their names:

"More rapid than eagles his coursers they came,
And he whistled and shouted and called them by name:
'Now, Dasher! Now, Dancer! Now, Prancer and Vixen!
On, Comet! On, Cupid! On, Donder and Blitzen!'
To the top of the porch! To the top of the wall!
Now dash away! Dash away! Dash away all!' "

SANDY: What spendid names! I must try to remember them. But what happens next?

FAITH: Why, the reindeer keep right on going, of course, and the next thing you know, they're on the roof! Listen:

"So up to the house-top the coursers they flew,
With the sleigh full of toys and St. Nicholas too.
And then in a twinkling I heard on the roof,
The prancing and pawing of each little hoof."

SANDY (*Excited*): Stop! Stop! Wait a minute! Do you hear anything, Faith?

FAITH: Of course not. Not a sound.

SANDY: I thought I heard a funny little noise on *our* roof. Didn't you hear it, Faith?

FAITH (*Laughing*): No, and you didn't either! It's just your imagination running away with you to keep up with the story. Now pay attention, and I'll read some more.

"As I drew in my head and was turning around,
Down the chimney St. Nicholas came with a bound.
He was dressed all in fur from his head to his foot,
And his clothes were all tarnished with ashes and soot."

SANDY: Oh, dear! Now he'll have to go to the dry-cleaner's!

FAITH: Not St. Nicholas. Now don't interrupt. Here comes the best part:

"A bundle of toys he had flung on his back,

And he looked like a peddler just opening his pack."

SANDY: Oh, I wish I could see him! I want to see him, Faith. Will he come here? Will he?

FAITH: I'm sure he will, Sandy. Old St. Nicholas would never forget such good little boys as you and Robbie.

SANDY: I wish Robbie would come and hear the story too, Faith. He'd love it.

ROBBIE (*Disapprovingly*): I've heard enough of that nonsense! Shame on you, Faith O'Flannagan, for filling our Sandy's head with such foolishness. Father would send you packing if he knew.

SANDY: But he won't know, Robbie. I'll never tell. It's the most wonderful story. So sit down and listen. Go on, Faith, read some more.

ROBBIE: I'll not listen! And you shouldn't either, Sandy. St. Nicholas is no more real than a ghost or goblin. Only silly children and foolish folks like Faith believe in him.

SANDY: Be quiet, Robbie. I want to hear the rest. Go ahead, Faith. Please go on.

FAITH: I—I—I really wouldn't want to do anything to displease your father, Sandy. If Master Robbie thinks . . .

SANDY: Oh, Robbie's just an old meanie. Father won't care. I know he won't.

ROBBIE: Don't be so sure of that, Sandy. You know how strict Father is about the truth.

FAITH: But it's true enough, Master Robbie. See . . . it's all here in black and white in the book. It tells just how he looks:

"His eyes—how they twinkled! His dimples how merry!
His cheeks were like roses, his nose like a cherry!
His droll little mouth was drawn up like a bow,
And the beard on his chin was as white as the snow.
The stump of a pipe he held tight in his teeth,

And the smoke, it encircled his head like a wreath.
He had a broad face, and a little round belly,
That shook when he laughed like a bowlful of jelly."

SANDY (*Laughing*): That's funny! I like that! Oh, Robbie, wouldn't you love to see him?

ROBBIE (*Almost laughing*): Well . . . maybe it would be fun . . . and he does sound ever so jolly . . . but . . . I tell you there's no use thinking of such a thing, Sandy. He'd never come here.

SANDY: Why not? Faith says he visits all the good children in the world.

ROBBIE: But Father would never permit it. So put that silly book away, Faith, before he catches you reading it to Sandy.

SANDY: Oh, no, Faith! Read the rest.

FAITH: It can't do any harm to finish the story now that I've started it. And you might as well listen too, Master Robbie.

ROBBIE: I must admit—I've heard enough to make me curious.

FAITH (*Reading*):

"He spoke not a word, but went straight to his work,
And filled all the stockings; then turned with a jerk,
And laying a finger aside of his nose,
And giving a nod, up the chimney he rose:
He sprang to his sleigh, to his team gave a whistle,
And away they all flew, like the down of a thistle.
And I heard him exclaim, ere he drove out of sight:
'Happy Christmas to all, and to all a good night!' "

FATHER: And that means "Goodnight" to you, Faith, and "Goodbye" as well.

CHILDREN (*In alarm*): Father!

FAITH: Mr. Marboro!

FATHER: It's plain to see you have disobeyed my orders,

Faith. It was distinctly understood that we do not fill the children's heads with fairy tales and falsehoods. You will pack your things at once.

FAITH: Please, sir, I was just trying to make Christmas for them!

FATHER: Whatever you were trying to do, you have succeeded in losing your place.

ROBBIE: But, Father, tomorrow is Christmas.

FATHER: My calendar says December 25th, but that is no day to have my orders disobeyed.

SANDY (*Crying*): Father, Father, please don't send Faith away! She was only reading a beautiful story.

FATHER: I am the best judge of the stories which are to be read to my own children, Sandy. Faith will leave this house within the hour, and I want both of you boys in bed before she goes.

ROBBIE: In bed? But it isn't even supper time.

FATHER: You knew as well as Faith that such stories are forbidden in this house. You and Sandy will both be able to think more clearly on empty stomachs.

SANDY (*Crying louder and harder*): Oh, Faith, please don't go!

ROBBIE: I'm sorry, Faith. We'll miss you terribly.

FAITH: I've done my best, Master Robbie. Now come along, both of you, and I'll tuck you into bed before I leave. We must not anger your father any further.

SANDY (*Sobbing*): Now St. Nicholas will never come! He'll never stop at this bad, wicked house. Never, never, never!

MUSIC: *Appropriate bridge.*

ANNOUNCER: But strange things happen on Christmas Eve, and one of the strangest was about to take place not too long after Robbie and Sandy had been sent to bed. As St. Nicholas and his sleigh full of toys approached the Marboro housetop, the driver suddenly noticed that the heavily-laden sleigh was pulling downward and slightly to the right. In vain he tugged at the reins and whistled to the reindeer! The sleigh still plunged downward and to the right. In fact, it seemed as if it would surely strike the Marboro chimney. Jing and Jang, old St. Nick's helpers, were alarmed.

JING: Better stop here, sir, before we have a wreck.

JANG: Something's wrong! Look out! Watch it! Watch it!

ST. NICK: Whoa, there! Easy now!

SOUND: *A sliding noise accompanied with a loud screech and jangle of bells.*

JING: Phew! That was a close one!

JANG: But we made a safe landing, sir. I'll hop out and look around. Do you know where we are?

ST. NICK: We're on the Marboro rooftop, if I'm not mistaken. But the name is not on our list.

JING: I'll check the reindeer, sir. Something must be wrong.

ST. NICK: Something *is* wrong, and no mistake! Take a look at Dancer. He's licking his right hoof. (*In a kindly, soothing voice*) Why, Dancer, what's the matter? Does your foot hurt?

SOUND: *Play any thirty-three and a third record at seventy-eight to produce a high, garbled "Donald Duck" sound which will serve admirably as reindeer language.*

ST. NICK: It does? You say something must be sticking in it? Well, let me see.

JING: What's the matter, sir?

JANG: Is there something wrong with Dancer's hoof?

ST. NICK: I can't quite see. He might have picked up some star dust or a very sharp icicle. Easy, boy, easy! Does that hurt?

SOUND: *Another snatch of "reindeer talk."*

ST. NICK: Now, hold still, and I promise to be very careful. There! Is that better?

SOUND: *Reindeer's answer.*

ST. NICK: No better? Well, I declare we can't go on like this. We can't have you hobbling along on a lame foot.

SOUND: *More reindeer gibberish.*

ST. NICK (*In amazement*): What's that you say? You want to stay here and rest your foot? Well, now, I don't know. That's a bit irregular, to say the least.

JING: Maybe it's a good idea at that. With a bad foot, he'll be a hindrance to the rest of the team.

JANG: I think the others would get along better without him. He keeps pulling them out of line, as it is.

ST. NICK: We could stop for you on the return trip, Dancer, after we've delivered the rest of the toys.

SOUND: *Reindeer talk longer and more agitated.*

ST. NICK: What! But that's impossible! What would people think?

JING: What does he want now, Sir?

JANG: What is he saying?

ST. NICK: Bless my whiskers! He wants to spend Christmas here. He says he's always wanted to see how children act when they open their presents.

SOUND: *Reindeer talk.*

ST. NICK: Yes, yes, I know. I understand. Of course, it would be fun to stay and watch. I've thought of it dozens of times myself. But it just isn't practical. Besides, this isn't a good place to stay. We never deliver presents at the Marboro house, you know.

JING: Why not, sir?

JANG: Aren't the Marboro children good children?

ST. NICK: Oh, yes, as good as gold. But . . . well . . . you see . . . it's their father. He doesn't believe in me. Stopped believing when he was quite a small boy, and now he doesn't want his sons to believe in me either. Naturally, we can't go against a father's wishes . . . so

. . . well . . . much as I regret it, the Marboro children are just not on our list.

SOUND: *A volume of reindeer talk.*

ST. NICK (*With a chuckle that turns into a roar of laughter*) : Bless you, Dancer! Bless you! I never knew a reindeer to have such a sense of humor! Come to think of it—it's a capital idea! Capital! The more I think of it, the jollier it is. Ho, ho, ho! Ha, ha, ha! I'd like to stay and see the fun myself! Well, Dancer, have it your own way. But remember, not a minute later than moonrise tomorrow. That should give you plenty of time.

JING: Plenty of time for what, sir?

ST. NICK: Plenty of time to rest his lame foot and teach old man Marboro a lesson.

JANG: A lesson?

JING: What kind of lesson, sir?

ST. NICK: You ask too many questions. Now come along and get Dancer out of his harness.

JING: Can't we stay too, sir?

ST. NICK: No, indeed. I'll need your help on my rounds. It's bad enough to lose one of my trusty reindeer but I can't spare my helpers. Look lively, boys, and loosen that harness.

SOUND: *Short reindeer speech.*

ST. NICK: Very well, Dancer. You do your best and we'll pick you up tomorrow night. Come on, Jing, back in the sleigh. Jang, you'll have to steady that pile of toys on the left hand side. Are we ready?

SOUND: *Loud jingle of sleigh bells and a piercing whistle.*

ST. NICK: Then away we go!

SOUND: *Sleigh bells up and out.*

ANNOUNCER: And so they were off into the night, while Dancer settled himself comfortably on the Marboro housetop to wait until morning. It seemed as if he had barely closed his eyes, when he was awakened by the voices of carolers approaching the house.

SOUND: *Fade in any Christmas Carol softly and under.*

ANNOUNCER: Dancer scrambled to his feet and peered around the chimney as the village children with their Choir Master drew near.

SOUND: *Establish Christmas Carol.*

ANNOUNCER: Suddenly one of the children caught sight of Dancer and let out a squeal of delight.

CHILD: Look! Look! There's a reindeer up on the roof!

CHILDREN (*Shouting*): Where? Where? I don't believe it! (*Etc., etc.*)

CHILD: Right there beside the chimney. He's real. He's looking down at us. Look! He's nodding his head.

CHOIR MASTER: Why, bless my soul! The lad is right. It *is* a reindeer!

CHILDREN (*Screaming with excitement and wonder*): A reindeer!

MR. MARBORO (*In anger*): Silence! Silence! What is the meaning of this? What are you doing on my property? Don't you see those *No Trespassing* signs?

CHOIR MASTER: You'll have to excuse us, Mr. Marboro . . .

MR. MARBORO: I never excuse anyone for trespassing on my property. You know I never tolerate carolers on my grounds. Now be off at once.

CHOIR MASTER: We'll be off at once, Mr. Marboro, but you have another trespasser who will doubtless prove more difficult.

MR. MARBORO: What are you talking about?

CHOIR MASTER: The visitor on your roof, sir.

CHILDREN (*Shouting*): Look! Look! The reindeer is coming close to the edge.

MR. MARBORO: By all the saints! It's a reindeer!

ROBBIE *and* SANDY: Father! Father! What is it? What are all these people doing here?

CHILDREN: Watch out! He's going to jump!

ROBBIE *and* SANDY: A reindeer! A reindeer on our roof!

SANDY: He did come, Robbie. He did! St. Nicholas really came! And he left us his reindeer.

CHOIR MASTER: Stand back! Stand back! He's going to leap!

SOUND: *A swish and a thud as of a heavy body landing.*

CHILDREN (*A long Ahhhhhhh of wonder*): Isn't he dear? Look at his big soft eyes. Look at his antlers.

CHOIR MASTER: Not so close, children. You might frighten him.

SANDY: You'll never frighten *this* reindeer. This is one of St. Nick's reindeer and he's not afraid of anything or anybody.

ROBBIE: How do you know, Sandy? How do you know he belongs to St. Nicholas?

SANDY: How else could he get on our roof? Of course he belongs to St. Nick and now St. Nicholas has given him to us for our very own.

ROBBIE: I believe you're right, Sandy. But do you think Father will let us keep him?

SANDY: I don't know, but I'm going to pat him and show him we're friendly.

CHOIR MASTER: Be careful, boys. Don't try to touch him. See. He's hurt. He's holding up his foot. Maybe he cut it on a piece of slate on your roof. Here, boy, here. Let me see your foot. Now, don't try to run away. I won't hurt you.

SANDY: Look, Robbie, he's pulling away from the Choir Master, and he's going straight toward Father.

MR. MARBORO (*Softly*): Come, fellow, come. Let me take care of that foot.

SOUND: *Reindeer talk, very softly.*

ROBBIE: Look, Sandy. He's putting up his hoof for Father to see.

SANDY: And it sounds almost as if he's talking.

MR. MARBORO: What's that? What's that you say?

SOUND: *More reindeer talk, a little louder and longer.*

MR. MARBORO: But I can't believe it. After all these years. It isn't possible.

SOUND: *Continued reindeer talk.*

MR. MARBORO: Your foot! Yes, I know, but . . . (*Joyously*) Oh, Dancer! Dancer! Is it really you?

SANDY: What did I tell you, Robbie? It is really one of St. Nick's reindeer. Father's calling him *Dancer.*

ROBBIE: But how could Father know his name?

SANDY: He knows all right, and Dancer knows him too. Look how he's leaping and frisking about like a puppy.

ROBBIE: His foot doesn't seem to hurt now.

MR. MARBORO (*Laughing*): Down, Dancer! Down! You'll knock me over! You must remember you're full grown now. No longer a little frightened fawn.

ROBBIE: Father, Father, what are you talking about?

SANDY: Does Dancer really know you, Father?

MR. MARBORO: Of course, he knows me. We're old friends, aren't we, Dancer, old boy?

SANDY: But doesn't be belong to St. Nicholas?

ROBBIE: Sh! Sandy! You'd think you'd know better than to talk to Father about St. Nicholas.

MR. MARBORO: It's all right, Robbie. Dancer says . . .

ROBBIE: You mean Dancer can talk?

CHOIR MASTER: Mr. Marboro, sir, are you sure you're feeling all right? I must admit it's a shattering experience to find a live reindeer on your roof . . . but a talking reindeer?

SOUND: *A barrage of reindeer talk.*

MR. MARBORO: Hear that?

CHILDREN: He's talking! He's talking!

CHILD: But what is he saying?

CHILD: It isn't the kind of talk we can understand.

MR. MARBORO: I can understand him all right.

ALL: You can understand him?

MR. MARBORO: Certainly. Every word.

CHOIR MASTER: Mr. Marboro, we'd better leave and send for someone to remove this creature. You're obviously upset.

MR. MARBORO: I'm upset all right . . . and it's good for me. In fact, it's the best thing that ever happened to me, sir. As for taking Dancer away, that would be impossible.

SOUND: *Reindeer talk.*

MR. MARBORO: That's right, Dancer. That's just what I was telling them. You belong to me, don't you?

SANDY: But I thought he belonged to St. Nicholas.

SOUND: *Reindeer talk.*

CHILD: What's he saying now, Mr. Marboro? What's he saying now?

MR. MARBORO: He's trying to tell you that he belongs to me, or rather that he *did* belong to me years ago, but that he belongs to St. Nicholas now. He's here for only a short while . . . to spend the day, in fact, and then he must go back with the others to get ready for next year's Christmas run.

CHOIR MASTER: This is most unusual, Marboro, and very hard to believe.

MR. MARBORO: Believing *does* come hard for some people, my friend. And I can speak from experience. You and the rest of the folk in the village well know that I have never pretended to believe in St. Nicholas, and Christmas trees and holiday treats, nor have I ever shared in the celebrations. My boys will tell you the same. Only last evening, I sent them to bed without their suppers and dismissed a loyal little nursemaid because I got into a temper over Clement Moore's *Visit from St. Nicholas.* Well, things will be different from now on, won't they, Dancer?

SOUND: *Reindeer talk.*

MR. MARBORO: He says, "You bet they will!"

SANDY: You mean you're going to believe in St. Nicholas from now on, Father?

MR. MARBORO: I guess I always did believe, Sandy, way deep inside. I'm a little too old now to hang up my stocking and write letters to St. Nicholas but I'm young enough to help two little boys do those things, if they'll let me.

ROBBIE: We'll let you all right, Father. I can't wait to begin.

CHOIR MASTER: But this animal, sir . . . this reindeer. Do you mean to say you actually think he belongs to St. Nicholas?

SOUND: *Urgent reindeer talk.*

MR. MARBORO: Yes, yes, Dancer. I'll tell him. I'll tell everybody all about it. You stand here by me where all the children can see you, and I'll tell them how I first saw you, many years ago when I was a little fellow no bigger than Sandy. You see, I believed in St. Nicholas then—believed in him with all my heart and soul, even though the believing was not always easy. We lived in a little clearing in the woods. Our house was small, and there were never any presents on Christmas morning. Year after year, I was disappointed, but then, the Christmas day that I was seven, I got Dancer.

CHILDREN (*In awe*): A reindeer in your Christmas stocking!

MR. MARBORO: Not in my stocking, but in our farmyard. There he was, a tiny, shivering little fawn, with those same big brown eyes he has today.

ROBBIE: You mean he's the same . . . the very same reindeer?

CHOIR MASTER: Impossible!

MR. MARBORO: It *seems* impossible, but Dancer has brought me proof. You see, we had a wonderful day together, Dancer and I . . . the happiest day of my life it was. We frolicked in the snow, we romped and raced and leaped over fences and had the time of our young lives. And all day long, I was thanking St. Nicholas in my heart for the wonderful, wonderful present. When darkness came, I built a little compound for Dancer near the barn. We said good night to each other and two or three times I crept out of bed and looked out the window to see if he was still there. The next morning I raced outside before breakfast, but he was gone. During the night, he had leaped the tiny fence . . . and in the early morning, the hunters got him!

CHILDREN (*Despairing*): Oh, no!

MR. MARBORO: I found his tracks in the snow, and the drops of blood trailing off into the forest, but I never found Dancer. And I never believed in St. Nicholas again. It was too cruel to give a present and take it away again.

SANDY: But it wasn't St. Nick's fault, Father.

MR. MARBORO: I guess I was too hurt to reason. But one thing I decided. No child of mine would ever be subjected to such a disappointment. It was better not to believe at all than to be hurt.

SOUND: *Reindeer talk—soft and coaxing.*

MR. MARBORO: Yes, yes, Dancer. Now, I know better. Now I know that something strange and wonderful must have happened to my little pet. Because here he is again, after all these years.

CHOIR MASTER: But how do you know it is the same?

MR. MARBORO: I'd know Dancer anywhere. And besides, he told me who he is.

CHOIR MASTER: That reindeer talk again! I can't see how you pretend to understand it.

MR. MARBORO: I'm not pretending, sir. I really do understand Dancer, and he understands me. It was like that from the very first. Besides, if I needed proof, there is his foot.

CHOIR MASTER: His foot?

MR. MARBORO: Yes. There is nothing really wrong with Dancer's foot. No slate! No icicles— No fresh cut! Nothing to make him limp. Nothing, that is, except an old scar from the wound the hunters gave him on that morning so long ago! Oh, yes, it's Dancer all right and we're going to have a wonderful day together . . . Dancer and Robbie and Sandy and all of you children who care to stay. In fact, if I had not sent Faith off in such a temper last evening, I'd invite you all for breakfast.

FAITH: Please sir, I'm still around. The gardener and his wife took me in for the night, sir, and I'll have breakfast ready in less time than it would take Dancer to jump over a hedge.

ROBBIE *and* SANDY: Faith! Faith! You've come back to us.

MR. MARBORO: I apologize to you, Faith, with all my heart. And if you come back to us, you may read *St. Nicholas* from morning to night if you like, on the condition that I may listen, too.

FAITH: You'd be welcome, sir. Now, I'm going inside to cook the biggest Christmas breakfast you've ever tasted.

MR. MARBORO: It's open house for the rest of the day, and you're all my guests for as long as you care to stay and play with Dancer.

CHILDREN: Hooray! Hooray!

CHOIR MASTER: It's a strange story, Marboro . . . a beautiful story in a way . . . but somehow, I just can't believe . . .

MR. MARBORO: Don't say that, sir. Don't ever say that, especially on the one day in the year that was made for believing.

SOUND: *Reindeer talk.*

MR. MARBORO: That's right, Dancer. That's exactly right. He says little children know how to believe in St. Nicholas and the spirit of Christmas without very much solid proof, but for older people it sometimes takes a house to fall on them, or a reindeer on the roof to convince them that there's a special magic at work around this time of year.

SOUND: *Reindeer talk.*

CHOIR MASTER: What's he saying now, Marboro?

MR. MARBORO: He's talking to you, sir. He says that a choir master of all people should know that the best part of Christmas is not the giving or receiving . . . but the believing.

CHOIR MASTER: Bless my soul, Marboro, he's right.

SOUND: *Reindeer talk.*

MR. MARBORO: Dancer says . . .

CHOIR MASTER: Don't tell me what Dancer said, Marboro. I heard him myself. He said . . . Let's stop all this talking and start having a merry, merry Christmas!

SOUND: *"Jingle Bells" up and under.*

ANNOUNCER: And that's just what they did, they had the merriest Christmas ever—a Christmas that lasted all day until the sunset faded, and the lamps were lighted. When all guests had gone home and Robbie and Sandy were tucked in bed, Mr. Marboro went outside to watch the Christmas moon come up and say goodbye to Dancer. But this time it was a happy goodbye and not a sad one. As the man listened to the faint sound of sleigh bells and saw Dancer leap onto the rooftop, he felt a warm little Christmas glow around his heart. And when he waved goodbye to the shadow of the sleigh across the moon, the Christmas glow did not fade, but grew stronger and steadier, especially when the sound of a chuckle reached his ear and a soft voice murmured . . .

VOICE: *"Happy Christmas to all and to all a goodnight!"*

ANNOUNCER: And in the morning, Robbie and Sandy were not too disappointed that Dancer had been called back to work. For there on their south lawn, right where Dancer had made his landing the day before, was a life-sized figure of the leftover reindeer, a constant reminder that someday, maybe he would come again.

SOUND: *"Jingle Bells" up and out.*

THE END

The Birds' Christmas Carol

by Kate Douglas Wiggin

Adapted by Lewy Olfson

Characters

GRANDMA BIRD
DONALD BIRD
HUGH BIRD
PAUL BIRD
MR. BIRD
MRS. BIRD
A DOCTOR
CAROL BIRD
UNCLE JACK
MRS. RUGGLES
PETER RUGGLES
SARAH MAUD RUGGLES
CORNELIUS RUGGLES
CLEMENT RUGGLES
PEORIA RUGGLES
KITTY RUGGLES
NARRATOR

NARRATOR: Many years ago, in a rambling old house in the fashionable section of the city, there lived a family by the name of Bird. They were as happy as birds, too, and the house in which they lived came to be known as the Birds' Nest. Christmas in the Birds' Nest was always a joyous event, but one Christmas was to be remembered by them long after all the others had been forgotten.

SOUND: *Ad lib of boys, excitedly.*

GRANDMA BIRD: Hush! Hush! All of you! You'll wake your new little sister with all this racket!

DONALD: I'm so glad it's a girl.

HUGH: When will we be allowed to see her?

PAUL: What are they going to name her?

GRANDMA (*Laughing*): Questions! What a bundle of questions you are!

PAUL: Why doesn't Papa choose a name for the baby?

GRANDMA: He chose the names for all three of you boys. He feels it should be up to your Mother to name the first little girl of the family. But I can tell you one thing; whatever name is decided upon, it will be decided upon today. For your Mamma never allows her babies to go unnamed overnight.

SOUND: *A boy's choir singing a carol, far off mike.*

HUGH: Listen!

DONALD: It's the boys' choir at the church next door. They're practicing for tonight's Christmas service.

PAUL: How lovely it is! I wonder if Mamma can hear it in her bedroom upstairs. It sounds as though it were a musical welcome to our new baby sister!

MUSIC: *Choir singing, swells, then subsides under.*

MR. BIRD: How are you feeling now, my dear?

MRS. BIRD: Oh, Donald, look! Isn't she the most beautiful baby you have ever seen?

MR. BIRD: That's to be expected, considering that her mother is the most beautiful woman I have ever seen. Why don't you name the new baby after yourself, dear? Perhaps that will help her to grow into the kind of woman her mother is.

MRS. BIRD: How sweet you are, my dear. But I had another thought: listen! Do you hear music?

MR. BIRD: Of course I do. It's from the Church of Our Saviour, next door.

MRS. BIRD: It has given me an idea for naming our baby. I had forgotten what day it was. She is a little Christmas child, and we will name her "Carol." Mother's Christmas Carol! Don't you think it is a sweet name?

MR. BIRD: I think it is a charming name, dear heart, and so like you to think of it. Welcome to the Birds' Nest, little Christmas Carol.

MUSIC: *Happy theme, in and under.*

NARRATOR: And so the Christmas baby received her name. Perhaps because she was born in holiday time, Carol was a very happy baby. Of course, she was too tiny to understand the joy of Christmastide, but people say there is everything in a good beginning. Her cheeks were as red as holly berries; her eyes were bright as stars; her laugh like a chime of Christmas bells, and her tiny hands forever outstretched in giving.

DONALD (*Thoughtfully*): Look, Mamma. Baby Carol is giving me a piece of her cake.

MRS. BIRD: And she will not eat hers until you have eaten yours.

DONALD: Why does she do it? None of us boys ever did.

MRS. BIRD: I hardly know, except that she is a little Christmas child, and so she has a tiny share of the most blessed birthday the world has ever known.

MUSIC: *Happy theme, in and under.*

NARRATOR: As the years went by, Carol became the darling of the family. But one year, Christmas in the Birds' Nest was scarcely as merry as it had been in the past. From the time little Carol was five years old, she began to complain of weariness; her color faded, and she began to limp ever so slightly. The illness was slight at first, and for several years, hope was always stirring.

MRS. BIRD: Carol will feel stronger in the summertime.

MR. BIRD: She'll be better when she has spent a year in the country.

GRANDMA BIRD: Don't worry; she'll outgrow it.

MRS. BIRD: Perhaps if we try a new physician . . .

NARRATOR: But at last, the facts had to be faced. The

cheeks and lips faded and the star-like eyes grew softer, for they often gleamed through tears. The doctor's verdict was cruel.

DOCTOR (*Fading in*): How old is little Carol now? Nine? What I have to say is not pleasant, but you must know the truth. Within a short time—it may be one year, maybe a little more—your Carol will slip quietly off to heaven.

MRS. BIRD (*In anguish*): Is there no hope, doctor?

MR. BIRD: It is no use to close our eyes to it any longer, my dear. Carol will never be well again. It almost seems as if I cannot bear it when I think of that loveliest child doomed to lie there, a helpless invalid, day after day. Merry Christmas indeed! It gets to be the saddest day in the year to me!

MRS. BIRD: Donald, dear, Christmas day may not be so merry with us as it used to be, but it is very happy and very blessed. I suffer chiefly for Carol's sake, but I have almost given up being sorrowful for my own sake. I am too happy in the child, and I see so clearly what she has done for us and the other children. Donald and Paul and Hugh were three strong, willful, boisterous boys, but now you seldom see such tenderness, devotion, thought for others, and self-denial in lads of their years. A quarrel or a hot word is almost unknown in this house, and why? Carol would hear it, and it would distress her, she is so full of love and goodness. The boys study with all their might, and why? Because they like to teach Carol, and amuse her. As for me, Donald, I am a better woman every day for Carol's sake. I have to be her eyes, ears, feet, hands—her strength, her hope; and she, my own little child, is my example.

MR. BIRD: I was wrong, dear heart. We will try not to repine, but to rejoice instead, that we have an angel in the house.

MRS. BIRD: As for her future, I think we need not be over-anxious. I feel as if she did not belong altogether to us, but that when she has done what God sent her for, He will take her back to Himself—and it may not be very long.

MUSIC: *Sad theme, in and under.*

NARRATOR: Because the Birds feared that Carol's tenth Christmas on earth might be her last, plans were made for the most enjoyable celebration ever. Carol was told that she might do anything on Christmas that her heart desired, and as a special treat, Uncle Jack, who was her favorite uncle, planned to travel all the way from England to spend Christmas with her. When he arrived, Carol was bursting with things to tell him.

CAROL: Oh, Uncle Jack, I want to tell you all about my plans for Christmas this year, because it will be the loveliest one I ever had. The boys laugh at me for caring so much about it; but it isn't altogether because it is Christmas; nor because it is my birthday. But long, long ago, when I first began to be ill, I used to think, the first thing when I waked on Christmas morning, "Today is Christ's birthday—and mine!"

UNCLE JACK: A fine thought that is, my dear. But tell me about your Christmas plans.

CAROL: Dear Uncle Jack, I am going to try to make somebody happy every single Christmas that I live, and this year it is to be the "Ruggleses in the rear."

UNCLE JACK: Is that the large and interesting brood of children in the little house at the end of the back garden?

CAROL: Yes. Isn't it nice to see so many together? When they first moved in, I used to sit in my window and watch them play. Then, one day, I had a terrible headache, and Donald asked them if they would please not scream so loudly.

UNCLE JACK: A reasonable request.

CAROL: And do you know what they did? They played Deaf and Dumb Asylum all the rest of the afternoon, so as not to disturb me.

UNCLE JACK (*Laughing*): What an obliging family, to be sure!

CAROL: Now, Sarah Maud comes to the door every day to find out if I am well. If I am, they play before my window. If not, they stay in the back yard and play quiet games.

UNCLE JACK: Is Sarah Maud the oldest?

CAROL: Yes; and Peter is next. He's a dressmaker's helper. And the pretty red-haired girl is Kitty.

UNCLE JACK: Which is the fat youngster?

CAROL: He's Baby Larry.

UNCLE JACK: And the one with so many freckles?

CAROL: Now don't laugh—that's Peoria.

UNCLE JACK: Carol, you're joking!

CAROL: No, really, Uncle Jack. She was born in Peoria, Illinois, that's all.

UNCLE JACK: And is the next boy Chicago?

CAROL: No, the others are Susan, Clement, Eily and Cornelius; they all look much alike, except that some of them have more freckles than the others. I do enjoy the Ruggles children so, and they are very poor, Uncle, so I have decided to give this whole Christmas to them.

UNCLE JACK: Give them your Christmas? How, little bird?

CAROL: I shall give a grand Christmas dinner here in this very room, for all of them. And after, we will have a beautiful Christmas tree, bursting with presents. You must sit at the head of the table, Uncle Jack, for nobody could ever be frightened of you; but Papa and the boys are going to eat together downstairs for fear of making the little Ruggleses shy. And after we've had a merry time with the tree, we can open my window and all listen together to the music at the evening church service.

UNCLE JACK: It sounds like a fine idea, Carol.

CAROL: Here is the invitation I have written to the Ruggleses. Would you read it, Uncle Jack, to make sure it is all right?

UNCLE JACK (*Reading*): Dear Mrs. Ruggles:

I am going to have a dinner party on Christmas Day, and would like to have all your children come. I want them every one, please, from Sarah Maud to Baby Larry. Mamma says dinner will be at half past five, and the Christmas tree at seven; so you may expect them home at nine o'clock. Wishing you a Merry Christmas and a Happy New Year, I am

Yours truly,
Carol Bird.

MUSIC: *Happy theme, in and under.*

NARRATOR: Never in your life have you seen such excitement to match that at the Ruggles' home when little Carol's Christmas invitation arrived. Mrs. Ruggles was determined that her children should look and behave as perfectly as if they had been to the manner born. Such scrubbing and tubbing, dashing and splashing, washing, sewing, reminding and explaining you have never seen!

MRS. RUGGLES: Now then! I reckon you young ones have never had such a washing and combing and dressing in all your life; and it isn't likely you'll have another in a hurry, either. Now then, we're ready to teach you some manners.

PETER (*Grumbling*): Why do we need manners? All we have to do is eat!

MRS. RUGGLES: Well, that's enough. There's more than one way of eating, let me tell you, and you have plenty to learn about it, Peter Ruggles. Larry, how many times must I tell you to stop pulling at your sash? Now look me in the eye, all of you. I've often told you what kind of a family the McGrills were. I have reason to be proud of *my* kin, goodness knows. Your uncle is on the police force of New York City, and my children have to learn to act decent! It isn't as easy as you think it is. Now you know, there aren't enough hats to go around, so nobody will wear any at all. You understand?

RUGGLES CHILDREN: Yes, Maw.

MRS. RUGGLES: Now when they ask you to take off your hats, Sarah Maud must say it was such a pleasant evening and such a short walk that you left your hats at home. Now, can you remember?

RUGGLES CHILDREN: Yes, Maw.

MRS. RUGGLES: What do you have to do with it? Did I tell *you* to say it? I was talking to Sarah Maud.

SARAH MAUD: Oh, do I have to, Maw?

MRS. RUGGLES: Of course you do. We won't leave anything to chance. Get up and try it. Speak up, Sarah Maud.

SARAH MAUD (*Stammering*): We . . . we . . .

MRS. RUGGLES: Quick, now!

SARAH MAUD: Maw thought—it was—such a pleasant hat that we'd—we'd better leave our short walk at home.

AD LIB: *Ruggles children laugh with delight.*

MRS. RUGGLES (*In despair*): Oh, what'll I do with you? Try it again!

SARAH MAUD: Maw thought it was such a pleasant—evening—that we'd better leave our—hats—at home.

MRS. RUGGLES (*With a sigh of relief*): Just say it over and over to yourself until you've learned it. Now, Cornelius, what are you going to say to make yourself good company?

CORNELIUS: Say? Me? I don't know.

MRS. RUGGLES: Well, you aren't going to sit there like a bump on a log without saying a word to pay for your vittles, are you? Ask Mrs. Bird how she's feeling this evening, or if Mr. Bird's having a busy season, or how this kind of weather agrees with her, or something like that. Now, as for the dinner: if they have napkins, Sarah Maud down to Peoria may put them in their laps, and the rest of you can tuck them in your necks. Don't eat with your fingers. Don't grab any vittles off one another's plates. Don't reach out for anything, but wait until you're asked; and if you never are asked, don't get up and grab it. Now, we'll try a few things to see how they'll go. Mr. Clement, do you eat cranberry sauce?

CLEMENT: Bet your life!

MRS. RUGGLES (*Sternly*): Clement McGrill Ruggles, do you mean to tell me that you'd say that at a dinner party? I'll give you one more chance. Mr. Clement, will you have some of the cranberry sauce?

CLEMENT: Yes, ma'am, thank you kindly, if you happen to have any handy.

MRS. RUGGLES: Very good, indeed! But they won't give you two tries tonight, so you just remember that! Miss Peoria, do you want light or dark meat?

PEORIA: I'm not particular about the color; anything that no one else wants will suit me.

MRS. RUGGLES: First rate! Miss Kitty, will you have hard or soft sauce with your pudding?

KITTY: Hard or soft? A little of both, if you please.

PETER: Both! Oh!

MRS. RUGGLES: You just stop your grunting, Peter Ruggles; that wasn't greedy; that was all right. I wish I could get it into your heads that it isn't so much what you say as the way you say it. Lord have mercy on you all, and help you to act decent! Now, is there anything more you'd like to practice?

PETER: If you tell me one more thing, I can't sit up and eat. I'm so full of manners now I'm ready to burst, without any dinner at all!

CORNELIUS: Me, too!

MRS. RUGGLES: Well, I'm sorry for you both. If the amount of manners you have on hand now troubles you, you're very easily hurt. Now, Sarah Maud, after dinner, once in a while you must get up and say, "I guess we'd better be going," and if they say to sit a while longer, you can sit; but if they don't say anything, you have to get up and go.

SARAH MAUD: Seems as if this whole dinner party sits right square on top of me. Maybe I could manage my own manners, but managing nine manners is worse than staying at home!

MRS. RUGGLES (*Good-naturedly*): Oh, don't fret. I guess you'll get along all right. It's a quarter past five, and you can go now. Remember about the hats. Don't all talk at once. Susan, lend your handkerchief to Peoria! Peter, don't keep screwing your scarf pin. Sarah Maud, don't take your eyes off Larry. Cornelius, hold your head up straight. And whatever you do, all of you, never forget for one second that *your mother was a McGrill!*

MUSIC: *Light-hearted theme, in and under.*

NARRATOR: Never in your life have you seen such a dinner party! The Ruggles children, who were very poor, were overwhelmed by the richly-set table, with its silver, crystal, china and snowy linen. When the food was brought in, their eyes popped out of their heads. Goose and turkey, soup and pudding, sauces and spices and sweets of every kind. Oranges, cakes, candies, nuts, milk and cider. At last, when no one could lift another forkful of food, the Christmas tree and the presents were brought in.

SARAH MAUD (*Delighted*): This box has my name on it. Books! "Little Women" and "Under the Lilacs." Oh, thank you, thank you, Carol.

CORNELIUS: Here's a tool chest with my name on it. How wonderful!

CLEMENT: Is this doghouse for my lame puppy? Thank you, Carol.

PEORIA: A doll! A doll! Here's one for Susan, too, and for Eily!

SARAH MAUD: Here's a Noah's Ark for Baby Larry, and some warm winter clothes for all of us. Dresses and coats and scarves. Oh, thank you, thank you, Carol. You're a Christmas angel!

MUSIC: *Happy theme, in and under.*

NARRATOR: That night, after the Ruggleses had gone home, Mrs. Bird looked in on little Carol to bid her good night.

MRS. BIRD: Now, my darling, you have done quite enough for one day. I'm afraid you will feel worse tomorrow, and that would be a sad ending to such a charming evening.

CAROL: Wasn't it lovely! From first to last, everything was just right. I shall never forget Larry's face when he looked at the turkey; nor Peter's when he saw his watch; nor that sweet, sweet Kitty's smile when she kissed her dolly; nor the tears in poor Sarah Maud's eyes when she thanked me for her books; nor—

MRS. BIRD: We mustn't talk any longer about it tonight, my dear. You are too tired.

CAROL: I am not so very tired, Mamma. I have felt well all day; not a bit of pain anywhere. Perhaps this has done me good.

MRS. BIRD: Perhaps. I hope so. There was no noise or confusion; it was just a merry time. Now, may I close the door and leave you alone, dear? Papa and I will steal in softly by and by to see if you are all right; but I think you need to be very quiet.

CAROL: I'm willing to stay by myself, but I am not sleepy yet, and I am going to hear the music, you know.

MRS. BIRD: Yes, I have opened the window a little. The boys' voices should carry up here beautifully.

CAROL: May I have the shutters open? This morning I woke ever so early, and one bright, beautiful star shone in that eastern window. I never noticed it before, and I thought of the Star in the East, that guided the Wise Men to the place where the Baby Jesus was. Good night, Mamma. Such a happy, happy day!

MRS. BIRD: Good night, my precious Christmas Carol—mother's blessed Christmas child.

CAROL: Mamma, dear, I do think that we have kept Christ's birthday this time just as He would like it. Don't you?

MRS. BIRD (*Softly*): I'm sure of it, my dear. I'm sure of it.

MUSIC: *Boys' choir singing a carol softly, in and under.*

NARRATOR: Downstairs, the family gathered to listen to the boys' choir in the church next door.

UNCLE JACK (*Fading on*): Well, I've taken all the Ruggleses home! This evening has reminded me of the old verse: "And a little child shall lead them."

HUGH: Softly, Uncle Jack. We are listening to the music in the church. The choir has sung "Carol, brothers, carol," which is the song they sang ten years ago when our Carol was born.

MRS. BIRD: I hope she heard it. But they are very late tonight, and I dare not speak to her lest she be asleep. It is almost ten o'clock.

GRANDMA: How beautiful it is. It is bringing tears to my eyes. Oh, I do hope Carol can hear it.

NARRATOR (*After a brief pause*): There were tears in *many* eyes, but not in Carol's. The loving heart had quietly ceased to beat, and the "wee birdie" in the great house had flown to its "home nest." Carol had fallen asleep! But as to the song, I think perhaps—I cannot say—she heard it after all.

MUSIC: *Boys' choir full to finish.*

THE END

Production Notes

THE CHRISTMAS VISITOR

Characters: 4 male; 3 female; as many Carolers as desired (offstage voices).

Playing Time: 35 minutes.

Costumes: Modern, everyday dress. The Remingtons wear expensive clothes. Laura wears a coat when she first enters. She wears a watch. She re-enters in a long dressing gown. Gerald puts on hat and coat in Scene 1. Sally wears exotic slacks and blouse. The Boy is bareheaded, and wears a shapeless coat. Charles wears dark trousers and white duck serving coat. He later wears derby and black Chesterfield coat. Mrs. Lester and Jamie wear coats.

Properties: Tinsel star, ladder, wrapped presents (one of them a child's carpenter set with hammer, saw, etc.), cards for Boy and Mrs. Lester, glass of milk.

Setting: The fashionably furnished living room of the Remington apartment in an expensive apartment building in a large city. A large, elaborately decorated Christmas tree dominates the room. A couch is at center, and an end table beside it holds a framed picture of Laura, smiling. A stereo is against one wall. The front door is at right, and beside it is a small table with telephone. The door at left leads to the rest of the apartment. A window is in one wall, and if possible, snow is seen falling outside.

Lighting: The room is brilliantly lit in Scene 1 and is dimly lit in Scene 2, and the Christmas tree lights are on. Some of the tree lights go out, as indicated in text.

Sound: Door buzzer, key in lock, telephone, recording of "Away in a Manger" and live or recorded singing of offstage Carolers, as indicated in text.

MERRY CHRISTMAS, CRAWFORDS!

Characters: 8 male; 7 female; male and female extras.

Playing Time: 35 minutes.

Costumes: Modern, everyday dress. When Father first appears, he wears indoor working clothes; before going to office party, he has changed into dress clothes, carrying hat and coat. Mother wears indoor clothes on first appearance, then puts on hat and coat before leaving for party. All visitors to Crawfords wear outdoor winter clothes upon entrance. Expressman may wear uniform. Bill Coleman wears working clothes.

Properties: Pair of straight curtains, ladder, Christmas tree, string of lights, Christmas tree decorations, 2 cartons containing various tree decorations and Christmas cards, radio, telephone, bicycle bell for sound of telephone ringing; pins for Myra; Christmas tree angel for Father; carton of broken tree decorations for Mother; hats and coats for Mother and Father; several gaily wrapped packages for Mother, Father, and Bascolms; large carton with torn wrappings containing a few smaller gaily wrapped parcels, pad, pencil, for Expressman; tool box for Bill Coleman; carton of tree decorations for Frances Saunders; bulging shopping bag for Mrs. Saunders; wrapped pie for Mrs. Coleman; candlesticks and candles for Jimmy Coleman.

Setting: The living room of the Crawfords' new home. In right wall is a window with straight curtains, looking out onto street. Downstage right is exit to street; at left is exit leading to other rooms of house. Fireplace with mantel is at upstage center. Upstage right is a partially trimmed Christmas tree, with lights on it not yet lighted. Near the tree stands a ladder and two cartons of decorations. Upstage left is a radio, and, near it, a small table with telephone. Other tables and chairs, etc., may be placed around stage.

Lighting: No special effects, except for Christmas tree lights which should go on, as indicated in the text.

A Room for a King

Characters: 5 male; 5 female.

Playing Time: 30 minutes.

Costumes: The traditional dress of the period.

Properties: Bundle (containing uniform) and coin for Jacob, key.

Setting: The yard of the inn at Bethlehem. In the middle of the left wall is an arched entrance which leads to the highway. In the middle of the right wall is a door opening into the inn. A door leading to the stable is on the upstage wall at left center. (A part of this wall should be so constructed that it may easily be drawn aside for the tableau at the end of the play.) Downstage center is a bench.

Lighting: No special effects except at the end when the tableau should be brightly illuminated.

Monsieur Santa Claus

Characters: 9 male; 7 female.

Playing Time: 25 minutes.

Costumes: Party dresses for girls and Mrs. Sutton; suits for boys and Mr. Sutton. Andre wears winter school clothes at first and a Santa Claus suit when he returns. Jay puts on a Santa Claus suit, while on stage. Delivery Boys wear uniforms. All wear coats, scarves, and gloves when they come in from outdoors.

Properties: Radio, and records of Christmas carols offstage; large book and "gift certificates," for Andre; Christmas packages, for Binky, Jay, Mim, Bev, Steve, Dorothy, Dave, Ruth, Ken, and Faye; envelopes, containing slips of paper, for Frank, Andre, and Jay; cardboard carton big enough for a boy to crouch inside and box containing Santa Claus suit, for Bev and Steve; tie and tie box, for Mim; large packing box, containing Andre in a Santa Claus suit, for Delivery Boys.

Setting: The comfortably furnished living room of the Sutton home. A Christmas tree stands in one corner, and the room is decorated for Christmas. There is a sofa against one wall. On an end table is a radio. Other tables, chairs, lamps, etc., are added to furnish the room comfortably.

Lighting: Lights should be dimmed or blacked out temporarily, when boys and girls think Andre is coming.

Christmas Spirit

Characters: 4 male; 4 female.

Playing Time: 20 minutes.

Costumes: Modern dress. When Tom, Bob, Miss Pennypacker, Mrs. Gray and Mr. Griggs enter they wear coats, scarves, hats, etc. Mr. Gillum might wear horn-rimmed glasses.

Properties: Long wrapped package, scroll, certificate, knitting, papers, pencil.

Setting: The living room of the Gillum home. At right is a fireplace. Downstage right is a large sofa. At center is a table holding books and magazines. At left is a well-stocked bookcase. On either side of the table are comfortable chairs. A door at right leads to the rest of the house, one at upstage center to the outside. Near the fireplace is a decorated Christmas tree with a number of wrapped presents underneath. Other Christmas decorations may be placed around room.

Lighting: No special effects.

The Trouble with Christmas

Characters: 3 male; 4 female.

Playing Time: 25 minutes.

Costumes: Modern dress for students. Miss Emily wears Victorian costume. Santa Claus wears traditional costume, but it is patched and shabby. He is thin.

Properties: Gift-wrapped package for Miss Emily; glass of milk and plate of cookies.

Setting: A conference room. Down center there is a long conference table with five chairs around it. Up right is a captain's chair with a small table next to it. Up center, against wall, is a larger table. There is a concealed exit behind it. Up left is a pile of Christmas materials, including a small fir tree in a stand, white tablecloth, folding cardboard fireplace, boxes of Christmas tree decorations, candlesticks with red candles, table centerpiece, and five gift-wrapped packages. There is a rocking chair near these objects. Exits are down right and down left, and concealed exit is at rear.

Lighting: Harsh bright lighting, dimming and softening, and spotlight on tree, as indicated in text.

The Humblest Place

Characters: 7 male; 3 female; extras for manger tableau.

Playing Time: 30 minutes.

Costumes: Everyday dress of the period except for the Wise Men, who wear more elaborate Oriental costume.

Properties: For the Woman, three small metal caskets and some silver coins; for Ethan, coins; gifts —fruit, eggs, flowers, etc.—for shepherds.

Setting: The yard of the inn at Bethlehem. The right wall is the front of the inn, with a door in the middle opening on the yard. The rear wall is the front of the stable, with a door left center. The left wall is the stone wall of the inn separating it from the highway. It has an arched portal leading to the highway. Down center, a stone bench. A part of the rear wall must be removable in order to reveal the tableau of the manger at the end of the play.

Lighting: No special effects except for the tableau, which should be brilliantly illuminated.

Little Women

Characters: 9 female.

Playing Time: 30 minutes.

Costumes: All, except the Hummels, wear the long full-skirted gowns of the period. The Marchs' dresses are all attractive, but very simple. All girls have long hair, but Jo and Meg wear theirs caught up in hair nets. Mrs. March wears a cloak and hat when she first enters, and all wear cloaks and bonnets when they exit at the end. Hannah wears a plain brown dress and a white apron, Aunt March wears a very fancy dress, cloak and bonnet. The Hummel girls are dressed in very ragged clothes.

Properties: Several sets of knitting, sewing materials, sketching materials, broom, old pair of slippers, coal scuttle, witch's hat, cloak, tablecloth, broad-brimmed hat, riding boots, salt and pepper shakers, poker, umbrella, three cups, tray, toasting forks, shopping bag, muffins, butter, bread, milk, dishes, wood, letter, teapot, cane, glasses for Aunt March.

Setting: The living room of the March home. It is a pleasant looking room, though the furniture and the chintz curtains are on the verge of shabbiness. There is a door left, leading to the hall, and one right, leading to the kitchen. There is a large window upstage center in front of which stands a sofa. There is a large fireplace at right and a comfortable chair and stool in front of this, upstage right. If possible there is a piano at left. There is a large table at center. Chintz covered chairs at various positions complete the furnishings of the room. There are several kerosene lamps, one on the piano and two on the mantel.

Lighting: No special effects.

Room for Mary

Characters: 6 female.

Playing Time: 25 minutes.

Costumes: Modern dress. Peggy wears outdoor winter clothing over blue jeans at first; later a skirt and sweater; then formal gown, and large flower in her hair. Jane, Martha, and Mary wear outside clothing. Anne wears sophisticated dress.

Properties: Duster; Christmas cookies; large wrapped box containing wrapped presents; box of baby clothes, including a bonnet; jewelry box; two suitcases for Martha, one containing a sweater, and one for Jane; perfume box in Jane's pocketbook; tea things and cookies on a tray; bassinet; box of baby toys, including a rattle; glove box; scarf box; doll wrapped in blankets for the "baby."

Setting: Average living room. A telephone on a stand, an easy chair, and a table beside the chair with a dish of apples and a magazine on it are near the door leading to the outside at left. Another chair is near by; at least two others are in the room. A Christmas tree almost completely decorated is at right; packages and gift wrappings are on nearby table. Sofa stands next to it against rear wall, and carpet sweeper leans against wall. Door right leads into house.

Lighting: No special effects.

Violets for Christmas

Characters: 1 male; 4 female.

Playing Time: 30 minutes.

Costumes: Modern dress. Maggie and Hen wear aprons and work dresses. Mrs. Dalton wears a hat, coat and gloves when she enters. The Santa Claus wears the usual red costume, and has a red hat with beard attached. Mrs. Pennington wears a fur coat with a bunch of violets pinned to the shoulder when she enters. She carries a purse and white gloves.

Properties: Small red boxes with bells attached to them, two mops and pails with water in them, record books, gloves for Santa, handkerchief for Mrs. Dalton, bills.

Setting: An office. There are three doors, one at upstage center leading to the street, another at upstage right leading to the room where the Santas wait, and a third downstage right leading to the employee's room. Downstage center is a desk with a chair in back of it. On tbe desk are some red boxes. Upstage from the desk is a clothes rack. Two office chairs should be down left and down right so that Maggie and Hen will have something to move about as they mop.

Lighting: No special effects.

Season's Greetings

Characters: 8 male; 3 female.

Playing Time: 30 minutes.

Costumes: Everyday modern dress. Mrs. Martinka wears a black dress suitable for an old lady. Jim may wear an elevator boy's uniform. Delivery Boy wears soiled white apron over old slacks, mackintosh and earmuffs. Mr. Tyler and Mr. Canfield wear outdoor clothing when they enter.

Properties: Typewriter, steno pad, pencils, newspaper, coat, hat, brief case, suit box containing Santa Claus outfit and mask for Kim; poinsettia, traditional Christmas painting for Jeff; envelope for Mr. Tyler; brief case for Mr. Canfield; small flat parcel for Mrs. Martinka; 4 brass instruments for brass trio; Christmas tree for Delivery Boy; easel, large, very gaudy cubist design, modernistic piece of sculpture, telephone, bicycle bell for sound of telephone ringing.

Setting: The living room studio of Joshua Tyler, Christmas card artist. The room is furnished in modernistic design. An easel, upstage center, displays a large, very gaudy, extreme cubist design, and a weird modernistic sculpture stands on desk downstage left, next to which stands the typing table. One or two decorative mobiles are on display. A small sofa stands at right. Small tables, chairs, lamps, etc., may be placed around the stage.

Lighting: No special effects.

The Master of the Strait

Characters: 4 male, 3 female.

Playing Time: 25 minutes.

Costumes: Clothes of the period. Windbreaker for William. Coat for Martha. Heavy wraps for carol singers.

Properties: Red tablecloth, books, sewing basket, lighted kerosene lamp, basket with fruit for Martha, candle and candle holder, kitchen matches, cookie jar.

Setting: Kitchen with two long, narrow windows at back. Doors left and right. Long table, front center, a few chairs.

Lighting: No special effects.

O Little Town of Bethlehem

Characters: 8 male; 3 female; male and female extras.

Playing Time: 25 minutes.

Costumes: All of the characters wear the traditional dress of the period. The shepherds have large wallets attached to their girdles. Simon has a crook; Samuel, a leather belt; Daniel, a coat.

Properties: Scene 1: Packages. Scene

2: A rather large toy lamb, sticks, brushwood, flints, loaves. Scene 3: Baby.

Setting: Scene 1: A village street. This may be represented by a simple backdrop that includes the door to the inn. Scene 2: A hillside. A few rough boulders are placed around the stage, and there is an open space in the center. If possible, a "fire" should be previously prepared at center; the "fire" should be lit when the shepherds eat. Scene 3: The stable. The traditional furnishings to be used here may be as simple or elaborate as desired.

Lighting: Scene 2: At rise, the stage is in semi-darkness. If possible, the shepherds' fire should be lit when Samuel starts the fire, so that a red glow will illuminate the children's faces as they eat. Gabriel's appearance is heralded by a brilliant light. After Gabriel exits, the stage is lighter than it was before. Scene 3: Spotlights should shine on Joseph and Mary.

Sing the Songs of Christmas

Characters: 21 male; 4 female; 7 male or female; 12 or more, male or female, for chorus. Most actors may take more than one part, if desired, or cast and chorus may be enlarged.

Playing Time: 35 minutes.

Costumes: Master of Ceremonies wears modern dress. Chorus wears modern dress or choral robes. Peasant, Woodcarvers, Jeanette, Isabella, and Children wear peasant's clothes; 1st Woodcarver also wears a brown cloak. Martin Luther wears dark trousers, a heavy coat, scarf, and gloves. Catherine Luther wears a blouse, shawl, and long, dark skirt. Luther's Sons wear old-fashioned nightshirts; Luther's Daughter wears a nightgown. Shepherds wear brown robes and carry shepherds' crooks. Waits wear long, red-hooded capes. Indian Braves wear simple Indian dress and headbands with one or two feathers; Indian Chiefs wear elaborate feather headdresses. Isaac Watts wears an 18th century English costume. Joseph Mohr wears black priest's suit, black overcoat, and scarf. Franz Gruber wears early 19th century suit. Phillips Brooks and Lewis Redner wear American 19th century clothes; Brooks wears a heavy coat.

Properties: Sprigs of fir or small red paper bells, for chorus; wooden spoon for one chorus member; coins, for several chorus members; Indian headdress, for one chorus member; drums, for two or three chorus members; script, for Master of Ceremonies; wooden box and bundle of hay, for Peasant; figures of ox, ass, and 3 sheep, for 1st Woodcarver; figures of the Holy Family, for 2nd Woodcarver; figures of 3 kings and angels, for Apprentice Woodcarver; flashlight torches, for Jeanette, Isabella, and Children; fir tree and stand, for Martin Luther; string of white Christmas tree lights, for Catherine Luther; small lanterns, big hymnals, and leather purses, for Waits; bows and arrows, for Indian braves; fur pelts, for Indian chiefs; large Bible, for Isaac Watts; two pieces of paper, for Father Mohr and Phillips Brooks.

Setting: The stage should be decorated gaily for Christmas. There are exits at each side and at rear.

Lighting: No special effects.

Holiday for Santa

Characters: 8 male, 1 female; male and female extras, as desired.

Playing Time: 25 minutes.

Costumes: Santa Claus and his helpers wear Santa Claus costumes and white beards. Santa has red and white striped socks. In Scene 2, Santa Claus wears a red bathing suit trimmed with white fur. Mrs. Claus wears an old-fashioned long house dress with a white apron, a white wig and steel-rimmed spectacles. When going out she wears a shawl and bonnet. Whole Wide World wears a pair of large, round placards, front and back with a map of the world encircling them. Boys and girls wear outdoor clothes.

Properties: Broom, pipe, writing materials, packs for Santa Claus and helpers, knitting bag, sleigh bells.

Setting: In Scene 1, a backdrop represents Santa Claus' shop, with shelves holding toys and dolls painted on it. In the center of the backdrop stand a pot-bellied stove with a shelf over it holding a clock, the hands pointing to midnight. Later in Scene 1, the children bring in a backdrop of a sandy beach with blue sky and water, a bright sun shining, and a couple of palm trees. The furnishings consist of a rocking chair and a small, unobtrusive footstool to be placed beside the stove.

Lighting: No special effects.

Adobe Christmas

Characters: 3 male; 3 female.

Playing Time: 15 minutes.

Costumes: Everday, inexpensive clothing for all. Outdoor wraps for Papa, Mama, and Mr. and Mrs. Rivera.

Properties: Box of crackers, for Rosa; large doll, with blankets, to represent the Rivera baby; handkerchief, for Mama; three packages containing small toys and fruits, doll, and dump truck, for Papa. The piñata is usually a pottery jar, shaped and decorated in some unusual way. For use in the play, however, a paper piñata, shaped and colored to represent some bird, animal, or figure, may be used. Small gifts and candy are placed in the piñata, and a long stick is used to break it.

Setting: A very plain room with simple furnishings: a wooden table and chairs, a fireplace in one corner, a cupboard near the table. There is a door upstage center. On each side of the door is a curtained window. At one side of the room is a manger scene, with a doll in the manger.

Lighting: No special effects.

Touchstone

Characters: 28 speaking parts. Most of the parts in the play may be taken by either boys or girls. Male and female extras may be used as additional Minstrels, Waits, and Children.

Playing Time: 25 minutes.

Costumes: All wear traditional costume of the period. The knights wear dark-colored cotton jerseys and tights, covered by jerkins. The jerkins should be sleeveless and may be hip-length with straight or scalloped lower edges, or may have knee-length front and back panels. The jerkins should be brightly colored and may have various medieval designs painted on them. The Minstrels are dressed similarly to the Knights, but their costumes are less elaborate in appearance. The Alchemist and the Servant wear dark-colored tights and smocks. The Waits are dressed in ragged clothes. The women wear long, full-skirted dresses.

Properties: Bottles, alembics, retorts, crucibles, brazier, bellows, tongs, tools, candles, touchstone, pouch for Sir David, pies, broom, kettle, rag. For Scene 4, the stained glass window could be handled in the following manner: The frame of the window, which stands on the table, could be made of stripping and should be lancet-shaped, about three feet by six feet in overall size. The frame could be surrounded by gray cardboard to simulate the stone work of a church window. At the inside of the frame there should be black cardboard verticals and horizontals, dividing the interior of the window into as many sections as there are individual apprentices. In this way, the work of each apprentice may be quickly set in place at the proper moment. The individual designs of the apprentices may be made of newsprint paper, painted with pure color in mostly reds, blues, and yellows. Each design should be framed by cardboard to strengthen it, and the individual design should correspond in size and shape to the section of the large window frame in which it is to be placed. The individual designs should be similar to those mentioned in the text of the play.

Setting: Scene 1: The Alchemist's workshop. There is a fireplace and oven upstage right. There is a door at left leading to street. At center is a large table and several benches. There are various other shelves and benches placed about the room. The room is littered with chemical equipment. Scene 2: A kitchen. This can be essentially the same set as that of Scene 1. The chemical equipment should be removed and cooking equipment should replace it. Scenes 3 and 4: A street. There should be an entrance at center to serve as the cathedral door and one at left to serve as the door to a house. The cathedral and the house could be painted on a backdrop. For Scene 4, a table holding the window frame is placed at right of the cathedral door.

Lighting: The completed window is illuminated from behind as indicated in the text of Scene 4.

The First Christmas Tree

Characters: 2 male; 3 female; male and female extras.

Playing Time: 15 minutes.

Costumes: The Carolers are dressed in bright sweaters and scarves, with typical carolers' hats. Johann, his mother and his sisters, all wear the simple peasant costumes of central Europe. The Child wears torn and ragged clothes. The Christmas Spirits are dressed in soft green robes and carry blue balls, tinsel and stars of silver. They wear bands of tinsel on their heads.

Properties: Log, packages for Johann, apples, shoes and stockings, coat, mittens, small pine tree.

Setting: Scenes 1 and 3 are in the snow-covered woods. A backdrop may be used or these scenes may be played before the curtain. Scenes 2 and 4 show the living room of a poor peasant cottage. There is a large open fireplace at center back, in which a bright fire is burning. Several pots are hung over the coals. There is a cupboard, table and chairs, and a rocker near the fire. A spinning wheel stands to the right of the fireplace.

Lighting: No special effects.

The Christmas Sampler

Characters: 6 male; 4 female; male extras.

Playing Time: 20 minutes.

Costumes: All the characters wear costumes of the Revolutionary period. Mistress Maltby puts on a shawl when she exits. Henry, William, and the Villagers should wear mufflers and caps when they enter. The soldiers wear the usual red uniforms, and Captain Hale has a sword attached to his side.

Properties: Needle, thread, sampler, rag dolls, wooden bowl, shawl, plate of cakes, guns.

Setting: A New England kitchen. Furnishings may include a table, several chairs and stools, a fireplace, etc. The room is decorated with Christmas greens. Upstage center is a cupboard with a door; the cupboard should be large enough to hold Henry Crocker when he hides.

Lighting: No special effects.

Keeping Christmas

Characters: 4 male; 5 female.

Playing Time: 15 minutes.

Costumes: All the characters should wear costumes typical of the early nineteenth century. When the children come in bringing gifts they should wear coats, scarves, etc.

Properties: Book, knitting, basket with cookies under a napkin, bundles, sack of apples, small tree, two red stockings.

Setting: The Arnold living room. Upstage center is a fireplace with a large mantel above it. At right is a large window. The only other furnishings necessary are a table and two chairs placed downstage center, but a desk, maps, and other chairs and tables of the period may be added.

Lighting: No special effects.

The Way

Characters: 9 male; 8 female, for parents and Innkeeper; extras, minimum of 25 children—parts may be taken by boys or girls.

Playing Time: 25 minutes.

Costumes: Everyday, modern dress appropriate to countries indicated. All wear outer clothing, except Innkeeper. Dutch family should wear wooden shoes.

Properties: Candle for window, stockings, wooden shoes, lanterns, piñata jug in shape of bird, stick, shawl, small candles for South American children, basket of goodies, sheaf of wheat, Yule log, evergreens, garlands, small Christmas tree.

Setting: Interior of an inn. Doors are at right and left. There is a window near outer door, a fireplace at center.

Lighting: No special effects.

The Chosen One

Characters: 7 male; 3 female; male and female extras, as desired.

Playing Time: 25 minutes.

Costumes: French peasant dress for Michaud family and Père Revnould. Philip and Carolers wear appropriate outdoor dress. Lady Elinor and Count Bernard are richly dressed, with wraps. Figures in Nativity scene wear Bible dress. If visible, Choir wears robes.

Properties: Two trays of Christmas cookies; shawl for Misé Michaud; crèche, toy lamb, carving knife, figurine of Christ Child for Felix; flutes, staff, bowl of fruit, pigeon cage containing stuffed birds, candles, for Procession; locket, ribbon for Elinor; bell or recording of cathedral chimes to signify midnight.

Setting: Scences 1 and 2 take place in a humble French peasant's cottage. There is a fireplace upstage center, with logs piled to one side. There is a window upstage right, an exit at left leading outdoors, and an exit at right leading to sheepfold. A table stands at center, with one or two chairs around it. A chair stands near the fireplace. A crèche occupies a prominent position in the room. Scene 3 takes place before the portals of the cathedral and may be played in front of the curtain. The curtain opens to display the chancel of the cathedral.

Lighting: No special effects necessary. If desired, lights may be dimmed for Scene 3, then brightened when curtains open to display Nativity scene.

Nine Cheers for Christmas

Characters: 5 male; 5 female; 9 male and female representing letters of Christmas (see directions in text); extras for Chorus (male and female).

Playing Time: 15 minutes.

Costumes: Everyday, modern dress. Each of nine letters of Christmas wears headband with bright cardboard letter of identification.

Properties: Letter for John; evergreen wreath tied with red ribbon for letter H; sack of toys (one for each member of Chorus) for letter S; small Christmas tree on stand, sparsely trimmed with bright balls and tinsel for letter T; handful of Christmas cards, each containing message to be read by Chorus, for letter M; tinsel stars for tree, for letter S.

Setting: Bare stage.

Lighting: No special effects.

The Twelve Days of Christmas

Characters: 50 male; 28 female; as many male and female actors as desired may be included in the court, or, if the cast must be limited, most of the actors may take several roles.

Playing Time: 15 minutes.

Costumes: The members of the court wear the traditional robes of fairy tale royalty. The Jester has on a tight-fitting costume of bright colors and a pointed cap with bells. The Pages may wear short full bloomer-like pants and stockings, the Maids, short full skirts. The Milkmaids may be dressed in blue and white and wear aprons and small white caps. The Drummers and Pipers can wear uniforms.

Properties: Paper and pen for the King; the following gifts made of cardboard: a partridge in a pear tree, two turtle doves, three hens with bows around their necks, four blackbirds, six geese, seven swans in a simulated pool on a cart that may be pushed onstage; five hoops covered with gold paper; pails and stools for Milkmaids; nine drums for Drummers; ten pipes for Pipers; robe for King to give to Jester.

Setting: The only furnishings necessary are two thrones at one side of the stage. The thrones should be placed on a platform so that the Jester can sit on the steps.

Lighting: No special effects.

The Legend of the Christmas Rose

Characters: 7 male; 3 female; female extras for Angels.

Playing Time: 10 minutes.

Costumes: Children wear shepherd dress. Wise Men wear rich Oriental clothing. Angels are dressed in traditional costumes.

Properties: Crook, white roses, for Madelon; 3 caskets for Wise Men; flute for Andres; basket for Michela; lily-tipped wand for Angel.
Setting: A snow-covered road near the field where Madelon tends her sheep. There is a well at left, and a large rock near center stage. White roses are concealed behind well.
Lighting: No special effects.

Granny Goodman's Christmas

Characters: 7 male; 5 female; male and female extras to be Neighbors and Children.
Playing Time: 10 minutes.
Costumes: The women wear peasant skirts and blouses. Granny Goodman wears a long skirt and has a shawl. The men wear costumes which give some hint of their occupations. The elves are dressed in green.
Properties: Christmas cookies, broken dishes, tins, handkerchief, red bandanna handkerchief, doll, leaves, Christmas decorations, cage-like rat trap, evergreen spray, Christmas tree lights, balls, tinsel, scrap of leather, knitting, scrap of bright green cloth, broom, little shoes, little socks, little coat, candles, pans, bowls, cooking materials, hatchet, and saw.
Setting: Granny Goodman's kitchen. There is a door at upstage left and a window at right. The window is not absolutely necessary as all entries may be made through the door. There is a large kitchen table at center and several chairs surround it. There are kitchen cupboards at right and a large fireplace at left. The room has been decorated for Christmas, but is disheveled in appearance.
Lighting: No special effects.

Twinkle

Characters: 4 male; 3 female; male and female extras.
Playing Time: 10 minutes.
Costumes: The stars are dressed in white or silver, and have cardboard stars attached to the fronts of their costumes. Star of Bethlehem's star is the largest. Ned and Ted wear brownie costumes, Santa, the traditional costume.
Properties: Brushes, cloths, pack for Santa.
Setting: The sky. Benches are placed end to end across the rear of the stage to represent the edge of the sky; they may be so labelled. A backdrop of stars may be used.
Lighting: No special effects.

A White Christmas

Characters: 9 male; 6 female.
Playing Time: 10 minutes.
Costumes: King and Queen are dressed in white with white or blue robes. They wear white crowns and their scepters are also white. Snowflakes are dressed in white; the girls wear full dresses, and the boys, white trousers and shirts. The girls have slippers with white fur or cotton trim, the boys white boots. All should wear white berets. North Wind and East Wind wear blue costumes with pointed caps and capes. Jack Frost wears green suit with white trim, and a pointed cap with icicles fastened on it.
Properties: None required.
Setting: All that is required are two chairs, covered in white, for the thrones. If desired, the sides of the stage may be draped with soft material to suggest the setting of a cloud.
Lighting: No special effects.

Merry Christmas Customs

Characters: 8 male; 2 female; male or female extras for Carolers.

Playing Time: 15 minutes.

Costumes: The boy and girl wear pajamas. Santa Claus wears the traditional costume. Martin Luther wears a dark robe. The Druid wears a light-colored robe. Sir Henry Cole wears tightly fitting trousers, a frock coat, and tall hat. Carolers wear costumes of different countries, including France, Italy, and Germany. Shepherd wears a simple robe and carries a shepherd's crook.

Properties: Bag of toys, candy, and packages, for Santa Claus.

Setting: A living room decorated for Christmas. There is a door to the outside at upstage center, and one at left to the rest of the house. There is a fireplace in the right wall, with two stockings hanging on it. There are two chairs near the fireplace. On the mantel are Christmas cards. A large, decorated Christmas tree is at left. A large sprig of mistletoe hangs over the door at center. Hanging on the outside of the door, but visible only when the door is opened, are sleigh bells. Tables, chairs, etc., are added to furnish the room comfortably.

Lighting: No special effects necessary. However, stage may be dimly lit when the curtains open, and children may turn on brighter lights and the Christmas tree lights when they enter.

Little Chip's Christmas Tree

Characters: 10 male; 9 Carolers may be male or female, as desired.

Playing Time: 15 minutes.

Costumes: Chip and Granfather wear old-fashioned peasant dress; Chip puts on coat before exiting with Carolers. Carolers wear bright outdoor clothing. Elves wear conventional elf costumes.

Properties: 2 sacks containing Christmas tree decorations; evergreen branches; recording of "Let's Trim the Christmas Tree."

Setting: Interior of a poor cottage in Ireland. There is a fireplace at center back with a mantelpiece. A window large enough to admit the elves is at right of fireplace. An evergreen tree stands at left of fireplace. The room is poorly and scantily furnished. Exit left leads to outdoors; exit right leads to other rooms of cottage.

Lighting: No special effects.

Old King Cole's Christmas

Characters: 7 male; 4 female; male and female extras as desired. Cast may have fewer characters if desired.

Playing Time: 15 minutes.

Costumes: Court costumes. The King and Queen wear the customary crowns and long trains fastened at the shoulders. Their costumes, those of the Fiddlers Three, and most of the others may be copied from illustrations in a Mother Goose book. Sir Algernon wears a dark suit with a wide bright ribbon across left shoulder to right waistline. Pasted or pinned to the ribbon are medals cut from gold or silver paper. He wears a dark cape, which, along with the ribbon and medals, is taken from him when he is deprived of the office of Prime Minister. The Villagers wear brightly colored peasant costumes.

Properties: Feather dusters for Rita, Lita, and Nita; tray with bowl and cushion with pipe, for servants; fiddles for the Fiddlers Three.

Setting: The Throne Room of King Cole's Castle. Two thrones, one for the King and one for the Queen, are upstage center. A small table is at the right of the King's throne. There is a stool down center, which is later removed by the maids.

Lighting: No special effects.

THE TALKING CHRISTMAS TREE

Characters: 2 male; 5 female; may be played with all-girl cast if desired.

Playing Time: 10 minutes.

Costumes: Pine Tree wears a green costume, trimmed with evergreen branches. A real pine tree may be used, with some of the branches cut out, where the child stands holding the tree in front of him. Fairies wear ballerina dresses and wings, and each has a wand and coronet. Snow Fairy wears white trimmed with cotton snow; Tinsel Fairy wears silver, decorated with tinsel; Bright Ball Fairy wears blue, decorated with Christmas tree balls; Jingle Bell Fairy wears silver or red, decorated with bells. Mark and Sally wear old, patched snowsuits and bright scarves and mittens.

Properties: Artificial snow, for Snow Fairy; tinsel, for Tinsel Fairy; bells, for Jingle Bell Fairy; bright balls, for Bright Ball Fairy; wheelbarrow and shovel, for Mark.

Setting: A clearing in the woods. A painted backdrop showing a winter scene in the woods may be used. The stage may be bare, or decorated with only a few evergreen branches, if desired.

Lighting: No special effects.

NORTH POLE CONFIDENTIAL

Characters: 5 male; 4 female.

Playing Time: 12 minutes.

Costumes: The five Santas wear traditional costumes. They might also wear signs of identification, such as "Santa-in-Chief," "Santa-North," etc. The Mrs. Santas wear red and white dresses patterned after the Santa costumes and they also wear signs of identification.

Properties: Four large maps, toys, tools.

Setting: Santa's Workshop at the North Pole. There is a door upstage center marked: "Santa-in-Chief—Private." On each side of the door stands a workbench. Two additional workbenches stand downstage, one at left, the other at right. In front of each workbench are two stools. The Workshop is filled with toys which the Santas are preparing for Christmas.

Lighting: No special effects.

MRS. CLAUS' CHRISTMAS PRESENT

Characters: 5 male; 1 female.

Playing Time: 15 minutes.

Costumes: Santa Claus wears the traditional red and white costume. Mrs. Claus wears a neat house dress with an apron over it. Santa's helpers wear short tunics and pointed caps.

Properties: Yarn, knitting bag, book.

Setting: The living room of the Claus home. There is a fireplace with a clock on the mantel. The other furnishings include a rocking chair, some other chairs (including one large upholstered one) and some tables. The exit at right leads to the kitchen, the one at left to the front of the house.

Lighting: No special effects.